DIVISION STREET: AMERICA

STUDS TERKEL

DISCUS BOOKS/PUBLISHED BY AVON

AVON BOOKS
A division of
The Hearst Corporation
959 Eighth Avenue
New York, New York 10019

Copyright © 1967 by Studs Terkel.
Published by arrangement with Pantheon Books,
A Division of Random House, Inc.
Library of Congress Catalog Card Number: 66-10415.

ISBN: 0-380-00279-5

First printing, April, 1968
Ninth printing

DISCUS TRADEMARK REG. U.S. PAT. OFF. AND
FOREIGN COUNTRIES, REGISTERED TRADEMARK—
MARCA REGISTRADA, HECHO EN CHICAGO, U.S.A.

Printed in the U.S.A.

This side the dark and hollow bound
Lies there no unexplored rich ground?
Some other world: well, there's the New—
Ah, joyless and ironic too!
                               HERMAN MELVILLE, 1876

We may either smother the divine fire of youth
or we may feed it. We may either stand stupidly
staring as it sinks into a murky fire of crime
and flares into the intermittent blaze of folly
or we may tend it into a lambent flame with power
to make clean and bright our dingy city streets.
                               JANE ADDAMS, 1909

You see, there's such a thing as a feeling tone.
One is friendly and one is hostile. And if you
don't have this, baby, you've had it.
                               LUCY JEFFERSON, 1965

Acknowledgments
and
Apologies

First, there's Cathy Zmuda, whose constant good humor was as important as her remarkable job of transcribing the conversations from tape-recorder to paper. Remarkable is the word because of my technical ineptitude. She performed small miracles.

Without the graciousness of Bernard Jacobs, general manager of Radio Station WFMT, and the three-month leave of absence he granted me, I couldn't possibly have met the publisher's deadline.

Among my casual, yet uncannily perceptive, scouts were Florence Scala, Hans W. Mattick of the University of Chicago, Edna Pardo, Jane Miller, Tom Kelly, Raleigh Campbell, Arlene Bouras, the late Bill Jankowski, Beverly Younger, Anne von Hoffman, Shirley Martinez, Fred Christy, and my wife.

Jim Unrath's comments, on reading fragments of the manuscript during the early stages, helped considerably. My collaborator in the making of radio documentaries, he appears ready and able for the working of this one when the time comes.

My apologies are extended to the more than a hundred fascinating people whose thoughts and attitudes I recorded but was unable to use. With each of these, I had a rewarding and pleasant experience. My omissions, I'm certain, were as arbitrary as my inclusions. The twin devils, time and space, worked against our collaboration seeing its way into print. Another occasion, perhaps . . .

With few exceptions, pseudonyms are used throughout.

Contents

EPILOGUE   403

· · · · · ·

Prefatory Notes

· · · · · ·

This book is in no way intended as a survey. Nor is it an attempt to spell out conclusions, joyful or joyless, about Chicago or any other American city. It is neither the believer's Good News nor the doubter's bad report. It is simply the adventure of one man, equipped with a tape-recorder and badgered by the imp of curiosity, making unaccustomed rounds for a year, off and on, trying to search out the thoughts of noncelebrated people (with a few "newsworthy" exceptions)—thoughts concerning themselves, past and present, the city, the society, the world.

My feelings toward Chicago have been wildly ambivalent as far back as I can remember. (I have lived here since I was ten. I am now fifty-four.)

Nelson Algren may have said it most succinctly and poetically fourteen years ago: ". . . it isn't so much a city as a vast way station where three and a half million bipeds swarm with a single cry, 'One side or a leg off, I'm gettin' mine.' It's every man for himself in this hired air. Yet once you've become part of this particular patch, you'll never love another. Like loving a woman with a broken nose, you may find lovelier lovelies. But never a lovely so real."* To determine how real or surreal this "lovely" is today was the purpose of my search.

The manner in which this book came about may be of

* *Chicago: City on the Make* by Nelson Algren (New York, Doubleday, 1951).

some interest. André Schiffrin, on publishing the American edition of Jan Myrdal's *Report from a Chinese Village*, wondered whether a similar communication might not be forthcoming from an American "village." It was a fascinating challenge. A Chinese village, an American city: why not? I had expected difficulties, of course, but none as formidable as the ones I actually experienced. The problems were not posed by the people I encountered. There was a shyness in many cases, in others a strange eagerness, but always a friendliness—once a few ground rules were established. The problem was the nature of the city itself. And the time in which we live.

In China, there was a specific you-can-put-your-hand-on-it event, the Revolution. The lives of the people, which Mr. Myrdal recorded with such profound understanding were lived by his informants Before and After. They had criteria for comparison, their own experiences: their lot, Before and After. What have we here? A *triple* revolution occurring *now*. There is a vague, uneasy—and in some fewer instances, exhilarating—awareness of the events. There is no Before or After. Perhaps, World War II was the great divide. Yet none of these Americans experienced Auschwitz or Hiroshima, its two most indelible mementoes. The several tattoo wearers I met had the exquisite legends *voluntarily* needled onto their arms. For the relatively few, popularly known as "bleeding hearts" (the frequent use of this phrase has always fascinated me and whetted my curiosity about the user), who sense the agony of others and thus their own tortured mortality, there is a Before: pre-World War II and pre-H-Bomb. They are the exception rather than the rule. So if there is no sense of Before for most Americans (some of the subjects vividly recalled the Depression; it was personally experienced), how can there be a sense of After? Or a sense of Now, for that matter?

A good fifteen years ago, Big Bill Broonzy, our greatest interpreter of country blues, was singing "Plow Hand Blues." The young in his audience walked out on him. There had been a noticeable scraping of chairs as the hipsters, cool and heavy-lidded, took to the pleasant air. Black and white together, they were not quite overcome. As Bill explained it over a bourbon: "Why should they listen to this old blues? To them it's horse-and-buggy music.

They never plowed no Johnson grass. They never had no mule die on them. Take me and the Bomb. People I met in Europe, they seen homes and family go. What do I know about the Bomb? The only bomb I seen was in the pictures. You gotta live through it to feel it."

On undertaking this assignment, I immediately called Dr. Philip Hauser, former chairman of the University of Chicago's Sociology Department, one of the country's best informed demographers. Is there a street in Chicago today where all manner of ethnic, racial, and income groups live? His reply—though a blow—was not unexpected. There is none. As late as twenty-five years ago, Halsted Street may have encompassed all these peoples. There is a quarter-mile radius on the Near North Side of the city that *might* fit these specifications; upper-middle-income high-rise complexes have sprung up with startling suddenness in the rooming-house heartland. They are adjacent to one another, *at this moment*. Still, the area I was seeking was a matter of conjecture, even here. The nomadic, transient nature of contemporary life has made diffusion the order—or disorder—of the city. The bulldozer and the wrecking ball have played their roles.

It finally came down to individuals, no matter where in the city or its environs they lived. Being neither a sociologist nor a research man, motivational or otherwise, I followed no blueprint or book or set of statistics. I played hunches—in some instances, long shots. Irvin Cobb observed, "All horse players must die broke." Here is one who will die astonished.

I was on the prowl for a cross-section of urban thought, using no one method or technique. I was aware it would take me to suburbs, upper, lower, and middle income, as well as to the inner city itself and its outlying sections. (I was about to say "neighborhoods," but this word has lost its meaning.)

There are deliberate omissions in this book, notably clergymen, college professors, journalists and writers of any kind. I felt that their articulateness and literacy offered them other forums. They had created their own books; my transcribing their attitudes would be nothing more than self-indulgence. It was the man of inchoate thought I was seeking rather than the consciously articulate.

I guess I was seeking some balance in the wildlife of the city as Rachel Carson sought it in nature. In unbalanced times, balance is as difficult to come by as Parsifal's Grail.

In no instance did I deliberately seek out the bizarre in people. It would serve as much purpose as visiting a Topless A-Go-Go (as drearily unrevealing). And yet: the part-time Syndicate tiger is as indigenous to our city—any large American city, I suspect—as the social lioness. Each has pertinent comments to make on urban life in the twentieth century.

So, too, with the window washer newly arrived to the middle class and the two ad-agency men, one of whom loves his job as much as the other loathes it; the tortured house painter—home-owner, who seeks respectability in his restricted neighborhood, and the wife of the ex-Wall Street lawyer, who risks respectability to integrate hers; the ADC mother seeking beauty, and the affluent steelworker for whom life's beauty has fled; the cabdriver finding his lost manhood in the John Birch Society, and the schoolteacher celebrating her humanhood; the Appalachian couple scoring in the big city, and the auto-body shop foreman who refuses to score; the blind woman who sees, and the sighted girl who doesn't; some going with the grain, others against.

Accident and improvisation played as much part in the making of this book as any plan. More. I had an idea of the kind of people I wanted to see: homeowners, home-makers, landladies, project dwellers, old settlers, new arrivals, skilled hands, unskilled, the retired, the young, the *haut monde,* the demimonde, and the solid middle *monde*—like Margaret Fuller, I was out to swallow the world. My world was my city. What with the scattering of the species, it had to be in the nature of guerrilla journalism.

A tip from an acquaintance. A friend of a friend telling me of a friend or nonfriend. A nursed drink at a tavern where a high-rolling bartender held forth. A chance encounter with a bright-eyed boyhood companion grown into an unquietly desperate man. An indignant phone call from a radio listener. A face, vaguely familiar, on the morning bus. A stentorian voice, outside City Hall, calling out my name. A wintry night in an Appalachian area, a hailed cab, the driver talking of a film, its impact on him, the meaning of courage; an appointment the following morning, a nearby bar. My seat companion on a bus, a Negro grandmother, bitter and strangely gleeful. The housewife next door, prototype of TV commercial heroines. An accidental shove on a crowded Loop corner, while awaiting the change in traffic lights; an apology; a phrase that holds my attention; we go for coffee; a life unfolded at the restaurant table. All these urban phenomena were factors in the making of this book.

An unexpected obstacle, in some few instances, was my identity. I had appeared on television and radio programs in the city and thus was a "celebrity." Possibly there would be a tendency in the other to say things he thought I wanted to hear. The encounter would, in this event, be wholly worthless. This was not so in most cases, though at such times I was impelled to use self-deprecatory profanity to clear the air. To many, my name and face meant nothing; that was a valuable timesaver.

I realized quite early in this adventure that interviews, conventionally conducted, were meaningless. Conditioned clichés were certain to come. The question-and-answer technique may be of value in determining favored detergents, toothpaste, and deodorants, but not in the discovery of men and women. It was simply a case of making conversation. And listening. Talk of childhood invariably opened the sluice-gates of damned-up hurts and dreams. From then on, there were occasional questions dependent on the other's flow.

There were, of course, key questions, asked idiomatically rather than academically, that would occur and recur. I had to be sure, though, that my companion was ready. It was in sharp contrast to conversations I had conducted on my radio programs with celebrated figures, who were everready. (This is in no way a reflection on the latter group. The themes were their professional as well as human concern. They were accustomed to talk as well as write about them.) It should be made clear, however, that a number of people in this book are highly literate; they're merely noncelebrated, that's all. As for articulateness, each person found it in his own way and in his own good time.

Often my companion introduced the themes himself: civil rights and Vietnam were two notable examples. Passions ran deep in these matters, even among the more diffident. Time itself and the flow of words brought them to the surface. Neither was much prompting needed for reflections on automation; here, too, strong feelings were quickly surfaced. The Bomb was something else again. In almost all cases, I introduced the question. The thought of it was simply too overwhelming for them to willingly put into words.

Surprisingly, God was an also-ran in their thoughts (again, with several exceptions). Like a stage mother, I had to push Him forward. Once He was introduced into the conversation, He was immediately and effusively acknowledged. (And in a few cases, rebuffed.) Whether God is dead or merely sleeping or really is a has-been is for theologians to have a high old time with. It is not the subject of this book. It is merely an observation. You will notice, too, that His son fares in a rather astonishing manner.

We come now to the role played by the tape-recorder. On occasion, it might have become an inhibiting factor, making for self-consciousness, were it not for my clowning. I'd kick it, not too hard, in the manner of W. C. Fields with a baby or a recalcitrant picket fence. With him, it was a state of war; with me, it was merely a matter of proving my ally's neutrality. Since the tape-recorder did not retaliate, its nonviolent nature was made clear to my companion. With most, its presence had no effect one way or the other.

When the recorder went wrong (this happened a number of times), I swore at it. During each of these instances, my companion laughed and seemed to feel more relaxed. (This may provide its own commentary on man's true feeling about technological advance.) I soon became aware that my playing Jacques Tati's Mr. Hulot helped break whatever tensions might have existed. (It came naturally to me, since I have never been able to drive a car, ride a bicycle, roller-skate, swim, dance, or engage in any such form of coordinative activity.) Yet, paradoxically, without my abused mechanical ally, this book would not have been possible. There is such a thing as base ingratitude—even to a machine.

The locales of these encounters were varied. Frequently it was the home of the subject, or his place of work, or a quiet corner of the radio studio, or my house, or a booth in the restaurant, or the front seat of a car. On occasion, there was coffee or a can of beer or a shot of whiskey, or in the case of a gracious elderly lady, a memorable meal. ("Even cooking takes love," she said.)

When I was a young boy, my mother managed a hotel on the Near North Side of Chicago. There were a few light-housekeeping rooms for couples, but most of the guests were single men. Many were skilled craftsmen: tool-and-diemakers, coppersmiths, chefs, master carpenters. They were a proud and stiff-necked lot. There were occasions when, for no likely reason, a fight would break out, a furious one—a pinochle game, a dispute over a nickel. The men earned what was good money in those days. Why, then, the fist and the blow over a lousy buffalo nickel? I didn't understand.

Now I understand. It wasn't the nickel. It was the harsh word, the challenging word, in the presence of peers: "Liar!" The nickel was not the matter, nor the dollar. Humiliation was the matter. Unless strong measures were taken. "Let's sit down and reason together" had no meaning while one had lost face.

Though there may be fewer such craftsmen today than there were then, face is still the matter.

Another recurring theme, to put it harshly and, perhaps, cruelly: the cop-out. "What can I do? Nothing." This plea of individual impotence had ironic overtones. It was voiced more frequently by those who called for a national show of potency and, indeed, violence than by the fewer others. Each of the subjects may have come to his belief or lack of it in his own ornery way; yet evidence seems overwhelming that mass media, with their daily litany of tribute to things rather than men, played their wondrous role.

Each of the subjects is, I feel, uniquely himself. Whether he is an archetypal American figure, reflecting thought and condition over and beyond himself, is for the reader to judge, calling upon his own experience, observations, and an occasional look in the mirror.

Although there is a Division Street in Chicago, the title of this book is metaphorical.

● ● ● ● ● ●

An A-B-C Guideline
for Non-Chicagoans

● ● ● ● ● ●

Chicago has a North Side, a South Side, and a West Side. There isn't much East Side. If you head too far that way, you're swimming in Lake Michigan—or drowning, as the case may be. Here are the city's beaches. The farther south you travel, the farther the lake recedes. Thus there is more East to the South Side than there is to the North.

Outer Drive is the thoroughfare that extends along the lake through most of the city. The city fathers are solicitous of the motorist's comforts and time problems. In seeking to serve him, they chopped down 800 trees in Jackson Park (on the South Side). One will soon make better time speeding through that area.

Much of the South Side and Near West Side comprise the black ghettos, the most expansive in the country. There are smaller such ghettos in other areas of the city. This is unofficial, of course. Mayor Richard J. Daley, on July 4, 1963, proclaimed: "There are no ghettos in Chicago."

The Near North Side, in the main, is an area of high-rise, high-rent apartment buildings and night clubs. Here is a concentration of bachelors and career girls, the latter often sharing flats. It is remarkably convenient, being close to the Loop, the lake, and "where the action is." It has much of the city's night life.

Old Town is an artsy-craftsy area, immediately north of Near North. It has a touch of Greenwich Village, with coffee houses, artists' studios, antique shops, restaurants, etc. Its phenomenal growth in recent years has—it is reputed—interested "the boys" (the Syndicate). Obviously, more than *kitsch* culture is involved here. The aimless young and suburbanites swarm all over this area on weekends. It has the spirit of a twentieth-century carnival, in which commerce overwhelms joy. Gentle people, who were the pioneer enterpreneurs here, are having an increasingly rough time of it. Early Old Towners, though somewhat disturbed, cultivate their gardens.

Chicago's large ethnic groups—Poles, Czechs, Yugoslavs, Ukranians, Germans, Scandinavians, Irish, Italians, Jews—no longer live in such homogeneous areas as formerly. There are still a few such sections to the south and west—and Germans and Scandinavians to the north—but the flavor is no longer lasting. Most of the younger generation of these groups have moved to the suburbs.

Uptown is located on the city's North Side, close to the lake. In recent years, transients in rooming houses and Appalachians in subdivided flats have provided it with a new atmosphere. Other Chicagoans of the lower middle and middle class encircle this area.

The North Shore suburbs are generally more upper "U" than the others, though there are considerable status differences here, too. The largest, Evanston, immediately north of the city, has its own Negro quarter. The others, give or take a token black, are lily white. Though Lake Forest is the uppermost "U," Winnetka is the wealthiest.

The suburbs to the south and west, varying in status, are, generally, ethnically oriented. A number of the southern suburbs have Negro communities; some are almost wholly Negro.

Hyde Park, of which the University of Chicago is the core, is one of the few integrated areas in the city. Income is playing an increasing role, along with the bulldozer. It is becoming more and more middle class. Rather than race, class is the factor here.

Bridgeport, where Mayor Daley lives, is on the Southwest Side of the city. It is near the stockyards. It is a lower-middle-class area that was once predominantly Irish. It now includes Slavic peoples, Italians, and Mexicans. No Negroes live here; they are "on the other side of the tracks" (the Rock Island Line).

The Loop (so called because it is encircled by the elevated tracks that then spin off toward the suburbs) is Chicago's Downtown, its mercantile and financial center.

Algren said of Chicago: "It's the city of 'I Will,' but what about those who say, 'I Can't'?"

DIVISION STREET:
AMERICA

PROLOGUE

• • • • • • • • • •

Florence Scala, 47

I was born in Chicago, and I've always loved the city. I'm not sure any more. I love it and I hate it every day. What I hate is that so much of it is ugly, you see? And you really can't do very much about it. I hate the fact that so much of it is inhuman in the way we don't pay attention to each other. And we can do very little about making it human ourselves.

What I love is the excitement of the city. There are things happening in the city every day that make you feel dependent on your neighbor. But there's detachment, too. You don't really feel part of Chicago today, 1965. Any more. I don't feel any.

I grew up around Hull House, one of the oldest sections of the city. In those early days I wore blinders. I wasn't hurt by anything very much. When you become involved, you begin to feel the hurt, the anger. You begin to think of people like Jane Addams and Jessie Binford * and you realize why they were able to live on. They understood how weak we really are and how we could strive for something better if we understood the way.

My father was a tailor, and we were just getting along in a very poor neighborhood. He never had money to send us to school; but we were not impoverished. When one of the teachers suggested that our mother send us to Hull House, life began to open up. At the time, the neighborhood was dominated by gangsters and hoodlums. They were men from the old country, who lorded it over the

---

* Jessie Binford, a colleague of Jane Addams, had lived at Hull House from 1906 until the day of its demolition in 1965. For many years she was director of the Juvenile Protective Association, which she helped found.

people in the area. It was the day of moonshine. The influence of Hull House saved the neighborhood. It never really purified it, you know what I mean? I don't think Hull House intended to do that. But it gave us . . . well, for the first time my mother left that darn old shop to attend Mother's Club once a week. She was very shy, I remember. Hull House gave you a little insight into another world. There was something else to life besides sewing and pressing.

Sometimes as a kid I used to feel ashamed of where I came from because at Hull House I met young girls from another background. Even the kinds of food we ate sometimes . . . you know, we didn't eat roast beef, we had macaroni. I always remember the neighborhood as a place that was alive. I wouldn't want to see it back again, but I'd like to retain the being together that we felt in those days.

There were Negroes living in the neighborhood even then, but there was not the tension. I've read about those riots in Chicago in the twenties—the race riots. But in our neighborhood it never did come to any kind of crisis. We used to treat each other as neighbors then. Now we look at each other differently. I think it's good and bad in a way. What we're doing is not understanding, some of us, what it was like then. I think that the American-born—the first generation, the second generation—has not hung on to what his mother and father had. Accepting someone naturally as a man. We don't do that today.

I think that the man who came over from Europe, the southern European especially, who was poor, could understand and see the same kind of struggle and have immediate sympathy for it. He accepted the Negro in the community as a man who is just trying to make a way for himself, to make a living. He didn't look upon him as a threat. I think it was the understanding that both were striving. Not out of some great cause, but just in a human way.

I'm convinced that the first and second generation hasn't any concern about the other person's situation. I think money and position are hard to come by today and mean an awful lot, and now they see the Negro as a threat. Though they may say he's inferior, they know darn well he's not. He's as clever as we are and does many things better than we can. The American-born won't accept this, the first and second generation family, especially among the Italians and Poles, and the Irish, too. Remember Trumbull Park? *

Through my teens I had been a volunteer at Hull House. After the War, Eri Hulbert, Jane Addams' nephew, told me of a dream he had. The Near West Side, our area, could become the kind of place people would *want* to live in, close to the city. Did I think this was possible? I said no, people didn't care enough about the neighborhood to rebuild it. But he introduced me to the idea of city planning. He felt the only hope for big cities, in these communities that were in danger of being bulldozed, was to sit down and look and say we have a responsibility here. He convinced me that you could have a tree on the West Side, see?

That's where my life changed. I became involved with a real idea and talking to people like the banker, the social worker, and the Board of Trustees at Hull House. But I suddenly realized my inadequacy. I simply couldn't understand their language, you know? I had to go back to school.

This is where I began to lose the feeling of idolatry you have about people. I think that's bad. I idolized the people that were involved in Hull House. I thought they could never make a mistake. I was later to find out they were the ones who could hurt me the most. I feel that people have to be prepared always for imperfections in everyone, and we have to feel equal, really, to everyone. This is one of the things lots of slum kids, people who came out of poor areas, don't have. Not to be afraid to say something even though it may be way off base. I did this many times and I'd be embarrassed, realizing I had said something that had nothing to do with what they were talking about. But Eri Hulbert kept saying it makes no difference. Just keep at it. You're as good as they are.

Miss Binford and Jane Addams resented being treated as special persons. This was the kind of thing they had to cut through all the time. Yet we insisted on treating them as special people, in an uncomfortable kind of way. These feelings of confidence, you know, ego, so necessary—most of us in the neighborhood didn't have it. Most of us hung back, see.

* Several years ago, a Negro family, having bought a home in Trumbull Park, was stoned out of the neighborhood.

In those days it was a new idea. You had to fight the politician who saw clearance and change as a threat to his power, his clout.* He likes the kind of situation now around Maxwell Street,† full of policy and hot goods being sold on the market and this kind of stuff that could go on and on without too much interference from authority because it's so oppressed. The rotten housing and no enforcement of codes and all that business. We had a tough time selling the Catholic Church, too. From '47 to '56 were rough years. It was tough selling people on the idea that they could do it for themselves, that it was the only way it could be done. Their immediate reaction was: You're crazy, you know? Do you really think this neighborhood is worth saving?

All the meetings we had were so much frustration. Eri Hulbert was trying to lead us in a democratic way of doing something about our city. The misunderstandings never came from the neighborhood people. It arose out of the Hull House Board's unwillingness to understand. He couldn't get his point across.

Eri Hulbert committed suicide before our plan was accepted by the city. His death more than anything else, opened a door which I never dreamed could open. You know, there's a real kind of ugliness among nice people. You know, the dirty stuff that you think only hoodlums pull off. They can really destroy you, the nice people. I think this is what happened to Eri, the way he was deserted by his own. I think it really broke his heart. What disturbs me is that I was a grown woman, close to thirty, before I could see. Sometimes I want to defend the rotten politicians in my neighborhood. I sometimes want to defend even gangsters. They don't pretend to be anything but what they are. You can see what they are. They're not fooling anybody, see? But nice people fool you.

I'm talking about the Board of Trustees, the people who control the money. Downtown bankers, factory owners, architects, people in the stock market. The jet set, too. The young people, grandchildren of old-timers on the Board, who were not really like their elders, if you know what I mean. They were not with us. There were also some very

---

* Clout: a Chicago idiom for "drag," "pull," "political power."
† Chicago's celebrated open market area.

good people, those from the old days. But they didn't count so much any more. This new crowd, this new tough kind of board members, who didn't mind being on such a board for the prestige it gave them, dominated. These were the people closely aligned to the city government, in real estate and planning. And some very fine families, old Chicago families. (Laughs.) The nicest people in Chicago.

Except for one or two of the older people, they made you feel that you had to know your place. You always felt this. That's the big argument about the poverty program today. You cannot have the nice rich people at the top passing on a program for the poor, because they simply *don't* understand, they *can't* understand. These people meet in board meetings once a month. They come by the main street into the building and out they go. They've never had anybody swear at them or cry or ask for help or complain the kind of way people do in our neighborhood. They just don't know.

In the early Sixties, the city realized it had to have a campus, a Chicago branch of the University of Illinois. (There was a makeshift one at the pier out on the lake.) There were several excellent areas to choose from, where people were not living: a railroad site, an industrial island near the river, an airport used by businessmen, a park, a golf course. But there was no give. The mayor looked for advice. One of his advisors suggested our neighborhood as the ideal site for the campus. We were dispensable. He was a member of the Hull House Board. It was a strange thing, a very strange thing. Our alderman, he's not what I'd call a good man—even he tried to convince the Mayor this was wrong. But the Mayor was hearing other voices. The nice people.

The alderman alerted us to the danger. Nobody believed it. The priest himself didn't believe it. They had just opened the parish, a new church, a new school. Late in the summer of 1960, the community could have been touched off. But the people were in the dark. When the announcement came in 1961, it was a bombshell. What shocked us was the amount of land they decided to take. They were out to demolish the entire community.

I didn't react in any belligerent way until little kids came knocking at the door, asking me to attend a meeting. That's where the thing got off the ground. It was exciting to see that meeting, the way people felt and the way they talked and the way—they hurt—to hear our Italian priest, who had just become an American. This was in February, we had just celebrated Lincoln's birthday. He had just become a citizen, he couldn't understand.

Though we called the Mayor our enemy, we didn't know he was serving others. It was a faceless thing. I think he'd just as soon have had the University elsewhere. But the pressures were on. We felt it as soon as our protests began.

A member of the Hull House Board took me to lunch a couple of times at the University Club. The University Club—lunch—me! My husband said, go, go, have a free lunch and see what it is she wants. What she wanted to do, really, was to dissuade me from protesting. There was no hope, no chance, she said. I had had a high regard for her. I've been thinking she's probably one of those on the Board who would have fought the people's end. But she was elected to convince me not to go on. The first time I went, I thought this was a friend through whom we could work. But I could see, you know, that she allowed me to be just so friendly, and there was a place beyond which I couldn't go. There was a difference now. I stayed in my place, but I said what I wanted to say. There was a place beyond which she couldn't go, either. See? I was glad to experience it anyway.

I think I understand her. She had strong ties with old Hull House and she was really a good person who ought not have allowed this to happen and she knew it. When the lunches failed to bring anything off, I had no more contact with any of them on that level. We reached the letter-writing stage. We no longer used the phone.

I shall never forget one board meeting. It hurt Miss Binford more than all the others. That afternoon, we came with a committee, five of us, and with a plea. We reminded them of the past, what we meant to each other. From the moment we entered the room to the time we left, not one board member said a word to us. No one got up to greet Miss Binford nor to speak to her. No one asked her a question. The chairman came forward, he was a gentleman, and showed us where to sit.

Miss Binford was in her late eighties, you know. Small, bird-like in appearance. She sat there listening to our plea and then she reminded them of what Hull House meant. She went back and talked, not in a sentimental way, about principles that must never waver. No one answered her. Or acknowledged her. Or in any way showed any recognition of what she was talking about. It's as though we were talking to a stone wall, a mountain.

It was pouring rain and we walked out of the room the way people walk out who feel defeat. I mean we walked out trying to appear secure, but we didn't have much to say to each other. Miss Binford could hardly speak at all. The shock of not being able to have any conversation with the board members never really left her. She felt completely rejected. She knew then there would be no help anywhere. In the past, whenever there was a serious problem in the juvenile courts, she could walk into the Mayor's office and have a talk with him, whoever he was. Kelly, for instance, or Kennelly, or Cermak. And never fail to get a commitment from him. Never. But she knew after this meeting, she'd never find that kind of response again. And sure enough, to test herself, she made the rounds. Of all the people who had any influence in town, with whom she had real contact, not one responded. They expressed sympathy, but it was hands off. Something was crushed inside her. The Chicago she knew had died.

I don't think we realized the stakes involved in this whole urban renewal system. The money it brings in, the clout necessary to condemn land . . . a new Catholic Church was demolished, too. It had opened in '59, built near Hull House with the city's approval. The church was encouraged to go ahead and build, so as to form the nucleus for the new environment, see? It cost the people of the area a half million dollars. The Archdiocese lends the parish money, but the parish has to repay. It's a real business arrangement.

Now the people of the area have learned a good deal, but it was a bitter education. The politicians' actions didn't bother us as much. We hated it, we argued about it, we screamed about it out loud. Daley gave the orders and the alderman followed it. This kind of thing we could understand. But we could never understand the silence of the others. A group wanted to picket the Archdiocese, but I felt it was wrong, because we were put into a position of fighting education, the University being built, you know.

35

Here we were in a big Roman Catholic city, we'd be looked upon as a bunch of fanatics. As I think back on it now, the instinctive responses of the people, who are thought of as being uneducated, were better than my own. I was very anxious we should not be looked upon as people from the slums, many of us Italians and Mexicans. We had to proceed in an orderly manner. We overdid that. We should have picketed the Archdiocese. We should have been tough with Hull House. We should have spoken the truth from the beginning.

Most of the people who left the area were deeply embittered. They said never again will they ever become involved about anything in their city. They'd had it. This was a natural kind of thing because it was a pretty brutal two and a half years. But I don't know now. This is a big question to ask: whether that experience gave any meaning to their lives? If they turn their backs on it, it's been a failure as far as I'm concerned. There's a danger of their becoming extremists in the self-indulgent sense. They'll be concerned with themselves and their own safety and nothing else. It has happened with some of them.

I don't believe so much any more. I don't believe so much in people as I used to. I believe in *some* people but not in all people any more. I feel I have to be careful about this business of believing in all people. That's the number-one change, I think. And I've found there are certain kinds of liberals who'll sell you out, who make life miserable for great numbers of people when they will not see beyond their narrow views. I'm thinking of Urban Renewal, and the huge Negro ghettos that have sprung up and have your heart break at the kind of overcrowding and rotten environment that's developed. It's an evil thing the liberal community does: it wants to see the slums cleared but doesn't fight to see housing for lower-income groups built first. It reinforces all the terrible things we're talking about in the big cities. Segregates the poor people, particularly the Negro people, and this goes on and on.

In an area like ours, the uprooting is of another kind. I lived on the same block for over forty-five years; my father was there before me. It takes away a kind of stability big cities need. Lots of the people have moved into housing no better than the kind they lived in. Some have moved into public housing. The old people have really had it worse. Some have moved into "nicer" neighborhoods, but they're terribly unhappy, those I've spoken with. Here, downtown in the Loop, everything is clearing and building and going up. And the social workers in this town, boy! I can hardly look at them with respect any more. The way they've knuckled down to the system themselves, because everybody wants a Federal grant or something. They don't want to be counted out. I'm sick of the whole mess and I don't know which way to go.

There are the little blessings that come out of struggle. I never knew Jessie Binford as a kid at Hull House. I used to see her walking through the rooms. She had such dignity, she just strode through the rooms and we were all kind of scared of her. In the past four or five years, we became close friends. I really knew the woman. It meant something to her, too. She began to know the people in the way she knew them when she first came to Hull House as a young girl. It really gave her life, this fight. It made clear to her that all the things she really believed in, she believed in all the more. Honor among people and honor between government and people. All that the teacher tells the kids in school. And beauty.

There was a Japanese elm in the courtyard that came up to Miss Binford's window. It used to blossom in the springtime. They were destroying that tree, the wrecking crew. We saw it together. She asked the man whether it could be saved. No, he had a job to do and was doing it. I screamed and cried out. The old janitor, Joe, was standing out there crying to himself. Those trees were beautiful trees that had shaded the courtyard and sheltered the birds. At night the sparrows used to roost in those trees and it was something to hear, the singing of those sparrows. All that was soft and beautiful was destroyed. You saw no meaning in anything any more. There's a college campus on the site now. It will perform a needed function in our life. Yet there is nothing quite beautiful about the thing. They'll plant trees there, sure, but it's walled off from the community. You can't get in. The kids, the students, will have to make a big effort to leave the campus and walk down the streets of the area. Another kind of walling off . . .

To keep us out. To keep the kids out who might be vandals. I don't see that as such a problem, you know. It wasn't the way Jane Addams saw it, either. She believed in a neighborhood with all kinds of people, who lived together with some little hostility, sure, but nevertheless lived together. In peace. She wondered if this couldn't be extended to the world. Either Jane Addams brought something to Chicago and the world or she didn't.

POSTSCRIPT

In 1964, Florence Scala ran as an Independent for Alderman of the First Ward against a candidate who had the support of both major parties. She received 3600 votes against her opponent's 8600. As she recalls: "There were people from all over Chicago campaigning for me, some people I never saw before nor have I seen since. A small number from the community had the courage to come out. And it took guts in a neighborhood like that, where clout is so important. But really it was . . . students, older people, the Independent Voters of Illinois . . . just a lot of people from all over, expressing their indignation not only about happenings in the First Ward but about the city as a whole. I think they were expressing support of what seemed to be an individual yelling out, you know, and they wanted to help. They weren't always people I see eye to eye with. There were some far to the right and I couldn't understand what it was in me they wanted to support. But there was something. I have a kind of sympathy for whatever it was that was frustrating them. I really do, because they felt themselves unable to count somewhere. And there were people way over on the left. But I feel most of them were moderates, who were responding to this thing."

......

PART

I

"THE
FEELING TONE"

• • • • • • • • •

Lucy Jefferson, 52

When I first came from Mississippi, I was so young
and ignorant. But I was freer, you know? I think I
had a little bit more room to move around in than I have
now. Because I think the white man wasn't so afraid then.
There wasn't enough of us. There's too many of us now, I
think that's what frightened him. Nobody noticed you
then. You were there but nobody bothered about seeing
you.

*She lives in the low-rise Robert Brooks Housing Project
on the Near West Side. Hers is described as a row house.
It was neatly furnished; some pies were in the oven; there
were books all over.*

My supervisor once said to me, "Now Lucy, you sit out
here at this desk and answer the phone. And I think you
should tell me what's going on because people here say
things to you that they wouldn't dare say to me. And because, after all, you're just part of the furniture." Oh boy,
did I give a chuckle. Yeah. I laughed to myself and I said,
now here's a chance for all the hate in the world. But you
know what really happened? I felt so sorry for the poor
thing. Some Negro went out to the steel mill and he shot
up a lot of people, and after that—Oh, I tell ya, I'm very
wicked—after that I'd take her arm and say, "Miss Pru-
ner, I want to talk to you about somethin'." And I
slammed the door and she'd freeze. I wasn't going to do

39

anything to her, but she . . . (Prolonged laughter.) I am just telling you how wicked I am. I'm an awful louse. (Soft chuckle.)

I walk down the street, I smoke a cigarette. Well, ladies aren't supposed to do that. But I'm no lady. (Laughs.) I just have the best old time. Sometimes, it amuses, you know. When I get blue and disgusted, I go get me some beer and get cockeyed drunk, stay at home. I don't go out. I don't believe in taverns. Then you say, why the hell do you drink beer? Because I like it. There's a lot of things that I don't like.

I just don't like doles. I wouldn't accept one dime from anybody. I'm not gonna raise my children on Aid. Why should I? There's enough money in America for me to raise my children. Now one is seventeen, one is twenty-one. And I absolutely refused to accept these handouts from anybody. How am I gonna teach these children of mine what a pleasure it is in accomplishment? Do you realize what it means if I'm gonna sit here and accept this check? We can't go to the zoo because there's carfare. Everything has to be pinpointed.

We took the little money that we made, brought it home, and we said, "Okay, Melvin would count it maybe one day, Corrine would count it the next payday." And they'd say, "Okay, what are you going to do this time, mom? Does the rent have to be paid?" And I'd say, "No, not this time." "Well, then, we can go to the show?" and I'd say, "Yes, we can go to the show this time. Meet me downtown when I get off from work." I'd go to the ten-cent store when I got off from work and buy a pound of candy, mixed. I'd meet 'em at the show. We'd go in. Now this means, this is about five dollars and some cents out of this paycheck. We don't go but about every two-three months. Or maybe less. I always had a picnic basket and picnic jugs and all this junk. Because these things are essential wherein they could get around and see what is happening.

I worked at Wesley Hospital for about eleven years. As an aid in physical therapy. I worked part-time and went to school part-time, as a practical nurse. There was this woman that was very kind to me. She used to tell me, "Lucy, why don't you get on Public Aid until you can finish school. Don't let your pride stop you." Maybe I didn't realize exactly what she meant by pride. But I just —gave it up. With all the stuff attached to it, maybe that's why . . . the publicity, the degradation, see?

Everybody's screaming now: Oh, these women on ADC. Why hasn't somebody told these people that they're on ADC because you gave all this money to keep from hirin' 'em? Years and years ago. This didn't just start, you know. You don't keep people in a certain category for hundreds of years and expect them to come out and do all these things. For generations and generations they've been just barely making it. Now what do you expect? Plums?

Hell, we're as poor as Joseph's goat, as far as that goes. We pinch pennies every day, but truly we don't think anything about it. When I get paid we know exactly what we're gonna eat for two weeks. I buy whatever sale is on, that's what we eat. I go to Hillman's or George's or something, whatever's on sale. Say for instance, we're gonna make spareribs today. That's okay. We might have spareribs and sauerkraut. If the steak's cheap enough, we might even have steak once in a while. But for two long weeks we know exactly what kind of meat we're gonna have. So what we do, we wrap it around, we got potatoes in the house, we got rice in the house, we got frozen vegetables in the house, so we build a meal around this thing. So far as being poor is concerned, boy I bet I got a monopoly on that. (Laughs.)

It's a very fashionable hospital, Wesley. The clientele there are usually people that's got money. To me they were fascinating. All those beautiful clothes. You know, I could dream and see myself in this role. Then naturally I continued to read, self-educated almost. This man came in one day and he suffers from a backache. He usually gets a heat and massage to the low back. He knew me and of course all the clientele called me by my first name, which I resented. But it turned out to be an asset. So he came in and said, "Lucy, what are you reading?" And I said, *The Status Seekers*. And he said, "Don't read the junk." And I said, "By the way, you're in the advertising business." I had loads of fun, loads of fun.

They call you by the first name, the students, everybody. You see, this was the policy to keep the Negro in his place. But I happened to be the kind of Negro that became controversial, because I read such things as *The*

American Dilemma and I walk around with the book in my hand, see? I defied them in so many ways. I almost terrified 'em.

You know, it got so every time I got on an elevator—"What are you reading? What are you reading? What are you reading?" (Laughs.) And I'd begin to enjoy this thing, you know. I was having the best old time. I was absolutely terrifying 'em. Everybody was yelling: "Lucy, Lucy!" Maybe that's why I say, the first name, it came in very handy. Because if they hadda just said, "Jefferson," nobody probably'd ever knowed it was me. But by making this so commonplace, here's this Negro woman, every time you see her she's reading a different book. You know what I'd do? I'd go to the library and get these books, and I'd just dash back home and read these. And truly it became a game with me. I don't think I ever had more fun in my life than I had working right there.

I guess I was darn near fifty then. That's the reason why I say I was havin' a ball. I'm carrying the book by Faulkner, paperback, in my pocket, you know. But this particular time I didn't realize that the heading of the book was sticking out just a little above. The students, doctors, interns got on . . . "Faulkner!!" (Prolonged laughter.)

What is it they're afraid of?

This is what—you are just breaking down this stereo thing that all Negroes are ignorant, they won't read, they won't do this, they won't help themselves. Once they see you're trying to do it . . . You see what? They're not really worrying so much about the Negro, they're worried about themselves. When I really want to fight them, you know what I do, I glare at 'em. They cringe. (Laughter.)

I have learned that a Negro woman can do anything she wants to do if she's got enough nerve. So can a white man. But a white woman and a Negro man are slaves until this day. I'll tell you why. The white man has set his woman up on a pedestal. He's trying to prove to her how superior he is. Truly he's not superior, he's just another little boy. She has to stay there if she wants to be anybody. But if she ever learns anything and she strays, she's an outcast. Me, you know what I can do? I can do any cotton-pickin' thing I feel like doin'.

The white woman is more a slave than you?

Oh, by all standards. The black woman has to have nerve, though. She has to have experience. And she needs a little education to go along with it. You know this is such a strange thing. I don't know why people like mystery. Love is so beautiful. It can be beautiful, with any group of people . . . Florence Scala and I can sit here . . .

We talk about all facets of our lives, things we wouldn't dare say to anybody else in public. And somebody else, even a Negro, walks in my back door, we shut up. Because it's taboo. They might say it was Uncle Tomming, or they could make it look ugly. These things are hard to understand. Two human beings could have so much in common that they can really sit down and talk about their own lives, their own failures, their own misgivings, and truly speaking tell you about some of my absolute traits that I don't like. Two women, we're just two women. So here is this cloak of mystery. Everybody, even the neighbors, gawking. When she comes in, you know. The curtains are moving, or they come boldly to the door and watch, as though, well, here is the enemy.

Florence, with Florence what I tried to teach in this particular neighborhood, here's a woman everybody says, oh well, she's Italian, she doesn't have the interest. Damn that, this is a woman that you *need* to talk to. She doesn't live on Lake Shore Drive. I tried to show them the little, simple, down-to-earth qualities about this particular woman. But, my God, this Petrillo,* whoever the hell he is, what are you going to tell him? The man has no interest in white or black. If you're poor, see? He's living in another world altogether.

This is the Berlin Wall right over here. You see, we don't even have a ten-cent store. Woolworth doesn't find it profitable. We don't have a bank. After all, everybody here is on Welfare. So if you want to get your check cashed, I go downtown to the bank. I usually go to Sears or Wards or somewhere where I've got a charge account.

* Donald Parillo: Florence Scala's victorious machine-backed opponent in the aldermanic election of '64. The two women met during this campaign.

43

This is where you get a check cashed, unless you want to go to the currency exchange and pay somebody to get your check cashed. Well, I don't make that kind of money to give somebody money to cash my check. We don't have any facilities here that poor folks need. On Michigan Avenue, where people can get along without it, you got your ten-cent stores. I did all my shopping in a ten-cent store when I worked at Wesley.

Here again, it's the white man's standards. You know, I laugh sometimes. Just like these books we have in our schools. Dick and Jane, here's this pretty rosy-cheeked white woman and she's got on a pretty dress and a lovely little apron and she's standing out on this lawn and here's this big huge driveway, goes to two, three acres. All this stuff, and she's waving goodbye to her son. He's off on his way to school, you know. And this is what they teach the children in projects. (Laughter.) Boy, this is really something.

I was trying to live by white man's standards myself. I didn't realize it. One day the school sent for me, I'm kind of a stickler for not laying off the job, so I sent my mother. The principal told her Melvin was a problem child. He must have been about seven then. When I got off from work at five o'clock, I chased myself home to fix supper. I couldn't see the forest from the trees. I was so busy trying to get home, trying to get dinner, trying to help with homework, trying to get him to bed, so he'd get enough sleep. Do you realize what a vicious cycle this is? I didn't realize what I was doing to my children. Because I was rushing them to death. I was rushing myself to death.

I asked for help. I realized that all the voices Melvin heard were female voices. My voice, his sister's voice, his grandmother's voice, his teacher's voice. I began to get frightened. I went down to the I.S.U. something, I talked with them. They decided I was the one needed the psychoanalyzing. They had me in a conference and there were about twelve psychiatrists, all around. Somebody was taking notes and what have you. Nobody said one word about tomorrow. I explained to the people that my child, he's wandering away and I'm afraid he needs male companionship. I'm not asking you to give him anything, just a few minutes of your time. Till this day I didn't get it.

This is what would happen at work. Instead of sending

a card: Mrs. Jefferson, come to school to see about your son . . . they'd call up. When the phone would ring, honest to God, you know what? My blood pressure would rise, because now I was so afraid. "Lucy!" Whenever a call came in, I knew something was wrong. And when this truant officer would phone, one of the girls would answer.

Boy, oh boy, here I go. I didn't like this, see? I was furious, because I thought this was invading my private life. The way I raise my children was my own private business. Let's say I was ashamed. This would be a better word. I wouldn't have admitted it then, but I can admit it now. Because, you see, the stigma of all Negro children are lazy, they don't do this, they don't do that, you know. See, I didn't want anybody to think my children wasn't up to par, or wasn't up to the white man's standards. Well, I blowed that long ago. (Laughs.)

I couldn't afford to go to the PTA meetings. They don't do a damn thing but drink coffee anyway. I like coffee and I like to drink it in the morning, but I have to go to work, and they had PTA meetings at one o'clock in the day. I couldn't lay off my job to go down there to chitchat with them. I think they had PTA meetings twice in the last ten years at night. They're no damn good anyway.

Melvin was doing very poorly and I was getting letters. You know, they send you all these little items. Come to see me, come to school, because your child is not working up to his capacity. I don't know why they just don't tell you the truth about it, instead of using all these vague, false phrases. I thought he was just being lazy, but the child couldn't read. He couldn't spell. He was at Crane High, out there in the ghetto. I laid off from work the next day. I got up, cocked my hat up Miss Johnny Aside . . . I wanted to let him know I was plenty mad then. Oh yeah, I visited Crane. Melvin was having three study periods in a row. Gee, this is kind of crazy, studying what? I went to see this study hall. And this is the auditorium. It has a false ceiling, and there's very few lights, and there's children everywhere, male and female, and about the only thing they can do there is make love. Most of the kids can't read anyway, but if they could, they wouldn't be able to see. So I went to the counselor and he said, "It costs $10,000 to put up this business of putting lights in and the school system doesn't have the money" and blah, blah,

blah. I said, "But in the meantime, what are you going to do about all these children in there, these boys and girls, these young men and women?" I said, "Maybe they can't read but they can do other things in there, such as getting babies." He said, "Well, well . . . we don't have anywhere else to put 'em."

You're talking about teachers. I bet he never had the same teacher twice in two weeks in two years. It's a disgrace to keep on calling these places schools. I think the best thing we can say about them, these are meeting places where people get up every morning, give their children a dollar, seventy-five cents, or whatever the heck they give 'em, and these kids go off. Schools you learn in. They could take a store front on Roosevelt Road or anywhere and clean it up, put some seats in there, and put some books in. But see, you can't learn anything where there is no books. Melvin went a whole year at Crane, didn't have a book. If I woke up in a house that didn't have a book in, I'd just turn it down, it wouldn't be any good. To me, they're my life blood. Types of caps, gowns, all that crap, it don't mean nothing.

Oh, what am I *really* looking for? For my daughter to have her baby. This is her first. Her marriage turned out bad. I would like for her to finish her college education. She's gonna need it to help her child, to rear her child. The only thrill left for me is to see my grandchild come and see what I can do about him. Won't that be fun? You know, I'll be able to afford things that would give him incentive to paint, music, literature, all these things that would free his little soul. Other than that, no bother. Melvin? Am I going to give him a chance to be a man or not? I took that chance when I let him go to Selma. I was scared to death. And I was very proud. I was afraid he was too young because he was only sixteen, to know what was really happening. But I couldn't afford to tell him. I wouldn't have given him a chance to be a man. This was his chance. And I didn't want to steal it.

Let's face it. What counts is knowledge. And feeling. You see, there's such a thing as a feeling tone. One is friendly and one is hostile. And if you don't have this, baby, you've had it. You're dead.

Gene Willis, 27

It's a very funny place. Lots of people here sit around and have a few drinks and just observe. Actually, you find half the people are observing and the other half are extroverts having a good time. They couldn't care less.

Bartender at a popular Near North Side tavern, patronized by "swingers." "To me, a swinger is a young fellow, young girl looking to have a real good time, open mind, just lookin' to have fun, regardless of situation, money or cost."

Most of the patrons are between twenty-five and thirty-five, unattached, and have good jobs: advertising agencies, banks, insurance companies—middle managers; the girls, airline stewardesses, schoolteachers, coeds. "The success of this place is girls, tons of girls. The high-rises are coming in bigger and bigger every day. More and more kids are coming down."

It's fun to watch. So many people are stiff and having a good time. It's gotten to be more like a neighborhood bar. Actually, Near North is very clicky. All the people that live around here know each other, and they get in their groups and have a good time.

The funniest thing you could ever imagine was to watch a young fellow sit there and not say a word to anybody. And eventually after he's sat there for two or three hours, when he has a few drinks, you just watch the expression on his face, as he loosens up and thinks he's gonna have a good time. He's trying so hard to let himself go and to enjoy himself. For the first three hours, he's wasted himself, it's time to go and he doesn't do the things he really wanted to do. That's the basis of having a good time.

I find that the average person can stay home and talk if he wants. But if a guy goes out, he wants to go where the music is loud as it can be, and you can see a chick walking by, and he can't hear himself think, and he gets pushed and shoved and he gets drinks—to him this is something different. It's having a good time.

· · · · · ·

Jan Powers, 24

She's on the staff of a magzine, popular with cool young men. Her job pays well and it's easy. She comes from a working-class family, and occasionally sees her mother and two younger brothers. She has an apartment of her own in a new high-rent high-rise on the Near North Side. She is engaged to Steven, a medical student.

I don't notice the world. I'm very bored. I really don't know how I feel. I'm nice and cordial but people sense something about me. I don't know, maybe I don't like them. Maybe I feel I'm above them. I can't think of anyone I love or respect. I can't be bothered with the news. I just can't get interested. I can't care less. I *should* care, it's terrible. (Laughs lightly.)

Vietnam? Isn't that a shame? (Laughs softly.) I saw a film on Vietnam, it showed the actual fighting. It looked ridiculous, just a bunch of kids. It was actually embarrassing to watch that, people were actually shooting and shouting. I saw Vietnam. I looked at a map once. I'm concerned with Vietnam if my brother has to go, otherwise, no.

My interest in life is me. It's a shame. I wish I could pick up a newspaper and read it. What I hear about things is heard from other people.

I hope I'll make it. I think it's marriage, to someone who is successful. Highland Park, * a couple of kids. I'm not too crazy about children, though. You're sitting in a room, and all of a sudden five kids'll come in and they'll go to another girl in the room. Same with dogs.

I'm worried about the next couple of years. Here I'm putting all this time and feeling into this relationship with Steve, and to have it not work out, it would be terrible. I don't know what I'd do. I'd probably find someone else and be just as happy.

Nothing touches me. I wonder why I don't care about these things. The Bomb doesn't bother me. I don't read the

---

* An upper-middle-class suburb on the North Shore.

papers. There isn't much I can do about it, so I'm not worried. What is important now is my friend and me. The rest of the world can go.

If I were God, I'd make a world with a lot of me's in it. (Laughs.) No, no, I'd leave it the way it is. We have to have war, there's been wars through all the ages, apparently everyone gets enjoyment out of it. If we removed this part from man, it would be boring. Otherwise things would be sort of dull.

I love my building, I just love it. If I'm on a bus going to my mother's, I look at these people and get a nauseous feeling. On Michigan Avenue, I respect them more. Home gives me a sick feeling.

It's a shame Negroes don't like me and children don't like me and dogs don't run up to me.

. . . . . .

Harriet Behrens, 66

It's getting to be very difficult for blind people. In the old days, streetcars were easy for people to manage, even visually handicapped like I am. You knew they were gonna stop at a corner or you knew where they ran. A State Street car ran on State Street and a Madison Street car ran on Madison Street. Now the bus can stop anywhere, there may be cars in the way or a truck or something, but you don't know and you have to run after it. You ask people and they don't always answer you. You ask the driver and sometime's he's busy and he don't pay no attention to you, so you don't know.

Mr. and Mrs. Behrens, childless, live at the Lathrop Homes, a low-rise public-housing project on the city's North Side, along the Chicago River. The apartment is startlingly neat; the phrase "genteel poor" comes to mind. The parakeet is chirping in counterpoint to the classical music coming from the table FM radio. A diploma from a music school, no longer existing, and an old-fashioned cuckoo clock are on the walls.

When I was a very little girl, may be five or six, I was studying violin. Playing at a concert one time, I received a large bouquet of flowers. I remember riding home in one of those open summer cars, sitting in the front seat, talking to the motorman. Telling him how I got the flowers and all about it. I remember those old cars.

Things seemed much simpler then than they are today. It may be that they were harder in a way because we didn't have so many timesavers, as they say. But I don't know, people seemed to have more time. They used to get out more, sit on their front porches and talk with the neighborhood. Front porches we don't seem to have any more.

Today, your stores are open on Sunday and people shop and they're crowded. Yet in those days, you wouldn't think of shopping on Sunday, and yet today they have more time. Why do they shop on Sunday? I don't understand. They have Saturday off, yet they're crowded Sunday.

Though I did travel alone, I don't remember having any trouble in those days. Maybe they are preoccupied with their own troubles these days or just becoming indifferent to others. There are a number of blind people living here. Totally blind, they have to go around with a cane. You'll see them standing on the corner and people go right by them. I can't see too well myself, but I've helped many of them across the street. They stand there otherwise for a long time. I don't know why. Some will attempt to cross by themselves, which they should never do because the cars today you can't hear too well, and they swing around that corner, so it's really dangerous. But they don't know what else to do. They stand and wait and nothing happens, so they attempt it themselves.

The self-service stores—now when I go to a store that I don't know, say a dime store, you're lost. You just don't know what to do. You ask the gentleman, where is so and so and he'll say, oh, over there in such and such. But you can't find it because you can't read it. Even in a department store. Wait on yourself. It's getting awful. A drug store, that's hopeless.

On the hour, the bird in the wall clock pops out and sounds off: "Cuckoo! Cuckoo!"

(Laughs.) Maybe he agrees.

One of my pet peeves is the automatic elevator. The other day I happened to go downtown. I guess it was Lytton's. Here was the elevator and it's got buttons. Well, there were a lot of people in, so I figured somebody must be getting off at the fourth floor. So I didn't know what to do, so I rode—well, I ended on the fifth floor. So I pushed the thing and I went down and got in again. So it stopped and I thought, well, this must be the fourth floor. It happened to be the third floor. Well, I pushed the button again and got back in and then I looked at it and there were great big numbers, I could see them. So I pushed Four and I thought, well, whatever happens will happen. It stopped at four. When you get into a building, say, like the Prudential, with those large panels, then I'm stuck. 30 North Michigan, that's another one. You get in there and they have so many numbers that I'm stuck, 'cause they're small. But Lytton's was a good one.

Down here in the medical center, they had a switchboard operator there. They're gonna teach switchboard to the blind. But they put in an automatic. Now that don't make sense. They're gonna teach switchboard, but don't use it themselves.

There's a senior center right up the street here in the elderly building. I work there quite a lot. We have a ruling though: no religious talk or politics. 'Cause we're liable to get into an argument. So, especially in weaving, we do a lot of talking while we're weaving and our instructor says: no politics or religion. I think it's a good idea where there's a crowd. Because somebody's gonna get hurt. And you don't want to hurt anybody, especially a senior.

Talk about the bomb, for example, is something I very rarely hear among seniors. Maybe they don't think they'll be around or something of that kind, but they don't seem too worried about it at all. TV is discussed quite a bit. They all have their favorite programs and they sometimes don't agree. We invariably end up with food, and then when we get in the middle of it somebody will say, well, how did we get back to that again? But somebody will say they had something and we're off on food again. There are some that are very proud of their children and grandchildren so they'll bring pictures to show you. But I don't know, we always end up with food.

There was a great deal of talk in our family when I was

51

young. They didn't have television. They didn't even have radio for years. So what else could we do but play cards and talk? Pedro and five hundred. I know they used to talk politics a lot. Today somebody's liable to say something to hurt somebody.

I think in the majority the young are fine people. We hear about delinquents all the time. Every day. When some youngsters do something real nice, that's not news, so we don't know about it. Therefore we're afraid. I notice elderly people here are afraid of teenagers. We have loads of them here and they're not bad.

We had a little incident out here in the parking lot back of the senior building. An elderly man had gotten out of his car out in the middle of the parking lot. He couldn't wait because he had to go to work at his church and he just left it there. Two teen-agers saw the car and they wanted to push it back. But they wouldn't touch it. They came in the building and asked if they knew whose car it was. The lady said she did. And they said, "Well, if you come out and stand with us, we'll push it back, but we won't touch it because as sure as we do, somebody will call the police."

My husband and I were just saying this morning that youngsters today don't have nearly as much fun as we did. We didn't have anybody supervise our play. We just made things up as we went along. Today they do certain things and it has to be supervised, and so on. I think that's because there are so many more children in the world and there are so many people coming in, migrants and all that. Population. Things were easier in those days when I was a youngster.

Some of these kids today resent the elderly being here. Maybe it's the fault of the elder person because they object to the youngsters making noise or playing ball and they antagonize the kids. The children resent this building.

I have noticed that if a blind person or a crippled person is in trouble, the colored people will be the first to come to help. Now there was a little girl that lived downstairs, she was a cerebral palsy girl. She was about in her twenties. She was working at County Hospital at the time and she couldn't get off the bus. Well, the bus driver didn't do anything about it, and the other people just pushed right by her. There was a colored gentleman across the street, came running out across Harrison Street, took her off, took her across and put her on the other bus to go the rest of the way. So I don't know.

When we first moved in at LeClaire,* we had a Negro family across the hall from us and a Negro family upstairs. Now we lived with those families, especially the one across from us. They finally moved to a larger apartment and we hated to see them go. He, Mr. Williams, would always say, "If you need anything, just let me know." And when we moved here, we had them next door. They had two small boys who were the nicest youngsters around. I never came to the walkway that they didn't run to the door and help.

I hear people talking all the time about them and it bothers me because it isn't true. I mean maybe some of it is, but then the same thing is true of white people. We're not all perfect, either. I don't like to hear people talk against the colored race or any other race for that matter. It doesn't bother me . . . but I don't do anything about it because I'm not about to get into an argument. It might be a good friend of mine and I just don't want to lose a good friend. Otherwise if it wasn't . . .

As for civil rights parades, I guess it's all right for priests, but honestly I don't think nuns should do it. I guess that comes from when I was little and I went to a Catholic school. I have the notion that they belong in the convent doing their duty and not out. I know they drive cars and everything today, but it just didn't seem right to have them out in front of that parade. Priests, it's all right.

The colored seem to have their classes, too. This one woman moved into a neighborhood on the South Side. At the time it was mostly white. She remarked that if the white people would only stay and try to get along with the few colored that were in there, they'd be very very happy, the colored people. But, she said, when the colored people start to move in solidly, she said, we're going to move out because we don't want to be with—she said, you get the . . . riffraff, is what the lady said. And, she said, we don't want to live with them. But we would like to live with the white. Now this wasn't a wealthy neighborhood, this was just an ordinary South Side neighborhood.

* LeClaire Courts is a public-housing project on Chicago's Southwest Side, near Midway Airport.

I notice classes more now. We weren't wealthy at all when I was a youngster. But it didn't seem to matter then. We didn't have a great deal of money, but we didn't feel that we were *poor* people. I suppose we would be by standards of today but we didn't *feel* that way. I think in Chicago it's going to be the very poor and the very wealthy, from the way it's going now. You put all these big buildings along the North Shore and you put the wealthy people in. And your middle class or upper middle class are all moving out to the suburbs, but the poorer classes can't afford it so they're staying here. You're gonna have the two extremes eventually.

People don't seem as neighborly now as they were when I was little. I guess people are about the same, but circumstances make it a little different. In this particular hallway here, and right through the project, they're all very friendly. We sit on benches together. But I didn't find that when we lived in apartment buildings. Most people don't know their own neighbors across the hall.

I don't like all this steel and glass that's going up straight. It don't look very warm or homey. I know they are inside, but they just don't look that way from the outside. It makes the city look cold, I think. People are moving to get away from people. I don't like the way we're going.

• • • • • •

Chester Kolar, 56

A technician at an electronics plant. There were glory days. Once, he had conducted a program over a foreign-language radio station. He was celebrated in his community then.

I'm cold to it, these Vietnam photos. And most of my friends, the technicians, are cold to it. The only thing is their remark: "What do you know about that?" If you're gonna worry about that . . . and today we got so many people that are so easy to falling in this category of worrying, that actually what makes a lot of people sick. Some people can't stand this. They shut the TV off. You heard of the guy who kicked the TV tube and took a pistol and shot into the—I mean, he was off his nut. I don't know if you ran across some of these people, they're very nervous-type people. As a matter of fact, if someone shouts, they jump. I'm cold to it.

These people sit around this radio and TV and they listen to all these broadcasts. I think this news we're having is doing us more harm than good. I'm speaking of those that are disinterested and it's being crammed down their throats. Over the radio comes a message. Special bulletin: so many people killed. I mean, what are they trying to fire up? This poor man that's trying to get his eight hours of work done to keep his family going, pay his rent, and buy his food which is high today, he gets all excited about what's going to happen. What does John Q. Public know what should happen? Let's not stick our nose into something we know nothing about.

Why should he worry about these things? We should know once a month, let's have a review of the news: what will happen and what has happened. These people are worried about something they shouldn't be worried about. They should be worried about painting their rooms and fixing something up where they could become industrious.

· · · · · ·

Elizabeth Chapin, 75

She was born in Chicago and has lived in the same house since 1908. A widow, her children married, she keeps a tidy place; a blooming geranium garden is in the back yard.

Don't cut off the nice things of the past. Why are they tearing down these old landmarks, the buildings, the trees? I don't call that progress. We must have something to build our life on, and our own ideals. I don't say foggy memories, no. Why do we tear down the water tower? I agree it's a monstrosity, but it's Chicago. It was a thing of beauty in its time. Is it because we've never been anywhere? Other countries seem to want them and hold them and retain them and be proud of them. I have in mind the

Garrick.* The Harding Museum,† what is to be gained in tearing it down? I don't call that progress. The need to go on and on. To have no *sitzfleisch,* as we say in German. No reposing.

The automobile, what could you do without it? In another few generations, people will have no legs, we won't need them. I take this dog for a walk every day. Walk a few blocks to the bakery shop. I have known people who live around the corner from the bakery, who take their car to get there. People are amazed when I tell them I don't pass a day that I don't walk three, four miles. It just wouldn't occur to me. There's so much to see, to observe, while you're walking. What happens to us that we don't see these things? When I take the dog for a walk, I see things. People's eyes are closed, with a film over them, or what is it?

Mothers don't take their children anywhere. *Do* something. Lady downstairs, I said put on your hat and I'll take you to Lincoln Park. I took another woman to the Art Institute. She hadn't been there in thirty-five years. These things are in our hands and we don't use them. I don't understand it. A month or so doesn't go by when I don't go to the Art Institute, maybe for an hour or so. It refreshes your mind again. It's provocative.

I remember one cathedral in the south of France, tall pillars. It was a kind of narrow cathedral. It reminded me of tall, stately beautiful women to be admired, and to be quiet as we passed by. I remember an old crumbled temple and I was terribly moved. I was standing and looking and thinking of many things. And finally I said to the children, "I think if I die now, I would be happy. I don't think I'll ever get closer to heaven." It was exactly the way I felt. I was never so moved in my life. (Laughs.)

I cried so many times in Italy, all these textbooks came to life. When we came to the Colosseum, I got up and cried and kissed it. We go by these things and we never see them. I can cry pretty easily. I don't cry for sorrow, that I can swallow and hold. But for real joy, I can cry.

---

* A theater created by Louis Sullivan. It was torn down to make place for a parking lot.

† A museum that featured armor and its history. At the moment it is a vacant lot, for purposes of urban renewal and the rerouting of a boulevard.

What is progress anyway? My idea of what progress should really be is to help the children, help the people who are out of work and find a place for them. Not to tear down beauty.

If I weren't independent, what would I do? Be a burden on my children? Or go to a poorhouse or something? Can you force your children to take care of you? You can by law, but would you want to? I don't know what's happened to our attitude toward older people. Do they figure they'll never get old?

The woman who lives downstairs, she gets less than $600 a year to live on. Seventy-three, seventy-four. What can you do on $600 a year? There's her gas, her electricity, her rent, food. I take care of most of her meals. She has no one else to go to. But she's a prudent woman. She has about $2000 stored away. That's for her funeral.

She carries with her a clipped newspaper photograph: a terrified Vietnamese woman, hovering over her child, as soldiers casually pass by.

I can't get this out of my mind. That woman has the same right to live and the same right for her—shall we say freedom?—or at least her chances to live and not be cowed down, protecting her naked child, while soldiers go by. That picture has moved me a great deal. Such contrasts. It's not the soldiers' fault.

When my son was injured in Belgium, he wrote to me from a hospital in London. He was cut by a saber from the ankle right up to his forehead. "Mother, you're all wrong. All men are not good, some are out to do you bad. I never saw this man before and I'll never see him again. Why did he cut me up?" My son didn't raise his gun, he was a paratrooper, but I don't think he would have killed. When he was in the hospital, there was a German convalescent there. He asked my son for a cigarette. And he wrote, "I didn't give him a cigarette. I thought he was my enemy. God damn propaganda! I had more cigarettes than I could smoke the rest of my life, but I didn't give that poor sucker a cigarette." Two strangers.

I shudder when I think what might happen in Vietnam. I can't understand, and never will, what gives the few men the right to **hold** all our lives in the palm of their hand?

What right have they got, what God-given right have they got? Just to press the button and say you've had it. And you think of your own son, who's just starting to live, and all these kids. Is it really freedom for them they're seeking? Or something deeper than that, something you and I won't express?

Don't you think at this time in our life, in our culture, we should be able to do something beside shoot each other? The ancient punishments, cutting off a thief's hands, did it ever stop thieving? No. How can they be so cruel to another man?

After all, the greatest tragedy in life is death isn't it? Why can't we make it a little less tragic? Every morning, when I open my eyes—I don't pull the shade, I like the light to come in—the sun is shining in. And each day I find sufficient.

. . . . . .

John Rath, 61

I come home to an empty room. I don't even have a dog. Go out, they don't care if you live or die. The only time they find out if you're dead is when you don't go down and pay the rent. There's been cases of the man being in the room for two or three weeks, till they were discovered rapping on the door: "Your rent is due." (Laughs.) You don't believe that?

A furnished room, somewhere on the city's North Side, a transient area. A stove, a single gas plate, a sink, a package of Quaker Oats, a tiny icebox. The plaster is peeling from the walls; the ceiling is cracked; the window shades are smudged. The man was rolling a Bull Durham.

You take a little walk. Take a drink if you can afford it. Stop in and have a cup of coffee. You can get one for a dime. No, this is not the kind of life I would choose. If a man had a little piece of land or something, a farm, or well . . . anyway, you've got to have something. You sit down in a place like this, you grit your teeth, you follow me? So many of them are doing that, they sit down, they don't know what to do, they go out. I see 'em in the middle of the night, they take a walk. Don't know what to do. Have no home environment, don't have a dog, don't have nothing . . . just a big zero. They're looking—no one likes to look to die regardless of how bad the situation may be. But that's what they're doin' anyway, just sitting down and waiting for doomsday. Which of course is on the way for all of us. But a man's gotta squeeze enough goodness in life, between the time he's born and the time he dies. Many never make it.

You get into these big cities, it's like a jungle. It's what they call the asphalt jungle. You're not even safe walking around. There are spots in this town I wouldn't even go in at night. But up there, in Luddington, Michigan, where I come from, there's a different class of people, I think. I mean they were more honest. They believe in that old-time philosophy, live and let live. You never hear that thing any more.

They don't care about anything. Money today is king. That's the only thing that matters, if you got the bucks. They figure, well, if everything's going to blow up they might as well grab as much as they possibly can, have a good time while it's here and while they're here, too.

Do you think the world's gonna blow up?

No, I don't think so. If there's a war, winner loses all, that new song says. I was just reading in a magazine the other day where one scientist claimed that all these nuclear bombs that have exploded in recent years are the ones responsible for the weather. You know, I don't have to tell you, you know what I mean. And another one says no.

Do you worry about the war in Asia?

They should—what did Goldwater say?—clean 'em out, didn't he say that? Well, I believe that they should. It seems the United States is the only one policing the world. Let this country be alone and take care of our own individual problems. You have problems, I have problems, everybody has 'em, but some have worse than others. I have greater problems, of course, than many men.

I've had a broken ankle, broken leg, broken collar bone. Feel this, see what it is? A fella hit me down on Clark

Street. I was going to work. For no reason at all he come up. I never seen him. I coulda knocked down a bull in those days. I could get hold of a man when he's unprepared like that. This was in 1946. Boom. I went down like a . . .

He socked you just like that?

Yeah, for no reason. It's given me a lot of trouble. Just put your finger in, so you can understand what I'm drivin' at.

Oh, I see it's broken all right. Wow.

Fully a half inch out of the way. And here I am walking around with a cast down from my neck down to my waist, see? No one tried to do anything for me. You can't try to fight big insurance companies. August 26 is when I think it did happen. Nobody was interested. The doctors for the money. Druggists sell you medicine, salves, whatnot.

You come across anybody who gives a damn?

No, really not, I mean, the way people are driving cars with no consideration for the pedestrian. Right around here, you ought to hear them screech around here at midnight. Oh, Holy Moses, I'm tellin' ya, up and down. It was only two weeks ago over here, two blocks that way, one guy was driving sixty miles an hour, on a Sunday morning, too. Oh, I don't know where he was going. He was in a big hurry. Boom, right into another car. The second car looked like an accordion. Telescoped it. Both cars were wrecked, one completely. The world's moving too fast for me.

That's why I gave up religion. I seen what was going on and how these religious people act. I was an altar boy for a good many years and I firmly believe it's a hoax. *H-O-A-X*. That's my belief. But I'm not a firm disbeliever. I'm what you call agnostic: a person who will not declare himself either way. He's not an atheist. An atheist, Thomas Paine was one. Clarence Darrow was another. I think Robert Ingersoll was a third one. There were quite a few.

I read extensively now, you know. I don't have anything else to do. There's a book that takes us back to the days when Manhattan Island was sold. (You'd be amazed at the conniving. All the way to Warren Harding where he got in with a bunch of crooks. I passed that place, halfway between Sheridan, Wyoming, and Casper.)

Teapot Dome?

Yeah, Teapot Dome. I stopped there a little while to look it over. Calvin Coolidge was vice-president at the time Harding died in San Francisco. I was there. Silent Cal. He didn't say nothing, he didn't do nothing. You take this governor we had. They spent over a million dollars trying to convict him. They didn't try, we know that. I told a fella, "You wait, you'll never see him convicted." 'Cause he's in a clique, he's what they call the elite. The elite, you know what I mean, they get by with everything. And I say they'll never . . . and they didn't either. So what is your opinion?

Do you see any hope?

When a man gets up in years it's not too important what's gonna happen a hundred years from now or even fifty years from now. It's the young people that gotta change this whole setup. That's my belief. Of course, when you get older, you talk to many older men and they don't care. (Too bad, too bad, and they go about their business the same as before. Because they know they can't change it and even if they did, they wouldn't reap any benefits.)

I'm tellin' ya, they wear you out fast. You're fit for the junk pile, that's all. You'd be amazed how many men I know in Lincoln Park, healthy fellas about my age. They look at 'em, they don't say your hair's gray, you're worn out, but that's what they mean. They say we'll accept your application, we'll file it. Boom, in the wastebasket. You're a machine, that's all. So a machine doesn't work out properly, throw it in the junk pile. Man, they throw you out the door.

I mean they're not working, they don't have money. I mean if he's getting a small pittance with the prices today, gone up about ten percent, twenty, thirty. They minimize, they always say, well, prices have gone up a mill, two mills, a tenth of a penny. Right? that's to make you feel better.

They sit in the park on the bench, that's all. Talk about

61

horses or whatever. Gotta have a little entertainment. Interest in life. There's not much else to do.

I would have stayed in a smaller city. I mean, not too small, but something like maybe 50,000 or 100,000 people, and I think I woulda gotten along better. In a big city, they don't know who you are or what you are. Neither do they care.

POSTSCRIPT

Outside the rooming house. It is twilight. Red neon cuts through the grayness. The window of the manager's office is open. It is a furnished room itself: the presence of a desk rather than a bed differentiates it from the others. There is, too, a slightly tattered divan and a TV set. The matronly woman in charge is watching a television program. Her manner is catatonic. Two guests saunter into the office; blond young men. There is no greeting. They, too, stare at the box. Their manner is desultory.

Across the street is a large sign above a building entrance: Montrose Urban Progress Center, Chicago Committee on Urban Opportunity. Mayor Richard J. Daley, Chairman.

· · · · · ·

Rita Buscari, 25

A schoolteacher. After hours, she was gathering signatures for a Paul Crump clemency petition.* She had been standing on West Side corner, near the County Jail.

After about two hours, I was able to know who was going to sign my petition and who wasn't. It's like Times Square out there. There are families coming, they've got kids in trouble, people coming out of County Jail, being released. I found invariably that the people that were eager, were proud to sign, were the poor people, the people who were in trouble, whose kids were in trouble.

I'd go up to a group that would be standing, waiting for

* Paul Crump, convicted of murder, had been in death row for nine years. Clemency was urged on the grounds of his rehabilitation. Among those so pleading was the warden of the County Jail, Jack Johnson. His sentence was commuted to life imprisonment.

a bus, and ask them. At first you'd get this: "What? You want me to sign? Am I important? Would my name be important?" "Oh, yes," you know, and you'd explain that every name is important. And they would sign. And a couple of women, they would actually start crying, and say, "Do you think this will do any good?" And we were saying, "Well, we hope so."

The people that refused to sign, were all the better-dressed people, the officials. And they'd look at you with such coldness, you know, and such resentment, like what are you trying to do? What are you trying to prove?

I took a tour through County Jail one time and when we saw the women, you know, the women are in one cell group. There were about a hundred of these women lying around, combing each other's hair and playing cards. I said, "This is one of the most awful things I've ever seen." And the others all said to me, "What do you want, Rita? What do you want to do with them, let them run wild? These are prostitutes, these are dope addicts, what do you want? This is better, we keep them all penned up."

And this was the attitude I would meet on the street. The poor would say, "Don't kill the man." I discovered, which is often the case, that the poor found it in their hearts to forgive. Whereas, the pure, the middle class, you know, haven't got it any more. Somewhere along the line, they've lost it. Like, you know, as if Paul Crump sitting there is a threat to them, and they had to keep the status quo. Don't rock the boat in any way.

The others, the dignity with which they signed this. Many of them were the young gang-member set. You'd rather cross the street than approach them, because they looked terrifying. Even they were like little children as they signed their names. With such pride, with such dignity.

There were about forty of us went down there to protest James Dukes' execution.* We had a very orderly, and I think, dignified picket line. We marched in two's up and down, very quiet. We rarely spoke to each other. But across the street were about two hundred people in their cars with the doors open, the radios blarin' out rock'n'roll music, with beer cans and with sandwiches. They were

* James Dukes, convicted of murder, died in the electric chair that night.

there all evening, and very often there would be jeers at us from across the street.

I was marching with a Northwestern student, who goes down to protest every time there's an execution. He said these people are there at every excution. Every single one. He said no matter how cold it is, there are approximately the same number of people. He believes they're there because the lights dim in the building, which isn't true, because the chair is rigged up to a different electrical system.

They stay there until the body is brought out in an ambulance. You got the feeling, you know, that this was the instinct that sent people to the Colosseum in Rome. And it's here, right here and now, present in our society. Warden Johnson said people call up and ask for tickets. Well, if tickets were sold, I'm sure it would be a sellout house every single time.

It was so brutish. I was marching with pacifists and ministers, and the quiet of these people compared to the crowd across the street gave it a nightmarish quality. At the time of the execution we all turned toward the jail and ceased conversation. And this was when the rhythm of the noise on the other side gained momentum. They had all the radios on, first of all because they wanted to hear the announcement. The sounds on the other side increased as our silence increased.

When the announcement came through on the radio, there was a big reaction across the street: Oh, that's over with. Oh, that's great. Especially toward us. It was a victory for them, you see? A great victory against the crackpots who were demonstrating across the street. You know: This is how much your demonstration has achieved, you're no place at all.

The next day, I read where Dukes had marked out a very moving passage, I believe it was Socrates—speeches before his death. He had marked out a particular passage to illustrate his feelings at the time And this was the man who was being executed.

You have this awful feeling: Will we ever get through? Will we ever be able to explain to people? Are you ever going to overcome people's desire for punishment? Because, in a way, this gives them a sense of security. And you want to say we've got to learn to forgive. And they just stand there. I had seen the chair and I could picture the scene, and you feel very helpless. And you pray. This is what you do. You pray for the man's soul. As the warden said, actually these men die with such grace upon them. Actually their death is not the tragedy. The tragedy is the people across the street.

● ● ● ● ● ● ● ● ●

Kid Pharaoh, 37

*He was standing outside his hot-dog shop, somewhere on
the North Side of the city. He was observing the sky.
"Think it'll rain?" I asked. "I'm looking at them high
rises," he replied. "Wish they were mine." During the conversation, I was rewarded with three fifty-cent cigars.*

Guys like me are the nucleus of the street. All the new-
comers are the real Johnny-come-latelies, are not familiar with the location, of what it stands for, of what it is.
I been in Chicago all my life, was born and raised here. My
dad was a speculator in the market, sometimes successful,
most of his life not. I'm an ex-prize fighter by profession.

I never graduated high school, and I missed absolutely
nothing. You learn nothing in school, nothing. The truth of
the matter is you learn it on the outside. A guy goes to
school, what does he want to be? A doctor? A lawyer?
These are the two biggest thieves in our society. One steals
legitimate, the other kills legitimate. Charge you what they
want. They never pay the Uncle what he's entitled to. Guys
like me they want to put in jail. Because I'm dedicated to
one principle: taking money away from unqualified dilettantes who earn it through nepotism. I work at this and I'm
good at my trade. I don't labor. Outside of being a prize
fighter, I took an oath to God I would never again labor.
But there's a million people on the street that want to be
taken and should be taken, and they're gonna be taken.

Me and my brothers have the same philosophy. We set a
snare, we trap these guys who come in. They're all either
biologically or physically insecure. They believe what they

66

read in the papers and everyone reads fiction and they're all scared. We sell two things: we sell the item of fear and we give them the security they never had in their life. And whatever they have, we take from them. They're more than willing to give it.

How did they get it? Did they earn it? Did they inherit it? Did they marry the boss's daughter? What's their qualifications? Half of one percent of America is qualified. You walk into any department store, for example, and you want to change a hat. He says, wait a minute, we'll send you to so-and-so. So-and-so sends you to the second floor, he's not qualified. By the time it's through, the whole afternoon is shot. Who's an authority? Who's really an authority that you know today? You can't name one.

During the Depression when I was a little boy, and I was hustling, selling newspapers or shining shoes or setting pins, or stealing ginger ale bottles off the Lake Shore Drive area, someone was the boss. Today there's no such thing as the boss. He's not really qualified.

My dad worked as a WPA man. We were on relief. I could see me and my kid brother going down to the Fair Store to get shoes on government stamps. I can see myself hustling food, luggin' oranges home and potatoes home. And this is the greatest thing that ever happened to guys like me. I mean, I loved it. This is what the system calls for, this is where you pick yourself up and go. Without money, you're a bum on the park, you're nothing. Who are you? You can't get yourself in an icebox. You can't get your hand out of one. You can't get your hand in one. What's the measuring stick of our system? He's a money guy, respect 'im. What do you do with a bum? Extend the evening felicitations. Is it a woman? She'll offer you a biological reward. If you've got currency, you'll offer her some luxury. The other mooch who got everything from his dad, the hell with him. Take it away from him. Hook, crook, slingshot, canoe, we must shaft this guy, got to take it away from him. But don't hurt him.

Now how do I survive? I live at the Belden Stratford, I manage a new car every year, I take my steam baths three times a week, I take a manicure, a pedicure. Now how do I get it? I don't break the law. If you steal it, you go to jail. You're in a trick bag. Now there are people on the street that have money, they don't know what to do with it. How do I take this money away from these guys? I play the Freudian theory, long may Freud live.

It's amazing, my reputation. People telling how qualified you are as Tom the Tough Guy and Pistol Pete. I got some good publicity as a prize fighter in the newspapers and I've gotten some bad publicity. People believe what they read. So then leave them think that way. My brother was in trouble recently. All the papers had him on the front page. He was on television. He was scared. I said, "Fool, you'll go out and raise all the money in the world." He came back in a week, he says, "You know, I made fourteen thousand?" "Double it. People want to help people, especially tough guys. They *need* you. They believe what they read. We know you're innocent, but let's take it from 'em." And we did. He was a celebrity. They worship celebrities. Tom the Tough Guy and Pistol Pete. This is the giant of their society. Who else is a giant? Some faggot movie star that puts powder on his face? What qualifies him? The entire country today moves on physiognomy. If you're attractive, it'll open the door. I can't get in. What's my best shot? The arm. I use it.

Everybody is really scared because they watch all this nonsense on television. No such thing as a tough guy, they're all dead. Now these people come in, say in the Old Town section where I bum in the late hours after I close this shop. We have a reputation of being some tough guys, but we're really not. We're very gracious gentlemen, we extend the utmost courtesies to everyone. But we don't tip our hand. As long as they believe it, leave them believe it. 'Cause their currency, we want to take it away from them, not by heisting them, but by encouraging them to do what they want. This boy who killed himself in Arizona, this MacDonald boy of Zenith. Now why couldn't I grab someone like him. We've often discussed it. He was insecure. Psychiatrists couldn't cure him, but we woulda cured him. We'd put a dent in him a little. Given him courage he never had. He had a Freudian complex of rejection. It was a broken-up family. And we'd of explained to him what to do with this type of money.

Why shouldn't we take it from them? Legally, with the semi-muscle. It can get you killed, but if you work it right, the greatest thing in the world is the semi-muscle. You put that fear in 'em that'll help them. I work on contracts, like in business. It's an oral contract. Now if they give me a contract, they come to me with some trouble. If called upon to perform, I perform. If not, I subcontract. Example. They're usually in debt. Or someone owes them money. Or they're extremely fond of women. Someone's cutting in on their girl. Their wife is an infidelist. There's all kinds of conditions. They're afraid, everybody's scared. I give them security. If their wife is an infidelist, I muscle the guy she's makin' love with. I run him off. If somebody owes him money, somebody's after him, I chase him away. See? Now this guy's in debt to me. The biggest mistake of his life. He should really paid 'em, because I've got him for the rest of his life. I'll always noodge him for some currency or another. I'll always go into him. You just can't imagine how many insecure people we have in this country. Say, in the Cuban crisis, remember? I was getting a manicure that day and my manicurist was so scared she didn't know if she was gonna have a heart attack. And I said, "Look, Louise, don't be afraid, sweetheart. They're gonna turn back the minute they get there, they're gonna make a U-turn." You know what happened? They got no chance with the Uncle. Everybody's scared—of something.

Are you scared of anything?

Absolutely nothing. And this is a dangerous society. People like to hurt people. Why do people go to Indianapolis Speed Race, two, three hundred thousand? To see the little guys run around in a car? Hell, no. They go to see people killed. If a man's brains can put a plane in the sky, why can't a man's brain kill ya? He does, he can use it, he's on the streets right now. Killers are stalking all day long, faggots are on the streets, peeking Toms are on the streets, teenagers are on the streets, you gotta use a baseball bat on 'em, guys like myself from the 43rd Ward, here in the Metropolitan area of Chicago. We don't believe in contaminating the morals. We run these guys off.

We don't want 'em around. If they come in a restaurant where we bum, or some faggot starts congregatin' around, they assemble—we run 'em off. We don't like 'em. I certainly have to protect my nieces and nephews. The law isn't qualified. The law protects these dilettantes and degenerates.

If I was a dictator, I would exercise genocide for all degenerates. I would slay them. Take most of these educated guys. Think they know what to do? You put them in Lincoln Park for three-quarters of an hour, and you'd have to take one of our little boy scouts who have to go in and take them out again. They wouldn't know how to get out. How does a man survive in a capitalistic system? Say you work twenty years on a job, you've lost it. What would you do now? My element can survive. Heaven forbid, we should live with a bomb, a fire, a flood, we'll survive.

How?

The mongrel and the pedigree. The pedigree will run across the street, is it not so, he'll get hit by the car? The mongrel will survive. He has the cunning to duck the car.

A dog, a mongrel?

Yeah, put me down as a dog, yeah. . . . You must be sincere in my element. Like Sam Giancana. Momo.* Now they've got this man in a trick bag, in a penal institution. They've taken his right away. It's unfair. It's not the way the American system works. The aggravation of putting this man away for no reason at all. He's my element. I don't prefer a lot of them because they're prejudiced toward their element of nationality. The same as the rise and fall of the Roman Empire. A one-way street cannot survive. He's fair with his money. He didn't forget people. Everybody who came out of jail he helped them, he made money for them, and he put them in power. He was qualified. Martin Luther King, put him away. What's he good for?

The American Negro not only has everything, now he's tampering with our white women. Women today seem to prefer pigmentation. I have two nieces, I'm worried about that. That some colored guy—and I'm the last guy in the world to be prejudiced—this guy comes to the big city and has a comb job on his head. They bust out in these attractive suits and they seem to have some sort of education

* Reputedly a leader of the Syndicate.

about them. Most of the girls who prefer pigmentation are not metropolitanites. They're from Ohio, Ioway, Indiana, or some of them buck towns.

Some war veterans who are laying in some basket in a hospital, they'll never go to him to arouse his biological urge or pat him on the back or give him a vote of confidence, a note of thanks, nonsense. What about the American soldier who went off to war? Who came back, who's in trouble with automation over his vocation? He's entitled to nothing, he's a mooch. What about the average layman who has labored hard and long in this country without an education, raised a family, sent boys off to war? He's in his vintage years. All of a sudden his building is worth thirty-five thousand dollars and he goes to bed feeling secure. In the morning, a Negro moves next door and his building is worth seventeen thousand. They've destroyed everything they've ever moved in. There's a revolt in the making, let me suggest it to you. When it will come, I don't know. How it will come, I don't know. Who will organize this revolt . . . but it'll come.

The best people for communities are the Japanese. They're never above a whisper. Their homes are immaculate. Show me a Japanese on the street after ten o'clock. Show me one, I'll offer a universal challenge to all. Did you ever see one arrested? Did you ever see one under the influence of an intoxicated beverage? Did you ever see 'em pregnant, Japanese girls who are not married? Of course not, there's love in the home. Say for the Negroes, they're animals. There's no love in the home. Not only wants to move the white man over, he wants to be there with him. They have a long-range plan of dissolving this pigmentation through intermarriage.

I thought you admired aggressiveness?

Yeah, but you ain't gonna muscle me. I'm a capitalist and they're gonna have to fight me and I ain't gonna lose. There's a lot of legitimate people like myself. My system may be outdated. I might have been a success at the turn of the century. Today with all the laws and Supreme Court rulings, I haven't even got a chance. If I was born forty years ago, I believe I would have been a multimillionaire. I shoot the same shot that Rockefeller shot while

71

somebody was tapping an oil well that was competitive to him. He put guys in trick bags. Got 'em in jail. There's a history written about these guys. John Astor, with his trapping, with his furs. Hitting guys. This is the way the system works. What else is there? These new laws are holding them back, destroying incentive. Our enemies are calling us capitalistic. We're not.

Capitalism ideally is for any bum in the park to come with an idea or be aggressive enough to find a place in the sun for himself, can go as high as he wants and as long as he wants.

Even if he has to step on others?

He must, he must. In our society, you must do it. It doesn't work any other way. People will hurt you, kill you.

To me the most important thing is helping someone who is in need. Financially, if I have the currency or any way shape or form, I can help people. And I do. Taking an oath before a high court and before God, we, we do it.

You believe in God?

I really don't. I'm a dedicated agnostic. Who was Jesus Christ? He was an excellent, I would say a con man. He learned hypnotism in India. When He lammed out of Israel, they wanted to shaft Him because He was causing all this nonsense and riots, He said He was the Son of God. Today they wouldn't kill Him. They would have offered Him psychiatric supervision, because the dear boy was in need of this. When He fed the multitude the fish, He hypnotized a half a dozen. They carried on the word. Who did He feed? He fed nobody. Who did He cure of leprosy? He hypnotized the people. They got up and they walked. He got Himself killed at thirty-two years of age. He couldn't keep His big bazoo shut. Did you know that Pontius Pilate offered to give this man a number? He said, "Now look, Jesus, you're a marvelous boy. Why don't you go off in the wilderness and cut this nonsense out, and go about your business. Quit causing all these riots." This man wanted to be killed. And he told Him, "If you want to be killed, I gotta hang up two criminals. So be it." Hit his hand on the table and they strung Him up. He was a rabble rouser.

Same thing with Martin Luther King. They asked the opinion of our great President, Harry Truman, and he said this guy was strictly a troublemaker, period. I thought Truman was marvelous. Because he was a guy that come up in the capitalistic system of politics from nothing to a giant. And this is the way our system works. From Daley here, from Kelly before him, from Nash before him . . . from the two Irishmen, Hinky Dink and Bathhouse John.* Boss Tweed in New York and what's his name in Boston —Curley. These were the giants that built the cities. These are the guys that built our country. They elect presidents. All these guys came up the hard way . . . shoeshine guys and bust-out crapshooters . . . shoot a shot against the blackjack. These are the guys we need in our country. Who needs educated mooches?

The greatest man in the twentieth century in my opinion—and I hope I don't offend anybody—is Mau Too Sung. He did something the world could never do. He feeds the multitudes. It's amazing about Peking. Like myself, the average layman in business for himself in a hotdog business, I'm always in trouble with flies. An ordinary fly who's a pest. Now Mau Too Sung has come up with a chemical. They've come up with somethin' which even us, the capitalistic system, does not have. There are no flies in Peking. He's a guy who's come up so hard.

You admire Harry Truman and Mao Tse-Tung and Momo Giancana.

And Daley. He's the greast mayor Chicago ever had. Here's a man dedicated to civilizing the city. He takes his paycheck and sits home trying to think how to do something for the city. He was smart enough and I believe intelligent enough and he fell into I must say luck, though

---

* "Bathhouse John" Coughlan and Michael "Hinky Dink" Kenna ruled Chicago's First Ward from 1892 for almost fifty years. This was the city's most celebrated vice district. The annual First Ward Ball was the social event of the season, attended by pimps, prostitutes, madams, political and social leaders—all the celebrities of the era. Tribute, material as well as spiritual, was paid to Bathhouse John and Hinky Dink on this occasion. There was reciprocity, of course: a wide-open area the year round.

qualified when called upon. Most of his competitors died off and he knew when to seize power. I'm for him a hundred percent. When mother died eight years ago, I got a condolence telegram from the mayor. It was humble of him to do that, very humble indeed. For the mayor of the second largest city of the world's greatest country to send such a telegram to an ex-prize fighter without a high-school diploma with the element that I'm in, my God, I should say yes.

Was he acquainted with you or your mother?

Of course not. My friend, Terry Boyle,* probably encouraged him. I'm a Democrat at heart anyway. I take the less of the two evils. Look at Chicago. There's all the sky rises and new roads and so forth. Qualified authorities tell me that a group of real-estate men control this urban renewal. I believe in slum clearance but this isn't the way to do it. All the benefits, no matter if it goes up, down, or sideways, they wind up with all the money. They all cut the pot together. They condemn the property they want to condemn and they throw in the high rises. They do it legally. I wish it was me.

There's a song I love. I never forgot it. "A man with a dream, a mighty man is he. For dreams make the man, the man he wants to be." You can be anything in this world you want to be, if you dream hard enough, long enough.

• • • • • •

Stan Lenard, 35

An actor, former interior decorator, he lives with his mother, who is unaware he is a homosexual. She and his two married sisters often urge him to get married. He hopes they never find out; it would hurt them. He himself is not ashamed of it. "You don't wake up one day when you're ten years old and say I'm going to be a homosexual. It's just something that comes. It's like a marriage that goes astray. A person doesn't pick a marriage that will

* Terence Ignatius Boyle. See Part XI: Celebrity.

fail, a person doesn't want an arm or leg amputated. It's something you learn to live with."

In high school and the army, they called him "Rosebud." It was done affectionately, not with antagonism. "I always felt they were laughing with me, rather than at me." And in deciding whether "to jump off the Michigan Avenue Bridge or laughing through it," he chose "laughing through it."

I can't remember anything that really hurt deep. Oh yes, when I walked into a straight bar . . . I feel I can walk into any bar, any house, either I'm accepted or I take the chance that I will not be. And if I'm not, it's not going to cut deep at this stage of the game. Nobody can love everybody. At this bar, there were some snide remarks made that cut deep, even though from perfect strangers. They didn't even know me. I just walked in and ordered a few drinks and the drinks were bad drinks and they came back that way about three times. Finally, I realized this was being done on purpose. Without having a chance to open my mouth, I was being stomped on. They are the ones without understanding. They may be much less people than I am.

I have avoided gay bars. They act as a depressant on me. I came up with a joke and I think it's a cute one: "Whatta ya mean gay bar? Nobody's laughing." (Laughs.) It's true. Nobody's having fun, nobody seems really human. I have seen older homosexuals. I don't really like what I see in them. There is nothing more ugly than loneliness. I've never been pretty or beautiful, thank God. I know homosexuals who are good-looking and are desperately afraid of losing their looks, their appeal, their everything. They're frustrated to the point of the drinking bit.

Loneliness doesn't get better, it gets worse. I can endure loneliness if I can find success, in show business, for instance. I found recently I'm happy giving myself in the theatre. I don't think I'll find one person I can love as much as I can an entire audience.

I tried loving an individual. My experiences with the female sex were disheartening. I never really knew what was expected of me. I didn't know how to give. I guess I just didn't want . . . It always seemed to be an invasion of my privacy, an invasion of my own path of life. I didn't know

75

how to think about anyone else except myself. I wouldn't go a couple of miles out of my way, if the girl lived a couple of miles out of my way, because it was taking up my time. It was taking up my life. It was doing something for somebody else.

There are a few women to whom I've been drawn sexually. But I was the one who was pushed away when it got down to those matters. I think love is a marvelous thing, no matter who it happens between. It happens between grandfathers and their children. It happens to mothers and daughters. Affection is a marvelous thing. I don't ever think it's anything to be pushed out of the way.

I'm getting at an age now when I realize that companionship . . . Lonely people are a sad thing. I don't know whether I can find anybody understanding enough. I don't know if I can really understand myself enough to be married to a woman whose life I might destroy. I know couples who are involved in that situation. They seem to be rolling along, but the mental strain is not worth it. It's not fair to the other party. If I ruin my life, that's not so bad as ruining somebody else's.

I live more by feeling than I do by reasoning. I feel there is less living with feeling nowadays. Whenever a city begins growing up, there's always going to be more loneliness. A lot of people walking alone. A lot of people doing things alone. Eventually, though, this lonely bit may be a good thing in bringing a better understanding of each other than ever before.

I was away from the church for two years, and I learned more about myself and my problems and the world than in thirty-five years of going to confession. The church always made me feel like I was better than anybody else because I was a Catholic. One day I realized: How can anyone feel they are better than anyone else and still be part of the world, able to give and take. I think this is why things are changing so drastically in the church. The last time I went to confession, I found a very understanding priest. He showed compassion.

I've bumped into other priests who were very different. It varied from the old hellfire-and-brimstone bit to "have you ever thought about getting married?" "Why don't you go out and find yourself a nice girl?" Have you thought about a psychiatrist?" (Laughs.) I feel if God is omnipotent and

76

full of mercy and has created us all, I am nothing but a creature of God.

I was very conscious of the sin bit when I was young. There are worse things going on in the world, murders. I don't feel guilty any more, but I feel being a homosexual is wrong. It's wrong because of the upheaval it creates within a person. I don't know how rich a life can be under these circumstances. It's wrong in that it limits the richness. It dulls it. What I want to do if I feel cheated to a degree is to push toward something where I can have this outlet and where I can feel I'm having a good life.

If I were God, I'd like to see the kind of world I remember. There's one time in my life when I felt absolutely pure white and clean and good inside and outside. Albeit fifty percent of this feeling was due to the white communion suit probably. (Laughs.) But it was my first Holy Communion Day. It was a marvelous feeling, because it was sunshiney, the suit was bright white, clean, the shoes were white, everything was white. And I was white and clean and good. I'd like to have that kind of world, where naïveté comes back in being. It's not a silly word. It's a beautiful word, really. And the kind where everybody could say whatever they wanted to say. I think we've gotten so wrapped up in all this jazz. (Laughs.) The world has lost so much . . .

An innocence, that's what's lacking in so many supposedly adult human beings today. So many people are ashamed to cry, ashamed to really have feelings. I must include myself in this group, because maybe this is the reason I have not been able to open myself up to accept anyone else in my life. You meet so few people who do have the capacity for it.

III

"DID YOU SEE LORD JIM?"

● ● ● ● ● ● ● ● ● ●

Dennis Hart, 26

"Did you see Lord Jim?" he asked. He's a cabdriver, working the night shift. He has an insect-exterminator business on the side. He has a wife and two children. He identified himself with Conrad's hero because it was about "a man finding courage. The most important thing in life."

He had known abject poverty in Chicago, where he was born, and on an Arkansas farm, where his family had spent several years. "I found an old potato in the back yard, I ate it like an animal. There was just nothing else." Poverty was crushing his spirit: "I lost face. I lost composure." His teeth are bad because of the Milky Way and Snickers bar dinners he had so often as a newsboy in the city. When the family had returned to Chicago, the slight Southern accent he had picked up led to ridicule by his classmates and to fights: "It was a matter of saving face. I lost more fights than I won, but you couldn't back down."

His father, whom he greatly admires, had left home at twelve, lived in hobo jungles, came up the hard way: "He didn't look rugged. He had that young determined look about him, about to gain a piece of life, a place for himself." What he finds most admirable in his father is his courage: he had worked as an FBI informer. "I was never very close to him. I don't think I ever panned out to be what he wanted." His two younger brothers were Golden Gloves fighters; he wasn't as good. "But I know he's proud of me today."

"I don't think you can ever stop proving yourself to

your father. More than that, you have to prove to yourself what you really are inside you: whether you're willing to die for what you believe. If the cause is great enough, you'd be willing to die."

In the last five years, I've become a Republican precinct captain. I also went on to become chairman of the Goldwater campaign in my ward. It was because I was trying to be somebody. I had these doubts about myself as to whether I had any courage in me at all or was I just gonna be a plant instead of a man.

If I die, I don't want to die a natural death that most people succumb, say at sixty years old. If I could die on some battlefield someplace, doing something good, I feel my life would be worthwhile. I want my death to be worth something. If the time comes, I want to die with some pride. I want to die like a man, not like an animal.

When I read Goldwater's book, I identified with my own experiences in life. Because he spoke of the hardship of the individual, things he endured. He himself didn't, he's more of an aristocratic family, but he seemed to understand me. An individual should stand for more than a handout. This is the way America is. You fight for what you get, and once you get it, you hold on to it: your pride, your bread and butter, and what not.

If they dropped the Bomb today, the man who would succeed most is not the man with the brawn but the man with the brains. I feel if this was a wilderness, I could make out quite amply—if I knew a little bit about everything. I'm not worried about them dropping the Bomb. I've lived in a wilderness all my life. Atheists are the most fearful of the Bomb. A man who is truly religious and believes in God doesn't run around worrying about these things. He knows there's a Hereafter.

Freedom is the most important thing in your life. We're facing an enemy today that's gonna annihilate us unless we retaliate in one way or another. We have to face up to it, Bomb or no Bomb. Otherwise, we're a bunch of cowards.

I am now a member of the John Birch Society. It is a great society, one I believe in and one I would fight for. The more it was criticized, it made me all the more want to become a John Bircher. I was hoping somebody would invite me to a meeting and sure enough it took place. I've never been prouder to join an organization in my whole life.

It was an image I saw in these people. When they speak, they speak sense. My grandfather never had much of an education, but he was strong enough to know right from wrong. These people are putting their cards on the table and calling an ace an ace and a king a king and saying exactly what they think. They're saying the whole problem is very simple. Life is complicated enough without saying it's more complicated than it is. The sooner we try to uncomplicate our lives . . . if you complicate things, you are only asking for trouble. But if you try to simplify things, you find solutions will come much easier.

Has this helped you overcome your self-doubts, your fears?

A man has to find himself. What caused my fears was the fact that we moved around so much. I never seemed to have found a home—until now. I used to be very scared. I've been saved three times. I fell into a dam once, when I was going to a Y camp. I was scared and I was saved. One time, out here on Lake Michigan, the undertow got me. And I had to be saved that time. At school, I was swimming, we were taking a test, and all of a sudden I tightened up. I got scared. I'm a three-time loser and I came through this. I can't fail again.

For the last five years, I had to take my family to the beach and go swimming. Every Sunday I had to lick this fear. I think I have. Boxing has given me a little bit of composure. I've been over to the Joe Louis Gym, I've been over at CYO. I've boxed a lot with my brothers. Boxing to me is the greatest thing in the world for composure—to lick one's fear and to go right to it. A lot of people think the important thing is knocking the other guy down. The important thing is to keep yourself from getting hurt.

You've been hurt a good deal?

Definitely. I got to the point when I found I was becoming very cold and this bothered me. I was afraid to see others be hurt around me and I was becoming very calloused to their feelings, to their wants, to their needs. More than anything else, beside my fear, this bothered me. I'd seen people cry and I felt no feeling for them. I didn't know what was going wrong with me.

I guess maybe it's growing old and realizing you're gonna meet your Maker sooner or later. You have to feel something for other people. There was a time in my early twenties, I'd see people bleed, I'd see people cry. I didn't feel anything. I began to hate myself. Now I feel I've conquered this also. Crying with this man when he's hit, I feel the punch. It keeps you young. Old people become calloused. A conservative feels pain for other people because a conservative is closer to God.

I think really what changed me was working as a guard in the County Jail. So many of the things are so unnecessary. You hear the train whistle coming through at three in the morning. Why are these guys here? They're so young. One fella said, "What time is it?" And I said, "Why? Are you gonna catch a plane or something?" After I said it, after I made the punch on the clock, I realized I made a damn fool of myself. I went back and I actually apologized to this guy in a roundabout way. A guard is not supposed to give in in any way whatsoever. You're supposed to stay above these guys. But I felt like a damn jackass. I think it was the human thing to do.

As I sat down, I had to think of a way to apologize. I didn't come out and say to this man, "I'm sorry for what I said." But I went back and paid a little more attention to him and he understood that I was sorry and I felt I was forgiven.

Do you ever cry?

Yes. I feel better any time I cry. I saw my grandfather cry, he was the most kindhearted and warm person I ever knew. He would rock me for hours on a rocking chair. I felt if crying is good enough for him, it's good enough for me. I don't feel one cries in the open, unless you're around friends, unless it's death or sickness in the family. Recently my grandmother was taken to the hospital and I cried like a baby in front of the nurses and everything. In order to be a man, I have to have a heart also. This is part of his composure. Every time I cry, I feel more like a man later on.

I have seen Negroes cry. Around Christmas, this one, his wife ran out on him, took the bankbook and everything. I remember he took me in like a brother. He ran a tavern. A young fella, very good-looking. I remember the tears in his eyes. I know they have feelings. I know that they love just as deeply as we love, if not more so.

I personally felt his grief more than if it was a white man crying. It's a rare incident to see a white man cry. I've known white people who make it a habit to cry to gain whatever they want to get. But I've yet to see a Negro cry for his own personal gain. If a Negro cries, he cries because he's truly hurt.

I feel the Negro will fight with us when the time comes. I think someday he's gonna make a great American. I have many Negro friends. One of my best friends, he says he'd kill for me. I don't believe in the demonstrations. I think this causes chaos. The Negro's goal is to join our society in a productive way. He will go out of his way to purchase things, and purchasing things, he contributes to the wealth of our great society. He wants to become part of it. The fastest way for a white man to be friends with a Negro is not to give him a dollar—and this is where I sympathize with Barry Goldwater—but to teach him something you know yourself. I've had Negroes working for me in my business. He wants to learn from the white man.

Why do you think they voted so overwhelmingly against Goldwater?

Because they didn't take time out to read his book. And also the strong feeling toward Kennedy. This is why the conservatives didn't have a true test. People, myself included, sat in front of the television set and saw a great man defeated and they cried. If they didn't cry openly, they cried inwardly.

I look at the white people and it irritates me. Every white man wants to make a million dollars. His goal in life is a summer yacht out on Lake Michigan here, a yacht and soaking up the sun out here. He has no goal. The Negro definitely has a goal in life. The white people have to find themselves, they have to keep looking and find out what it is, because if they don't, the communists can take over this country without a shot being fired.

How do your conservative friends and your John Birch colleagues feel about you and your Negro friends?

Nothing was ever said in front of me. They knew how I felt. Maybe they made an exception in my case because I deal with them in my business. Even if this wasn't, they'd have found it in their heart to accept it. I really think there's good in all people.

Do you feel your fellow John Birch members have joined for the same reason you have—to overcome fear?

I don't think so. Maybe they just don't show their fear. This one fellow I know very well, he's a member of the Knights of Columbus. He's done very well for himself. He's not yet thirty, he's well-to-do. Most of these are middle-income people, who have found their place in the sun and who want to grasp onto it, they see an enemy and they feel there's a need to destroy him. Not destroy him physically. If they knew a communist on the street, a John Birch would be the last one to throw a stone. The average individual, if he saw a communist on the street, he would pick up a stone and throw it at him. A John Birch member would identify him and he might try to bring him back over to capitalism. Communists only know what they're taught. If they knew what it was, they'd probably come over because this is a very fruitful life in America. They would want a piece of it, instead of trying to chop the cherry tree.

People just like myself, hard-working people, seem to have more of a goal than the average white person today. They have a goal, they know what's mapped out before them. Martin Luther King scares me because he's done destructive things in peaceful ways. I've talked to many white people who despise him. In the white race, he stirs up resentment. They feel he's going too far, upsetting our society as we know it. And I think nuns and priests who've been demonstrating are being taken in. The type of peace they're advocating is going to cause havoc and destruction and this is what the Commies want.

What kind of leader would you like?

To me, the ultimate would be General MacArthur. I wrote a biography about him when I was in school. He was what every young boy wanted to be when he grew up. He was debonair. He had pride in what he was doing. He loved his people, though he never showed emotion, though it came out in his voice. I feel he got a rotten, dirty deal from some of our own people in this country. He was a man that could not be bought out. He didn't care what the majority of people wanted in a democracy. He knew what was right and he did it.

Didn't you work on behalf of Florence Scala?

Yes. There was a warm person here. She was the greatest personality I've ever known among women. She made you feel you were fighting for more than just one cause. I convinced many of my young friends and my young brothers to come out with me on this. We expected trouble. We faced the Syndicate. They're tough and they throw their weight around.

We came into the polling place. The policeman was fifteen minutes late. It was his duty to be fifteen minutes late, that's how he got his job. So the dirty work would take place before he showed up. They started to fight with us. It looked like it would be a free-for-all, there was even guns. We didn't back down. Toward the end of the day, we received compliments from our opposition. It was the greatest experience of my life, in courage. Not only was I going to try to prove to myself that I was going to be a man, but I was doing it for a great person and a great cause.*

* See postscript to the Prologue. Page 10.

TWO LANDLADIES, A COP, AND THE STRANGER

• • • • • • • • • •

Eva Barnes, 56

It was dark. There were dim lights and vague television noises in the one-family frame dwellings; off the highway, on the far southwest side of the city, recently incorporated as part of Oak Lawn. Dogs barked along the unpaved roads. Nobody seemed to know where Eva Barnes lived.

At the tavern, a barmaid, a weary forty, mumbled sullenly, "I dunno." A man and a woman, on adjacent stools, vaguely pawed at each other. They were out of focus. In the process, a bottle of Hamms was toppled onto the bar. The other man abandoned the shuffleboard and, after a rough sea journey across the room, found us, at last. Genial, he offered directions: a graceful wave of the arm out toward the scattered dim lights. On the TV set, above and behind the bar, a Western with a high Nielsen rating was on. Nobody watched.

Eventually, we saw her, hugely silhouetted against her doorway.

Yeah, just a few yards away. And they sit. If you go in there and talk, they don't talk nothing but sex. I won't even go in there. I rent the tavern out. That's mine. I go in there a coupla times, and the kind of people that hang around, I don't have no use for. She probably don't know because she never seen me.

It's a league of nations. But as far as Negro, not in this section here. There is in Oak Lawn, I don't know where. We have truck drivers, I think the majority are truck drivers, drivers for newspaper companies and drivers for big oil companies and building trades. All ages. You can find from newlyweds just married months up to married fifty years, or I guess more.

I don't go in their homes visiting them. But I know them. We meet at the mailbox, say hello. We meet in the store, say hello. I don't go to church, so I won't lie and say I meet 'em in church. Maybe that's one reason, too, that there's a little resentment, because I don't go to church and they know it.

The biggest change I saw? Oh gee, supermarkets. (Laughs.) And it seems like people are more afraid of talking to anything to progress us, you know. If you talk about improvements, your neighborhood or anything, right away they're afraid of being called a communist. That this is the word they're afraid of.

I remember in 1951, when my husband was paralyzed and our septic system got clogged up in the tavern over there . . . if it wasn't true, it would be funny. I couldn't get anybody for any money to open the tiles up. 'Cause the water was backing up in the tavern. And I was working out there and you know how the tar is out from the sewer, and it clings to your skin. (Laughs.) My poor nine-year-old son was up to his elbows, he was all covered with that black tar. And myself.

I had the tavern closed up that day. Because I couldn't go draw a glass of beer with these dirty hands, run and wait on people. So then my neighbors came in, Mr. Hanson and a couple of other neighbors, walking down the street, saying, "Look at her, working like a communist." I thought to myself, Gee whiz, why do they have to say I'm working like a communist? I'm tryin' to keep this goin' myself. I can't get nobody to work. Why do they brand me like that?

She was born in Riverton, Illinois, near Springfield. Her father was a miner. "We moved like gypsies from one town to another. I would go crazy mentioning all of them." She scores off the names of ten mining towns. She remembers a girl friend who was widowed seven times in mine disasters, as well as losing a father and two brothers; company stores and scrip; five brothers and sisters dead at

*infancy; babies' nipples out of cheesecloth; hired out for
housework at nine; going to seventh grade at school.*

I came to Chicago all by myself, two months before I
was twelve. And it was wintertime in 1923, and I had sixty-five cents in my pocket. And the next day, girl friends
that I had gone to school with, older than me, they come
over and they took me to look for a job. So I got one at
Omaha Packing, piecework. And I don't think I'd ever got
the job, but I was an overgrown girl then and I looked big
for my age then.

And I got in line there. I think there was about two
hundred and fifty people, Negro and white. Standing on
the platform waiting to be picked up for a job. There was
no union in those days. And this employment manager
comes out and he says, "Hey, you big one over there"—he
points his finger at me. "Hey, you big one." I turned
around and he said, "Don't turn around, I mean you.
Come here." And I says, "Me?" And he said, "Yeah, you.
How old are you, about nineteen?" I says, "Mmm-hmm."
(Laughs.) I was afraid to open my mouth. I was only
twelve years old. They hired me as a nineteen-year-old.

He says, "You know how to sharpen a knife?" Well,
back in the coal mines, we used to butcher our own hogs
and our own beef, and I said, "Sure, I know how to
sharpen a knife." And he hands over a knife to me and I
start sharpening. So he says, "Okay, go to work." So I
worked Omaha Packing Company for quite a while, piecework. I was making good money. My first paycheck, I
made so good, I don't remember exactly how much it was,
but it was an unusually big check. And I got scared. I
thought the company made a mistake, so I quit the job.

I done practically everything in the stockyards. I
worked till they started organizing the CIO. They took us
off piecework and put us on bonus, which we didn't like.
Because bonus you had to work harder than you had to
work piecework. Nobody represented us. So the men were
organized, but we women weren't. So there was a fella,
Bob Riley, he come up and he asked me, "Eva, how
would you like to organize your women?" By then I was
about twenty-one years old.

Oh, in those nine years, I was married and divorced before I was eighteen. And married a second time and I had

two children. My first husband was a coal miner and he was an alcoholic . . . how can you build a home when the man is not responsible? . . .

My first wedding, I'll never forget as long as I live. Went back, married this coal miner from Bullpit, and we got married in St. Rita's Church, that's just a few miles near where I was born. I was sixteen. Of course, I won't go into the ages of the man. But the wedding we had in those days was more than a week long. The neighbors all pitched in. We went to the farm and bought a whole calf and a whole pig. I think it was 150 chickens and home-brew and homemade wine. Everything was homemade. And we got married in church with everything, brides-maids and High Mass and everything. The whole works. In fact, even the coal company superintendent, he brought silver for a present for us. And because I danced with him, he gave me thirty-five dollars if I would sell him my wedding shoes. I sold him my wedding shoes, everything was sold. (Laughs.) I was sitting in only my slip, even the dress was sold for me. Just to raise money for the new-lyweds in those days. This was 1925. And of course there's a lot of pictures taken, we were in the *State Register* in Springfield, paper there.

The shivaree, I don't think they do this no more. But we had shivaree every night. Maybe two, three o'clock in the morning, they would be banging cans and making all kinds of noise. The rule was you couldn't sleep at all. And the next morning, you go around and you figure you won't be able to face these people. You know you're ashamed, the wedding is still on. I think there was more fun in the wedding then. Nowadays they go with cars around tooting the horns and everything, but I still think 1925 was nat-ural wedding days.

It was different then. Sure, miners lived poor and the only ones that really had money is the woman that has lotta boarders and women that bootlegs, this is prohibition time. But the woman that didn't bootleg and had boarders, she just lived from hand to mouth, like here in the city from pay to pay. But I remember we'd go out picnics, we'd go out fishing, all families. Everything for the picnic. And then when you went to the picnic, there was no money exchanged, no commercial, everything like one big family. They'd cook a pot of mulligan stew and everybody'd share out of that. That was a picnic. Today you go on a picnic, what is it? It's commercial. You buy your ticket, you buy your popcorn, you buy your beer. If you haven't got a fistful of money, you haven't got no picnic.

Anyway, my wedding was the biggest wedding in Sangamon County in 1925. They said that nobody has a wedding like St. Rita's, the church was dressed up real beautiful. These were the days when I was a very religious woman. And not long after that, when the priest told me to hit my husband with a skillet in the head because he asked for meat on Friday, I thought, well, bad as he is, I still loved him. I didn't think it was right for the priest to tell me to hit my husband in the head with a skillet. (Laughs.) I didn't go for that very much. I thought, what the heck kind of priest is he? So right there, I didn't believe in fighting or hitting. I said, no. So I better don't go to church, I just quit going altogether. But my children were Christian-raised. . . .

I think they put me to work at every job in the stockyards. Pork trimmer. I worked in the laundries. I even worked in the offal. It's where all the guts and everything come in there. This is Depression time now, it's in the Thirties. This is when they bumped a Negro girl to save me a job, 'cause I had two sons. And I didn't like the idea, but then there was a fella named Dick White, he was cutting the pigs' heads and he says, "Don't worry about it," he says, "we're used to it already." He was colored.

And working on these guts, you know, open, and I had to sterilize and wash them. And the ones that were condemned you couldn't touch it, if you did, you would get a hog itch. And you had to keep your hands in a cold shower on them all the time because to get that hog itch off you. I was sick to my stomach and my children used to say when I got home, "Mommy, we love you but you smell awful." But you get used to it. (Laughs.) You work in it so long, you can't smell nothing no more.

But this I'll never forget, this colored boy—not boy, man—Dick White, I'll never forget his name. I don't know what happened to him but he saved my job. And he says, "You'll get used to this job. Just don't think that that's what it is, pretend it's some flowers or something." (Laughs.) And I got used to it. . . .

And then we started organizing the women in there be-

89

cause the men were organized. And then this Bob Riley said, "Don't organize so fast." I had forty women the first day I went out. I said, "They all want union, they want to get better wages." I said, "We're doing the same kind of work men are doing, trimming meat, sharp'ning our own knives, why don't we get paid the same like the men?" They're only paying us, I think, twenty-eight cents an hour. Identical work. And the men were getting fifty-nine cents an hour. So I told him, I said, "When we get union in, we're gonna get the same wages."

That's Depression time, then Roosevelt came in. And I was carrying the biggest Roosevelt button. I was working for a radio company then. Assembling radios. I go to the job, and didn't know that the company was for the opposition. A big Roosevelt button, they told me to take it off. I said, "No, I'm for Roosevelt." They said, "You're for Roosevelt, you get out, you don't get a job." So I got laid off.

And this is election day, the day Roosevelt's election day. I just got through voting for Roosevelt and I lost my job. I had a job all the way through the Depression, and now the first day Roosevelt gets elected, I lose a job. So this is when I met my second husband. He died.

And both of us were looking for a job. He got a job himself as a beef lugger. A man that carried half a steer or quarter, hind or front, from these hooks that are in the freezers and puts them in the truck. It's heavy work and my husband was a pretty strong guy. But it took him. Later on it come up on him.

And then it was funny again. All the time after we got married, we're looking for a job. He's too old and I'm too fat. I was young enough, but too heavy. So what are we gonna do? So we went into the tavern business.

John Woods, he heard me singing in a Legion club, and he says, "Eva, you're singing for somebody else making money. Why don't you open your own tavern?" I said, "I haven't got the money." He said, "You find a place, I'll back you up." And I said, "Well, I got a place on 31st and Halsted, my old neighborhood, lot of people knew me there." * He said, "Fine, as long as you know the people.

---

* The area known as Bridgeport. Mayor Daley has lived there all his life.

Give me two days, I want to look over the place." He says, "Fine, good location."

So we got everything practically. All the beer, all the liquor, everything. New Year's Eve, we want to open, no electric, no gas, we're in the dark. (Laughs.) And I called him up, I says, "John, they need fifty-dollar deposit for gas and electric and I haven't got it." He says, "Jesus Christ, you woman, you got everything, over a thousand dollars worth of equipment in that place and you forget a measly fifty dollars." So we opened the tavern on candlelight. We had candles all over the place.

Those days, I don't know . . . today, I don't think I know anybody who would do that, the cooperation of people. And here this big manager of a brewery company helps me out. And then the whiskey houses, they brought in all the whiskey and wine and liquors and everything. And the lady across the street, the tavern lady, she closed her own tavern up. She knew we were new, we didn't know how to mix drinks, we didn't know how to make a highball, we didn't know nothing. (Laughs.) She closes up her tavern, takes her bartender, takes all the glasses, we run out of glasses, she comes across the street, put her bartender behind the bar. Frank, from 24th and Halsted, he brings his two bartenders, Steve on Archer Avenue, he's got a tavern there today yet. Steve, Frank, Rudy, the three of them behind the bar, they told us to get out and go with your guests. They took over the bar.

I never heard of anybody today going out helping anybody like that. Right here, say, I lived all these years, and when my husband was paralyzed all these years and sick, he never turned down neighbors of anybody passed away, for a flower piece, a sympathy to the neighbor. And yet when he passed away, nobody came to my door and said they were sorry to see Herman go.

The answer is selfishness and greed and jealousy. My own tenants, six months they don't pay no rent. He can't pay no rent, he's a truck driver and he's behind. Got four kids, I feel sorry for them, but I have to do something. I gotta pay taxes, I can't keep up for nothing. But he says, "Gee, what the heck you bothering me for this rent for. You don't need the money." He said, "You're loaded with money." Now this is the idea, you're always loaded with money. They don't know.

91

But it's deeper than this, the more I think about it. It's this fear, fear of everything. Fear of the war in Vietnam, fear of communism, fear of atomic bombs. There's a fear there. I am not afraid of nobody or nothing. The only thing I am afraid of is in case there should be an atomic war, if it hits me or anywhere close, I hope it hits me fast. And that's all, there would be nothing of me. Just like striking a match.

Myself, I get confused. The President tells ya that he don't want no war, it's peace. You pick up a paper, they're bombing children. And television, the guys being interviewed, talking about peace, and the picture shown where the women and children are being bombed and slaughtered and murdered. How long if I think that way and I have a bad feeling, how long will other people that their mentality's not strong enough, to separate the cause of it? Fear. What's gonna happen to our kids, our grand-children?

Lotta them are afraid of their jobs, losing their jobs. Because the government's maybe got some contract with some company. For example, we got one fellow here works with the government, with this here carbonic gas or whatever it is. If he opens his mouth up too much, he can lose his job. And the senators or congressmen, they personally don't take interest in their own country, right here, what's going on.

The colored. We had a tavern on 61st Street and State, three and a half years, Negro neighborhood. I tell you I never was insulted no place by not a Negro person over there. They respected me highly. It took a white fella to come in and insult me because I wouldn't serve him beer, he was too drunk. And if it wasn't for these poor Negro fellas, I'd a probably killed this man. (Laughs.) Because he called me a dirty name.

It just burns me up when they say, Woo! Those Negro people! My kids would go out in the street, my little girl would be out on the streets, nobody bothered, nobody touched. One day I'm lookin' for my little girl, and she was only four years old then, and I went to the back yard. They had a quilt spread out on the lawn and had my little girl sittin' in the middle, 'cause she had a white organdy dress on. (Laughs.) Little colored girls and boys all around, so she don't get off and get her dress soiled. They were watching her. (Laughs.) They don't care how dirty the quilt got but just don't get her dress soiled, watching her.

Today I had an argument. I just got mad because I heard them back and forth and they started telling: Those Negroes, they're so filthy. Everything is the Negroes. I said, "Do you ever stop to think that the white trash of the white people do the same thing?"

I know they sit in taverns and booze all night long. That's why we never did make a lot of money in taverns. My husband couldn't stand it. If he knew there was a family man or woman, he'd tell 'em, "Get out and go by your kids. You drink two, three glasses of beer, that's enough. Go home, watch your children." "What's the matter, don't you like our money?" they would say. "We don't have to come here if you're like that." So we never made any money.

In Bridgeport, I know what's going on over there. Old-timers that have homes, and they're afraid that the neighborhood's gonna be run-down. That's what they're afraid of. Because they listen to the reputation of State Street.

I don't know how to explain it. I was never anti-Negro, because I don't remember when I don't know a Negro living next door. When I grew up, there was nothing for my father to bring a couple of Negro fellas that he worked in the mines in the gang with, for supper. Or my dad taking us by the hand Sunday morning after church, and it was nothing at all to spend Sunday morning after church to go by them. The first time I tasted homemade cornbread was by a Negro family.

Just because my skin is white, that doesn't make me better than he is. Or it doesn't make him better if his skin is black. A lot of people think, my skin is white, I don't even have to go to school. . . . One particular woman in this neighborhood, when her daughter wanted to go to school so bad, she said, "You don't need no high school. What do you need high school for? Get married and raise kids." "Gee whiz," I said, "she'd make a better mother if she has an education. Don't deny her. If she wants to go to school, get an education, give it to her, let her go. If you can't afford it, it's different." But, "Oh, no, she don't need it." Today what is she? She's just a baby factory, that's all she is.

Education is very important. Always, always. I raised my children in the rottenest business a child can grow up in. They grew up and all got education from that tavern business. I could thank Roosevelt for it. If it wasn't for Roosevelt being elected and repealing the Eighteenth Amendment, well, I'd still be bootlegging. (Laughs.) When I was sixteen years old, I knew how to make moonshine and home-brew. (Laughs.)

Oh, I done everything. I was a riveter during the war. I worked even in a rubber factory. In those days, they used insulation rubber around the automobile, around the windows, I was the trimmer on that. And I made steering wheels on a great big bandsaw. I don't know how I didn't get my arms cut off. (Laughs.) Made steering wheels and working in a candy factory. Now listen, just I'm telling you. . . . I wasn't a bad-looking girl, I mean, I had opportunities. . . .

You're not a bad-looking woman now.

Thank you. When I hear people say, ah, the children are bad, delinquency from broken homes, and girls turn bad because they have nobody. . . . I had all the opportunities in the world to become bad. All of it. In fact, one case worker, Irma Cline, I'll never forget. . . .

. . . During the Depression, there was an old couple that needed a stove. And she wouldn't give them the requisition to get the stove to heat their place up. So I went to the relief station and put that Cline against the wall. I got her by the throat and she suggested that I come in for the stove. And she said, "You're not a bad-looking woman. Why don't you get yourself a job and buy a stove yourself?" She thought it was for me. I said, "It's not for me, it's for an old couple." I said, "I'm helping them all I can. I can't help them no more." And that's when she made the suggestion that I am not a bad-looking woman. She said, "Why don't you get married?" I said, "What do you want me to do? Get a mattress on my back and walk up and down 35th Street?" This get married. I had all the opportunities in the world to become bad. I didn't. I worked.

I don't see why people should have to struggle for everything that's important to them. In the Constitution they tell us that under the Constitution. . . . I found out by being arrested, when you're arrested you have no Constitution.

Why were you arrested?

For to end the war in Vietnam, with the students. I was demonstratin'. I think it's good. It's good exercise for me. (Laughs.) The only way I get my exercise is in these demonstrations. Marches, and for a good cause, I don't mind that.

What made you join it?

Well, I tell you, my first husband, though he was no good, I don't know if it was the First World War or what had to do with it, but he was wounded in the First World War real bad, that he was pensioned. Old Soldiers' Home, all crippled up. Decorated in some kind of medal he got over there, to end all wars. So his sons won't have to fight in the wars. Well, along comes Hitler, so then my oldest son, before the end he was old enough already. Thank God that my first one come home safe.

And my second son, when the Korean War started, he was old enough to get in the Korean War. He had this thick, bushy hair head, when he come back, I think two and a half years, when he come back he was bald-headed. And he's a different boy altogether. I think this Korean business had to do. Well, he isn't . . . how should I tell you? 'Cause maybe he's a man now. He isn't jolly any more, he isn't . . . (she has difficulty here) . . . he's very strict with his own children, it's just like a bully . . . the army training, the meanness is in you. And left in you. He's not . . . the meanness is not taken out of you when he comes down to civilian society. But maybe I'm wrong, I don't know. . . . He was never a bully, now he's a bully. And I guess they train 'em like that.

Now this boy I got, this last one. He's a good boy, he's never given me trouble. He's never missed a day of school. He's never been late to school. He's never harmed anything. I tell you what kind he is, if there's a mosquito, he won't kill the mosquito, he says, "Oh, let him go." (Laughs.) And gets along with everybody. And little kids, they're just crazy for him.

95

Yeah. He always wanted to be a policeman and I . . . He's a boy, I never let him have a toy gun. I says, "I don't want my children to have guns." I won't buy a gun, I won't allow in my house a gun.

I never did fight, I'm not a fighter, I never fight with policemen even. (Laughs.) I left my husbands to it, but I never fight with them. I'm afraid. I'm too big, I weigh three hundred pounds, my husband weighs 150 pounds. If I hit 'em, I could kill 'em.

I don't want my son to go to Vietnam. All right, he's got a dangerous job, he's a policeman. So I feel different about it. He's got a gun on him, he's doing everything what I'm against. But as long as he knows . . . he knows I don't believe in police brutality. No way. *No* way. If I ever hear that he's brutal in any way, I don't care he never got a whipping—but I would beat the shit out of him. I would. You got to defend yourself, but you don't have to provoke it.

Because when I was picked up after that demonstration, there was a lot of them police were there, trying to provoke us on. Even the matrons, they'd come to me and say, "Now, missus, why are you demonstrating with these Commies?" Students. And here's a priest, nuns, marching along, and police calling them Commies. I don't see that. She's got the upper hand, the matron, she takes my purse away, takes my glasses away, then she says you can make one phone call. I said all right. Then they lock me up in a cell, everything taken away from you. I says, "Can I have a paper cup so I can get a glass of water." This is four o'clock we were picked up. No, I wait till ten o'clock.

But then she takes you again, they just move you from one cell to another cell, and then they fingerprint you and take your picture and all the time, they're talking, they says, "You ought to be ashamed of yourself. Why don't you stay home and mind your own business? Why don't you take care of your family, instead of going mingling with all these bunch of hoodlums and bums?" This is the only time I ever come in a bunch with the intellectuals, the educated students, university students. Here I'm in this neighborhood sitting here, I could become a dummy. And there I learned something. I learned geographical locations, the games we played. That I haven't played since we were kids, you know, in spelling class. (Laughs.) But this was not a spelling class. And all these different freedom songs. But the beauty part of it is they take your glasses away, then they come around and bring Bibles for you to read. And you can't see your hand in front of you, how you gonna read the Bible?

And I said to her, the matron, I says, "You got the upper hand all right, I'm not gonna argue with you." "Shut up." I says, "I'm not saying nothing, I just said you got the upper hand." "Shut up." That's all what they know, just shut up. I could probably buy and sell her if I wanted to. . . . I pay her taxes, I pay her wages, I pay big tax, I pay $1200 a year for taxes, how much taxes she's paying? But I can't talk to her. I have no right to say nothing to her. I've seen people get arrested in southern part of Illinois. My father was arrested for bootlegging. I never seen him treated like that. And here, I'm marching peacefully, and he says, "Are you gonna move or you don't move?" I says, "I'll move."

The cop?

Yeah. So I moved a little bit. He comes back again, he says, "I told you to move." So I moved again. I says, "I'm movin'." He said, "Are you gonna walk to the patrol wagon peacefully or do we carry you?" (Laughs.) And I took a look at him and I says, "Look, I don't want your officers get ruptured," I says, "I'll walk." (Laughs.) And then he recognized me at the HUAC. . . .

At the anti-HUAC, we weren't doing nothing. We were just marching because they were persecuting the doctor.* I don't even know the doctor, I only know his reputation. I don't know him personally, but I know what I read about him, what a good doctor he is, what a humble man he is. And so I said, "Well, I gotta go defend that man. I gotta be one of the people to be counted." I can't set home. The students that were arrested were marching here. They were happy to see me. The police too. . . .

* A distinguished physician conducting research in heart disease for the Chicago Board of Health, who was cited for contempt by the House Committee on Un-American Activities.

He said, "Hi, there." He called me by my name, the policeman. I said, "How'd you ever remember my name?" He says, "Aren't you the little lady that didn't want my officers to get ruptured?" I said. "Yeah, gee." Then he smiled. And every one of the officers, they were real nice to me. I thought, you know, maybe they'd get snotty or sarcastic or stuff, but even some of them were singing freedom songs.

But I can't see why they allowed them Nazis, like all right, one of the Nazis that were demonstrating against us, here he took his hand and grabbed by his privates and he went and shook his privates at this lady that was behind me, a Negro woman. And I said, "Boy, that's a very intellectual guy doing that." And he says, "To you, too." And the officer was looking at him doing that, and if he was on our side, somebody doing like that, they probably would put him in jail. *They* can do it. So whose side is the law on? We don't know for sure whether Hitler's dead or alive. (Laughs.) We got a lotta them here.

Was that the first time you were ever arrested? When you marched for peace?

First time in my life, and I've done some things that I shoulda been arrested for. (Laughs.) Like I said, I was sixteen years old, I cooked moonshine, and they could smell it. The chief, who lived right across the street, never pinched me. I made home-brew and they never pinched me. And I ran parties all hours of the night, and nobody had me arrested. For peace, they arrest me. I said, "My God," I said, "I wonder if I murdered somebody in Mississippi, would they arrest me?"

You see, how I got arrested. . . . I had $750 worth of savings bonds in my purse and about $470 cash money. Then I had the title, the deed to the property that I was changing. I went to take them out of one box and closer to home. In the meantime, this demonstration was going on. And these students see my peace button and ask if I could help them make the amount of people look bigger.

In the cell, I hear a banging on that steel wall. And I'm a heavy woman, but tacked onto this steel wall is the other cell. And every time I move, that wall would move and shake. (Laughs.) And some voice from this other cell hollers, "Hey you, quit moving in your bed. Every time you move, you knock me out of my bed." Her bed would bounce up, you know. And she said, "What are you arrested for?" I said, "I'm arrested for peace." I said, "What are you arrested for?" She said, "Me, too. Soliciting." I said, "Without a license?" She says. "Why do you need a license?" I said, "Where you from? You from Chicago? You gotta have a license for everything." She said from Long Island. I said, "When you come to Chicago, you go County Building and you ask for a solicitor's license. Then nobody can arrest." (Laughs.) Then the matron comes, she said, "Will you shut up?" (Laughs.)

Later on, she said, "You was kidding me." And I said, "Yes, I was kidding you. I know what you mean." But I said, "You girls are foolish anyway." I said I had a tavern on 61st and State and I used to see girls get picked up and they picked them up, the police themselves. And these are white policemen, I've seen 'em. And they come in and tell my husband, get that streetwalker out of here. They call her worse names than streetwalker. And my husband would say, "If you know she's such a woman, why don't you put a mark on her, so people could tell? I don't want to get my face slapped, going to tell her, you so-and-so. Listen, she's not doing no harm. She comes in, spends her money, just as good as anybody else's."

I've seen where the policemen picked up these girls and the girls would flip their wallets over the bar and let my husband hold their wallets for them, because the policemen would take their wallets from them, take them a couple of blocks around and drop them off in the alley some place: "Now, next time you better have more money. See?" They'd take the money from 'em, encourage it: go ahead some more. In fact, if you don't have more money, they're gonna give you maybe with a billy club, the beating or something. Yeah, the vice squad. Now this I live with, I seen it. And if it went on then, it's still going on now.*

Maybe some day I will get hurt. I don't distrust nobody when I'm out. I never turn around, like a lot of women, turn around to see who's following them. This is a funny thing, the matron, she asked me, she said, "You with all

* During 1965, two Negro prostitutes were found slain. An accusation was made of police involvement. The case is unsolved.

this real-estate property, all these deeds and titles you're carrying, you ought to be ashamed of yourself. How are you not afraid to walk the Chicago streets with all this in your purse?" I said, "Lady, you're a matron and you don't have faith in Chicago?" I walked through State Street, Cottage Grove, and Halsted many times, nobody bothered me. I could tell a person if he's out to hate me or he's friendly. I mean, is he gonna be taking me? When I was in the tavern business, you had to be that way. And yet I lost. Somebody, some I trusted. . . .

Most that disturbs me today is when I talk to some of my neighbors, none of them, they don't like this Vietnam going on, but here's where they say: "What's the use? Who are we? We can't say nothing. We have no word. We got the President. We elected him. He got congressmen in there. They're responsible. Let them worry. Why should I worry about it?" It's already pounded into them, you're just a little guy, you vote and you're through, it won't do no good anyhow.

I think different. I think, like they say, that if I'm a voter, I should have a say-so in this. In everything. . . . But anything good for the people is never given easy. Never given easy.

I saw coal miners come out of the coal mines all crushed. I saw in the First World War. My mother had seven young boys come from Europe to stay with us, worked a little while in the coal mines and they were drafted into the American Army. They were young boys, I think, twenty, twenty-one years old and they never came back. My mother had seven stars in her window. Instead of saying they came from Lithuania, they said they came from Ledford, Illinois. So they sent the stars to my mother, and whatever little belongings they had, little chains or something. . . . Just enough, there is death enough. I don't like to see nobody get killed. I don't like to see nobody get hurt. This world is beautiful to live. . . .

POSTSCRIPT

I asked her about that one phone call she was allowed while in jail: "About two or three o'clock in the morning, the matron come up to me and asked me if I was gonna have that phone call made. I said, 'Yes, make it.' 'Well, who you want us to call?' I said, 'Call my son.' She says,

'You want us to tell that he should come and bail you out?' I said, 'No, I don't want him to come bail me out.' I said, 'Tell him to take the beans off the stove, because they're gonna get spoiled.' It was hot that day."

· · · · · ·

Gladys Pennington, about 50

We were seated in the front room of her home on the Near North Side, a five-minute bus ride from the Loop. It faced the huge, modern high-rise complex across the wide boulevard. The furniture was old-fashioned; some toy dogs, wide-eyed, were gaping at us.

I'm a very bad landlady because I always put a middle-man between me and the victims, because the victims always hate the landlady, and the landlady always looks dimly upon the victims because they don't appreciate what she tries to do.

I'm on little side streets and I am far north. Out on the West Side, I have colored property. I used to live there myself and it was delightful. It's real healthy-type property. So I've gone through the whole gamut of fixing it up and having them rip it down, fixing it up, rip it down. I have a store there, with a magnificent tenant who is a real business woman, beautiful, stunning, sensational.

Every time I get tenants in there, I rent to two people and twenty-seven people occupy it. I'd done everything I could for the house, but now I'm letting the city tear it down. I've given up, I can't cope. Because my own tenants will just knock out the windows with their own fists. They'll pay the rent, but then they'll say fix this, and knock it out.

Everything's condemned. If you can't keep it in A-1 condition, it's condemned. I buy the garbage cans, I chain them to the wall. I have big slabs of wood like telegraph poles put on the wall. I chain the lids to that. I chain the cans to that. And the next day, guess what? There's nothing there. (Laughs.) I used to visit the place once a week. Terrible people. Four adults, all with jobs. Four cars. All better than mine. Cadillacs, Oldsmobiles . . . I just adore the colored people, but unfortunately I never find what I want for tenants. All they do to me is just wreck everything.

On the same block, I got the best tenant you ever saw. Her lease is going to run out and I haven't spoken to her because I'll let the city tear that down, too. I don't know what she's up to, but she drives a fantastic car and she's very zippy looking and very brilliant and turns it off and I'll tell you I think she's taking policy slips and horse bets. Anyway, she just goes on mailing in the rent and stays there and I don't say anything to her and she doesn't say anything to me.

You have several pieces of property in the area?

From the boulevard to the alley. The half-block, and all of it is a pain in the neck.

Doesn't it bring you a . . . ?

Since she's there I don't get any violations on her . . .

Doesn't it bring you a fairly good income?

She's got the voting part, too. She runs the whole place.

She has clout, a woman of influence, then?

She's a dream.

You and she understand one another?

No. Every time I've ever went out there, she's always given me the rent in small change and in a paper bag, small change and bills, and then I would have the kid along, and between me and the door she would have four men with knife scars running here, there, and what not. So I would take the money and the boy would count it—he was in eighth grade, the boy used to go out with me once a week—I'd let the kid count it, all the pennies and what not. And I would put it here, here, here, I had eighty-seven pockets in, you know, the pocketbook. And then I would have to walk through four fierce-looking boys to get out to

102

the street. So Bill finally said he didn't think that was the place for the boy to be, out collecting rents. Without the boy, I can't go out there. He's attending Groton now. He was thirteen then. So I gave her a dollar off a month and she sends me money orders, and it comes every month.

Now, I have a perfect tenant up in the new hillbilly section, Wilson Avenue. Blight area. So the city has come around and said you must put it back to a six-flat building. So her lease ran out May first and right after that, what did I do? I took an ad in the *Tribune*: six-flat, putting it back to its original thing. So I give up, you know. I'm not going to go on fighting the city. I'm a little, weak, stupid woman. My tenant has been in there twenty years. She's been renting the whole building, it's broken up into one's, two's and three's. They all share the one bathroom, the one's, two's and three's. So I talked with her yesterday, we had a long let's-bleed-from-the-heart conversation. I said, "I have these fantastic replies, they all want to move into this apartment. You're not letting me make apartments, what are you still doing there?" (Laughs.)

I've got these fantastically lovely replies from these wonderful people, lawyers, teachers at IIT, fantastically lovely people. And they can't see the building. (Laughs.) She won't let 'em in. They might dirty up her hall. The building is marvelous, it's so clean, the bathrooms are all, you know, itty-bitty tiles and you could eat off her toilet seats. I mean, the whole thing is the cleanest thing you ever saw. This old woman, she says, "My people have been with me nineteen years, look at this, isn't this marvelous." Of course she never got any violations and I used to think she was Swedish, but now I think she's Norwegian. She's cleaner than the Swedes. Even the furnace is painted white. So this is a labor of love. She doesn't want to go. The city's doing this to get rid of the hillbillies. Now she's got nineteen old people in there and they all use the same bathroom and . . . the city says you've got to put it back the way it was. So she's got a beautiful plan going and it just breaks her heart, so she's crying. I'm crying. Everyone's crying but the city.

Everybody's spending a lot of money over here. (Laughs.) One man bought a building for $25,000 and got $50,000 to improve it. And only paid the down payment on the $25,000. Of course, he's going to jail for seven years because he didn't do anything. But along here two doors down we have a darling neighbor who is borrowing $80,000 and making apartments. He's renting them as fast as he's finishing them. They're better than the brand new sterile-type across the street. (Indicates high-rise complex.)

This area isn't transient any more. Everybody has to sign leases now. I've had letters from suburban people wanting to come back. "If it's a good neighborhood," they write. What's a good neighborhood? I'm living in a very good neighborhood now. We have the ultimate in police protection. But even I worry if I have to go out and leave the house. And the vandals will get in and the people who just break windows for fun. So you just can't leave property in the city. You just can't leave the house vacant for one second, or they rip it to shreds.

Bill saw a woman thrown out of an apartment here on the coach house by the alley and he ran in to phone for an ambulance and they told him he couldn't use the phone because they didn't want to get involved. So he had to come all the way back home and phone and the lady was Appalachian and all she did was lay there with a broken back as far as we could deduce. In the alley. She lay there mouthing curses and her husband closed the glass window, but he'd already busted the screen throwing her out. And no one ever came to see Bill after, no one was interested. But I understand from the landlady that the lady lived and went back to her husband. (Laughs.) So it really turned out roses in the end.

I don't believe these hillbillies are of no worth. They have the best names, they have the old English names. These are the original settlers. They're really a very precious people. Their children are beautiful. They neglect their children, they neglect their wives. They act like they're on a holiday all the time, because I guess they're just like Tennessee Williams' plays, kind of played out. But really, they're a delicious people.

My experience with Negroes that come from the South is that they're very loyal and decent and wonderful. But Negroes who've lived in the North and haven't bothered about anything are pretty hard to get along with. But elegant Negroes are so good, so great, so fine that my husband always says to me, "Drop them, you can't measure up to them."

We went on a cruise and we got on the boat and there was only one very small, same size as my boy, dark little boy. I found him and I said, first thing, I'm being very careful, I said, "Are you a Haitian?" After all, I don't want my child slit through the gullet stretched out tomorrow morning. (Laughs.) And he said "No, I'm from New York City." So they were both ten and he was traveling with his mother for the cruise. This is a beautiful and darling child. So momma turns out to be very Bergdorf Goodman and way above my social aspirations, dressed to the teeth, and what wonderful underwear.

She's got a little boy and I've got a little boy, so we're tied together. And we have 150 Southern Bell Telephone executives and their wives aboard ship—who cannot see us. We're a completely blind foursome. Nobody can see us on the boat. We were invisible. A McKinley Republican can recognize the facts of life if you get two little boys. (Laughs.)

She's a great woman. I can recognize this although I'm just stupid. Somebody who's out to do something. But her boy isn't on any picket line. Her boy is in the safest place she can put him, like my little boy is in the safest place I can put him. And we're not teaching our boys to go out with a picket sign. She's not out there laying down and bleeding and I'm not sure I think this is a great thing. I don't believe we're ever going to win anything except that people should be superior. Her underwear was better than mine, her clothes were better than mine. Obviously, she's superior to me.

We went into this dining room in this Jamaican hotel and the man came up and said, "You can't sit here." So she looked at me and she had just bought all these *New York Timeses* to read and I said to the man, "Why can't we sit here?" And he said, realizing that he was up against loyal opposition, "You can't sit here unless you're going to eat." And I said, "Who in the hell told you we weren't going to eat?" (Laughs.) "Blow, bud." So he went. He recognized the symptoms of the old soul, Sewell Avery— let's be carried out before we meet defeat.*

* In 1944, Sewell Avery, chairman of Montgomery Ward and Company, was involved in a controversy with the government. He con-

I don't believe any place has a right to object to Bergdorf Goodman clothes, just because the skin doesn't match up to the specifications. Now what I object to is what I get in my own tenants when they break the window out and say fix it, just because it's fun for them to torture me. And push me around. My child has been pushed around many times by drunken colored gentlemen. I bruise very hard and I'm not particularly afraid because they don't really want to kill me. They want to live there. They all want to live there.

I marched in the Kennedy Parade. This is hard for a Republican to admit. We always make political parades, because my child adores them. The most objectionable colored gentleman in the world came along, and he tried to start a riot with me. Of course, he picked the wrong girl. I've been pinched and poked before. So I was able to say, "Get lost, bud." After all, I'm a Republican, what do I care if he has a riot or not. The only way I could get away from him was to get out and join the parade. So they gave Billy a torch to carry and they gave me a sign, which I brought home and Bill had around for a long time. So he burned holes all through his little winter jacket from carrying a torch. But the only way to get away from this guy who wanted to start a riot, and I knew he wanted to start a riot, was to just get out in the mob and become one. I think there are troublemakers out, always are troublemakers out.

I don't have any fears about America. There are more good people than bad. They'd be an awful dangerous type underground if anyone ever conquered us. These men are good shots and they're healthy and capable. We aren't all married to men who would fight, but I think 99 percent of the women in America are married to men who would.

Let's not have another Cuba. I think we should have said, "Now look, little pal, we've got all this American money in this country and you better behave to start with. And if you're not going to behave, we're gonna hurt you." And we've let it go so long, you see, that now we're in an intolerable position. Johnson's realized this in Vietnam and he's going to put a stop to it. We ought to do what the

tended his mail-order house was not involved in war work. The plant was seized, and Avery, declining to leave his office, was carried out, still seated in his executive chair, by two soldiers.

government says or we're dead. I either throw out my good tenant of twenty years and convert to six flats or I'm done for. I get fined $200 a day to the year eternity. I must do this even if I don't want to. But he's the big government and I'm a little citizen and they're a little country and I'm a big country. Mayor Daley is big enough to whip me any old time he wants to, but we were big enough to say to Cuba, "Now you knuckle down and behave. We've got all this money here. *Of course,* the Hilton Hotel belongs to Mr. Hilton. *Of course* these things belong to these Americans. What are you doing? How can you take them? 'Cause we're big and you're little." But we didn't do that. What we put money into belongs to us and we should have it. I'm not worried about the Hilton Hotel. I don't have any Hilton stock. It's just this idea, all this American money is there. We're a big, strong country. We should say, "Now kids, you've made us angry. We are a little irked with you and you better behave or else." And then or-else them. I got nothing against Cuba. It's a delightful country. I was there. But politics are politics. No, I feel if there's a riot going on in front of your house and you can't quell it, you call the police.

I think Chicago's got many things that are better than anywhere else. Many things are worse. Our taxes only come up, they never go down. But I think we have some of the greatest schools in the world, and everybody is condemning Willis.* The citizens are least likely to admit that we do have good schools. Bobby went so long to Latin, the most expensive private school in town. He switched over to Ogden for the seventh and eighth grade. Public, and a real great school.

This civil-rights revolution came as a shock to me. I went to all these high schools and never realized there was a problem. I feel that there never is any problem except education. If you don't know anything, nobody wants to go near you, no matter what color you are. You could be purple, which is quite a novelty, and they'd still put you in a cage. If they read books and they like words and they like people and they like living, why then it's no problem.

---

* Chicago's superintendent of schools. He had been accused by Negroes—and various church and civil groups of the city—of fostering de facto segregation.

But if they're looking for a fight, there are always people who will give it to them. I'm one.

I think this is a real great country. I think most people are on the ball. I think most people love their houses, love their families, love their lawns and their shrubs and their plants and their mode of life, and I think they'd do anything to protect them. There are those, the unsuccessful few, and they hate everything. But the majority of people like it the way it is, corrupt, maddening, aggravating, horrible, we would fight to keep it that way. We wouldn't have it any other way because we can still go down and blow off steam to some little minor bureaucrat when something aggravates us. And if nothing comes of it, we don't get locked up for it. But we still do have our moderately free speech and when they reach a peak like poor old LBJ, there he is, poor, beautiful kid, he's got to be a pretty good guy, too. Even though I did vote against him.

If we have anyone threatening our way of life, it's our minor bureaucrats and politicians. And we're acquiring more of them every day. And what is our way of life is also everybody else's way of life. Everyone just wants to live their own life. We only want to think about politics a couple of days out of the year. We're not concerned. We don't care really. We know that if we need new sewers then we get mad and go down and say, "We need new sewers. Do something." Then we're made.

• • • • • •

Tom Kearney, 53

An apartment in a high-rise complex on the Near South Side of the city, adjacent to Michael Reese Hospital. A well-thumbed copy of Gunnar Myrdal's An American Dilemma *was on the coffee table.*

I've been a policeman for twenty-three hard years. You have to work odd hours, often long hours. Yesterday I was assigned to the parade, the astronauts, White and McDivitt. We reported for duty at six-thirty in the morning and weren't released until five o'clock in the evening. That was without any time off at all. No lunch period or anything.

I worked as a patrolman and a detective. Then I was promoted to a detective sergeant and from there I went to the traffic division. So I've covered all bases so far.

Sometimes you're disenchanted, you're disillusioned, you're cynical. When people attempt to offer a bribe. I know I've been negligent in my duty because I should have arrested the person. At the same time, that's universal, everywhere. I turn it down. I told him, you know, "No harm trying. But I just don't go that way." (Laughs sadly.) It's a corrupt society.

You think you're a wise guy until you run into situations where you shoulda known better and didn't. The night before I went on my vacation, I was out in the squad car, and you travel alone, you know. The radio signaled for a police officer. They needed help on a 10-1. So over the air came this signal, a couple of blocks from where I was. I got there and found an officer struggling with two young men and they were giving him a pretty good battle. So I joined in. At fifty-three, when you take those blows, you absorb them, you know. You just don't shake them off. I went on my vacation the next day with bruises. Shins all beat up. But there's nothing else I can do, you see?

I was born in Chicago, my father was born in Chicago, and my grandfather was born here. His father came to America to dig the Sag Canal. They were promised they could have farmland where they could grow anything. In the winter, they'd dig the canal. Unfortunately, it was all rocks. So they wound up with a rock farm.

There's something you gotta understand about the Irish Catholics in Chicago. Until recently, being a policeman was a wonderful thing. 'Cause he had a steady job and he knew he was gonna get a pension and they seemed to think it was better than being a truck driver, although a truck driver earns far more than a policeman today.

Someone had to be police, you know? They sacrificed anything. They just knew that so-and-so in the family would be. It was another step out of the mud. You figured at least you'd have some security. They felt they no longer worked with their hands. They weren't laborers any more.

If the Depression hadn't come along, my father would have been able to do more educational-wise for us. He couldn't provide. There was no money for two years. At that time, the firemen and policemen weren't paid. My father was a fireman for forty years. They were the only ones who didn't get their back pay. Whoever could work and earn anything at all . . . that's what kept us going.

I recall the hunger marches. I remember the police at that time, they had mounted police. I had a job at Madison and Canal, and they were marching, trying to get into the Downtown area, from the west to the east. The police charged them. Whether they were right or wrong, I didn't know than. I was too much concerned with my own self. 'Cause things were rather brutal and you expected that, you know.

I remember at Blue Island and Ashland—there's a lumber company there now—that was a big transient camp. I remember the food lines. I also remember getting off the Elevated and men waiting in line for the newspaper. If you were through reading it, they'd take it. They had a little code among themselves. After you got your newspaper, you moved away from the line. What they used them for was probably to sleep on. . . .

There's no colored there [Bridgeport]. A mixture of white—different ethnic groups: Polish, Slavic, Irish, Italian, anything and everything. A few Jewish families. In the old days, it was all Irish. The streets, the names were Irish. The street my grandmother lived on was named after one of my father's sisters who died very young.

We moved farther south, to Roseland. My father was assigned there. It was a community begun by people who had left Pullman. They had rebelled against the company by moving out. If you worked for him you had to live in one of his Company houses. You bought from the Company store. If profits fell below a certain level, wages were cut. The rents weren't lowered, the rents remained the same. Now, of course, there's nothing much over there.

My father was one of the radicals. Even though he had status, you know, being a fireman and the fact he got a pension, he used to say, "Why should I get a pension when the fellow next door doesn't get one?" He was a good Irish Catholic, so he wasn't a Commie, but at the same time he used to say, "You know, maybe they got something over there that we should know about, because they keep on talking about how bad it is over there."

My family wasn't devout. Certain things my mother, of

course, insisted upon. On Good Fridays, you had to sit in a chair in the kitchen. In those days they didn't have any foam rubber seats. It was hard wood. And you had to sit there till about five minutes to twelve. Don't laugh and don't talk. You sat for three hours. She had some of an idea that it helped you spiritually. But I don't think we were deeply religious.

I find myself at odds with the Church at various times. I knew the nuns taught me some things that weren't true. At the same time, I realized they themselves didn't know whether they were true or not. They were simple women, you know. You say you'd rather have your son go to a public school because he's gonna have to get along with those people and he might as well start young. The same as going to school with the colored. You're going to have to get along with them. They're here, so you might as well go to school with them and get along with them.

How do you feel about young nuns and priests taking part in street demonstrations?

They have every right to do so, although not to violate the law. I'm not saying that because I'm a policeman, but simply because having been in parochial school all my life, all I ever heard was: "Don't do anything wrong." Respect for authority.

Today things are changing. If one married outside the religion I remember this: "Oooh, tear out all my hair. I can't face my friends, we gotta move." Oooh, terrible, terrible. And what happened? I have five brothers and one sister. Of the brothers, one is a bachelor. The rest of us married Protestants. My sister married a Protestant. My older brother had two daughters. They raised one a Catholic and one a Protestant. The girl raised a Catholic married a Protestant and the one raised a Protestant married a Catholic. Today, for convenience's sake, my brother and his wife go to the Catholic Church. She hasn't been converted, but just goes for convenience's sake. It isn't any big deal any more.

It's changing rapidly. Look at the city. Of course, everyone resists change, good or bad. Even if it's good for them, they resist it. Take the color situation today. The whites, they're only fighting a rear-guard action. The walls are coming down, that's all. The tragedy is that the program of the colored is still negative. There's no reason to lead a march or sit in the streets any more, as I see it. Because they've won, there's no question about it. They've got to find a way to have the whites accept them.

Unfortunately, the colored man came to the industrial North just too late. He came after there were so few jobs to begin with. The Caucasian immigrants came with nothing but their hands and they worked in steel mills and maybe they were snapping cinders, which is one of the most difficult jobs and the lowest paid. They watched another fellow do a job and they learned his job and climbed up. Well, the colored man didn't have that opportunity after the wave of migration from the South. There were so few labor jobs that he could start out from and learn how to get up. The machine took care of that. They didn't need him any more. One man can do the work of ten today.

What do you think the objective of the colored is?

The same as mine, the same as mine. I can see where they'd want to move away from a completely colored neighborhood and integrate. I can understand that. He also understands that his family is gonna have to live with whites and if he doesn't live with the whites he can't understand them either. The colored man says: "Well, you don't know us." Naturally we don't. They don't know the white either.

I think people are intelligent enough to accept integration. We've done one thing, it's a bad thing, but I can't think of anything better. The quota. It's bad because you have to exclude someone sometimes, but the whites wouldn't have any fear of being overwhelmed. And the colored wouldn't have any fear that the white would run. This high-rise complex I live in now works on a quota. It's highly controlled.

Most of urban renewal is bad in a sense. People were displaced. Yet it had to be done. Where we're sitting now was one of the foulest slums in America. It was worse than Calcutta, believe me. I've been in here as a police officer on many occasions. Right across the street, they had a fence to protect the institution there. It must have been eighteen feet in the air, with barbed wire.

Actually it's not really integrated now because there's no community life here at all. You don't know the fella next door usually. Your wife may meet them or something like that, but you yourself come and go, that's all. There's no way for people to know one another. You at least vote together, you know, at election time. Well, each building is its own precinct. So people just go in and out. There isn't any standing outside like you do normally at an election. There's no church in the immediate vicinity. Most people, they have to go several blocks to an known place. And these complexes have very few children. An adult population, more or less concerned with their own problems. When we first moved in here, I thought I'd go insane, being cooped in and actually nowhere to go, because the neighborhood is sterile. It's not a neighborhood at all.

People don't want to become involved. Most people have had some dealings with court, like traffic courts. People have sat for long periods of time, waiting for their case to be called. In criminal court, they've found themselves returning there and then continuances being granted after continuances. This man, he loses his day's pay from work. If it's a woman, she becomes frightened, that they might retaliate in some way. The fear. Like many cabdrivers that don't report a robbery, 'cause normally they might not have eight or ten dollars when he's held up. He won't report it because he'd lose a day's work if they finally apprehended the offender and the loss is a loss.

This fear of involvement. I wondered why there were so few colored in the crowd greeting the astronauts yesterday. Most of the fellows said, "They don't care if anybody went to the moon. They don't have any feeling about it." I said, I don't think that's true. We were briefed to search for colored people who might be a threat, you know. It was the week of demonstrations. The average colored person is just like you and I. If there was a great crowd some place and there was a threat to all people wearing blue shirts, you certainly wouldn't go down there in a blue shirt.

Do you have any colored friends?

Oh yes. Yes. (Pause.) I *say* colored friends and I *think* colored friends . . . but actually I really don't know.

113

Not really. I can understand that. Because if I were colored, I'd be bitter, too. I *think* I'd try to control myself, try to be rational about it. I remember one night, a colored schoolteacher I know, we're at a party, an interracial party, very nice. She forgot the potency of martinis and I was sitting talking to her and suddenly she looked at me very hard and said, "You're my Caucasian enemy." Very indignantly. Of course, I realized, you know . . . I mean, she just didn't realize how potent a martini was. So you really don't know.

Some guys that I know, colored, we talk and discuss the family and how things are going, and how their wives are and things like that, but I don't think I know. (Pause.) I don't think I know.

My son, a twenty-two-year-old boy, who's been going to college, I really don't think I know *him*. I think he knows me better than I know him. That's one thing he really doesn't like. I think he'd like it the other way around. The younger generation doesn't think too highly of us. They think we made a mess of things, which we did. We seem to lead disorganized lives. Most of us dislike the work we're doing. Most of us are anxious to go someplace else, thinking we could leave our troubles behind. They love us, our sons and daughters. But at the same time, they don't think we did things correctly. They're critical of us. They discuss things far more intelligently than we do. They think for themselves.

One day he brought up a charming little blond girl, not overly dressed, but not ragged or beatnik type. She was going down South to teach in one of the Freedom schools. Very much enthused about it. And she seemed to have a good idea why she was doing it. I mean she wasn't looking for publicity or anything like that. She really thought she should be doing this. And then again, he met a colored girl, a beautiful creature, who also had a brilliant mind, you know, straight-A student, one of those types. And she had absolutely no interest in civil rights. None. Couldn't mean less to her, although she identifies with the colored people. She makes no attempt to pass, 'cause she could very easily. And then he has a friend whose sister and

114

mother are both active in the civil-rights movement. The sister was arrested twice in the last week.

Did you have to arrest her?

No, I . . . (Laughs.) It woulda really been funny, you know. I asked her, "Now what is this about police brutality?" And she said, the way some policeman talk, you know, and then I suppose holler at them at some degree or another, I mean to keep them in control and get them in the wagon or something. But I said, "What happened to you?" I mean, the voice means nothing, I mean, I holler at people, too, you know—stand back, or something. Well, she said, "When the policeman arrested me, he said, 'Now come along, honey, step up in the wagon.'" (Laughs.) That was police brutality.

. . . So the difference in them, more freedom. You never say, "Go to your room, I want to talk to your mother." When I was a boy, when they had company, I was always excluded. Today, even when our son was young, he sat in on conversation and he learned to judge and evaluate things. In my home, when my father was there, he got the paper. When he was through with it, you got it. That's all. Sometimes he didn't get through with it until you were in bed. About the only thing that was discarded was the comics on Sunday. They didn't think you were interested in other things.

I was surprised to see what these young people were thinking. Civil rights. Some couldn't care less. Others were militant. Then others like himself approved of what was going on but didn't participate. They had some very good ideas about it. Some of the most controversial things, Vietnam, Cuba.

They began wondering. Of course they have more time. You and I have to make a living. But their level of conversation is much higher than the adults' level today. I think we tend to be more humorous, even if we force it, probably because of age and years of work. I find myself in a group, visiting, where there's very little conversation of any depth. Did you hear the latest Polish joke? or things like that. Or talk about some play or movie. You know, there's no . . .

But these young people really have a feeling. They trade

115

views. I find they seldom argue in a—in disagreement. They give and take, back and forth but they don't stand on their points. They want to know the other person. They seem to accept other people more easily than we did.

The only thing is there's a great many pressures on them. The fear of the draft is always there. It's stupid, they feel. It doesn't accomplish a thing, and why do it. They don't seem—outside of this one girl who was arrested twice in one week for sitting in the streets—they don't seem to have any great drive. I mean, it's a problem. Everything is so complex.

They see all our values changing. Just as we see the city changing, with the expressways and with the high-rise living, which I never thought I'd live or could possibly afford.

You're two years away from retirement. Do you look forward to it?

Not particularly. I do in one way. I'd like to take up something else if I can. Be able to enter—this sounds sort of corny—more of a community life, in a smaller community where you participated more, you know. *In doing something.*

I myself haven't done everything a man should do. Some guy once said the four things a man had to do: he had to be in love, he had to get married, he had to have children, and he had to fight a war. So you accomplish these things, and I did. Now there's the Bomb. As far as I'm concerned, I'd hold on as long as I could. I don't think this is as serious with the older generation, this fear, as it is with the young. They believe here's a possibility of working your way out of this intelligently and we don't seem to work toward that end. We're constantly in turmoil. That's the older generation. After you're fifty, it's all the way down, no speed limits. That's it, you've had it. I mean you have nothing left.

A policeman starts out young and very impressionable, and you see people at their worst, naturally. You don't go into the better homes, because they have fewer problems, or they keep them under control. Sure, a man and wife argue, but usually it's on a quiet level. In the poorer classes of homes, frustrations are great, pressures are tre-

116

mendous. They turn on the TV set and they have these give-away programs and someone's winning thousands of dollars. Or if they're watching a play of some kind, everything's beautiful and lovely. They watch this and they don't have any of it and they can't get any of it. Then when an argument breaks out, the closest one to 'em, he's gonna get it. We were taught, you know, if my mother and father argued, my mother went around shutting down the windows and the doors because they didn't want the neighbors to hear 'em. But they deliberately open the doors and open the windows, screaming and hollering, and it's a release from their emotions. So when they have an argument, it's a good argument and it necessitates the police coming to quiet it down. Naturally, the impression of a young police officer is that they aren't really people, you know, get rid of them.

I've often worked with policemen who became very angry when we'd arrest a narcotic addict, a burglar. And then have to notify the parents. This one police officer, he used to get insane, he'd be so mad. Why couldn't you do something with your son? One day I finally said to him, "What would you do if your son came home and said he was a junkie?" He wouldn't know what to do. He wouldn't know why his son did it. The son would know, but he wouldn't. You understand?

• • • • • •

Carlos Alvarez, 33

He had come to the United States from a small Puerto Rican village sixteen years ago. He had worked in New York and Chicago as a hat blocker, assembler in a radio manufacturing plant, waiter at a fashionable Catskill resort, and clothing salesman. "When you first come to this country, you have to learn something from people all over. I have been among people of both states, they show they are very friendly."

For the last six years, he had been a night watchman at one of Chicago's smaller museums. "I enjoy work for them, otherwise I can find a job for more money any other place."

117

On a pleasant autumn morning, there was an unexpected encounter.

It was about six o'clock in the morning when I was getting ready to go home. I walk out about five feet away from the back door out there, at Academy. A police was approaching to our parking lot over there. The first question he asked me was what I was doing there? I told him I work here. He asked me if I have any identification. I said no, we don't have any right now. He asked me if I had the key. I said no, I just left it with the relief man. When he don't believe me, I ask him to come in and ask the relief man. He says in a kind of very rude manner, he pushed me against the car, he said he heard that before from other people, and he pushed me against the car again and called for help.

About six other cars answer his call. Another sergeant drop in, and this man grab me and put my hands in the back, cross my hands, throwed me into that holdup car. My cheek hit the glass, the hood. And my arm was hurt by the side of the car. And they were laughing about asking what my nationality I was. They were laughing, walking back and forth, back and forth, in a way that, like making fun of me. One particular fella was laughing and walking back and forth and he was trying to show off with the sergeant. He was talking to the other guys who come to help him, and he said, "Leave this one up to me, I'm gonna get him in jail, no matter what."

When I called the relief man and asked him to call Mr. Baird, who is the curator, Mr. Baird arrived about five minutes later. And he asked the police what happened. Nobody answered him any question. They asked him if he recognized me. He says, yeah, he worked for us for many years and we know him very good. What happened? Nobody happened to answer him. He went inside to call up the director.

When he went inside, there was about seven more cars, fourteen cars altogether, about fifteen policemen were surrounding me. I was innocent, I don't know what to do with myself. They were talking there for a good half an hour before they decided to take me to the station. I told the station, I think my arm is broken. And I need medical attention. One sergeant, he pushed me and told me, he

118

said, if you need medical attention, we'll take you to the Cook County Hospital and lock you in there till tomorrow morning and you get your attention there, and you don't gonna be in court till tomorrow. Or you gotta wait over here till nine o'clock when the judge arrive. I say I rather stay over here in jail till nine o'clock and not wait till tomorrow.

They took my fingerprints, my name, my address, where I work, how long I been working here. They put me in a room, second floor in the back, where all the bums from Clark Street, there was about seventy-five or a hundred bums there. I was the only one in there clean and decent. Only one washroom, in the middle of the floor, for everyone to use there. I asked one of the bailiffs to please change me from this pigsty to another room, not to be between so many bums in there. I was sick in there. He said, no, here is where you belong. He pushed me against the wall and close the door.

About nine o'clock the judge arrive. Everybody in line, like a pig, went to the courtroom. The courtroom where nobody is admitted. The public is not allowed to there. Behind bars. The lawyer was not allowed to go there. My cousin was not allowed to go there, even Mr. Baird was not allowed to go in there. When I went there, they push me back into the room again because the police who was involved in my case was not there.

Once I wait there for ten minutes, they call me back again. The police was there, four policemen show up. They were the ones who talked. I wasn't allowed to say a word. When I tried to defend myself, they push me, they say, you have nothing to talk in here. When I wait for my turn to come, the judge said. They talk all they want, they said I tried to punch the sergeant in the mouth or in his face. When I was even handcuffed in the back. Which was not true, because I could do nothing myself when there is a man armed with guns, and so many men around me, for no reason at all. I was tired, nervous, exhausted, I didn't know what to do.

They talked so dirty in a way over there to the judge. And the judge, the only thing he asked me was if I have any family. And I say, yes, I have a family. He said, well, I'm gonna give you guilty with a suspended sentence. When I asked him guilty for what, he said, that's all, you're not allowed to talk any more. I say good-bye and I see you later.

My cousin drive me to the hospital and I stayed there from ten o'clock in the morning till three in the afternoon, waiting for the X rays. The doctor find out that I have a fracture in my arm, about two to three inches cracked. I came home, I don't know what to think, I don't know what to do, I don't know what to say.

Next day, what I did, I wrote to different personalities, who runs the city of Chicago. Also I wrote to Congress of the United States in Washington. I wrote the President and I wrote to the governor of Puerto Rico. I explain in three full pages what happened and how it happened. They all answered to me. It was kind of a glad lift that they answered to me and at least they did something. They wrote to Superintendent Wilson* and they said that he said he will do everything in his power to be sure that something has to be done to the person who was involved in my case.

How long ago was this?

Four months already. Nothing has happened so far because I'm waiting for the doctor's discharge. I will know for sure what's wrong with the arm. There's 15 to 20 percent shorter, not only shorter, but curved. It still hurts when the weather is kind of damp and it's kinda cloudy, you know.

I took three weeks off. When I came back, the assistant director calls me and he says, I'm afraid we have to tell you right in your face that you have been fired. He said, I don't know if you receive a letter or not. A registered letter. The only reason that they said is that the insurance company complained that I cost the insurance company too much trouble. To my knowledge, this is the first time I ever had trouble with an insurance company.

The first time, the director, he was very shocked about what happened. He didn't believe it. He asked me how I feel and after a while he said, this happens to you for being against the police. And I told him I have nothing against the police. And I say, you talk this way because

_____
* Police Commissioner of Chicago.

this doesn't happen to you. And the answer he gave me, he turned his back, he said, "They do this to me and nobody will have a job at that police station." That was his answer.

One day Mr. Baird, he was talking about me, about the same case, the director said, "Well, he cannot ever deny that he's a Puerto Rican." And also one day, when the director mentioned the case to the board of directors, one of the women's board said, I should go back to Puerto Rico, what was I waiting for here in Chicago that I didn't go back to Puerto Rico where I belong. They are the biggest society in Chicago.

This situation is the one that hurt me the most. I loved walking, and I enjoy walking in summertime and wintertime, I don't care. Sometimes police follow me in cars, asking me what I'm doing that time of night. But never have any trouble. They've always been very friendly to me and very nice to me, till now. But this change in the police station, to me they are nothing but like hungry dogs looking for a piece of fresh meat. Those two hours in the police station, that's the biggest experience in my life. I have been nervous ever since.

When this happened to you, were there other people around? Did they watch?

No, they don't watch. They keep walking, because maybe they might be afraid that the police might grab them and say, well, you are involved, too. They walked by and they didn't pay much attention. Maybe they were afraid to stand by because the police might throw them in the can too.

If a person is wrongdoing, it's all right, the police should do what they're supposed to do and what the law tells them to do. But if a person is just coming out of work, minding his own business, now why do the police beat him up for no reason at all?

I think the way the police acts is a very very low way of doing. I was waiting for a bus about six weeks ago. Now a black car happened to drive north up the street. The police stopped the car. The man was well dressed, he come out of the car, he had a five-dollar bill in his hand. He just hand to the police. The police say **no,** I cannot do

121

that. The guy put the money in his hand. The policeman's hand is against the handle of the motorcycle. Drove away about a half block south. He put his hand in his pocket, the money in his pocket, and the other guy drove north.

● ● ● ● ● ● ● ● ● ●

George Drossos, 66

He sits near the window of a small Greek pastry shop, on the Far West Side of the city. He seems out of place in this area, as does our hostess, an old woman. They are part of the old Chicago Greek community, whose neighborhood, Greek Town, in the Hull House area, had been bulldozed to make way for the Circle Campus of the University of Illinois.

For almost fifty years, he had lived in the old neighborhood, along Halsted Street. He had been the principal and guiding spirit of Socrates School, known as the Greek School, though English was also taught there. He is a teacher emeritus of languages and history at one of the city's public high schools, having been urged by the Board of Education to continue another five years.

The new neighborhood is middle class.

We are here now, but it is not the same as it was there. We Greeks, most of all things, love *nostos*. *Nostos* means the feeling you have when you return to your country. For all these thousands of years, the Greeks held that feeling most near to their heart. From that comes the word *nostalgia*. When you feel pain because you cannot return. In Greek, anything that is nice, sweet, good taste, we call *nostimo*. It partakes of the feeling of *nostos*.

So, we Greeks, when we settled down there in that part of the city, which we called Greek Town, we felt we were in our country. We gathered together, there were centers there, and all the places . . . Especially the so-called intellectuals, we gathered together and we called that "The

Academy." We spoke and we discussed all subjects, from politics to philosophy to anything—on Halsted Street.

There are no centers here where we can gather. We are dispersed now. We are in the *diaspora*. We can't see each other. Now, two times a week, I go down Halsted Street, Tuesday evenings and Friday evenings, to meet some old friends there. We meet in a coffeehouse there. And then we go to one of the restaurants and eat together, and feel like old times. To meet my old friends and talk to them, but it isn't the same. It is in miniature now.

If they would do as we planned—I was a member of the planning board down there with Scala and the others*—if they did that, then most of the Greeks would have settled there, but now they are dispersed.

I don't see too many of my friends in this neighborhood. I see some of them, but this is no togetherness here as it was there. We felt safer, we felt like we were in a Greek town. You came out of your house to the street and you would meet so many people, who would say hello to you, and you knew them although you were not so closely connected with them. But just the same, they would speak to you. And you would go out anytime, night or day, and you felt safe.

Here, you come out and you look around and see who is—because you hear so many holdups all around. Even in the best neighborhoods of the city. You come out here out of your house and you look around and see if you're safe or not. You feel more of a stranger here. Although this is nearer to the school where I teach, I don't feel so comfortable here. When you went out, you could see your friends, you could go any place and you could find people you could talk with and understand each other.

What is the biggest change you've noticed in the city since 1917, when you first arrived here?

Of course, this renewal. People were more settled at that time. Now everybody's on the go. That's the feeling now. Although, of course, the city has progressed a lot, so many things changed to the better. But for individuals—

* A reference to the neighborhood committee, with its plan for rehabilitating the Harrison-Halsted area. It was ignored by the city authorities.

now all these people who lived down there, I don't think any of them is happy now. Because it's the same as you leave your country where you were born and you have to go abroad, go to another place. Same feeling.

All of them have a transient feeling. Not settled, not happy. It's not a question of money. It's a question of social feeling. We don't feel that here.

I remember when I left my little town in Greece, to go to Constantinople to study. I felt I wanted to cry. But I kept myself, I just wanted to be courageous, and I held it back. As soon as the boat departed, as soon as my parents and the others went away, then I started crying to myself. I remember that. Yes, it's a bitter feeling when one leaves his own surroundings, his own country.

I never wanted to come to America. I heard of people coming here, uneducated people, and they suffered a lot, hardships. This wasn't the place for me to come, but I decided this would be an adventure for me. And for the sake of my family, who were refugees from the Turks. They had to have somebody to support them. So I came here.

For many years, I had thought of going back to Greece, but there were so many upheavals there, so I had no chance. In the meantime, I became a member of the Greek community here and of the Greek church. About 1936, I introduced Greek in the high schools here. I was the first one to teach it. I taught Greek for about twenty-five years. Later on, I learned Spanish and taught Spanish. I learned German and taught German. Latin, I knew. French, I started to learn Russian—and what else? (Laughs softly.)

When I started teaching in the American high school, I knew I wasn't going back to Greece. It was too late. It is a calamity, you know, for a person who leaves a country of birth and goes away. . . He's a stranger *here,* and if he goes back, he'll again be a stranger *there.* So he's a man without a country.

In leaving Greek Town here, did you have the same feeling as when you left your native village for Constantinople?

No, not as much. Then I was a boy, it was different. That broke my heart. And when I came to America, it was a new country. I had to acclimatize myself and so I was busy doing things. When I lived in Greek Town here, sometimes in the summer I would take a trip, to go to other states, to stay a month or so, and then I felt the *nostos* for Chicago. I wanted to come back to Chicago. Now, in this neighborhood, to come back to what?

Throughout the conversation, the sound of automobiles, motors revved up, roars. The old woman, at the pastry counter nearby, is continuously startled.

Do you look forward to retirement?

I did several years ago, but now that I came near it, I don't care very much. The Board of Education wrote me a nice letter: We need you, it's an honor for us to ask you stay, and so on. That made me feel good. But when I accepted, I said to myself: How am I going to do it? When I started teaching in September, I felt better. So, if anyone retires and does nothing, he doesn't feel so good.

I always had in mind writing some textbooks and I may start doing that in five years, when I fully retire. Or write the history of the Greeks in America, especially the Greek community here. Nobody ever wrote it to do it justice.

My wish? I would like peace to prevail all over the world and I would like my native village to be free from the Turk, so I could go there and contemplate those old days when I was a child there and I was happy. Because now, wherever you go, you're not in peace.

Nostos is the most I seek. I can't ever have that. Only in dreams, I have it. Those are very happy moments for me, when I dream.

• • • • • •

Lucky Miller, 19

He has lived in the same neighborhood all his life. He is a loner who, until a few years ago, did a great deal of walking through the streets of the city, often as many as fifteen miles a day: "I'd delight in taking those long walks." He now attends a college in town and works evenings at a chain supermarket.

Here I am talking like an old-timer. In my younger days, when I was four or five, everything seemed like it was peaches and cream and there was no evil in the world. I remember I used to think that to the west of Halsted Street—we lived just east—was a Garden of Eden of some sort. I thought that as one went west, the scenery became more lush.

I never knew what was on the other side till some years later in my life. I discovered it wasn't much different from what was east of Halsted Street, really. I always used to wonder what the rest of the city was like. I really didn't know.

The city is beautiful, yet it's ugly. Maybe it's the ugliness of the city that makes it so beautiful: within the ugliness there's a beauty. Do I make sense? There are a lot of boosters, Chamber of Commerce men, who use the words *seamy side* as meaning ugly. Its exterior is ugly and the people live in misery, but ever so many of these areas have their own color, their own life. I don't mean these conditions should exist, but the people there seem to be more lively than the others. That's how it appeared to me, during my long crosstown walks.

One of my fondest memories was of Chris, the grocer. I remember what a congenial old fellow he was. He was probably in his seventies, a short fellow with a shock of white hair and little rimless glasses. Every time he'd see me, he'd lift me toward the ceiling in his arms. I remember one thing that used to fascinate me was pulling the strings of his fluorescents, with the little Seven-Up tags at the end of the strings. And then he had this old female tabby he called Helen.

There are so few of them [grocers] around any more, it seems. Those that are left just seem sort of depressed. All the life has gone out of them. Most of the small independents today just aren't getting business any more. As a result, you find the men who own them putting in eighteen-hour days. They're tired, haggard, the life has gone out of them. They just have to work constantly to make ends meet. So there's no life in them any more, no spirit.

Getting back to the old grocery store—I was about four or five—I remember old Chris, he used to have this assistant, a young fellow named Booby. He loved to chase me around the store with a feather duster, got the biggest bang out of it. And I loved being chased.

Now I work in a supermarket. If some mother were to bring in her kid and I were to be seen chasing the kid around the store with a feather duster, chances are I'd be reprimanded. After all, this is a big, impersonal supermarket, and we're there so they can get as much work out of us as possible. Of course, we're paid well for it, I must say that. But there is no time for that sort of cordiality. If a customer asks where something is, you tell her and that's that. She goes on her way. There's no time for any conversation. *Everything* these days is getting more impersonal, it seems.

• • • • • •

Billy Joe Gatewood, 19

He came to Chicago two years ago from a town in eastern Kentucky: population, 2,500. His mother and stepfather, Mr. and Mrs. Thurman Parker, followed one year later. He is one of fifteen children of his mother (fourteen surviving); she has twenty-one grandchildren. He had gone to work at the end of his first year in high school. He works in the city as a "stock chaser"—a shipping clerk.

The three are seated near the front window of the flat, facing a street of other Appalachians. On the worn davenport, across the room, his skinny, child-faced, eighteen-year-old sister-in-law dandles a lively baby on her lap.

They had come to Chicago because "the mines were worked out." There is a shyness and formality in their bearing, though their hospitality is quite evident, even to the proffered cola.

Chicago, hit's a place you can labor and work an' make a livin' at. We have better things in life than we did down home. I have everything I can wish for. I still have my mother. I have my stepfather. I have twelve good brothers and two nice sisters. And work every day an' make fine money. I eat good. I can't seen anything else a man can ask for. As long as I'm workin', I figure everything'll be okay. The only thing I have against Chicago is that maybe there's too much alcoholics around here. An' maybe too many young boys runnin' around.

They haven't got nothin' else to do besides running the streets. They don't have no mother there at home to keep their house clean and to have their meals ready when they come in. So they go out, maybe spend a couple bucks after the evenin' when they get off from work, an' mess around like that.

I have a few friends, they never enter into anything like that that I know of. We mostly run around, maybe nine or ten o'clock at night, we ever stay out. We have a good time at the movies and bowlin'.

I always try to respect my elders, but as I've been walkin' down the streets, I've heard other boys my age, talkin' about people older than they are. I don't see no sense in it myself. Down home, very seldom do you find a young man that didn't have respect for his mother and father and older people. After the boys gets up here, they think they're it or something.

There was an old man walkin' down the street, I know of, an' he was fairly well crippled up. And I knowed some guys jerked his hat off and run around with it. And I don't think that was the right thing to do to the old man.

They're up here by theirself. They get out an' drink a couple of beers an' maybe they tried to grow up too fast, like I had at one time. When I quit school, I thought I knowed as much as anybody else, an' I could do a man's work. Now I wisht I'd a went to school, because a lot of places today, that's the first thing they ask: my educational record.

They come up here too soon, which I did. So they get up here and that's about all they do, run around in gangs. I know maybe five or six guys from maybe the same home town an' when one of 'em gets in a scrap, well, all of 'em is gonna help the other, that comes natural.

Down home, we'd get four or five together an' go to a drive-in movie an' spend the evenin'. We'd never run around together other than that. We'd stay close to home most of the time, or we'd be in fishin' or go huntin', or maybe go swimmin', there'd be a gang of us. Other than that, no.

From time to time, I worked with people, it's even said, they ought to take sub-Thompsons and walk up and down the street and shoot all the hoods off and throw 'em in jail. That ain't no way to treat 'em. I think they should have more recreation than they do have. Anybody can go to a bowlin' alley an' bowl. An' if while they're down there, how many beers they're gonna drink and things like that. You get tired of doin' the same thing all the time. I know I get bored of goin' bowlin' or shoot pool or goin' to the movies all the time myself. For boys my age, there ain't nothin' in a movie to go see. You seen the same movie maybe twice or somethin'. It ain't no fun to go back an' see the movie.

If they had a place to go swim, through the winter. Maybe like a rifle range some place. I know I like to use guns myself. If we had a small rifle range, then we could go out and shoot a few shots and that takes attention off a man's mind a lot. The biggest thing on my mind is I work nine hours a day and I come home an' the tensions build up and I don't know how to get it out sometime. That's the biggest thing that worries me.

The colored don't worry me. I never had no trouble from them, I never did give them no trouble. If there's a big bunch runnin' round, I don't know if I could get along with them or not. I've never associated with them. I've heard tell of one colored family moved on this block. It doesn't bother me as long as they stay on their side of the street and I stay on my side of the street.

Suppose they're on the same side of the street?

(Laughs.) I imagine we might be able to be pious and get along pretty good.

Mrs. Thacker interjects, "The same sun would have to shine on both of 'em, wouldn't it?"

If anything happens in Vietnam, I'd have to go most likely. Maybe there'd be some there with me as well as our own race in there. That's most of my dream now, someday goin' into the service and makin' a career out of it. I'll wait till they call me in the service before I go.

Vietnam, I do think about it pretty often. I sort of pick up a paper now and then or listen to the news about it. As far as going over and dyin', I think every man, even though he's a sinner or a Christian, he looks forward to his judgment. So I figure, if he's in Vietnam, that's his duty. To die.

• • • • • •

Thurman Parker, mid-fifties

Gaunt, bespectacled, he speaks softly, deliberately, as though unaccustomed to the process.

What if a boy's called to service, he goes and he kills someone? What would that be in the sight of the Lord? I think the feller that called him, that forced him into it, would have to face the Judgment there, for this boy. Forcing him in there and he's forced to kill.

• • • • • •

Mrs. Thurman Parker, mid-fifties

She is seated in her rocker, the matriarch, bearing a remarkable resemblance to Ma Joad. Her voice is a young girl's.

We don't get out very much, Mr. Parker an' me. I'm very well satisfied with Chicago, but I liked down South the best. I don't like this hoodlum business that's goin' on in Chicago. I'm always afraid the boys will get out and get into trouble. Down home, as critters as we are on earth, we very seldom do have such as that goin' on. I think it's too many people, so many people.

I miss gettin' up and gardenin' an' things like that. Getting it ready for summer, I miss that most of all. I can live anywhere my children is. I have four here in Chicago. Oh, they're all over the world. I've got 'em scattered everywhere. Back home, one daughter-in-law is all. Everybody's gone. I write home, I get in touch with home. I know a few neighbors here, very few. A lot of people from home, somtime I see 'em, sometimes I don't.

I figure someday to take a trip across-country in one of them diesels. I won't get to drive it, but I might take a trip. I'd sit with the driver. That's my dream. I'd like to be a cross-country diesel-engine driver myself. I'm too old now. When I was a little girl, I wanted to be a nurse. I'd still like to be, but I'm too old now. I married young. I was in first year high school. That ended the dream.

We didn't have very many colored people back home. I got one son, me and him argue about it all the time. I ain't got nothin' against the civil-rights people. I've had boys in service all the time. And the colored boys goes and fights for us and I tell you I think they ought to have just as much rights as we've got. Go fight and lay down besides our boys. I say stand up with 'em here.

Course, sometime they do get unruly. They do things we don't like. But still, if they have to fight like our boys, I think they ought to have the same right as our boys. They have to die just as our boys has to die. And they got a mother, too, you know. She has the same feelin' for hers as I have for mine, even though she's black and I'm white. That's the way I feel about it. I don't know how other people feel about it.

But I think they ought to stay in their place. I don't think they ought to go to school together. I'm not used to it, because down home they have their own schools and we have ours. They have as nice a school as we do. Nicer. It's strange, though. Now we had one family, it went to Indiana and the children felt hard toward goin' to school with colored children. But they got used to it. They didn't mind it after they got used to it. I guess it's just that you have to get used to them things.

I know several colored families in West Virginia. They were all right. Best neighbor I ever had was a colored family. She always took good care of me and when I was down sick . . . I was always on to her. We always associated.

But these young, I mean all colors, I just couldn't tell you. They just don't know where they're goin'. They live too fast, too dangerously. They just figure they're not afraid or somethin'. I don't know what's wrong with 'em.

It's a very sinful world. I think we're living in the latter days of time. I don't think it'll be too awful long before there are a lot of things the Bible speaks of is fulfilling every day. I never think about that, the Bomb. Because if it's comin', we're gonna get it. You just can't let it worry

132

you. I got one over in Korea now. I'm just little in the picture. I just don't figure that it pays me to worry about it, can't do nothin' about it.

I think in time it'll be used. It won't be in my day, but Billy Joe may live to see it. (Her grandchild howls with delight as he is thrown into the embracing arms of his uncle, Billy Joe.) The little ones, well, they'll have to suffer just like anyone else. If the end of time comes and they're not ready to go, he has to pray to be redeemed. Man wasn't born to live, he was born to die. We're each and every one of us born to die. I'd *like* to see 'im live in a peaceful world and stop this fightin' an' all that. Stop our boys havin' to go overseas and gettin' killed. For nothin'.

· · · · · ·

Bonnie Dawson, 34

On New Year's Day, 1964, she came to Chicago with her family: an ailing husband and six children. Stopover, an eastern Kentucky town of 2,000, in Pike County, had been "home" all her life. "Nothin's there now. The mines are all worked out. I didn't see a future for the children at all because there's no work for me nor him."

Her eldest, the thirteen-year-old boy, returned to Kentucky to stay with his grandparents. He could not adjust to Chicago. "The other kids understand we've got to stay here and make a livin' for them and their future."

The rent for the furnished three-room flat (there are twelve such apartments in what was originally a three-flat building) $24 a week. She's a machine operator at a plastic plant in a western suburb; the only woman on the floor. "I ride with the guys works out there."

I get up about quarter to five. Don't get home till about seven. When I get home, I cook, wash dishes, sweep up. I don't have time to rest. I don't have time to watch TV. Go to bed about eleven. Wash dishes, make the bed, cook, clean the house, bathe the babies, pin up my hair—why, it's eleven o'clock. You don't know where it went. I work myself to death on Saturday and Sunday, catching up with my back housework. Sunday is my catch-up day. I enjoy it. I never been Downtown. Two years and never been Downtown. (Laughs.)

Ever hear of Marshall Field's?

No.

You know what it is?

No. But I been to the Lincoln Park Zoo once. (Laughs.) Oh, I 'pologize. I been to State Street once. Me an' a girl friend. We took a subway there. Lookin' for employment.

Ever hear of the Bomb?

I've heard tell of it. Don't worry about it. I got no time to worry about it. I got too much work to do.

• • • • • •

Benny Bearskin, 45

The American Indian Center. It is on the North Side, an area of many transients—elderly pensioners, Appalachians, and many of the nine thousand American Indians who live in Chicago.

Here, on a winter's Saturday night, such as this one, are ceremonial dances, songs, and stories. We're seated in the office; families are assembling in the hall.

It is the Center's purpose, in the words of Benny Bearskin, "to preserve and foster the cultural values of the American Indian, at the same time helping him to make an adjustment to an urban society."

Getting urbanized. I like this term. It means you have to learn the ropes, just like a person moving out from prairie country into the woods. You know, there are certain dangers in such a transition, and it's the same way in a city. You have to learn the ropes. And once you become urbanized, this means to me that you're gonna settle down, and you have to have a goal to look forward to. Otherwise, I think it would drive you crazy.

I'll tell you the extent to which I'm urbanized, after being here for seventeen years. Some years ago, we went back to Nebraska, to my wife's parents' place. And for three or four nights in a row, I'd wake up in the middle of the night, feeling that there was something drastically wrong. And it puzzled me until I began to realize: it was quiet, that's what was wrong. There's no fire engines or police sirens passing by, no street noises. It's funny.

I was raised all the way from the Winnebago Indian reservation in northeast Nebraska, to Iowa, Minnesota, and Wisconsin. My father was a laborer. He moved his family whenever there was employment. So I got an early introduction to the melting pot.

In those days, I didn't give discrimination much thought. Since we moved around quite a lot. The one thing that stands out in my mind is that every new school we attended, we had to go through an ordeal. The toughest fellas wanted to see how tough we were. So we got kind of oriented that way. And if we could whip the toughest kid, why then, we had it made from then on. We had a lot of friends. Of course, that didn't always happen that way, either.

I came to Chicago in 1947, after I had been married, and later on I sent for my wife and my one child and since that time we've lived here in the city. The most important reason was that I could at least feel confident that perhaps fifty paychecks a year here . . . and you can't always get that way. Even though it might be more pleasant to be back home, for instance, Nebraska.

What do you call home? Do you call Nebraska home?

Yes, I think this is one feature most Indians have in common. They have a deep attachment for the land. This has been so for a long, long time. Many different tribes of Indians are now residing in Chicago, but most of them maintain ties with the people back home. Even in cases where the older members of their families have passed away, they still make a point to go home. Many of them make the trip twice a year to go back to the place where they were born and raised.

Some Appalachian whites in this neighborhood feel the same way. Home is not the city, but where they came from.

I guess there is that one similarity. When we were in Minnesota, we listened to the Grand Old Opry on these long winter nights. My brother and I used to play fiddle and guitar for square dances. I guess that was the only phase of my life when I was interested in music other than Indian music. As a matter of fact, I still own my violin. I kept it probably for sentimental reasons. I think the country fiddler was expressing some mood to his instrument. And Indian music is similar in that way, too. There are songs that we have which might have a sad mood to it. There are others that are very joyous and sort of light-hearted. And I found that this country and hill music had this sort of appeal for me.

. . . You know, the federal government has made mistakes . . . and one time, dating back to 1887, under the Allotment Act that Congress passed, they thought that evidently all the Indian needed was a plow and a pair of horses and harnesses and some seed and he'd become a farmer overnight. This didn't happen by any means. So judging by this, I would find it very difficult if I were used to the Southern hill country and then make an abrupt changeover and finding myself in a large city.

I was fortunate in that, as I grew up, at least part of my youth was spent in a city. I did a lot of common labor the first few years, and then the war came along, the Second World War. And I picked up the welding trade, worked in a shipyard, worked in a powder plant. And after following the welding trade for some seven years, I moved to Chicago, and I became a union boilermaker, which I am yet today.

I believe, in the long run, automation will affect my trade. Because in the length of time that I've been at it, design has changed so radically in the last few years. They can erect a powerhouse perhaps twice the size of a powerhouse that was built ten years ago, and they can do it with several thousand man-hours less. And, you know, in the long run, this process of change continues, it's gonna have a great effect on the tradesman.

On the basis of my experience, I'd say about nine out of ten companies judge you solely on your performance and only about one out of ten would have any reservation because of race. This doesn't say much, because I don't know what happens to anyone else.

The one out ten? Well, they come up with some kind of excuse that we think you can do the work, and we'll call you whenever we have an opening, and that's the end of that.

You put down on the application: INDIAN?

Yes, always. I think that's a source of pride. I think a lot of fellas think this is a source of pride, because we enjoy the distinction that no other person has. We are at home, while everyone else came here from somewhere else.

And I believe that, as time goes on, that society becomes more and more complex, there is that need for a basic pride in order to have something on which to build character. If you don't have that pride, well, then you have no identity. We understand that all the states have these mental institutions that are bulging at the seams. This is evidence of social and psychological maladjustment. So we have to have some values, I believe.

There is possibly a class of Indian youth that doesn't have these values. I've seen signs of this in my travels. Back in 1961, I covered about ninety-five percent of the reservations to the north and a little to the west. During these times I saw the cultural deterioration that some of these children are growing up with.

There are some areas where the transition from Indian culture to white culture is going on, and some of the children are born into a situation where the old values are already lost. There being no basic economies in these areas, there's much poverty. And nothing of the white culture is available to them. So they're lost in between.

And it is this type of young Indian who is ashamed he is an Indian. Because he doesn't realize, there's nobody ever told him: his ancestors were a noble race of men, who developed over many centuries a way of life, primitive though it was; it existed without prisons, hospitals, jails, courts or anything, or insane asylums or currency or

137

anything. Yet an Indian back in those days was able to live from babyhood till all the hair on his head became white, and he lived a life of complete fulfillment. With no regrets at the end. You rarely see that in this day and age.

Four of our children were born here in this city, and yet, I think, they're oriented as American Indians. I make it a point to take them on my vacation trips in the summer, always to a different reservation to get acquainted with the people of the tribe. We take photographs, we record the songs that are sung, we participate in dancing and compete for prizes. . . .

I have five now. My wife is a full-blooded Winnebago. I met her on the Nebraska reservation.

(Laughs.) Oh, one time we had a little trouble with housing. In 1960 the work was kind of slack, there wasn't anything going on about that time. So I got together with three other boilermakers, and we went up to Pierre, South Dakota, where the U.S. Army Corps of Engineers had this dam-construction project going on. While I was up there, the rents were raised where I had been living on the West Side. Well, my wife, with the help of the parish priest, found another apartment.

But I was kind of worried about being eight hundred miles from home, so I jumped on a train and came back to help her make the move. We made the move, and it happened that weekend the American Indian Center was holding a show. So after we got everything moved, we all went down to the theater. And after the show, we all went to the Center and had coffee and a good visit with everyone.

When we went back to the apartment on the West Side, the first thing we discovered that most of the windows were smashed. Well, I called the Chicago police. The police came out there, and we had a police car in front of the door for about two weeks, I guess. But . . .

I still don't know who did it, because it was done at night. They evidently thought we were Mexicans. Well, when the police asked me about this, I said I was sorry to disappoint anybody. As much as I admire Mexicans, I'm not a Mexican. I'm an American Indian.

And, well, during the following days, there were representatives of many different organizations who came out and talked to us. There was a man from the Chicago

Commission on Human Relations, the Illinois Commission, from the National Conference of Christians and Jews, American Friends Service Committee, Bureau of Indian Affairs, Catholic Interracial Council. You know, there was very little that they could do.

If I didn't have any children to worry about—they would have to walk to school about four, five blocks—I think I would have stayed. It was one of those arrangements where the thing was operated by a trust. Even the newspapers couldn't find out who was the actual owner. But I found out later that this was right inside the battle lines that had already been established. It was an old Italian neighborhood, and just across the line east of us were Puerto Ricans, Southern whites, and to the South were Negroes. And since we were different, we posed a threat. They thought we were breaking the dike or something. It was kind of enlightening, really, after it was over.

The most amusing part of it was the Chicago *Defender**
ran a cartoon. Yeah, there was a picture of an Indian family leaving a neighborhood in an old jalopy, and the people were all shouting. And then the label said, the caption said: These fellas just got off the boat. (Laughs.) The fellas just got off the boat were running the first Americans out of the neighborhood.

If we go back three generations in any given family, you see that perhaps our grandfathers had no education at all. But your fathers had a little, and we've had a little more than our fathers have had, and our children are getting a college education. We also see the pattern in the last two states that granted the Indian the right to vote: New Mexico and Arizona. Strange, but these are the two areas where the Indians really get out and vote when an election comes up. They realize they can swing an election in some areas of the country.

The Indian has little in common with the Negro, other than they are both minority groups. The American Negro, according to Indian observation, is that the Negro's culture, his entire culture, is obtained from the white man. *Whereas,* the American Indian still retains his own culture. For instance, you go back to the first sit-ins at lunch counters. During these periods, Indians felt that this was

* Chicago's leading Negro newspaper.

kind of ridiculous, because I mean after all, what was a lunch counter from an Indian's point of view? Or the front seat of a bus? Or the freedom to sit in any railroad car you want to? The Indian, in his mind, possesses values that the white man never dreamed of, which are much more important to him.

Some Indians take a stand for or against the Negro Revolution. But there are many who do not take a stand, they want to wait and see, and watch with interest. I believe that they understand, because they have an innate sense of justice, because of their heritage.

I think those Indians who retain the greatest amount of their cultural heritage are really very fortunate, because they feel that it's more important to retain one's dignity and integrity and go through life in this manner, than spending all their energy on an accumulation of material wealth. They find this a frustrating situation. I think the Indian is the only nationality under the system who has resisted this melting-pot concept. Everybody else want to jump in, they view this idea, jumping in and becoming American or losing identity.

I don't think the flame has ever went out. Of course, we do have exceptions. We have many Indians who have been orphaned at an early age, who have become completely acculturated and know nothing of their heritage.

No, I don't think there's much bitterness retained toward the white man. I think that certainly some of the older people can recall some of the—*many* of the atrocities that were perpetrated against the various tribes. But they more or less view it as being part of an era.

I believe the Indian sees irony in specific situations. What appears to be ironic to him is the recent Supreme Court ruling on prayer in public schools. I think the Indians felt that we almost witnessed the white man meeting himself coming back, so to speak. Because in the beginning, the foundation of this nation is supposed to be a belief in God. I think that you read some of the historical accounts of how the Puritans wiped out whole Indian tribes, burned them out, and burnt everything to the ground, and then proclaimed to the world that this is a nation so founded under God.

We then arrived at the point where the Supreme Court said you can't do it in public schools. But whether you're an atheist or not, they put the Bible in your hotel room. Indians certainly have a view in regards to things like this. During the early periods, the main motivation in the building of these big schools was one of competition for the soul of the Indian. I was baptized a Christian. Episcopalian.

I think we all share the knowledge that the Bomb has grown all out of proportion to its creator. And certainly it's nothing like warfare in the early days when warfare was pretty much of a sporting proposition. Now it's just a matter of pressing a button. And some of the older Indians point out: in the earliest times, humility was preached and practiced, which was supposed to attain nearness to one's Creator. How in the world is a man who can kill thousands of people just by pressing a button going to be humble enough to think of his Creator? It can't be done.

It's so impersonal. I think this makes itself felt in many situations. For instance, when you become urbanized, you learn how to think in abstract terms. Now when you get here on Broadway, to catch a CTA bus going south, you subconsciously know there's a driver, but you take no interest in him at all as a person, he's more like an object. And it's the same way in schools. The teacher is there to do a certain function. And I think the teacher also feels that these pupils are like a bunch of bumps on a log. You know, this can be a difficult thing, specifically for an Indian child, who, in his family life, he learns to establish relationships on a person-to-person basis. And he finds that this is absent in the classroom. And frequently parents go to talk to the principal, to talk to the teacher; it's just like going over there talking to a brick wall. They feel you just aren't hip. Something wrong with you, and if you don't conform, it's just too bad.

It would have to be a very unusual teacher, I think, who would see the capabilities of an unusual child. Unless the child came from an acculturated family, where you go by the rules, just rules only, instead of person-to-person. Then the Indian child would sail right through without any trouble because he'd be behaving just like the rest of the kids in school.

Of course, the adults accommodate to it, they can adjust to it. But there are exceptions to that, too, and this leads to personal problems: alcoholism and other such symptoms.

Poverty is not merely the lack of wealth, a lack of money. It goes much deeper than that. There's poverty in reservations and where there are no reservations, and where there are no Indians. What we try to do here, at the Center, is to some way, somehow, get people *involved*. Most of these people are coping with their problem on a day-to-day basis. The future is something rarely enters their minds.

I think that perhaps my early training in the home impressed me with the philosophy of our forebears. It was taught to us that if one could be of service to his people, this is one of the greatest honors there is. I think this has been a strong influence on my life. I'll never know all the answers. I'm still learning the answers.

I think there will be some radical changes taking place. We have a younger generation, in the age bracket of my oldest daughter. I think in the future Indians will make a bigger contribution. It's been pointed out that Indians should feel that if it was not for the land which *they* owned, this would not be the greatest nation on earth. . . .

• • • • • •

Sister Evelyn, 26

A second-floor apartment on Kenmore Avenue. The neighborhood, on the city's North Side, is increasingly Appalachian. The apartment is simply furnished, neatly, old-fashionedly appointed. The telephone, as well as the doorbell, rings constantly.

Three young Glenmary (R.C.) nuns live here: Sister Marie, Sister Gerald, and Sister Evelyn.

Their habit is unconventional: a gray suit, street-length; a diaphanous veil, set slightly back, showing their hair. "The degree of being set apart doesn't have to be so monumental that we become isolated from people who, we tell ourselves, we're here to serve."

We're here in this neighborhood because the Appalachian people are here. Our community was established to bring service where the Church has not been able

142

to provide it. This means, for us, areas in Appalachia itself. To offer any service to the Appalachian people back home, we have to confront the problem of migration. That's why we're here on Kenmore.

Theologically, we're here because Christ must be wherever mankind is. And certainly mankind is on every block in Chicago, and the witness of Christ, the incarnate Christ, is there as well, or should be. There is a special necessity for having Christ-in-my-brother present in this neighborhood.

We started in the Appalachian South twenty years ago. We're in Chicago because a large percentage of these people have come here.

As Sisters, we became involved in the notion of a new Church: a certain willingness to question given structures; a certain uneasiness with institutionalized answers; a certain acceptance of the ambiguity of not having answers; and the necessity of making a concrete choice.

Any person who attempts to shake an institution has to be willing to take the consequences. We certainly don't look upon ourselves as prophets. We look upon ourselves as people who are testing a situation. But in the testing, we have to infringe on certain notions that have become traditionally accepted as the way sisters do things.

We hope that we will be able to be primarily a neighbor on our block, of being with the rest of the people, a Southerner in Chicago. I think this is meaningful to our people here. Because we refer to letters we get from back home, from the mountain counties of North Carolina, from the mining counties of Virginia, and this is back home to many of the people here.

Proselytizing isn't part of this?

No, no. I think almost everyone on this block knows we are Catholic Sisters. Most frequently, though, the people refer to us as "the Christian women."

Do you encounter, because of your unconventional approach, opposition, spoken or unspoken, from the hierarchy?

After we had been in Chicago about three months, we

had the privilege of meeting with Cardinal Meyer. This was shortly before his death. The Cardinal was most gracious to us. The three of us were with him for almost half an hour, just discussing his concern for peoples in need in Chicago. We also had meetings and discussions with Monsignor Egan.* Very many other priests and sisters offered us encouragement. There also have been those who ask us questions, certainly to help us in clarifying our own goals, sometimes touching seriously on what we're doing here. Occasionally, bewilderment, but I don't think opposition . . .

Why don't you sit behind those cloistered walls . . . ?

(Laughs.) I think that's been communicated verbally and nonverbally.

What has the attitude of the neighborhood people been toward you?

Most beautifully Southern, I suppose I could say. We, I think, are pretty well accepted as neighbors. Sometimes, prejudices about the Church come to the surface. Mostly, people are expressing to us their surprise at finding the Church presenting itself this way, when they had perhaps known it in some other aspect, or had not known it at all.

After first moving here, we made ourselves known the way any other neighbor on the block would. We frequented the places that Kenmore frequents. We did our laundry in the laundromat around the corner, which is the real communications spot for many of the women on the block. We shop at the little store around the corner. We've set out and walked down to the L station with them. After some identification was achieved, we felt that maybe the most significant thing we would attempt to achieve on the block would be creation of some sense of community, a sense of welcome of the stranger. That's part of the Appalachian heritage, and this was something that was strangely lacking on Kenmore. We felt that if we could bring it to

* Monsignor John Egan, head of the Archdiocesan Department of Urban Affairs. In January, 1966, he was transferred to a parish church by Archbishop Cody, successor to the late Cardinal Meyer.

Kenmore, it would present something which was most needed by the people here.

Our efforts, since that time, have been to serve as liaison on Kenmore, between neighbor and neighbor, in pulling together small projects. The first step to the more significant exchange.

The initial reaction of an Appalachian in this big city is one of fear and frustration. It intensifies the normal isolation that a new group would have coming in. I think the city of Chicago is a big unanswered question. This is in the mind of many Appalachians. The complex network of relationships, which those of us who have grown up in a large city take as part of the way world turns, is a new experience for the Appalachian people. It's a system which I don't think many of us who have been raised in a city take time out to explain. Primarily, because it doesn't need explanation to us. We've grown up with the taste of the city. But this is a new flavor, I suppose, for the Appalachians. And it will take them a while before it becomes something that they're willing to open themselves up to.

My acquaintance with the problems confronting the Negro is not as great as my understanding of the Appalachian. I think there are several areas of similarity and perhaps, a few differences. I'm sure that many Southern Negroes, similarly, come up from a rural background and a rather isolated one. Perhaps not as isolated as the Appalachian community, but with the same results. Neither is used to the complex community of Chicago.

A difference between the two groups might perhaps be that the Southern Negro most often would come to the city, having divested himself of many of his ties back home. This is not true among the Appalachian people. They came to the city out of necessity, too, but would wish to be back home. I'm not sure if this is true of the Negro community.

Is there one overwhelming fear that you sense among the Appalachians in the city?

Oh, it's a conglomeration of many elements, which could perhaps be listed under just a strangeness. An unknowing, coupled with a realization that they're not exactly welcome. They bear the burden of a stereotype similar to

145

the one that the Negro bears in Chicago. Theirs is the stereotype of the uncouth, uneducated, immoral, violent hillbilly. It's interesting that many of these elements are part of the Negro stereotype as well. Maybe they're just the stereotype of the oustider. They're culturally unaccepted, socially unaccepted traits, and if we can locate them in a group that we're not willing to accept, we have some justification for being unwilling to accept them.

There is a certain cynicism and hesitancy about people. I think maybe the reason we experience this here is that often . . . when we first go into an Appalachian area, we are the outsider coming in. He is at home and pretty much in command of the situation. He can open himself to hospitality because he is secure in his position there. In the city, he has been made to feel *he* is the outsider. He has also had some experiences which would make him hesitant about the people with whom he finds himself involved in the city: which perhaps explain this certain withdrawal from the open, spontaneous hospitality and attitude toward people that has always been characteristic.

The Glenmary Sisters really began in Cincinnati. Appalachia was at our doorstep. It was a natural progression out of Cincinnati to the South. I think this led to our continued involvement with the Appalachian as he now makes his movement away from the South, back to the urban areas from which many of us came.

I'm from New Orleans. Memories? I expect I went through the normal phase of what every little girl wants to be, a school-teacher, a nurse, certainly a mother, and perhaps later, the adventurous careers—*apparently* adventurous to the young girl, careers of secretary or an airline hostess, a journalist, perhaps. I can't remember any particular career that captured my fancy more than just a few weeks at a time.

The telephone rings for at least the dozenth time.

There is no one answer as to why a person would become a nun, or how involved as an individual she sees herself. We, as Sisters, make a commitment which involves promises of a life of chastity, or virginity; we do not marry. It involves a life of obedience. It involves a life of

146

detachment in the use of what has been called the goods of the world. But what is the reason behind this? What justifies a woman in the twentieth century choosing to give her life energy in this direction? For some of us, I speak only for myself, the commitments that have been taken are to make us more adequate in this struggle in which mankind finds itself—I mean, in which mankind *endeavors* to find himself.

We are not married. Is this simply an attempt to avoid the pain and ambiguity of a sustained human relationship? If so, this is travesty of what it means to be a Christian. A Christian must be involved in sustained human relationships, because this is where Christ is found. But if our commitment to remain single enables us to give more of our time, more of our energies, more of our concern to mankind—or that limited area of mankind in which we're concerned—then it is valid.

If our detachment, our relationship to money and goods, means simply that we have retired from the strains and stresses of facing the monthly mortgage payment, or having to worry about will this check cover the emergency hospital bills—if it is merely a removal of ourselves from this pressing immediate problem of most of mankind, then I don't believe this is it.

But if it means that we can live in a way that closely resembles the lives of many people in the world, in which our finances are as limited as theirs are, under the human limitations that other men live out their lives, then I think our sign and symbol makes sense.

If our obedience, our relationship to the Church, points to the role of cooperation and personal responsibility that each man must eventually face as corporate mankind realizes its humanity, then, again, I think we have a message to give.

If it is simply an attempt to shy away from the responsibilities of making a lifelong decision, for which we will live out the consequences, then again, we're invalid as witness.

I think we, as Christians, who have come of age, within a mankind that is coming of age, must speak in terms that can answer the questions of those with whom we live and work. Certainly none of us live up to the full ideal of the incarnation, but as we struggle with what it does mean to live out the central mystery of Christianity, in the twentieth century, in Chicago, on Kenmore, then I think our struggle, our witness, is valid.

I can remember when I was in high school, the first attempt to take my life in my own hands was upon me. I can remember that I felt that my life was going to be too short, and given the short span of time, I would have to be pretty sure that each day's struggle and small conquests would have to have some meaning beyond myself. The choice I made was through religious life. And it's certainly not the only one. This realization that I'm not enough of a meaning by myself was part of the decision. It has grown and I believe has deepened. But I believe there was some seed there in the beginning.

Have you ever had any second thoughts?

Yes, certainly. The human situation demands rethinking at various times. We are in the community for three years before we make any sort of promise to remain. Then our promise is made for just a one-year period. So for a total of eight years, there is the yearly opportunity to rethink.

There have been periods of questioning, sometimes, I'm sure, coming from questions inside myself, sometimes from concerns outside myself. Each year I have felt the weight of ambiguity a little bit heavier, but I think I have felt more sure of my response. I think it's just part of the growing-up process.

My family wasn't enthusiastic about my choice nine year ago. Since that time—I hate to say they've become resigned, this doesn't indicate an acceptance. (Laughing.) I'm not sure that all of my family understands, have the same vision of my life as I do. But again, each man lives his own life. I think that my family has a certain assurance that I am happy—and that my choice reflects their own concern for humanity. That's I'm sure where I got mine. My family is satisfied. Hopefully, as our communication continues, I'll be able to express to them a little of that interior vision, of why I am a Sister. Not only to those whom I serve, but those closest to me, my family.

I've been away from New Orleans now since 1956. Back for a couple of visits, but certainly not enough to be part of that community any longer.

I can remember as part of my desire to become a nun —when I was in high school—the feeling of outrage at the position of the Negro in New Orleans. New Orleans was a town that prided itself on hospitality, it was a town that claimed a large heritage of culture, and a large heritage of religion as well. Yet I had seen some areas of New Orleans . . .

I know there were many people my own age who were actually sensitive and there were many who were not. And I have as yet never been able to solve the problem of why some people feel that we are our brother's keeper and others feel that we're not.

My father is from West Virginia, an Appalachian hillbilly himself, I suppose. Probably he's had firsthand experience with what's become known as the race question. He came to New Orleans to go to school. My mother is a native of New Orleans. My grandmother and grandfather on her side were before her. I think my mother has very strong personal feelings on the whole question, but I think it was her hesitancy to inculcate these in myself and in my brothers and sisters, which have put us in a position now, of being in some dialogue of controversy with my parents and grandparents.

I'm sure we owe much to my father's native sense of justice and my mother's realization of her responsibility to permit us to make our choices freely.

Sometimes I wonder if it's just nostalgia, but I can remember the feeling of being at home when I returned to New Orleans. I'm sure it must have been part of my growing-up experience there. But it's interesting that I sometimes can feel something very similar walking on Kenmore, after being away a week or two on a trip.

(Laughs.) Sometimes if I'm Downtown and meet someone and I say I'm going home, it means Kenmore. Occasionally, when I refer to going home, it would be to our headquarters in Cincinnati, and then I think of going home, and it's New Orleans.

I truly feel Kenmore is home for me now. Though our present involvement will be three years.

POSTSCRIPT

The phone rang continuously: a student who had visited

eastern Kentucky coming over to tell of a mine workers'
organization at a newly opened company truck mine; a
folk singer planning to organize a country music group in
the area; a neighborhood mother with a personal problem;
a call from JOIN, a chapter of the Students for a Demo-
cratic Society, working with Appalachians down the street.

"It has to be a one-to-one relationship," she said. "We are
approaching one another face-to-face as individuals. Then
some of the fear and hesitation and suspicious on both
sides will be allayed. And giant steps toward creating a
sense of community might be taken. The small steps are
being taken now, the necessary first steps. . . ."

At the door, I put the question: "If Jesus Christ came
back to the world today, what do you think would happen
to him?" She laughed: "Well, I hope that He would come
to visit us on Kenmore. I think that He would be most at
home here. I think that if He came back, or Christ as He
is here now, is asking us that He is to be met in our broth-
ers at this level."

VI

HOMEOWNER

• • • • • • • • •

Henry Lorenz, 53

*Mid-North, adjacent to the artsy-craftsy area, Old Town.
A frame house, two and a half stories. It has seen better
days; yet the siding salesman's offensive has been hurled
back. Outside stairway, wood, steep. The Lorenz apartment is in the process of being painted and refurnished. A
White Sox ball game on TV was switched off as the conversation began. "We weren't watching it anyway," said
Henry. A Java bird in a cage; a set of the* Book of Knowledge; *a set of* Great Books of the Western World.

*His was a hard childhood, one of a family of thirteen.
"I was lost in the shuffle somewhere." At twelve, he
dropped out of school and became a workingman: a bed
company, an iron foundry, the state roads, "swinging a
sixteen-pound sledge in the sun for ten hours." He had
been a carpenter and is now a house painter.*

We've lived in this neighborhood twenty years. First,
we had the old German area, people who were here
for years and years and years. I'm talking about people
who were here thirty to sixty years. Then after the war,
we had this terrific influx of folks from Europe. These
people were so unaccustomed to the life they found here
that the—making a quick dollar became a mania with
them. It didn't take them long to become aware of the
housing shortage.

I know one family bought the house we lived in for
$6500 and a very, very short time later his asking price
was $24,000. I think he got about twenty. A good forty
percent of the property in this area in the past twenty years

have changed hands four to six times. All of a sudden we started getting this other type of people: professional people, artists, doctors, lawyers, sculptors. You see, we had a period from the lowest to the highest. But the lowest are being priced out.

In this block here, we have something in common. Each one is trying to do something with the house he's living in. Trying to progress as rapidly as he can, and so on and so forth. When you find you have something in common with your neighbor, you take time out to know it. No strangers. I know just about everybody around here. When someone is ready to sell, there are a half a dozen people ready to buy it. We are entering on a threshold of permanency again. I feel good about it. I'm part of it. I welcome this change.

The city has changed for the good. You know, I'm not sure what good is any more. See? Traditions of the past, there are some that I miss. Chicago was a big city before and yet it was pretty much like a small town. Neighborhood after neighborhood, you know, were like small towns themselves. People integrated, relatives visited, you had more friends, you talked more, you got to know each other. You know what I mean? You miss this. There was more music, homemade music, you understand. You were able to develop yourself to a far greater extent. We knew everybody in the neighborhood.

Families do very little today. Years ago, when you were a kid, on Saturday nights, Sunday, you invariably went to somebody's house or somebody came to your house. You played cards, you picnicked, you maybe talked. All these things. You used to read more. You had no other ways to entertain yourself. You don't find that today.

We generally stay home, watch the television set, for three-four years we were fans, real TV fans. But the television set broke down. I'm telling you, we were literally sick. We didn't know what to do. We became desperate. We yelled at each other. Some of the arguments we had took place at this time. Suddenly there was something gone. It was like, gee, I don't know what. Something died. What are we gonna do? Where can we find a television repair? Will he be able to get here on time? It was a real tragedy.

What did you do before you had a TV set?

Oh, that's easy. She played a guitar. I played a harmonica. We used to play, we used to sing. Instead of going to bed at one or two in the morning, we might go to bed anywhere from nine-thirty to ten-thirty in the evening. We'd lay for three hours and talk, back and forth. We got to know each other pretty well. I haven't talked to her since we got the television set.

The boys have grown up pretty much with it. I don't think it's been detrimental to the kids, oddly enough. They know there's more to the world than what's across the street. You understand? They see many, many, many things. They witness things we never could. They begin to speak . . .

I have tried to analyze my boys. I found I did not father any geniuses. This is definite. I've established this. Not only my sons, but neither am I, right, Hazel? So I asked myself where do we go from here? So all right. The door to college. If you can't make college, you've made an honest effort in high school. Then get into a trade, one of the trades.

Frankly speaking, if they did this, they'd be far better off themselves and their future families. I think this college bit is overrated by far. Because I know of my own experience. Say, thirty-five to forty years ago, if a boy told you he was a high-school graduate, he stood out in the crowd. Is this correct? He stood out in the crowd. But today . . .

The man on the bread route not long ago told me there was an opening to drive the truck but a college education was necessary. It's becoming so commonplace. What college actually is doing today, it's becoming the equivalent of what was formerly four years high school, nothing more.

No, I don't long for the past. Much of the past has been a trial, more or less. . . .

The big question in my mind is how long I'll be able to sit comfortably here—in this neighborhood. How long this is going to last. I have an instinctive fear, I don't know why, that it could end at any time. I feel very uncomfortable living in the big city. For some reason or other, I—I dread the thought that me and my family will find ourselves swimming in some kind of blood bath. There's not a question in the world about it. Any thinking man or woman will see this. If they don't, they're deaf, dumb, and blind to the facts of life. In black-white relations. We haven't got a solution and I don't see any solution in sight. Because man is thinking no different than he ever thought.

My feeling about the Negro is this: I never try to think of him in terms of is he equal to me or isn't he equal to me. I don't know and he doesn't know. I admit to this: I am a man and he is a man. I can't say to a Negro, "You are equal to me." Some are, some aren't. The average Negro is not. I am not saying he won't be and that he might not surpass me one day. My father came here when he was seven years old from Europe, couldn't read or write the American—the English—language. He had no relatives whatsoever, outside of one cousin who was just about in the same boat he was. Yet he made his way. Scholastically, he got nowhere. Insofar as making a lot of money, he didn't get anywhere. But this is one of the lessons I've learned, it is not so much what you make or how you make it as it is what you do with it after you've made it. And here is where the Negro is not very smart. Because the average Negro's mind, when he gets a given amount of money—he could forward his education with it—but the average Negro thinks about how big a car he could buy, how many clothes he could put on his back, and whether or not he could afford a diamond or two.

I fear the Negro today. By and large, the Negro represents violence. I don't think the issue involves civil rights any more. It's gone beyond. Right now in the heart of the average Negro is vengeance. You better believe it. They intend to make me pay for what my great, great, great ancestors did to them. I am completely innocent of this. Even the so-called good Negroes. In their hearts they are too timid in themselves to come forward, so we don't think they feel this way. But you would be amazed, if we could open and bare their hearts, how many of them have this feeling for revenge in their hearts.

We talk about this constantly on our block. In tones of how can we stop it? What can we do to stop it? But there is a feeling of defeatism in everything they say. You detect it. A feeling as if they have been sold out. They feel as though their government has sold them out.

154

I tried to analyze this in my mind and I see the Negro is going to make great strides by virtue of the fact that he has the force, the militant force of the government behind him. This is the only reason he is going to make these strides. I am going to gain access to your home, but only because there is a man strong enough to break your door down behind me. You fear the man behind me. I haven't gained much in admittance, have I?

Now it's an odd thing, the white people on every hand are screaming about what we owe the Negro, they're telling us the wrongs we have done, the wrongs we have committed against the Negro in the past, and they're doing everything in their power to alleviate this thing, to change it, to make it right. But each damned one of them, you better believe this, each one of them is wondering how much money have I got at my command? Where can I move if he moves next door to me? How far can I get?

Depending on where they fit in the economy, where they fit distance-wise from the Negro, you can tell who is going to speak the loudest and the hardest for the Negro. The farther he is away from him and the more money he has, the more harder he will fight for him. But let the Negro breathe down his neck!

I am afraid that in the future somebody is going to come up. I don't know who, I don't know what. Some kind of a man is going to come up and be a leader. Who knows? I really don't know. Goldwater, if they're lucky. They had their chance to be lucky, and to my way of thinking they were very unlucky. They had their opportunity to be lucky and they rejected Goldwater. *He sounded like me myself.* A Goldwater could be a wonderful thing, but look out, I'm afraid it could be someone more like the John Birch Society. Today it's condemned, tomorrow it's our religion.

The Birch Society, there are many things to be said for it and there are many things against it. They're not all wrong. Just like the murderer like Hitler was, he wasn't all wrong. But he certainly fell short of right, wasn't he?

You'd be surprised how easy it could happen, how easy. You can get people in the right state of emotion, this is all you need. Then reason goes out the window. Because you can't experience the two things at one and the same time, can you?

Maybe this is some form of sin on my part, I don't know.

The average white person, you ask him about integration, is the Negro equal? He wants to scream *NO*. But he thinks back and he's a Christian. Now he knows in his heart that he doesn't believe he's equal, but all this Christian training almost forces him to say yes. He's saying yes to a lie, but he has to come face-to-face with the truth someday. We in our lifetime won't find the answers at all.

I was raised in a Bohemian Catholic family. I remained a Catholic until I was about thirty. And then certain things became untenable. So I grew away from it. Maybe I'll be condemned to a certain kind of damnation, I don't know.

The world should take Christianity and ban it for a certain period of years. Just shelve it for a while, give it a rest. Give Christianity and God a rest and teach man he's living in a world that belongs to him, and he's only going to get out of the world what he puts into it. Teach man that in order to stand he's got to stand on the two feet the good Lord gave him and not use the Lord as a third foot or a third hand: "What I can't do, oh Lord, you will do for me. Or help me to do."

Religion has been holding the Negro back for many, many years. The Negro has been taught to sing the Lord's praises, you understand. And he's been left with an understanding that whatever his shortcomings are, the good Lord will compensate for them. Or the talents he refuses to use. He can't expect God to solve his problems for him.

I tell you for every ounce religion has served, it held man equally back as much. To me the biggest sin has been committed by religion itself. Number one: instilling fear in men. Fear is the biggest killer of all. Every time I turn around, they tell you you should do things because in fear of God. It's how wrathful He is, how much He can be, how He can punish an eye for an eye and all these sort of things. And then in the same damn breath they tell me that God is Love. I can't reconcile the two, I can't. You understand what I mean?

They tell me about the omnipotence of God. He is all things, on heaven and earth, He is all things. And then in the same breath, they tell me about the Devil. Now if God is all things, there is nothing that exists outside of God.

156

Where do you place the Devil? Where is he, in God? I can't conceive of the Devil being within God. Does He embody the Devil, too? I don't believe this stuff, I can't . . . can you?

Man is a creature of habit. He gets something, he grows to like it, he possesses it, he hates to give it up. Sometimes he'll defend a thing to the death rather than to give it up and it actually may not be worth anything. You've got to release some of the old ideas. If something's going to live, you've got to let something die, too. I mean, you can't have life without death.

Yesterday was Good Friday. Tomorrow is Easter Sunday. What do you think would happen to Jesus Christ if He returned to earth tomorrow?

If Jesus returned to earth tomorrow and the average person were to see Him on the street, they would look at Him, point a finger and say, "You lousy bum, why don't you go back to Old Town? Why don't you shave? Why don't you take a bath? Why don't you wash the garments you're wearing." You better believe it. I think He'd be crucified, condemned as being some kind of crackpot. This I'm sure of.

• • • • • •

Lew Gibson, 50

Lawndale, an area on the West Side of the city; once predominantly Jewish, it is today almost wholly Negro. The apartment is on the first floor of a old two-flat building. On this Saturday night, it has an air of business.

Lew Gibson has been a packinghouse worker for about thirty years. He is now on the staff of UPWA, handling grievances.

An upright piano, in the front room, is at the moment covered by plastic; the TV set isn't working. On the shelf, a row of the World Book. A small boy and a small girl are watching; an older boy and his companions hurry past, eager to try out handmade scooters. The lady from upstairs is at the door with a question. Two men are holding up a hand-painted sign: "Clean-Up Week."

157

I was drafted as chairman of the block club. We have a so-called precinct captain. We don't see them people until election day. White precinct captains that used to live here, they keep their fingers in. They'll take one Negro guy and they'll make him precinct captain, but actually *he's* the precinct captain.

The few politicians we have here are very disturbed by the block clubs. It's a threat to the status quo. The precinct captain here he's worried, he knows he's not doing his job.

A lot of these people are working in laundries, working housework. They don't even make minimum. They come to me. Getting down to these poor people, the people who are giving up . . . if more guys go down into the bowels of the community, knock on their doors—that's what I admire about Jehovah's Witnesses—and let these people know what's possible, we could be a lot further than we are today.

One of the problems in Lawndale: I think this building was originally a one-flat, housed a maximum of six. Now with my family, it's five of us. And I think a minimum of eight upstairs. Made for six, housing thirteen, fourteen. The sewers, the hot water, the lights, everything is overtaxed here. These other places is eight times as worse.

You got taverns, you got policy, you got store-front churches. You just got everything popping up. The block clubs are trying to combat this. But it's fighting with the politicians and the graft.

The main thing is to teach the people to clean up, not only their personal being, but their home, their yard, to plant grass. Personal pride. We're in no position to challenge the politicians now, but if we keep on working the people's grievances and their own responsibilities . . .

Then you have no place for the kids to play and they have to be out on the street. And thing that's a contradiction, everybody's got a car, though. The car is a symbol. On a good, warm day, they'll be out, they'll wash the car, they'll polish it, but they won't take a broom and sweep up, you know. A lot of them will do a lot of things to keep up the impression. Most of them are not paid for, I know that. (Laughs.) Including mine. It's on time payment, easy down, dollar down. Some fellas live on this block, but the car's parked three blocks away to keep the guys from picking it up when they don't make a payment.

Buying things on credit, especially Negroes, I always feel very keen on this, because my mother was only making fifteen dollars a week, she was really took for this furniture we bought. I think it was five hundred bucks. On fifteen dollars a week, she couldn't meet the payments and she was fired from her job. Unions were unheard of in those days.

In this area today, they'll buy a television, they'll buy a car. They'll buy it one place and a couple of days later, he sells it to a finance company, who adds more and more. . . . They don't read the contract. You can't read it because if you go in to borrow money, open a credit account, if you ask too many questions, they won't give it to you.

Most of these people here are from the South Side, who have come from the South. I came here because instead of paying $150 a month just for rent, you could start buying a house for a small down payment. In buying these homes, you can buy them on contract, like $500 down. Most Negroes, he has no choice. He says if I can get this place, then I can make it. But the little print, they don't understand they should have a lawyer to check it out. We encourage them to do it, but most of them don't.

When we were renewed out (laughs), on the South Side, they gave us preference when they built the projects. We had to live some place till the projects were built. I came here. But my children—you see these two here—I'd hate to see them on the seventeenth floor of a project. Some Negro kids have been hurt, the porch gave way, the elevator . . . These high-rises, it's like the Jews had in Warsaw, I imagine. If you dropped one bomb, they could kill ten percent of the Negroes in Chicago from 32nd to 55th.

I came from Jackson, Mississippi, around 1918. That's when the race riots were. We used to live in the backwoods. We went to this apartment building on State Street, when we got off the Illinois Central, and we knocked on the steps instead of the front door. Our people was living on the third floor and we was knocking on the steps down at front.

Sometimes I wonder how we made it on fifteen dollars a week. When my mother lost the job because of the furniture, we had a couple of milk crates to make the house look, you know—to sit down. We went on relief. You

159

know how relief workers in those days were trained to investigate the recipients. . . .

Me and my brother, we was twelve, fourteen, and we had two or three old caps in the house. The relief worker came in and she said, "It seems to me there's a man in the house." So my mother told her, "These are my sons', I got two sons, they're growing up. So there won't be no misunderstanding, these two caps belong to my sons. So you'll understand I'm a woman like you."

In those days, relief paid one month's rent. We would live one month, and the second month we would go to court. And at the end of the second month, we had to move some place else. I was always afraid the people at school might find out we was on relief. All children have pride, you know.

The incident most vivid in my mind was when the bailiffs came to our house. About six guys in a small truck. Our grandmother was living with us. So just on the spot, we decided to put her in bed. She was sick already, but she wasn't that sick. We put a wrapping around her head and doused her with water. And we begged them not to put us out. So they had a conference and said, "We'll be back. We can't put you out today."

In those days, you couldn't walk three doors without walking into people's furniture. This was in the Thirties. They evicted a lady, she was sick and she had ten or twelve children. They sit her out in the middle of the street. White, colored, they came from everywhere, they had a meeting in front of the house. What I saw was thousands of people gather there and put these people back in their home. They turned the gas and lights on and took up a collection. The police wagon drove into a crowd and it turned into a riot. I heard the shots. Four people were killed. Mayor Cermak came out and the eviction was halted at that point.

I think the poor class of people, both Negro and white, as bad as I hate to say this, being a union man, I believe they've forgotten a lot of these things. In those days, if you had a car transfer, nobody threw away a transfer. They would put it where somebody else could get it. Nobody threw away a cigarette butt. It was awful hard to find a cigarette, but if a guy had one, he would choke it and give it to the next guy. Everybody was very friendly at that time.

Today, based on the war economy and the unions, some people make a few dollars, and the feeling, the atmosphere is different. Labor's respectable now, it's status quo. If you fight against these guys, you're labeled. Fear. A lot of fellas want to know how come George Meany don't walk together with Martin Luther King, you know, in these demonstrations. We evade the question. (Laughs.)

There was a meeting downtown where all the business agents were, labor leaders. I thought they were gonna pull Mayor Daley's pants down and kiss him. These guys go overboard. And they were raising a question of why we wasn't organizin' more. Why there wasn't more than five Negroes out of two, three hundred guys! So I finally got up enough courage to get the floor. (Laughs.)

So I told 'em, "Looking around the room here, you guys got all diamond rings, manicures." Honest, I didn't know Bill Lee* had a telephone in his Mark IV, air-conditioned, chauffeur, everything. (Laughs.) And I said, "The image of so-called labor leaders is not what it was in the old days. Now you can't tell 'em from a businessman." So they accepted the criticism.

And the Butchers' Union, they have separate locals. I'm not talking about the South. Negroes can cut meat in this neighborhood, but they can't cut it past Belmont.† And barbers. I said, "Some Negroes got hair like white people. You can't tell the difference. Negroes got all kinda hair and white people got all kinda hair. So the Negro barber can cut any kind of hair there is, but he can't cut hair no more than in the Negro area." Today they got separate locals. So they ruled me out of order. So I took my seat. I didn't have no support anyway. (Laughs.)

Labor, the poor, in the old days, were closer to reality. The way I visualize it today it is like a guy standing there with his left foot on poverty and his right foot on prosperity, and everybody's trying to make the big jump. Some feel they can do it through politics, some feel they can do it with the boss, some feel they might win a sweepstake ticket. In those days everybody knew who the common enemy was. (Laughs.) They all had grievances with relief. It's not as tightly knitted as it was, the feeling.

Of course, other things I remember, too. Assembly Hall

* President of the Chicago Federation of Labor.
† Mid-North, Chicago.

161

on Thursdays in school. And everybody salutes the flag: I pledge allegiance to the flag, for what it stands, you know. I wasn't conscious I was a Negro at the time I saluted the flag. After I graduated, my pastor gave me a letter to one of the big stores Downtown. I felt through my church work, I'd get the job. Anyway, I went with my graduation ribbons, with my letter. I was almost physically thrown out of the store: "We don't hire your kind," and I don't want to use the name that they called me. But "We don't hire you people here." That was in the Thirties.

And I used to buy Sunday school cards, and I saw Samson and I saw Jesus Christ and I saw Joseph and Mary, and everyone was white. I asked my grandmother, who was one of the church leaders, "Do they have any black angels?" Brother So-and-So died, Sister So-and-So died and we've been to many funerals, and we were told they were smiling out of heaven. And all the cards I get are just white people. And she said, "Don't ask those questions. God will punish you." I think she felt when a Negro starts asking questions and resisting some status quo, it might hurt me.

My first packinghouse job was with Swift and Company. I was about nineteen. They put me on the butcher's job. I made one mistake. I joined the union the first day out and put my button on. Once the boss saw you with the button on, you were a marked guy. They took me off my job and put me on the most menial job for two years. Driving hogs. The crap was about one to two foot deep. Every day I'd come up and raise the question to the stewards. What are you doing about my grievances? I felt I was a good butcher. So the guy said, "Look, why don't you come in and help us?" From then on, I lived at the union hall. From then on, I was elected chief steward, grievance chairman, plant steward, president.

Automation and the packinghouse, what impact?

I got calluses and blisters on my hand, I've got scars on my back, shoulders, as a result of the manual strength that was needed. The same job that I had, now is easy. Automation helps the worker, that's number one. On the other hand, they used two men, now they use one. In some instances, where they had ten they use one. One machine replaced thirty-seven people.

Now that's a crime. I seen two or three of them today. We call it a scrap heap. There's nothing in the making now to rehabilitate these people. Some of them, they took their little money and opened up a newsstand. These people are lost, they have no hope. One thing they hope is to live long enough to be sixty-two, sixty-five. And get that ninety or whatever it is a month. Like tonight, I'm lookin' for six men, $2.54 an hour. They want young men, I can't even find them. But the older guys, that I know need the jobs, they won't even talk to them. If you're forty or over, they'll give you a blank, but they ain't gonna hire you.

Some of these guys are good butchers, good automobile mechanics, and all things, but after a while they give up. They say, what the heck. If a guy's got five, six or eight kids, he'll get a job for $1.25 an hour, you bring home thirty-five a week. He'll do better on relief. This would explain a great deal of welfare. The relief budget only allows for potatoes and beans. Now who the heck wants to eat potatoes or beans every day? Like a friend of mine said, "There's more on a hog besides its tail." (Laughs.) You know, oxtails, pig's tails, pig's feet. You want something else.

I went to a PTA meeting and the young schoolteacher was telling ADC mothers, mainly, "You young mothers, when you send your children to school, you get a calico dress for the girl." And then dress the boy so-and-so. "When they come in at noon, give them milk and crackers and in the evening give them broth." So I'm sitting in the audience. (Laughs.) I know I was out of order, but I said, "First place, young lady, these people you're talking to here, if they have a job, they're making $1.25 an hour, they can't buy all this you're talking about. And broth, they don't even know what you're talking about. Say soup." She had no understanding, a Negro teacher, she had been to college. . . .

Give you an idea what I'm saying. The other night, a Negro businessman, I met him when he started years ago, we got into quite a debate. He said, "You labor guys cause too much trouble. You want to picket, you want to demonstrate. If a white man misuses you, take him to court and sue him." (Laughs.) So I told him, "One thing about these cases, if you sue, it might take fifty years. You'd be dead before you can win the suit."

Yes, this is one of our big problems. Right in this neighborhood, right across the block, these are the social elite, the Negro leaders. They got jobs with the school, some of them don't make as much money as I do, but they don't see themselves. . . . We had several people here, they couldn't stay here and face the problems we face, so they moved in the suburbs. But they come back here: "Oh, how you all doin'?" He thinks he's escaped, see? He's got one foot up here, you know, and one down there. He can't get up *here,* and he's just a little above *this,* so he's just in between. Removed from reality.

For example, my kids and everyone else, they see these people on TV. They got a maid, they got a two-, three-car garage, they got a butler, and this glamour. I remember my classmates, some of the young ladies. They took up sewing and basic cooking, they were gonna marry some of the young fellas graduating. They didn't know these young fellas would be making $1.25, if anything at all. They see all this glamour. The babies come. So these broken homes, these ADC's. He can't produce what she thought, and things ain't like he thought. The reason he leaves is the dreams are shattered.

I met my wife on the picket line back in the Forties. We have three children. I don't want them to look to the packinghouses and steel mills. I'd like to see them as teachers, scientists. . . .

My personal wants at this time is security. I don't want to be a millionaire. I don't want to be a bigshot. If I'm disabled, I'd like to see the home taken care of. That's all. I like the car I've got now. I could have a Cadillac, you never pay for 'em anyway. (Laughs.) But I've got just an ordinary car. As long as it runs, it takes me where I want to go, I'm satisfied.

But I'll tell you, I do a lot of traveling. It's a little better now, but when I go into a small town, a new town, if I want to go to any motel or get a sandwich, when I go in, I get little butterflies.

I'd like to be able to come home, play a little music, look at the ball game, meet the neighbors, go out in the back yard and talk with the guys—without these economic things hanging over my head. That would be heaven to me, when I come home and pick up a few notes here on the piano. . . .

He walks over to the piano, removes the plastic cover, and noodles some roughhewn blues chords as he talks.

I call this culture. That's my best definition of culture. When people are oppressed, sometimes they have to have some way. Mahalia* is a typical example of what I'm trying to say. Like when my mother died, her music made me cry, but it gave me hope. I think that's one of the things that keeps, at least, the Negroes . . .

• • • • • •

Mike Kostelnik, 36

His home is on the Far Northwest Side of the city, bordering the suburb Norridge. An area primarily of one-family dwellings of a new middle class.

He is a window washer, earning $160 a week. He has worked eighteen years for the same contractor. He has a wife and two children, a boy and a girl.

I'm losing a very good neighbor. He's a fireman, captain, and he's retiring. As a matter of fact, he's leaving today. So before I went to work this morning, I even had to say goodbye to him and his wife. They had one boy, but he's gone now. He's married, you know. So he decided to retire, a man fifty-some years old. He's doing very well. Shelby, Michigan. When you're owning individual property you have a community feeling. Everyone's more interested because they have more at stake. And when you come outside, I mean, there's Joe Blow or whatever his name is, he's doing a concrete job. Well, the thing to do is go over and give him a hand. I've got a neighbor across the way, well, he can't do heights, so I cut his trees. So the next time the guy comes over my house, he's gonna do my plumbing.

We had our street paved where we were living. Now

---

* Mahalia Jackson, the gospel singer. She had a large following among the poor Negroes of the country years before she became officially popular.

everybody had to do this, because you wanted the block to look right, you know. And if you didn't—'cause a couple were real slow at it—all the rest of the people looked at them: "Hey, when are you going to get yours?" A month or two and you see the guy's not doing it, so you, well, you sort of look it over every time you go by. You give the guy a subtle hint that this should be done. You know. "Lookit, uh, why should you leave it this way? You like the area? That's why you moved here. You like the area? Keep it up." I mean, why should you go into an area that you pick and then right away let the weeds grow, you know? Why should I be a noncomformist? You have to conform to society.

What makes people scared of the colored race is they're scared of deteriorating property. Now if these people just go ahead and show that they're intelligent enough . . . And there are a lot of wonderful people. I've done work for colored lawyers, educated people, and you couldn't find a better group of people. These people don't like their own type, they don't like their own people in their own race. Now there must be a reason for it. I have quite a few Negro friends. I've discussed this basic thing with them. I know a parking-lot fella here. I've met a lot of wonderful Negro people, don't get me wrong. It's never a question of color, it's the way a lot of them live.

So why should anybody tell me, the property I'm sweating for right now and I'm working every day and sweating for . . . why should I be told who to sell it? Where are *my* civil rights? There's the twister. Why should I be told what I sweated for and earned—this is against the constitution actually—how I should dispose of it? Don't you think that's wrong? I don't want to infringe on any man's freedom. But I also don't want mine infringed on.

Suppose a neighbor left and sold his house to a Negro?

I would not run. But I tell you one thing, he better keep up his property, because then I'd get disturbed. I'd be one of the first guys on the phone and keep on calling City Hall and telling them: "Here's your man now, let's see how he keeps up his property." 'Cause I bought my property and I want my property value to be up. I'm taking care of mine and so are all my neighbors. Now if this gentleman conforms to this type of situation, there's no restriction. Of course, his moral code I would watch out for, too. . . .

Maybe I've gotten in contact with some poor ones, but the few of them have left me with a very poor idea. It seems the biggest thing to do is to live with two, three women. Well, maybe I'm a little old-fashioned, but I've been married to the same woman for sixteen years and I'm pretty happy with her.

Now, I'm just a window washer, okay, I'm just a bum window washer, some people would say. But I'll tell you one thing, when I walk away from a building, I like it to look like it's been done. Follow me? It might be a simple thing to other people, but when it's done, it's done. I mean I can go up and take a look at this glass and say, great. And then I don't have to take back seat from my boss. I do my work. No brown-nosing, no nothing: "If I'm not doing it for you, I'll do it for another man. I stayed here for eighteen years because you wanted me and I enjoyed being here. But I don't have to kowtow to you." And this is the point of pleasure. If you're willing to do your job, everybody wants you.

Window cleaners, like I told you, they're independent people. And they love challenges. They'll match against each other to see how much speed they have. Now I'm getting a little out of the stage, but when I was a little younger man, I used to enjoy it. When I was eighteen or nineteen, My God, the worst thing that could be told about you was he could beat you. You were the Johnny-on-the-spot, man, you went and moved. To show him that you were as good as him, if not better. Personal pride in work. This we're losing in window cleaning. And when we used to race like this, against each other, any streak on the window, that window was discounted. These were the challenges, this is what made your job interesting. A different group of men, they were big, burly men, rough, big drinkers, and all this . . . but they had a feeling about it, they took pride in their work. Today, a lot of it's gone.

It's a new age. Automation's the big thing. People who're really getting hurt are the office people, as of now. Factory workers was hurt before, now it's got to the office field. You know I heard this—they said something Henry Ford said to Martin Luther . . . no, it wasn't Martin Luther . . .

No, no, the big union man. Walter Reuther, that's it. He took him through the plant. I heard this story somehow, it hit me pretty good. He said, "I like that machine there," he says. "It does the work of six men." "And yet," as an added remark, he tells him, he says, "it doesn't have to pay union dues." And Martin Luther told him, he says, "Yeah, it's a good part. But you tell me how many cars that machine will buy. You can produce all you want, but you have to have a market for it. And if you don't have a market for it, you're not gonna sell your products." So . . .

They can work a man, heat, cold, snow. You want a job, you want to earn a living, you go in, go do it. You know these machines have to have a 72 temperature. So they talk about a working man fighting for better working conditions. Here's a machine, just don't work, has nobody to support. It doesn't have to work. It just sits there, unless you give it the proper working conditions, it just don't work. . . .

My kids are gonna have a better education than me. When my boy hits a certain age, when he's qualified to be a window washer, which I hope is another two years, he'll be working with me in the summer months, picking up about a thousand dollars for the summer months. He's hoping to get a scholarship through football.

He told the boys he didn't want to have any part of smoking, because it kills his wind, and he intended to play football. These are things that make a man feel good. He doesn't have to impress anybody. His size impresses, you know what I mean? He doesn't have to make like a bully. Nobody picks on him, because anybody in his age bracket doesn't want no part of him.

Today he's got a beautiful arm on him. I like strength myself. I'm one of these individuals that enjoys a good Indian rassle or a handshake, or stuff like that. If it's a nice bout or challenge. I enjoy it. My son, I guess he gets it from me. We've been doing this—God, since he's about ten years old. Now he's got an arm on him, he could take a grown man, at fourteen, you know. And this is the fun of it.

I've got an insurance policy, this will guarantee his education, the one I couldn't get. This will make him a better man. And this isn't done overnight. My dad was a laborer all his life. He came from Poland. We used to speak it in the home. I read and write it. My dad never owned a home. My dad never owned a car. I own all this. And this is true, generation after generation.

Yet, these kids today . . . I've got four nephews in the teaching profession. One, he's six feet two, but at times he's a little scared. He says a fifteen-, sixteen-year-old with a switchblade sort of scares you.

A regular school, not only colored. Maybe a Puerto Rican kid might do this or another white kid. We're talking about people. What did it do to these kids? When I was a kid, I came from an awful rough neighborhood. You don't like someone, man, you matched up against him with your fists. If he whipped you, you knew him better next time. But this idea of switchblades and knives and what have you, it scares a man.

And these kids come from good homes. What is a good home? If you don't spend your time with those kids . . . no, I'm trying my best. For all I know, maybe next year, or two years from now, my son might change and become one of these big bullies. Right now, he's a wonderful kid. Who knows what happens to a kid? Who knows what happens to anything?

● ● ● ● ● ●

Mrs. James Winslow, early fifties

On her father's side: a distinguished Eastern banking family, one of New York's Four Hundred. Pre-Revolution Americans. On her mother's side, the aristocratic antebellum South. She had attended Sweet Briar in Virginia, as did her mother and sisters before her. Mr. Winslow, a Yale man, came from an old, respected Pennsylvania family.

Twenty years ago, the Winslows, with four small children, moved from the East into one of the most fashionable areas of Evanston, Chicago's largest suburb—a city in itself. "We were very much in the mainstream of the social life and all the goings-on" as well as in community and Episcopal Church work. She had served as president of the school's PTA; he had been a scout master as well as general manager of the posh Fourth of July Celebration.

"However, all along we realized . . . I don't like to use the words 'closed society' . . . but it was somewhat." She noticed, "You had to be very careful, if there were home meetings, what do you do? Is the Negro mother (of the PTA of the colored elementary school) going to open her home? Or will people even go to the meeting in the Negro mother's home? I resented this." She noticed how quickly clubs were chartered, when the subject of social dancing came up. "Yet, the youngsters (who had joined these lily-white clubs) were asked to give talks on brotherhood. I thought how hypocritical this was, knowing that fifteen percent of Evanston is Negro, and look around and see not one Negro in that entire, packed, huge, white Protestant church."

The Winslows were becoming profoundly disquieted, especially in the matter of housing. One of his Negro clients—there were very few Negro lawyers in the suburb —was denied the right to add a bathroom to his house by the zoning board. "Why in the world would the board not allow a Negro to upgrade his home?" Further study revealed that not one Negro block was zoned for single-family dwellings. "Yet this was Evanston's great drawing card: the ideal. The family picture of Evanston, the one-family home." They discovered that the board discouraged the one-family housing idea among Negroes. "They could change single families into multiple-dwelling families, but, you see, it would all be within the same area, and you could just overcrowd more and more. . . ."

"There was a subtle feeling that people knew how we felt about this. There was no way in which he could come out. Jim finally, working through the Council of Churches, tried to get an open-occupancy ordinance in Evanston."

The actual incident that brought us before the Evanston people as now being antisocial and dreadful, not to say communist . . .

A doctor from South Chicago asked Jim if he could find him a home in Evanston. They had two children they very much wanted to get into better schools. They were concerned about their education. This was a highly cultured family. The wife was a talented musician, both children were studying music, and she knew in Evanston schools of the great opportunities. This is why they called Jim. One of his clients had suddenly left for Florida and said, "Won't you see that my house is sold?"

The house had been put in the hands of a real-estate agent, too. If Jim found anybody that would like to buy it, he would refer these people to the agent. Jim went ahead and showed the house to the Negro couple. They were very pleased with it. Jim is honest and open. He does not approve of a white person buying it and transferring it to a Negro. He feels you should do it on an open basis, that there is nothing to hide, so why hide it?

When he returned the key—perhaps this is Jim's naiveté as many people will say—he said to the agent, "I have just showed the house to a very nice Negro doctor and his wife and they seem to think that it's very nice."

He had no sooner left the house when the telephone started ringing. By the next morning, he had been accused of being deceitful and underhanded, trying to move a Negro family into this white area. Jim has gone to our rector, because these Negroes happened to be of the same denomination as we. He thoroughly approved because he wanted our congregation to be aware of the need for more brotherly recognition of all people. It was surprising that people who were so vilifying were the ones who went to our minister and said that if Jim were not excommunicated, they would leave the church.

This was the first time we realized how cruel your closest friends could be. How fear, and it was fear, you see, that their houses would lose property value—that through fear, they can vilify people. It's really devastating.

From then on, we really knew where we stood. We knew why we stood the way we did. This was one of those things we were going to have to stand on. You have to become hardened to the hate you're going to receive, even from those people you would like to call your best friends.

On the other hand, from unsuspecting sources, you receive great strength. People that will never come and talk to you will come up and say, "What you and Jim are doing is wonderful. We're not able to speak out, but we're behind you all the way." And this is the thing that sustains you.

Jim and I have always felt the Church meant a great deal in our lives. If you have a faith, it must be a faith that

171

controls your life or else it's not a faith. It has been heart-breaking for us. People of your own church will reject you for things you feel you're doing because of God's love. I think it's harder than anything else, really.

When we first came to Evanston, after about a year, Jim was asked to be on the vestry. He has been known throughout the country as a devoted church person and knowledgeable. There were study groups at the time. You submitted suggestions in writing to the rector, who would read them at the vestry meeting. Nobody knew who the suggestion came from. The second year Jim was on the vestry, he suggested that one of the courses during Lent be the study of peace. That was about 1947. He felt it was high time that Christians talked peace. When this was read by the rector, the entire vestry blew apart. (Laughs.)

One man jumped to his feet and said anybody who wrote such a thing must be a fellow-traveler, that Christians don't talk peace. Another jumped to his feet and said the *Tribune* would have it in headlines the next morning and no one ever again would step foot into the church. Jim, of course, admitted right away he was the one that had written the letter. The rector again stood up for him, the same gentleman that stood up for him during the housing mess. He spoke to them sharply that peace was indeed a topic Christians should be concerned with. And calmed them somewhat. This was the first time that Jim was known for his—idealism. (Laughs.)

We were told indeed never to speak about peace again or we'd be run out of the church. We have not stopped talking about peace since and people know that we believe in peace. However, Jim was put off the vestry and has not been asked to be a member since. Until about a month ago. . . .

About three weeks ago, he was asked if he would serve on the vestry. He was surprised and delighted and said that he would be glad to. He was the only one of the four nominated who received complete acclamation by the committee. Four are elected every year on a rotating basis. They only nominate four for four positions. There has never been a contested election in vestry.

The parish meeting was held two weeks ago. The committee reported their choices and then, as is usual and proper, nominations were open. There was a silence and

172

then a gentleman stood and nominated another member. This was a very conservative quiet-spoken person, who you never see at any of the church functions. (Laughs.) This had never been done before. Jim ran fifth.

Of course, it was a perfectly proper election. But what happened was this: at the parish meeting Sunday morning there had been a great deal of whispering from person to person, this kind of thing. But everybody said, "Oh, this will never happen. You know, they're always talking like this. Even though we may not always agree with Jim Winslow, he's really the only Christian we have in church." (Laughs.)

The element that recognized Jim's work in human rights felt this could never happen. So they did nothing about it. The others apparently had to call twelve men before they could get one to accept. Our telephone the next day rang constantly. People called to apologize for not being at the meeting, that these were usually automatic, that they didn't realize . . . how this showed that indeed they should become involved.

Many times when Jim would write a public letter—it's difficult to do your marketing and be completely repelled by people you had worked with in PTA and liked—mothers of friends of your children—and know perfectly well that they just despise you. It's very difficult.

These are respectable people . . .

Very respectable. Pillars of society. Jim's been denied membership in the University Club, which is one of the luncheon clubs of Evanston. He's been blackballed. We, of course, have never applied for membership in any of the country clubs. We realize we would make this a difficult thing for our friends. You don't want to put your friends on the spot. Jim set some sort of precedent by being denied inactive status with the Kiwanis Club, when he was busy establishing his first law office.

I think, though, the hardest part of all of this has been when you have to see your children denied invitations to social events that they would love to go to. Our children have been simply magnificent about all this. Still . . .

Jim Winslow had come to the Midwest after several years

173

in Washington with the government, as attorney for a trade association. After eight years, he resigned so as not to embarrass his colleagues, to feel more free in expressing his opinions. It was a solid, secure job. There were some qualms in the setting up of his own practice, but not too many. After all, he had been a Wall Street lawyer.

He was forced to move his office from the center of Evanston, where he was establishing a growing practice. The realty firm, managing the building, objected to his colored clientele as well as the fact that one of his three secretaries was a Negro girl. The realtor is "one of the gentlemen who sits right across the aisle from us in church every Sunday."

Last Saturday, we were invited to one of *the* social events in Evanston. Five socially prominent couples invited their friends to a tea dance. We happened to be on the list of one of these couples. I'm sure they're sympathetic with our view, but they would never be able to be as outspoken as we are. They're one of the silent, supportive people.

We had to make a decision whether to go to this dance and be rebuffed, take it and smile sweetly. You can easily say you're busy, sit home, and not undergo this. On the other hand, we felt, people must know that we enjoy social events as much as any human being, that we know how to behave. . . . We decided that this was the time we should go and greet our friends, and greet as though, indeed, we expected them to have opinions and they could express theirs and we could express ours. This is the way we feel society should be, and so we would just go.

As we walked into the main room, it was very interesting. Some friends, members of the local bank, would look right through you, just as though you weren't there. Now I'm a very large woman, I'm very difficult to see around, but they do this with great practice.

Other people were startled to see the Winslows included in this. They looked at us and it was funny. Either their eyes would open wide or sometimes their mouths. They would turn immediately to the couple they were with and you knew perfectly well what they were saying: "Mercy, do you see who I see at the door? How do you suppose they ever came?"

Jim and I walked to the table to get a glass of punch. As we approached the bowl at the other end of the table, the president of the bank was talking to a friend of his. I could see immediately they were talking about Jim and me. But they weren't quick enough to turn their heads. I looked squarely into this gentleman's eyes and nodded. After all, we did know him. We had known his children in school, I had worked with his wife on various things. And I just said hello, across the way. It was quite a distance so I'm sure he didn't hear the hello. But he recognized that I was greeting him and he nodded and actually smiled at me.

Later on in the evening, after Jim and I had danced— we did this so that people could see we were not going to stand in the corner, that we were going to enjoy the party, too—he came over and shook my hand. I said hello and smiled again and he went on with his group. I think that all this is part of a change in attitude. I cannot help but think he came up and was not quite able to speak to Jim and say, "Jim, you are doing magnificent things and I wish we could support you more openly." I think he was doing it through me.

Another man came over and actually kissed me. This man, I'm sure, had had quite a few cups of punch. He had been a warden at the church. Some time ago, he might have said good evening, but to have shown any other kind of recognition would have been impossible for him. Again, I'm sure this was a demonstration of his feeling that maybe things we were talking about are becoming acceptable.

I think Evanston is changing. There are younger people moving in. People know integration is coming and they're beginning to face up to it a little bit. They really are. The outpouring of concern when Jim was rejected by the vestry is an illustration. I don't think this would have happened five years ago.

I'm sure all this bewilderment, antagonism, ambivalence toward us stems from housing. Jim and I wondered whether we should buy a house in a Negro neighborhood as a form of witness. We've come to the conclusion that it's more of a witness to be living where we are and entertaining Negroes, accepting them as our friends, involving them in all of our lives. This is more of a witness than

175

buying a house in a Negro neighborhood. We would then be in an area where we could not witness to our white friends, who we feel are bigots and might be changing. They need changing because they have not had our opportunities to meet and know the magnificent people of other races.

I guess Jim and I have found the peace that we hope other people would find. We know that they're seeking. . . .

I'm sure without Jim, I could never have done the things I've done. He is a Christian with strength untold. It is the thing that keeps him going. He keeps me going, and I guess that's just the way we are. That's all there is to it.

FASHION NOTE—*"We stood in front of the North Shore Board of Realty every morning for two or three hours. Protesting restrictive covenancy. A silent vigil. While we were picketing, a woman came by and said, 'Mercy, look how they're dressed!' It absolutely convinced us that whenever we go picket hereafter, we were going to put on our very best Sunday-go-to-meeting clothes and be very respectable. I never, never thought white gloves were a necessity for picketing. (Laughs.) However, this seems to be one of the things the North Shore requires: well-dressed picketers."*

• • • • • •

Bob Carter, 38

Downers Grove Estates, an unincorporated area west of Chicago. A lower-middle-class section. He is the foreman of an auto-body repair shop. He built his own house. He is still in the process of completing it to his satisfaction.

I leave the house at, let's say, ten after seven usually in the morning. And seven, seven-fifteen, I get home at night. And Tuesdays, that's firehouse. I'm available every time there's a fire, volunteer. Tuesday's our training night. I go down to the firehouse from about seven-thirty till . . . well, there are times when we play poker or something like that, you know. And it's usually around twelve o'clock at night when I get home from there. And the rest of the week, I'm just beat, actually. That's what it amounts to, and I just don't have time to do anything. It's just like a vicious circle, you just get started on something, and by the time you get started, it's time to go to bed.

I don't have much. What I have is my own. Nobody's gonna take it away from me. If I can't build it, I don't want it. I don't care what people think of my home. I fix it the way I see it, and I do things the way I see fit. And I don't want anybody telling me how I'm gonna do it.

That's the thing that's a sore spot with me, that status symbol. New car, boat, and all that, I can't see it. Who are you trying to impress? Why should I go into debt where every dime I make is going to some loan shark? I know a lot of people out here who do it. Everything is charge accounts, and I think if the economy was to bust in two today, every one of them would lose everything they got, everything, I would say, across the street there, the fancy homes and all, new cars and everything they want. If the husband lost his job and he couldn't get another job for a year, they'd lose everything. They'd be beggars on Madison Street. I guarantee it.

I could live that way without any trouble, because I think I make as much money as they do. But my problem is I do things myself. I can't see hiring somebody to do my work. I like to do my own. I like to work with my hands. I think if I was tied down behind a desk, I'd go crazy. I have to be moving, I gotta be doing something. Even before I went into service, I loved to pull things apart and put them back together, make them work, that's how I like to do things. Cars, I don't know, cars have always intrigued me.

He recounts his work experience after coming out of the Navy in 1946. He had worked fourteen years for a Packard dealer in Cicero, becoming foreman of the shop. His boss, a retired lieutenant colonel, decided to finish his college education, and "closed the doors" on one week's notice. "Sure it hurt, you work in a place fourteen years and there were times when the guy was like a father to me." He remembered his boss coming through when he, Bob, had TB. Though he lost out on the bonus due him, "the other things compensate a heck of a lot more." He's been at his present job four years, foreman for the last three.

177

I don't care what my neighbors think. My father, he didn't care what people thought. He figured if they were his friends, they didn't care what he lived in. But when they came to our house, they were treated like kings and queens whoever they may be. That's the thing that was in his mind, to treat people decently. I guess that's where I got it.

I'm an outcast down at work almost, because I can't see what's going on. That stuff really burns me up, just burns me up. Everybody you talk to is against the colored, and I've worked with colored people all my life. Every job I've had has been with colored people. I mean, I've never worked side by side with them, but they've been around me. And they're decent people, they're good people in my book.

I had this job in Cicero at this Packard agency. This one fella who musta been around fifty years old, a colored fella, Eddie François was his name. One day we got to talking and he said, "Boy, I'd like to come out and see your house." And I said, "Well, whenever you want to come out, you let me know." I said, "You could come out with me on a Saturday afternoon and have dinner with us." The rest a' the fellas in the shop looked at me kinda funny. I don't care. He's a friend of mine. I don't care what color his skin is or anything else. And he says, "Fine, I'll let you know." I guess he figured I was just pulling his leg. So I left it go for a couple of weeks and he never mentioned it, so I thought maybe he just doesn't want to come out.

So one day I says, we got to talking about something, I don't know how it come around, and I said, "Oh you lousy skunk, you. You'll never come out to my house. You think you're too good for me or something." And he says, "Can I come out to your house?" and I said, "You're doggone right you can come out to my house." So he said, "I don't want to cause you any trouble." And I said, "What do you mean, cause me trouble?" I says, "You want to come out?" He says, "Yeah." And I said, "What about this Saturday?" This was during the week. So he said, "Fine, okay, I'll come out." I said, "Okay, we'll leave here right after you're through scrubbing the floors." That was his job on Saturday. We got through working at twelve o'clock and he usually got through about one.

So I hung around till one o'clock, and I told Therese, "Make some fried chicken." 'Cause he loved fried chicken, he could eat that seven days a week. So she made some fried chicken and I come out with him. And the neighbors were out here and nobody said anything. But when I pulled in the yard with him, man, you could see them, looking all over, boy, their eyes were just about popped out of their heads. I guess they got the idea I was probably gonna sell to a colored man, see? But he came in here and had his dinner, and like I say, he was a friend of mine. I don't care, the color of his skin didn't make a damn bit of difference to me. The neighbors never said anything but you could see something was bothering them.

So one day we had a, you might say, picnic out here in the yard. And we got to talking about the colored, and they had to bring it up, "What was that colored guy doing here?" And I said he was a friend of mine: "I brought him out to dinner." You mean he ate in your house? "You're doggone right he ate in my house. What the hell, he was hungry." That's all that was ever said.

From that time on, that colored guy down at work, if I told him to dig me a ten-foot hole, he woulda dug it for me. Just to show his appreciation, I guess. I didn't want that. I mean that wasn't my idea of bringing him out. It wasn't my idea to show the neighbors that I can bring out colored or do anything like that. I did it because I liked the man, that's all.

He got fired from the job anyway, and that was the last time . . . I never seen him since.

Over here, at this shop, the boss, he's a year younger than me, and he owns the business, and he's always coming around with these stories about the niggers, what he calls them. The niggers are gonna have a march down 22nd Street and he's gonna be one of the ones in line to help them bust it up. And I said, "Well, the only thing I can hope for, Bob, is to have one of them so-called niggers bust a bottle over your head."

Oh yeah. I speak my piece. I figure this way: If he doesn't like what I say, that's too bad. I do my job. I make him money. If that isn't good enough, I'm sorry. I have my own feeling about certain things and I don't want anybody to tell me what I can do or what I can't do. I just can't see just for the sake of a job . . .

What he'll do is sort of needle me all the time. He'll bring up Martin Luther King, he shouldn't have got this Nobel Prize. And, oh, the different colored entertainers. You take Bill Cosby or Godfrey Cambridge, I tell ya, I could listen to those guys all day long. And this John Bubbles, I love him. There was a time I liked Sammy Davis, Jr. But it seems that he's pulled away from the rest of them, like he's maybe getting too good for them. Setting himself up on a pedestal. I don't like that type. Same with the white. I mean the class of people who want to set themselves up as better than anybody else.

I mean you've seen a lot of people that are poor that you wouldn't even give breathing space to. And I've got them right here in this area. But the class of people that think they're better just because they have money, I can't see that either.

I've got one brother, especially, I swear he's a communist. I mean, the way he talks. He works for the gas company and he says he was working in the colored district in Joliet and he saw those colored kids running around the truck, and he said, "If you colored kids don't stop running around that truck, I'll run you little bastards over." I said, "Ronnie, are you going out of your mind? Those are kids." "Ah," he said, "they should take them all and put 'em on a boat and drop them in the ocean. Ship 'em back to Africa where they belong." We go round and round every time.

With me, one instance in the Navy maybe had something to do with it. I was in Charleston, South Carolina, and a buddy and myself were gonna go to the show. We walked in the theater and they said standing room only. What the heck, we'll stand, we didn't care. The place downstairs and the mezzanine were jammed, you couldn't get a fly in there. So there was a balcony upstairs. So I said, "Let's take a walk up there, see if there's anything up there." We walked up there and there was all kinds of seats. So we sat down and watched the movie. I was comfortable up there, I mean the seats were nice.

When we came down after the movie was over, well, there must have been fifty, sixty people standing downstairs there, waiting to get in. When they saw us, they turned around and started laughing, you know. It still didn't dawn on me why they were laughing. I don't know what possessed me to turn around, but I turned around and there must have been about twenty-five colored people coming down the steps behind me. I was so mad at the time when I realized what was going on, I think if I probably had something on me, I'd a probably hit somebody. I was burning no end. I can't express it. But it was a feeling they were trying to say they were better. The whites were trying to say they were better than me and the colored 'cause I was sitting with them. See. I think that was the one thing that really set me off on this.

After we walked out there, when I went to the door, there was a colored man, and I waited, thinking he was gonna walk out, but he grabbed the door and opened it for me. I thought he was gonna go out. I'm standing there waiting for him to go out. You know how you see somebody in front of you, you go to put your hand on 'em, to more or less guide them through. And the minute I put my hand on him, he looked like he was gonna drop, you know? I guess he thought I was gonna hit him or something. But he didn't flinch or anything, it was just that shyness, you know. I said, "No, go ahead." I guess then he realized I wasn't from that area. And he went ahead of us.

You see, he was older than I was, and my dad always taught me to respect my elders. To this day, I don't dare call any of my uncles by their first name. It's always Uncle Charlie or Uncle Elmer, and I'm thirty-eight years old. I've got cousins that will call my dad by his first name. He's never said anything, but you can see he doesn't like it. He wants the respect and that's something he's always wanted.

Are you respected out here?

Oh, yes. I've never heard anyone talk bad about me. Maybe they do behind my back, but I've never heard anything from anybody else. I'm a lieutenant at the firehouse. I could be higher, but I don't want to be any higher.

I'd like my kids to be better than I am in a way of working. They don't have to work with their hands. I mean, if they want that, fine. If Bobby wants to be a body man, fine. I'd welcome it, actually. But if he wants to be an engineer . . . I'm trying to get him into electronics, I think that's a good thing to get into. I'd just as soon have them have a white-collar job. Not where they're looked at, where you live in, say, the slum area of a town, which this is. That's what this amounts to. This is a low-class section here, and I don't want my kids to be where they think they're better than anybody else, but I'd like them to have something a little better than I have, that's all.

I like my work. I mean I couldn't do anything else. I could do carpentry work, but I've seen some carpentry work today and it's actually a sin. If things aren't just right, I guess I just don't want to do it. You can see it even in my line. How would you say it? There just isn't any pride in what they do. I think that's the biggest trouble today. No pride in what a person does. It's just slipshod, everything's slipshod.

I think personally myself that people are too interested in the money end of it than the actual skill. Just to get it out, just to produce. You have flat-rate shops, like in my line. You see the workmanship that goes on in them shops. There's no comparison to a shop that's on straight time. A man who's on straight time, he knows what he's gonna make at the end of the week, so if he takes ten hours to do a ten-hour job, he's not hurting himself, but he's gonna make sure the job is right. Because if the job isn't right, he's gonna get screamed at, and maybe even lose his job. So he's gonna make sure he's doing a decent job and he's getting a decent wage. That's why I can see the difference between your flat-rate shop and your straight-time shop.

"I'll tell anybody the amount of money I make a week. I could ask the people here what they make and I could never get an honest answer. They would never tell me. But I don't care if they know mine. Money doesn't make that much difference to me. Like I told Therese, even before we got married: I want food on the table, I want a clean house, I want clean clothes for my kids, and I want bills paid. That's all I want with my paycheck.

If Christ came back to earth, what do you think would happen to Him?

In this day and age, I hope to God He doesn't. It'd be the same thing all over again. He'd be crucified. Because the temperament of the people today, you just can't de-

182

scribe it. They're your friend today and they're your enemy tomorrow. There's no friendship today. Like I say, it goes right back to the status symbol. If you don't have a new car or a new home, you don't belong. You may be invited; if you do show up, why there's a doubt in your mind whether you should have gone or not. It's not because you don't think you're as good. It's the idea that you can see they weren't expecting you. They give you the invitation because you're supposed to be a friend, but when you do show up, you get the impression you weren't welcome to begin with.

I have friends. I don't think any of them would ever let me down. But there are times when it seems like the friendship, it's not given willingly. Whatever the favor you do, or they do for you, isn't done willingly. It seems like, well, you're a friend of mine, so I have to do it. It isn't because I *want* to do it. I feel like I *have* to do it because you're a friend of mine.

If I were God, I would take this feeling of superiority out of people's minds and make everybody feel they weren't better than anybody else.

What would I like to do? Therese bought me a wood lathe for Christmas. I've had it now fourteen years and I've yet to use it. One of these days, I said, when I built the garage, I'm gonna put up a bench and I'm gonna start working with that wood lathe. And it's still setting in the corner. I still don't have the time, that's all. As much as I'd love to do it. One of these days I'm gonna get next to myself and start that thing going, 'cause I love to work with wood. If I could be a cabinetmaker, now that to me is the thing I'd like to do . . . I'd love that.

VII

HOMEMAKER

• • • • • • • • •

Therese Carter, 35

*The kitchen of the Carter home, Downers Grove Estates.
The children, two boys and a girl, are asleep. Bob, her
husband, is in another room. On the wall is a kitchen
prayer:*

> *Bless the kitchen in which I cook*
> *Bless each moment within this nook*
> *Let joy and laughter share this room*
> *With spices, skillets and my broom.*
> *Bless me and mine with love and health*
> *And I'll ask not for greater wealth.*

Sometimes I wish the neighbors weren't as friendly as
they are. I would like to have friends that you don't
have to feel that you've always got to be real happy and
smiley and everything. When you feel like not talking, it's
all right, too. Bob and I went on a vacation last year for
the first time, for four days, and that's okay that you went,
but what did you find to talk about? For four days? Well,
you don't have to talk all the time. You talk when you feel
like it, and when you don't, you don't say anything, that's
all. I like to be alone most of the time. Be alone, just to
think.

Oh, I think about everything. First of all, I keep changing my mind about things all the time. Oh, you know,
maybe about Vietnam and things like that. But the more
you read, the more confused I get until I really don't
know. I couldn't say how I feel. Because when I hear

about anybody being killed, hurt, I don't care who it is, it drives me wild, and yet I don't know what . . .

Not just Vietnam, not just big things like that. Even little things, just anything. There's always problems about something, and you'd just like to have a little peace and quiet and just like to have everybody happy, that's all. It sounds real corny, but it's the only thing I can say.

I mean, can you ever just pick up a newspaper and read it and not find about two million problems on the first couple of pages? It's with everything. Maybe it's because I haven't tried hard enough to even do anything. Just right here, I wouldn't even know where to start. Because it just seems that everything is just one-sided out here, and everybody who would even think a little bit different is . . . Well, for one thing, I'm not supposed to know how to read a book. If you do that it's just a waste of time, to read a book, *to do anything* even. To sew is even too much for some of the women out here, I don't know. And I don't think I'm that good, I'm so dumb and I've got so much to learn yet, but I would at least like to learn these things.

I can learn about the John Birch Society any time I want, just by calling up a friend of mine or something. But that's not really what I want. There's this one lady that was always passing me literature last year. I just kept ignoring her, but I'm sure if I encouraged her on, maybe she'd be friendly. I met her through the Girl Scouts.

I'll betcha there's three or four on the block that wouldn't know what I was talking about. I think there's very few, anybody that really tries to think for themselves. There's no way you can even talk to them. The things they hear, that's it, there's no way of swaying them at all. I argue back but it doesn't do any good. The thing they always say is: You don't know, because you don't have any colored living around here. I had one here for dinner years ago. And I made the biggest mistake in the world. He said he loved it out here so much, and I said, "Well, why don't you buy the lot next door?" And he said, "They wouldn't want me here." And I didn't know what to say then. That was the only colored I knew.

You say things like that here, they don't pay any attention to you. I mean, they don't stop talking to me or anything, they just think, well, maybe you're kooky or something. That's all. They leave you alone. (Laughs.) Well, maybe I am, I don't know. (Laughs.) I have more fun this way.

About the worst thing you can do is read a book. I've got a neighbor that's had a book three years and hasn't finished it yet. And I have only one neighbor that ever reads anything. This other neighbor, she has only one boy and he's fourteen years old. If she washes clothes on a Monday morning, she has had it for the day. Now I wash clothes in the morning, get rid of the clothes so I can do something else. They have no outside interests at all that I can see. They go visiting a lot, you know, back and forth.

They talk about what's gonna happen to somebody on the television tomorrow, or they had a big wash, or they had a big ironing. And those things are important. I'm a housewife, I enjoy even that. It's nice to see an empty ironing basket, it's nice to see an empty hamper. But that's just the end, I mean . . .

I wanted to be a teacher. Oh, yes, I'm going to be a teacher. I'll probably be the oldest one, but I'm gonna be one. Bob said it would be all right, and I thought maybe as soon as David goes to school all day in September, I wanted to start doing something.

You want to go back to school?

Yes. Why? Don't laugh.

I'm not laughing.

Everybody else would. I wouldn't even tell anybody.

Why wouldn't you?

Because they would think it was the most ridiculous thing any woman would want to do. Because why would anybody do that when they're married and have kids? There just wouldn't be any sense to it, that's all. Why would anybody want to do anything that ridiculous? Maybe I wouldn't tell anybody I was going, but I would just go and come home and bar the doors and do my homework and that's all.

I would as long as I could. I know that sounds terrible,

but I really would. Because if I told anybody, they would just all go around and everybody would know, and then they'd all laugh. They're just not the kind to think those things are the things to bother with. Like I say, they would shop seven days a week if they could, and they're not even good cooks. I don't know. That's why I've tried to figure out, what do they do all day? 'Cause I never have enough hours in a day. If I could get by on four hours' sleep, I'd be real happy.

Well, I get out of bed and make breakfast for Bob, I make his lunch. When he goes off to work I either usually have ironing to do before the kids get up. I'll wash, I read, I sew. I make almost all of Cathy's clothes, almost all of my own. I read . . . I won't read anywhere near what I would like to, I'd be the first to admit that.

What do you like to read?

Anything, anything. Matchbook covers, if there's nothing else. Oh, I read everything. Because when I talk to anybody else they're almost all much smarter than I am. There's so much more I'd like to know. And I don't want anybody to tell me what I should or what I shouldn't know. I want to find out for myself.

It's the same with this Vietnam deal. Why, I was all for Johnson throwing in everything he could throw in there, and yet the more I hear, the more I read, I get wishy-washy. And I still think he's good, but I can find things, faults with some of the things he's doing, and before that I couldn't. Everything he did, to me, was just perfect.

I might question it, but I don't know how I could stop these situations or anything. I figure, does it do any good to write a letter to the editor? I don't know. What else can I do? Because most people, when you talk about Vietnam, they really don't know enough. I don't know all about it either. I just try to keep finding out more and more and more.

You hear millions of dollars a day or a week or whatever, my God, it's just . . . it seems to me it wouldn't take that much to make peace as it does to make war. I just keep hoping there won't be a nuclear war. I don't know if you can stop anybody from doing it if they want to. I would like to see everything stopped, but how? There's one thing I can't understand, is they've had this test-ban treaty and it's worked. We had to take the Russians at their word, and we did. I really think that they won't want anything to happen any more than we do. They're humans, they're not robots or anything, they're humans, too.

Bob and I argue about these things. Bob thought it was all right if they picket for civil rights. He just didn't like them laying in the streets. And I said: Well, what about on March 17 or whatever it was, St. Patrick's Day, when Mayor Daley held up traffic for three hours? (Laughs.) That was just the same. No, it doesn't bother me. Where else can they turn to? I don't know how else they can do it. I mean, even if you're against it, at least you're talking about it and maybe something will come about. I don't know what other way they can do it any more.

Suppose your neighbors heard you say this?

They would agree with me because I don't think they even know enough. All they ever talk about is getting a new car and going on a vacation. Oh, they talk about their jobs. All their kids play pony league and things, like that, that's all. Their husbands? All they do is drink beer and go play golf and bowl and that's it . . . and coach Little League. In this Little League, I don't know, I think maybe the parents are trying to show themselves through the kids or something. But it's just a game, they're kids. Does it matter if they win or lose?

Everybody's just really only interested in themselves. I've never really needed anything, really desperately, from any of them, but you get the feeling that maybe they would help you if they had to, but then everybody would have to know about it, too.

Do you have a friend you could trust, let's say, in a crisis?

No, I don't think so. No, I think they would all be good in a little pinch, like if you needed a ride or something, but no real big crisis, no. Mmmm-hmmm.

When I listen to Bob's dad talk sometimes, and he talks like people during the Depression years or something, like if they had something, it was shared. But I don't know. I just don't think people would be that way now.

I'm not saying they're not happy, 'cause sometimes I think they really are. And yet they spend their time being miserable. Because I see people who have a lot of things and they look at each other: oooh! like they can't stand each other; their kids, they're screaming at them all the time. I holler, too, but . . . It's just like they don't enjoy anything. They have furniture, they don't enjoy it. No matter what they have. I can't figure out why. Maybe it's something else they're looking for. But I mean, if it would be like paying off a mortgage or something, well, everybody would be happy with that. But I mean, they get a car, and you would think they would be so happy because they've got a car. But they don't get any enjoyment out of that. They buy things for their kids, and the first screw or nut or bolt that comes out of it, they're all . . . they just can't be happy. They buy a barbecue pit and they can't be happy with that. I just can't understand that.

From what I read and hear, I guess people will always be banging up their cars, and if Bob's happy fixing them, I guess we're all set for a while. I suppose there's always gonna be some people that will get a raw deal when automation takes over. But when you come right down to it, there's still nothing like a human being when it comes to certain things.

. . . I feel like the average man would be good, and they could be a lot better. You hear more about these days: I don't want to get involved. Maybe the same thing happened years ago, and we just didn't hear about them. Maybe I could be just the biggest coward in the world, if I was to face something like that, I don't know. But I think I would try to do something.

I don't know, maybe there's a bigger group of people that think the way you do. I think maybe it kind of stimulates you into doing something. But when I think that there's one here, like me, and there's maybe twenty miles away from something . . .

The greatest day of my life was the day I went to see a Pete Seeger concert. I think he's good. But to me the biggest thrill that I got was the fact that here were that many people together that felt a certain way. And I've never been in a crowd where everybody felt that way. And yet at the same time, how come . . . You could read in the paper that so many people felt like you do, yet you could never yourself meet anybody that feels the same way. That's what I told Bob, I said, that was one thing I thought he missed, that night, whether he likes him or not, the feeling that you're in with people that think the way you do. . . . I could just stand up and cheer. It makes you feel so good all over.

• • • • • • •

Helen Peters, "slightly past forty"

A middle-class area in the city. Two-flats and three-flats are being suddenly surrounded by high-rises. It is near the lake.

She came to Chicago in the early Forties from a farm near Pontiac, about a hundred miles southwest of Chicago. "Most people leave. The town isn't progressive."

She does market research a couple of days a week, thus a second car has become necessary for the family. One of her discoveries on the job: "The more successful a man is and you can tell by going into his office how successful he is—the more anxious he is to help you."

She is active in the PTA, a neighborhood bowling league, and numerous fund-raising activities. She keeps house for her husband and two children. Her eldest daughter is married and has "two babies."

We have right on this street almost every class. I shouldn't say class because we don't live in a nation of classes. But we have janitors living on the street, we have doctors, we have businessmen, CPA's.

Take janitors, for instance. The ones we have contact with and happen to know are very class-conscious. And it's not because people make them feel that way. It's something . . . they have come from a family of janitors, they feel they have to prove themselves, that they are as good as the next person. One of our mutual friends calls this the janitor syndrome. (Laughs.) They are constantly trying to prove that they are as good as someone else. Well, that isn't necessary. Just because he cleans boilers or carries garbage, he's making an honest dollar.

My husband, as he says, is a Jack-of-all-trades. He's assistant to the president of a corporation right now. He's primarily interested in over-all management. He's very machine-conscious. He's a sort of systems-and-procedures man. It expedites things. I mean, he's a firm believer, do it the best way possible, the fastest. And he—blowing my own horn—is a very smart man.

I think when your children are small, a woman's place is definitely in the home. But once they're partially grown a woman is foolish if she sits around and stagnates. I think you become unhappy.

I know many women who have become bridge bums, they've become alcoholics, or they are doing clubwork which they do not enjoy. Because it's the thing to do. There are women who play bridge every afternoon. They also play bridge every night. Their whole life, their whole outlet, is bridge. And I feel that if these women don't have bridge, they would be hitting the bottle quite hard. In fact, there are a lot of so-called bridge players that are very heavy drinkers. And some of them take dope, too.

Also in PTA, there are women there are in their sixties that are still in the PTA. Their grandchildren must be out of PTA. I feel sorry for them. Their life must be so empty that their only outlet is PTA, and they are to be pitied.

. . . The kids . . . I wonder if they're getting the proper education. I went to a country school, out in the country where a teacher taught all eight grades. I learned the eight parts of speech when I was in grammar school. I could still give them if I had to. Most kids in school now don't know there are eight parts. They do not teach grammar as such.

You know, nouns, verbs, prepositions, and so forth. But the kids are not taught to diagram sentences, that is no longer considered necessary. I don't know, they just aren't taught. If they write a composition, if it's correct, it's strictly an accident. Not by thought, word, or deed, shall we say? It's a subject I think should be brought back. We hear all children say, "I don't got any" —and, mine included, until I could strangle them.

My boy is sixteen, he likes to go out. I trust him. I know he won't go out and steal or break into a car, what do you call it? Mug somebody? But maybe he's going to be the one who gets mugged. I don't know all his friends. You can't possibly know. Most of them have been to the house. But you can't keep them in the house all the time.

So I'm one of those worrying mothers who stands in the window and watches (laughs) for them to come home, and if they're five minutes after curfew, yell, "If you're picked up by the police, you can stay there all night."

And especially with an eleven-year-old girl, you worry about some mentally deranged people. I'm not neurotic about it. But if they come home later than they should, then I'm always, shall we say, a little upset.

I love Chicago, contacting people, talking to people. Despite the violence. If I go out late in the car, and I can't park right out here on the street, I jump out and run in the house and get Cliff and say, "Come on." (Laughs.)

. . . I would think it was all right if a Negro family moved next door to me. If he moved on this street to begin with, he's going to have to have a job that supports himself and his family in order to pay the rent around here. Rents on this particular street are not excessively high, but they are not low. On the next street, there is a colored woman living, did you know? She is married to a white man, she came to the PTA the other day, and I'm very sorry to say there were only three of us who talked to her. We invited her to join our bowling league, and as you know, asked her to please come again. She is very nice. She is a very pretty Negro woman.

In Pontiac, we knew one Negro man down there. He was a junkman and came out and I imagine he made as good a living as anyone else. Buying and selling junk. Probably better than most people, during the Depression. (Laughs.) But somehow or other, well, there was an incident when I was a child. A colored man shot a white man, and they put a curfew on the colored people. They had to be off the streets at six o'clock. Whenever this man came, we weren't exactly afraid of him, because we knew he was Les Summerville, he was the junkman. But he was different. If he was at our house collecting junk over the noon hour, call it dinner hour on all farms, Les was asked to come in and eat with us, and he ate with us at the table. And I can remember as a child that the insides of his hands were white, which amazed us when we were small. That the insides of his hands should be so white and the backs of his hands so dark.

We have a neighborhood school policy. I believe in the neighborhood school policy. I also believe in open housing. I think a man should be able to live in the neighborhood of his choosing, where he can afford to pay the rent. Like they say, water will seek its own level.

But I think these demonstrations are horrible. I don't think they prove a thing. I don't know how much patience I could have if I were a policeman, with these people laying down in the streets. When they are asked to move, they will not move. The demonstration in what was that place, the so-called ghetto, in the West Coast? Watts. I think that was the most disgraceful thing that ever happened in any country. I think the National Guard were within their rights, if they just mowed them down wholesale with machine guns.

I think somebody has come in and stirred these people up. I know they are not brilliant people, they are easily led, they're poorly educated. A lot of them are from the South where they really have been forced down. They really don't have rights in the South, but I think here, I mean, everyone has the opportunity to go to school, he has the opportunity to go to college if he chooses. I'm sure if they want to work and earn a living that they can.

I think it's highly possible that there's a communist influence here, that if you don't have, go out and take it. It is your right, which these people did by looting and taking things out of stores, that that man was walking away with a couch on his back. (Laughs.) It's horrible even to think, but I really couldn't have blamed those troopers if they had . . . because they were being shot at by snipers.

About that march in the South . . . this woman that was killed from Michigan. I think that's awful that the Ku Klux Klan, we know they're a violent group, but to shoot people in the dark, it's not . . . it sounds trite to say, it's not nice. She felt, from what I read in the paper, that she was helping those poor people. Each one has his own compulsions and drives, and maybe she felt it was her moral obligation, maybe she had a feeling of religion about it. I don't know. But she did have a home and five children, and I don't feel she had a place down there.*

* Stacy Goings, twenty-two-year-old Negro cosmetician in a Loop department store: "This man was talking to me one day about this lady from Michigan who got killed in the South. He probably was thinking it himself, but he said, 'My wife said she just can't see how any woman would leave her family to go to participate in some-

193

Do you and your husband talk politics much?

We have mixed politics in our family, and the name of Roosevelt can almost turn my husband purple. I think he's the greatest president, or what have you, that ever lived. Of course, I think Truman is, too. And I like Johnson. We are not solid Democrats or Republicans. We both vote a split ticket. But primarily he's a Republican and I'm a Democrat, and we have friendly arguments. We also have, shall I call them discussions?—like what year did Baumholtz play for the Cubs, and I'm up in the middle of the night looking up references to find out. (Laughs.)

At parties, Vietnam always makes a good topic of conversation. I think it has to be cleaned up. It just cannot continue and continue. And even though my son-in-law is going to have to go—by the first of the year I know he will have to go—he's in the Strategic Air Command, and SAC is stationed on Guam, where they take off, these big planes, B-52's. They're going to have to get more men in there and just clean it up. War can't go on forever and ever and ever, and you get sick when you think, gee, Cliffy is only sixteen, in two years he's going to have to register. And he's going to be seventeen pretty soon. And you think: Holy smoke, I would hate to have to see him . . . I lived through that Second World War, it was horrible; the Korean War was horrible. But now your own kids are coming up into it again.

I don't think they will come to a truce. They're going to have to clean out all the guerillas, and something has to be done. It's too much a drain on our young men, too much of a dollar drain. We have to get enough boys in there to bring things to a sudden halt somewhere along the line.

We're told that H-Bombs today can destroy the world. Does it ever bother you?

Yes, because in August of this year we went to South Dakota. We were lucky enough to tour Ellsworth Air Force Base. We saw these terrific bombers, these tremen-

thing like this.' When people say things like this it kind of gets next to you. That one human being can care so little about another that they can set and say something like this."

194

dous B-52's. We went through the bomber. It amazed us, all the equipment that is in this plane. The plane is so loaded down, if I'm not mistaken it can carry only two bombs. This multimillion-dollar thing. Then we drove up the country of South Dakota. We saw these, they're called silos. They're the missiles, I think they're called. They're out in the middle of wheat fields, Evidently at a moment's notice a button can be pushed and these things will be shot off.

It makes you feel, oh, aren't we lucky to have such an organization as SAC. And then you see these young kids, these eighteen-year-olds, and they're responsible for your safety. But they are put through rigid training. So you feel, gee, aren't we lucky? That we have this.

You feel so insignificant when you see this tremendous B-52 plane, with eight engines, four on each wing. And the wingspan of the plane we were under. We went out and saw the launching, and they take off on their practices within fifteen seconds of each other, and if you think that isn't a sight! To see these tremendous big planes come at you. The first plane you can see, the second one, in the fifteen-second time that it takes, is completely blacked out because of this jet take-off from those eight engines. You see it come up out of this black mess, and when the third plane comes up, it is wavering because of the air current. But they all get off and they're gone, but you're so glad that they're for out side.

You feel so insignificant, you said?

Yes, I wonder if we'll ever come to a time that will be like the Dark Ages again . . . it's highly possible. And I don't think I do one lousy, miserable thing. Look how crazy Hitler was. We could get another man like that. We don't know the Russians. Red China, probably. Or one of those little grubby hungry countries that are playing both sides against the middle: "If you don't do this, we'll go over here."

So the individual feels helpless?

I think there are a lot of people in very prominent, important places that can cause an awful lot of trouble for the whole world. I think these Vietnam protesters ought to be taken home and whipped with a strap. (Laughs.) Really I do. I honestly do. These boys are over there for something they believe in, and these smart-aleck upstarts, because we have freedom of speech, are allowed to go and more or less demoralize people that are over there. They're doing our country an awful lot of harm. This gives us a black eye in the eyes of the world.

I think that some people are professional dissenters. They take the opposite point of view whether they believe it or not, just for the sake of argument. There are those who dissent because they are looking for the overthrow of our government. (Almost whispers.) They infiltrate all our organizations, even the PTA.

You feel that?

It's a known fact.

Communists, you're talking about now?

Yes, and Birchers. I think Birchers are an obnoxious lot. I came in contact with one on our trip to the West. He cannot come out openly against or for anything, so he's a fence rider, he's not a member. But I tell you he's the biggest John Birch leaner I have ever seen. I think that the John Birch Society flourishes in small communities where people have no outlet. This is a town of only nine hundred people. If someone comes in with any highfalutin ideas and all these people that don't get anywhere . . . every day they're out working in town, in the little post offices or courthouses, you know, that probably has four rooms . . . they think this is marvelous. Why, he's right. I think they are easily led because they have not come in contact with the world.

Yes, I'd like to see a peaceful world. I mean, a world without war, the terrors of war and the abject poverty that comes from war. There'd have to be a meeting of the minds. It brings Kennedy to mind: his meeting with Khrushchev, where these two men of two great nations grew to respect each other. They knew they couldn't walk on each other. Do unto others as you would have others do unto you.

Maybe I've grown to appreciate more things. I think we

all grow as we grow into more understanding people. You learn to be more tolerant of your fellow man.

• • • • • •

Diane Romano, 35

A mother of six children, she is separated from her husband. Her seventeen-year-old boy "is feeling too much woman in the house and he's resentful." A devout Catholic, she is awaiting Vatican approval for a chance at remarriage, though it is out of the question for the immediate future. She provides for her family with a county job as "baby-sitter" for jurors. Though the job is political, she is conscientious and, according to her boss, he's never had anyone better. She reads law books all the time, listens to hearings in courtrooms, and hopes one day to go back to school and become a lawyer, "even if I'm sixty."

During the summer, she takes her children to concerts in the park, two, three times a week. She collected classical records until recently, when the company started sending her Masses and they weren't "even Gregorian chants. They were awful." Often she takes the children to the Art Institute.

She has lived in the same neighborhood on the Near West Side all her life. It is predominantly Italian, with some Mexican families nearby. A Negro community in the same general vicinity was "renewed out." Though this neighborhood has been declared by the city as a "conservation area," few of the residents believe it. The "betrayal" of the Hull House district people is too fresh in their minds. Many of their close friends, who lived there, are now scattered throughout the city. For this reason, there is little rehabilitating of homes. She had participated with Florence Scala in the losing battle.

The area has the feel of an island: to the north, an expressway, to the west a medical center and new high-rises, to the east the Circle Campus of the University of Illinois. "So much building going on, you don't recognize parts of the city any more. This morning when I went to work there was a red-brick building. When I came home, the building wasn't there. It was flattened. I can't decide whether it's all for the good. All I know is there's a feeling of a loss, a lot of things leaving us."

I was thinking of moving, but if something happens to one of my children, what neighbor am I going to call? If my washing machine pops or my wringer . . . or if one of the kids gets a cut or something, who's gonna bandage them? In a strange neighborhood. Over here, I got my next-door neighbor, Angie, I got the lady across the street. I got everybody on this block that would do something for me. If one of my children were sick, I wouldn't feel any compunction of waking up the man across the street to take me to the hospital. He expects this. He would expect me to do this for him.

One night I took my daughter to the hospital at eleven o'clock at night. Next morning, at least eight people, on my way to work asked me how my daughter was. When I got home it was worse than that. It took me an hour to get home. Because everybody wanted to know about Christine. Did the doctors do anything? Did I need anything? I get a cheery hello from everybody. Old ladies, when I get dressed to go out or go to work: "Oh, how nice you look." Old and young blend together here. In the summertime, everybody's outside. There's no fear here. I have friends who live in the suburbs, they wouldn't dare be out in the dark.

I know friends of ours, who've moved away from here, who bitterly lament their predicament now. They've got beautiful homes—I guess the city planners would say they've done better for themselves. Their plumbing works, their electricity is good, their environment's better . . . supposedly. If you're a type of person who considers a mink stole and a fountain in your living room and big bay windows, front lawn beautifully kept, all these things mean something to you, well . . . To me, we're more concerned about people. I don't say we get along fine all the time, we have our quarrels, God knows. God and I have a real good relationship going. He knows all about me. I think things could be a lot worse if He wasn't smiling at me. I know He smiles on me quite a bit, because it's no easy job raising six children and for them to be as good as they are. I know my strength comes from Him. . . . How I'm gonna manage, not so much the financial part of it, just the thinking part? This one has to be talked to this way and this one has to have a crack because this is the only thing this one will understand. Karen's a dreamer, I don't wanna bust her bubble, it's gonna be busted soon enough. Cathy, on the other hand, is a fun-fun girl, she needs the reins tightened on her. Christine is a shy-shy girl and pulled herself out of her shyness only to be a pest to people. But basically, she's very shy.

I've attended three different social agencies to tell me if I've done the right thing and none of them told me I was doing the wrong things. So I can't clap myself on the back, somebody's gotta get the credit, so I guess it has to go up there, where it belongs.

Why can't you give yourself credit, too?

Because I'm not that smart. Maybe. He's my strength, my pillar. Everybody has to have somethin' they can lean on. Some people have thir parents, other people have financial backing. I don't have any of that, so what I got is God. He's not just *a* God, He is *my* God. Sometimes I wonder why He's given me all these problems: like with them, two allergies and an infected ear and a broken arm at the moment. There must be some reason. I'm not a big enough person to understand why He's doing it.

Everybody gets the impression that I'm so strong. My mother thinks I'm a pillar of strength. Twice in my lifetime, I cried to her over the phone. Once was when I had my sixth. She wasn't at all sympathetic. She said, "Ah, go on, you can manage five, you can manage six."

I definitely feel there should be birth control. Because the church is making sinners out of 85 percent of the Catholics. You know darn well 85 percent of the Catholics are using some kind of birth control, so what they're really doing is making sinners out of good Catholics. A person that cannot afford more than three or four children, why in the Good Lord's name have them if you can't take care of them?

I don't see what other great changes are being made, other than this Luci Baines Johnson when she was rebaptized, it created quite a furor. Pope John's my sweetheart, but that New Mass was something. I don't like it. Like there's no melody. I know a young fellow who's going to be a priest and he said they're using a lot of the old tunes, some of them Protestant tunes. And they're trying very hard to make the Mass a little better, because it's awful, somebody singing one tune and you're singing another. And nobody knows how the tune goes. I don't like the Mass in English, it doesn't sound resonant.

No more white communion dresses for the little girls, this was a big blow for all the mothers. It's like taking the incense and vestments away from the priest, that's what they'll be doing next.

I don't like having to be the leader of the family. I'd rather be second in command. I'd love to have a man in the house here. But I'm in no hurry, I make spiritual communion Sundays, so I feel okay. Like I say, I feel a rapport with God. Who knows, someday I might have a great big church wedding, who knows? (Laughs.)

The only thing that gripes me is the nun at school told the children that all divorced women will go to hell. So I called the school, because my little girl came home in tears. She was hysterical: "Oh mamma, you're divorced, you're gonna go to hell and it's hot down there and you're gonna burn up." But I explained it was all right, that she had nothing to fear for me. She's a little girl, last year she was seven.

This is my primary concern, the image for the children, and they're too young to understand the divorce and the whys and wherefores, this is what really bothers me. When I'm introduced to somebody who I'll probably never see again, I have such a shame about divorce, I have said I'm a widow.

I felt very proud of myself when I did something that the kids could look up to me for. Like `at the time I worked with Florence Scala. They stuck to the television set and they watched everything. I never saw myself on TV. When I come home, they'd be so excited: "Mamma, we saw you on television." We don't have a man image in the house and I tried to tone down the "mamma" bit and let my older boy take the masculine part. . . .

I feel I've grown since I started out with this Hull House thing. I happened to be sitting at a meeting because somebody asked me to go. I heard Florence speak and I thought: This is a woman I'd like to help. I felt that she kindled something in me. She started the motor going inside of me. What am I sitting here doing nothing? This is my city, my community, too. How can I sit back and moan and cry if something happens to the community, if I don't do something, too?

It wasn't easy. I had to get my breakfast, dinner, and supper made early in the morning to be at the march at ten o'clock. So I wasn't neglecting my family or anything.

We may have lost, but I feel a lot of us won. When it all started, they figured it was just a bunch of irate housewives going down to sit in the Mayor's office. I know for one, Florence is looked up with respect as a leader of the community. And me, who'd've thought that me, a mother of six kids, would get up and speak at the city council? And I did, I made three speeches. I went down to the polling place in the morning to challenge Mr. Fiorito.* He was throwed out of the box. Had nobody challenged him, he might have been alderman now. It was two o'clock in the morning, and someone said, "Don't you think somebody should go down there?" And everybody looked at me and I said, "Well, all right, I'll go." So I came home, got two hours sleep, and I walked in. When Fiorito came in, I plumped myself up next to him. I guess their mouths popped open. I was shaky inside, a nervousness, a little business, but I felt my cause was just. Lose, win, or draw, it must be God wants it that way. I was surprised when I spoke up, my voice was so strong. It has to be a little spirit inside that's doing that talking.

Too many people are being led around by the noses. How can so many people not think? How can so many people believe what the man tells them to believe? When it goes to the polls, it always works out the same way. The powers that be are the powers that are.

I think they got the perfect system. They got the Negro vote, and they are the ones that have been keeping them in, and they are the ones that are hurting the Negro the most. I've marched with them and I'm in sympathy. I'll go march, if it's something big.

I don't use the term "nigger" in the house, and I never allow it. I don't know if my oldest is testing my authority, I know he has to conform to the rest of his group. Their parents are not really anti-Negro. It's just fear of the un-

---

* The machine's first choice as alderman. He was declared ineligible because of nonresidency in the ward.

known. If they moved in a project around here, okay. It's not owned by Mrs. Palumbo or somebody. People here are afraid of the new. They wouldn't like new neighbors. I know changes are coming and it's not all bad. I feel just as sorry for the white people who are scared as I am for the poor colored people, who don't have much of a chance in the city.

A Negro girl is a good friend of mine. I've invited her to the house four or five times. Definite dates. "I'll expect you Sunday three o'clock and you'll have dinner with me." She always said the same thing. You see she was concerned with my welfare. "Now what do you want me to do, come up your front stairs, and stay half an hour and have your windows busted before I leave?"

I don't know what my neighbors would do. I believe I'm well liked and respected by the majority of the community. Now she's married so I'll have to invite her husband, too. But I want my children to see these people are no different from any other people, that they talk and they have manners and they eat like we eat, and they think and they have feelings, and they're sensitive and they're artistic, and some of them are strange and some of them are dumb, they are just like we are. And I think I'll do it before the summer's out. So that everybody will be sitting outside and they're gonna see these people come in. This is the step that's gotta be taken. Somebody's got to take it.

• • • • • • • •

Barbara Hayes, late thirties

Number 1510: a doorway facing out on the gallery.* An apartment in the world's largest public-housing project: the Robert Taylor Homes, on south State Street, extending from Pershing Road (39th Street) to 54th. We're in the kitchen of a six-room flat. Somewhere in the vague distance a child is whimpering. "The little one," murmurs Mrs. Hayes. "Her afternoon nap." A small boy of four or five is observing us.

She has eight children, four boys and four girls—includ-

---

* Gallery: the official name for the balcony that extends out on each story of the building. The words *porch* and *gallery* are used interchangeably.

ing a set of twins—ranging in age from sixteen to the baby. She has recently been separated from her husband and is on ADC. She came to Chicago in 1954, and all these years she has lived in a project.

She had attended Southern Illinois University in Carbondale, where she was born. Her father was a coal miner, "When there were mines." Her mother was a teacher. She was the first Negro cheer leader the university ever had, helped edit the newspaper, and played in the school band. "My classmates would always take me into their confidence, though they had come from towns that were really Southern." A white girl friend's grandmother objected when she wanted to take Barbara home with her during a vacation. "Don't feel guilty," I told her, "because my grandparents are just as prejudiced as yours are." So she said, "You're all right with me." And I said, "You're okay with me, too."

It's about two in the afternoon. The place is in semi-darkness, the electricity having been cut off. Fortunately, the battery of my tape-recorder was fully charged.

T hey said I hadn't paid my bills on time, and when you don't pay your bills on time, you get a black record. So they don't bother to send you a second notice. They send you your bill and then they send you a final notice. This is the first time mine's been cutoff. We're in darkness tonight.

If one of the kids wants to read a book . . .

No, they can't read a book. They can't watch TV. They can't listen to the radio. If we didn't have a watch, we couldn't tell what time it was, because we have electric clocks.

In about three hours, it'll be totally dark. What happens?

They'll light a candle. We'll probably eat by candlelight. And just before it gets dark, they'll straighten up their rooms and change their clothes and lay out their school clothes for tomorrrow. And this will be it. Then we'll sit in here, I suppose.

. . . I like children and I always thought that mothers

needed a lot of understanding. I wanted to be a social worker because I realized people had so many problems that they needed somebody to listen to them, to talk to them, to help them. This was a busy world. People don't have too much time to listen. They have their own problems.

On a bus, it's easy to strike up a conversation. You don't have to say anything. Just look as though you'd listen and people start telling you, oh, something the boss did, or somebody on the job, or what the landlord, say, or complain about prices—they might've just left a sale, you know. People want to talk; they don't have to know you.

But as far as life in public housing is concerned, I don't think it's a very good place to raise children. They can't make noise, they don't have freedom. They can't do like they can in a small town. They can't lay on the grass, they can't climb trees. . . .

The phone rings. It was the first of many such calls during the conversation.

That lady was not of this building. She's in the 5200. I'm chairman of this building's council. She called about the course in cashiering. The Joe Louis Milk Company is offering it. If we could get the people. I told them this is no problem. The women here would like to work. People think people on Aid won't work. If you have three or four children and you really care anything about them, you want to be sure when you go to work that they're taken care of. People will accept your money and say they're taking care of your children, but this is not always so. I think I've talked to about thirteen people who say they want to take the course. But one of the questions they ask: Where's the last place you worked and how long ago? If you haven't worked in six or seven years, who's gonna hire you? (*B-r-ring!*) Excuse me.

"She just got fired from the CHA—the Chicago Housing Authority. She was a janitress. Quite a thing going on here —among the row people, too. They have a tough supervisor and they don't want the employees to show any insubordination, whether they're right or wrong. There's a great deal of unemployment. Most people who do construction

work, they're off quite a bit. It's seasonal. The others who work at the post office or at some stores don't have too much trouble—I don't think."

The people here want to do something. Last year, we had a garden project, seven acres. They raised their own vegetables and flowers. Quite a few of the ladies canned the vegetables. They were so pretty. Some of them had freezers and they had a whole family dinner. I think they enjoyed it because a lot of the people are from the South. They had done farming and this might have carried them back to, you know, memories.

I don't like the Taylor Homes. It's too crowded, there are not enough activities. Who does the child have to talk to at home? Mother's got other kids. If the father's there, he's working or on relief and this he doesn't appreciate. So who wants to be bothered with some kids? So they say: "Mama, what is this?" And: "I don't know, don't bother me. Go play." So they send them out on the porch or downstairs.

The kids have been shoved outside. So they break windows, destroy property, fight—anything to get some attention. That's how you get the gang leaders. Everybody wants recognition. You get it whichever way you can.

We had some teen-age boys around here that were pretty troublesome. Whenever we were going to have something, I'd ask those boys to keep order so that nobody would start any confusion. They were the ones who started the confusion, so by having them look out for the others, I didn't have any problems. They enjoyed this. And they respect you, too. I started out one evening for class and they were roughhousing downstairs and one of them said: "Cool it, here comes Miz Hayes." I hadn't gotten two feet away and they started again. But at least they let me pass. (Laughs.) This is the same group of boys that I would say: I need your help now.

You push them outdoors, out in the galleries: You can't play ball—no roller skating—you're making too much noise by the window. So they go downstairs: You can't sit on the benches—you're not supposed to be around here. Or somebody throws something down: You're not supposed to be hanging around out front. So what are they gonna do?

You can push them so far. Then they're gonna push back. But if they had more to do . . .

The turnover's so fast, you know. In a crowded place like this, you . . . oh, so what? You want to stay by yourself. You don't know about the people next door. You don't know what they're like. A lot of people are kinda suspicious. Maybe they resent conditions. A lot of them are on Aid, a lot of wrong things go on. So they stay to themselves and don't have to worry about it getting out.

Often the elevators don't work. I think we have one working today. It might be working at noon, two o'clock it might be out of order. Three o'clock in the morning it might be out of order, you hear bells ringing. Children and adults get stuck in them. Sometimes they get frightened. Kids know how to stick the elevators. They make a game out of it. They find a kid who is afraid and they stick it.

I've walked fifteen flights quite frequently. When I first moved in, I did it for the exercise. I do it now when I have to. It's not too pleasant. You never know who you're gonna find on the stairs. People from off the street. The stairs are open. You might see people sleeping on the stairs, you might see people gambling on the stairs, you might see drinking on the stiars. You never know what you're gonna meet on the stairway. The light might be on, they might be off. If they're off, you're gonna come up those stairs, you know.

Suppose somebody gets sick, needs a doctor, and the elevator doesn't work?

They're just sick then. You have to take them down the stairs. Or, if somebody really gets sick, they'd just die, I suppose. I often wonder what's gonna happen when we have a fire? * I wonder what's gonna happen when they

---

* From the Chicago *Daily News*, December 11, 1965: "Two children were killed Friday in a $200 fire in a Robert Taylor Homes building at 4352 S. State. The victims, Timothy Larde, 5, and his sister, Regina, 3, suffocated in their tenth-floor apartment, firemen said. Neighbors pulled Regina's body from the apartment. Timothy's body was found under a pile of clothes in a closet where he apparently sought refuge. The children's mother was at work, firemen said, and a girl who came to baby-sit discovered the fire. It was confined to the Larde apartment." This item appeared months after our conversation.

have a fire and the elevators don't work. It'll take 'em longer. We had one in Taylor when a couple of kids did die because they couldn't get an elevator.

They say kids play on 'em and people put 'em out of order; but if this is the case, certainly CHA should do something about it. Put some operators on. They have repairmen and electricians and maintenance men. Wouldn't it be less expensive for the CHA? Of course, it would be more convenient for the resident.

We can't get cooperation from management. Our council has gotten parents to say: We'll operate the elevators during the day, if they put some people on in the afternoon. We did this for two weeks. And they say you can't do anything with the kids. This is not so. After we had been on there for a week, the kids knew when to come down to the first floor instead of going to the third floor to get on. Came to the first floor, lined up and waited. In a matter of fifteen minutes, we had all the school kids home. It was working out.

We asked management to send some people up in the evenings. We were gonna help them, too. The kids had gotten used to seeing the parents down there, so they would straighten up, they wouldn't push. They'd get on and wouldn't touch the buttons. They'd tell you what floor. They didn't scream and just make a piano board out of the buttons as they do now. The management didn't object. They just didn't co-operate. They didn't care.

We had a meeting to find a method of keeping the galleries clean. Kids drop food, paper, and so forth. It wasn't swept. The janitors don't do it. They make good money— $441, assistant janitor, it used to be. I think they got a raise. The head janitor makes five something a month. We don't know what for. They don't sweep the galleries, they don't keep the laundry rooms clean. In this building, we have a defective incinerator. When it's smoking, you can't put anything down. You've got two choices: either leave the garbage out there or bring it back into your apartment. Most people leave it out there.

We tried to get the people to keep the porches clean, and we asked management to go along with this little story: Everybody would get fined five or ten dollars, everybody on the floor, if there was any debris found outside. We circulated this story through the building for about two or three weeks. You could tell the difference. But there was never this follow-up letter from management. The people would call them to see if this was so. Nothing. They enforce the rules they want to enforce. Just like we say: Don't overcrowd the elevators; nothing was said or done by them until one of the painters was injured and then *they* said: Don't overcrowd the elevators. Until someone from management is affected, there's nothing done.

People would care for things, would keep things clean, if they were given encouragement.

You tell people: Keep your porch clean. You're subject to hear this: "Who are you to tell me what to do? You live here just like I do. Who gave you authority? So they're paying you now?" But management can say: You pay more rent or you get a five-day notice. Can't they say this, too, if it's for the betterment?

If kids come out of this environment stable, emotionally stable, they're lucky. It's very difficult. All the pressures, you know. Say, I live on the fifteenth floor. You can't make too much noise, the people downstairs complain. You can't go out to play. You have to study, watch your little sister. Be careful, don't talk to a stranger. It's an open neighborhood, anybody can come through. The building is like a street. Not just your friends and your bill collectors, but everybody's you know . . . salesmen, anybody.

The people here don't know how to resist. They'll come by with something they know you want, or maybe you need it, you know, but you really can't afford it. And they high-pressure people into taking it. On the installment. No money down, or a dollar down, dollar a week, make it sound so simple. Yeah, they always pay more than what it's worth, you know. Sometimes they can't keep up with the bill and then comes this pressure from the company. They take it away or they pressure you about making a payment. So you have to take your food money or something else to pay them. They want to get paid, they don't really care. You pay for bein' poor.

I don't have time to worry about the H-Bomb. Sometimes you say So throw the Bomb. Who has time to think about the Bomb, when you have to think of how the kids are doing at school, are they gonna make it home all right? Are the elevators working? Where's the next pair of shoes comin' from? You gotta take one of them to the dentist's. Somebody's gotta go to the clinic. These things. Are you gonna . . . how's this kid gonna turn out, you know.

About 3:15. The older children have been coming home from school, one at a time. A burst of energy and news. Suddenly entranced by the presence of the tape-recorder on the kitchen table.

Was it '62 when there was so much talk about the bomb? We talked about these air-raid shelters and so forth. What are people in Taylor Homes supposed to do? I said: Is this a booby trap? Is this one way of getting rid of a whole lot of Negroes? So you press a button and they're all gone. Too many people in this world, they have to do something about this. This is a good way to get rid of a lot of people.

Time out: Each of the kids has his moment of glory at the microphone. Name, grade, favorite subject, snatches of songs. Much giggling and clowning as voices are played back.

I guess the Bomb bothers a foreigner more than it would me, because the people who have been exposed to war, you know. We see it on TV, it's just a movie. To me, it's just a story. If we get bombed, a lot of people will get killed. Yet, it's a threat. But you just don't worry about it. . . . There's nothing I can do about it. Other people control those things anyway.

Who?

The politician. They have a job to do. The people in power tell them what to do.

Who are the people in power?

The people with the money. People that control the hiring and firing, those people. Take Taylor Homes, just one place, for instance. Okay, it's election day: Are you gonna
209

vote? Yeah. No, I'm not gonna be bothered. For what? If agencies would educate the people on their rights, it would be a lot different.

It's not a cause for Negroes. It's a cause for everybody. I don't feel you can keep one person down without keeping yourself down. You can't think of being down and progress at the same time. You got to think one way at a time.

What do you want most in life?

For my children to get a good education—where they'll not have to be pitiful on public aid. And I hope to move from Taylor Homes into a place where I can have my own day-care center. Not just a baby-sitting thing. Expose them to the fine arts. And take them on trips.

Beauty. It's really all around. You just have to find it. Look around and see. Some think the sun and a bright day, that's beauty. Not necessarily. I'm quite sure *this* would be a scene of beauty to an artist. With his canvas. He can see so many things we don't see, you know.

POSTSCRIPT

The elevator going down was crowded. A number of jerky stops. Two women, with Deep South accents, forlorn, lost. Their plaint: the obstinate elevator failed to stop at the fourteenth floor; they had pressed the button again and again; they had been going up and down, three times; yo-yos. "Lotsa time it don't work. I walk up fourteen floors, more'n I can count." One talking, the other nodding: "'At's the truth, Lawd." Young Negro, in the hard hat of a construction worker, gets off at seventh floor. His departing comment over shoulder: "President's Physical Fitness Program." There was no laughter.

VIII

NOBLESSE OBLIGE

• • • • • • • • • •

Mrs. R. Fuqua Davies,
age handsomely indeterminate

We are studying Chicago's skyline from the Davies' town apartment on one of the upper floors of Marina Towers.

This is a city that is progressing so fast. (Laughs lightly.) Perhaps this is true of any city you can name, any big city. But, of course, this is where I live. So this is where I sense the change. It's a city that is so on the move, it's so stimulating to live in it for that reason.

We've lived here since 1938. I was born and raised in Grand Rapids. My parents came over here a great deal. They didn't bring me very often, but they were very interested in music and they always came to the opera season, and then they always came back with presents from Marshall Field. (Laughs.) This was sort of a city of promise. My mother had been to the Columbian Exposition when she was a young girl and she actually never forgot that experience.

I don't really remember my impression as a young girl. I really didn't see it terribly often. I began to come here quite a lot when I was at Vassar, because I had a roommate from Winnetka and I used to come over with her for some of the debut parties.

I can't think of any specific change today. The thing that does impress me is the constancy of change. I mean it's always changing. This may sound like a funny thing to say, but one of the things that I love most about it is that everything hasn't been done yet. I felt that coming from

New York. It was such a contrast. Here was such a wonderful city and a great big city, but you could get hold of
it. And it isn't that I want a sense of power or domination
in a city. (Laughs.) But I think you feel happiest in a city
where you can identify with it and feel that you're doing
something a little bit constructive about it. This city invites
audience participation, so to speak.

There's so much that's being done that's beautiful. But
it's a long way from being Paris or New York. I just want
this city to be the finest in everything, you see. We do
travel a great deal and then when I come home I say, oh,
I wish we had fountains like Madrid or I wish we had
beautiful buildings like Paris, etcetera, etcetera, so that it's
some sort of divine discontent.

That's the thing that keeps alive, I guess, the love affair
on my part with the city. I really adore its strength. Somebody once said a very disturbing thing: about how Chicagoans love . . . really secretly revel in the vice of their
city. They like this wicked aspect of it. I occasionally
probe very deeply into my mind: Do I really find that
kind of exciting? I remember the first contact that I ever
had with anything of this sort, when I lived in Grand Rapids. Of course, half the people who live there make furniture, you know, and somebody—a friend of mine—had
reported that he was making dining-room chairs for Al
Capone and that they had a little slab of steel in between,
that the wood was laminated (laughs), bullet-proof steel. I
don't know, all these sort of picturesque, dreadful things
maybe do add up to a legend that we are secretly half-
proud of.

Oh, I find more vitality now. I know the city better. I
think the business community is an enormously vital community. I hear that mostly through my husband, of course.
They just work their heads off, you know, to improve the
city in one way or another, and they really love it. They're
not accepted unless they get in there and pitch. It's really
part of the job. Plenty of people make a lot more money
than the kind of man I'm talking about, but in order to
gain prominence in this city—and by prominence, I mean
admiration and acceptability—you've got to put a certain
number of man-hours into the public till, don't you think?

You live in a North Shore suburb, Lake Forest, and you

have an apartment here in the city. Do you see two different aspects of Chicago?

Oh, yes. Very different. I must say, before I say anything critical, I absolutely adore living in Lake Forest. It's a beautiful community, and I have many, many friends there. I like to have the best of both worlds. I don't think any suburb can possibly offer the kind of excitement that a city can. I love to golf and tennis, and I love to have a garden and so on. But it isn't all of life for me.

Is there anything about Chicago that bothers you?

Oh, yes. The main thing that bothers me is the ugliness. I'm delighted by the beauty, which is sort of a mask on the city. I mean, you feel as though [if] you ripped off this beautiful Lake Shore mask—that it's so ugly back of that. Of course, there's hope in that area because this is changing all the time. But in general there's a lot of tastelessness in the city. Do you think so?

I'm talking about surface ugliness. I'm not talking about sociological problems. I know that's a big problem, but I haven't experienced it myself, so I'm not qualified to talk about it. I think people are very eager to overcome racial difficulties. They move very slowly, but I think most people proceed with pretty good will. So I can't talk about any ugliness except the surface.

I think the whole civil-rights thing is long overdue. I'm completely in favor of the American experiment. This is the exciting thing about our generation. It's more exciting to me than flying to the moon or anything else . . . to really try to put this American experiment to the test where it hurts. And it hurts quite a lot of people in very deep ways. I mean, to absolutely overturn your convictions and prejudices is a difficult thing. The fact that it is being tried and, I'm sure, being accomplished, testifies to the vitality of our whole system.

Do you ever talk about this at parties or gatherings?

Yes. Oh, three or four different times, we've had a full day of field trips. So that people have the opportunity of seeing Negroes in a way most just don't. We've gone into their homes and we've seen their charitable enterprises and their business enterprises. We've invited a number of women to do volunteer jobs at the Art Institute. They have to be interested, they have to be qualified, and they have to have money. I mean, these boards, let's face it, are created to raise money. I don't know if it does any great good for the Negro race, but it at least brings some of the leaders into an integrated life.

The subject comes up at social gatherings, too. And I'm sorry to say it often comes up with quite a lot of ill feeling. It depends on who you're talking to. I have many friends who are passionately devoted to this cause, and I have many who just absolutely writhe at the mention of it and wouldn't conceivably lead an integrated kind of social life. We have many times been privileged to be invited to mixed parties and found it perfectly delightful. Just not different from any other party, you know. Nice, attractive people that we've enjoyed and they seem to have enjoyed us. But I do know a great many people still who will never come to this. They don't realize the enrichment that there is to the lives of people who do adventure a little bit.

When I hear people talking with violent prejudices, it doesn't mean that I'll never see them again. I do see them. If you're in a social pattern anywhere, you do see people whether you like them or not. But I always hold reservations about them. I know they're not really my kind of person. Because these feelings, they show the inner you. More than anything else.

Demonstrations, what's your thought on these?

I want to see them make their point, but I'm disgusted by the lack of taste. I can't stand the sight of people lying in the streets and being hauled off by their hands and feet. It just really sets the cause back, I feel. The reason I'm so disgusted by it is that I care about this cause. I want it to succeed. And it offends me terribly to see slovenly behavior in the name of a good cause.

The great cause I've worked for most of my adult life is planned parenthood. I traveled around the world with Margaret Sanger. But this was after she was quite old and I wasn't so young myself. (Laughs.) It wasn't a social, a fun thing to do. I think that's true with all the big social movements now.

In the civil-rights business—I don't know if one goes out on the limb for civil rights in this part of the country. I'm sure the Southerners do. But here I think, oh, it's pretty safe, I don't think anybody's going to be read out of the party.

In the early days, there were some women of influence, social leaders perhaps, who backed people like Jane Addams in highly controversial matters. This is not so of their granddaughters, is it?

Women were really embattled at that time. The Suffragettes were an absolutely marvelous band. I'm sure I would have loved marching with them in those days. They worked so hard for this cause, and then there was so much to be done in the labor movement. They got the whole picture. They saw all the things fit in together. Once women got the vote, they felt they must go on and take up all these other causes.

So many things happening today . . . does talk of the H-Bomb . . . what effect does it have on you?

Absolutely none, I hardly hear anybody talk about it. I think to let your life be frustrated and destroyed by some horrible thing that might happen, I think that's just the way madness lies. I mean, you have to go along, (laughs) live your life in some sane and sensible way. Maybe it's a mistake not to be fretting about it all the time, but I just feel this thing is too big for me, (laughs) and I can't do anything about it.

Do you feel that if it comes, it comes?

Yes, I'm afraid that I do sort of feel that. I know that isn't the right way to feel. And maybe that's a very bad thing not to be protesting and writing to this editor and marching and so on. But I think I feel the futility of the people that do protest.

I've had the privilege of visiting the Strategic Air Command headquarters. General Power was in command.

Seeing that perfectly marvelous nerve center—and it's quite security-minded—you feel that we are protected. On the other hand, the thing one needs to be worried about is whether this thing is going to be carelessly dropped somewhere. You're pretty well persuaded that it isn't, when you've had a chance to really be there. It's a terrific operation.

It's only fair to say there were two different views. The two or three that felt differently were very liberal. I would say, almost professional liberals. Marvelous women, all smarter than I. Women who I admire very much and love very much. So I don't discount their opinion. My own feeling—and this is the majority feeling—was that our military was doing an absolutely fantastic job. It was beautifully run, just from the point of view of somebody organizing an outfit. There seemed to be so many safeguards. These were all spelled out to us.

The general was a very outspoken person, the archetype of what a fine military man should be. Which is not what you think the head of the United Nations should be. An absolutely different sort of person. Very respectful of the fact that it was not his decision to push this button. There are checks and counterchecks before any of these things can be used. That wasn't too clear to me before I saw this, so . . .

Well, I'll tell you something parenthetically—one little remark. Somebody said, "Do you think Red China will attack?" And he [General Power] said, "We should be so lucky."

Really?

(Laughs.) Yes, that we'll never take the offensive.

I could be . . . I'm very vulnerable to disillusionment. I usually go through life in a general state of euphoria. I know perfectly well that my defenses are really very low. I could be terribly hurt. But, goodness, look at all the years I've been living, and I haven't been. So naturally I maintain a very bright view of things, in spite of reading everything to the contrary.

The world is different than it was. Having been born in a quiet Victorian era and now living in this jumping age, well, I'm different too. So naturally the young people are not going to be the same today as young people were some other day. I don't view them with any alarm at all. I think they're terrific.

You're God. Re-create the world.

Most pretentious thing I ever heard of.

How would you like to see the world, had you the power to change it?

I've told you I was a conservative. I ought to stick up for the status quo. I'd probably like it is, because the variety of it and the constant change and the knowledge which has come in the last few generations, is so vitalizing. It's so exciting, the constant striving toward something better than we have—I think really makes this the best of all possible worlds.

IX

EX-DOMESTIC

● ● ● ● ● ● ● ● ● ●

Lois Arthur, early sixties

A middle-class Negro neighborhood on the Far South Side of the city. Rows of neat one-family dwellings, well-kept lawns. She has brought out the picture of her fourteen-year-old grandson.

Chicago is a lost town. It's too big and too out of hand. Nobody can live in Chicago and feel like they're living in a place where everything's going to be all right. Everything's wrong in Chicago, everything. You find individuals trying to do the right thing, but the over-all picture of Chicago is wrong. The leaders, they have no principle . . . Everything is run either by gangsters or by . . .

I lived in Chicago since I was six years old, and it hasn't changed. It's grown, but it hasn't changed much race-wise, as I feel some of the cities of the South have changed. Chicago is more typically a Southern city than many cities of the South. They have their own political party, they have their segregated neighborhoods, they have their segregated schools that are going to stay segregated as long as there is one political party in Chicago.

I don't care how disgruntled people are, there's nothing they can do about it but move. No, I'm too old to move. But I'll tell anybody that's young, when they tell me, "We're looking for a different place to live," I say, "You are very wise." I wish I had done it a hundred years ago, because Chicago is hopeless.

There's nothing but undercurrents and topcurrents. Everybody's dissatisfied in this neighborhood. In Chatham,* everybody's dissatisfied. I'm not speaking of the high-rises, where those people are afraid they'll get thrown out or cut off their relief. I don't know how they feel because they go along with everything. With the high-rise projects and those votes guaranteed and in the bag—nothing that you can do about it.

Fear, that's the thing. I used to be afraid, too, when my children were smaller. I used to say, "Oh, I would like to do something. I would like to vote differently, but maybe I better not. Maybe this will be changed and it'll be good." So I can understand the people down at the projects and their reasons. But now that I'm older and the children are grown, if I could just tell some of them: *Take a chance!* Take a chance, you won't die. The whole Negro race is awakened, whether you act like it or not, you are awakened to the fact that we are in a revolution, and I'd say, just take a chance.

I stopped being afraid when I got my first good job. When I got my first big, good—I don't say a big one—the best I ever had, when I got in the defense plant in World War Two. I got a good salary. And I didn't realize then how wonderful it was not to be afraid. I didn't even realize it until . . . later days. But all of a sudden I was just automatically doing what I wanted to do, for the first time since I had had children. But it was money. It was a good, fat paycheck, taking it home every week . . . every week. And it made me feel, well, I was free.

I remember when I went out job-hunting for the first time in my life. They had an ad in the paper. I think it was a cosmetic company. The man, the watchman, was downstairs, and he said, "What do you want?" I went early and the other employees were coming in. It was an early time, and I figured if I got a job, I'd be there to start work. So anyway, he said to me, "What do you want?" and I said, "I read the ad in the paper." I had it with me and I said, "I want to see about getting a job." And he said, "What?" And I repeated it and showed him the ad. And he began to laugh. And he didn't say anything to me, and the people were coming in there to work, I remembered then and thereafter, they were all white. So he said to a couple of the guys, "Come here, she wants to get a

* Another Negro middle-class area in the city.

job here." They didn't laugh, but they all smiled and walked on. And he said, "Oh, no, you can't get a job here." And I said, "Well, they said they needed girls," and I said, "I need a job and I thought I could get one." And he said, "Oh, no, they need girls, but they don't need *you*."

And even then I didn't realize. I thought maybe I was too short or something. It didn't even register with me until I went out and was walking, maybe a half a block away from the place. And I wondered why he gave me the brush-off. Then it hit me: I'm colored. He was trying to tell me that they didn't need me because I was colored. Well, I was floored. Something like that had never crossed my mind. I figured if you wanted to work, somebody needed somebody, go and apply for the job and get it.

Well, after that I didn't look for a job any more. Because if they don't say it in the paper, white only, as they started doing after that in lots of companies, you didn't know whether to go or not go. That was my first and last trip out to look for a job . . . of that kind. And that's why I went out and got a job as a domestic.

I like individual people whether they're black or white or green, according to how they act and how they treat me. How they treat my people. I worked for one family twelve years. But they were more like my family to me than they were strangers. I still see them. I was just like a person to them, and they were just people to me. If I needed a favor right now, if I needed somebody to do something for me, I would call him before I would call any colored person, because he has proven himself. I like individuals. But so far as the white race as a whole, no. I don't like them.

I think there are some that are just wonderful, with their hearts. But they're not enough. They're in the minority, the great minority.

The majority? That gray old white man—since Washington, not even gray any more—I tell you, I see him as a monster. When I just think about the horrible things that they do, and it's forgotten with the turn of a page. A thousand years from today, if there's another world, if it starts like America is today, it'll be another hideous mess.

The white man does not like the Negro and the Negro does not like the white man. There's more hatred between the men than there is between the women. Males, naturally, are beasts, you know. Yeah, he's a beast. You didn't know the male was a beast? Sure, he's a beast. He'll get out there and kill, he'll destroy, he'll murder, he'll dump people and lock people up in trunks of automobiles and leave 'em there. What won't he do? He'll kill his mother, he'll kill his child.

Women don't make these wars. It's the man that's the beast. And you get him out of the world and keep him out. I would say: Keep men out of the world for ten years, and we would see some peace and love. He keeps the world and keeps the nations at each other's throats. From Johnson on down, a man wants to do nothing but fight, fight, fight. They're not happy if there isn't some kind of a fight. And it's pitiful that they have charge of things in this world. If women could rule it . . .

. . . Women can get together, yes, and talk. The women get along with all of us: the white woman getting along with the colored man and the white men getting along with colored women.

We went to white schools and white churches. Most of the Negroes that went to the Catholic Church in those days were the Creoles and the lighter Negroes like us. But as I grew older I met them, the darker people. I found out that color has nothing to do with it. I am as black as the blackest Negro in the world. In fact, I am blacker. If you want to see a black Negro, look at me. Because I tell you, I'm black from my heart. Yes. And I will never, never, never change. I want to be what I am, a black woman. I am a dark, dark Negro in this revolution, with my money as much as I can spare, with my presence and with my help and with my thoughts at all times.

I'm praying and hoping only for just one thing: that the white man does not get to the moon, if there's anybody up there. They don't have to be colored, black, just different. I certainly hope that the white man don't get up there with his prejudices and spoil the moon . . . spoil the heavens.

Does the Bomb worry you? . . . that the earth will be no more?

Tomorrow will be all right with me. I don't see anything to stay around for. I like the Bomb, because it's not prejudiced. All I say is: When it lights, make sure it doesn't drop on only me. It's a frightening world. And if the Bomb is going to be dropped, which I do think someday will probably be, the end of the world . . . I guarantee you the white man will be at the helm. Every place America goes, it's hard. No, America's not capable of settling the problems of darker peoples. Uh-uh. Too white.

And that's what bothers me. Why is he able to oppress so many people? Who—from whom does the white man get this strength? Somebody's in his corner.

If Jesus Christ came back into the world, what do you think would happen?

He'd take a look and go on back to Heaven where he come from. He couldn't stay here. There's too much wickedness. He would take one look and say: "Well, this has gotten completely out of hand. I've got to go and report it to My Father." That's all He could do. No, He couldn't manage here at all. Unless He would just assert Himself and use the power that He has. Because He could just lift His hand and just wipe it all away. That's the way man has pictured Him. As being able to do anything. But just to come here and live like a man for thirty-three years like He did when He came, oh, no, He wouldn't last here. In the first place, they'd kill Him. He couldn't get to first base here.

They'd kill Him just because He's different. I know that. And another thing: He wouldn't be lily white like they picture Him, because He was born down there around Africa, and that sun doesn't allow for lilies to be white. So He would be a dark man, so He would be a condemned man. So He couldn't stay there, and if He did, He'd have to stay with us. He'd have to stay with the Negroes in the ghetto.

But just coming into the world, and from Africa where He was born, in Egypt, down there in Bethlehem, and to come here, no. These whites would take one look at Him and He would have to get out of the white neighborhood before dark. Otherwise the white policeman would be questioning Him: "Why are you over here?" No, He couldn't stay.

If I were God, I would have put only love in the heart of men. They say that all people are born in sin. I wouldn't have done that, because I wouldn't have allowed

222

any apples in that garden. I wouldn't have had any forbidden fruit. There is no difference in any tree, for all of them are the fruit of love.

But everybody hates. Instead of loving, you hate. I'm speaking of myself, too. I don't have enough love. But I would have, had I been God. Everybody would have had love and we'd live in a beautiful world.

. . . The young are the ones that are going to change things, much to the old folks' sorrow. The young people are not as prejudiced despite the fact that their parents are telling them daily. I'm talking about my own granddaughter. I'm talking about your own children. My granddaughter is not as prejudiced as I am. I want to say that. And I want to say to white people we Negroes are prejudiced, too. Just like the white people. We act, and we're just like them. But so far as young people are concerned, they haven't been in the world long enough to be as hardshelled as their parents or their grandparents. The grandparents are the worst of all. Yes, the older you get, the harder your shell, which is natural. But the young people coming along are going to fool a lot of their foreparents. And that's going to be a good thing. Black and white.

My granddaughter goes to Mercy High School. They have quite a few colored now. But when I was graduating, they wouldn't accept me. Now my granddaughter goes there. She said to me the other day, it tickled me, she said one of her girl friends was gonna call her. "Grandmother, you were on the phone so long, my girl friend's gonna call." I said, "Who is it?" She called her name, and I said, "Oh," knowing by the name that it was one of her white schoolmates. So I said, "Forget her, let her wait. She can wait." And she said, "Grandmother, you're just saying that because she's white. You're against the whole world." So I told 'er, "I'll get off the phone right now so you can talk." (Laughs.) But it was funny just to hear that she says I'm against her. But I'm glad she is like she is. She goes there and she gets along with all of the children she comes in contact with. And it's a good thing. She came from St. Columbine, and that's a colored school. But she thinks Mercy is great and she's just as happy there as she can be.

Yes, she's different from me, because I have grown bitter, and I don't want her to.

X

EXECUTIVE SUITE

Bill Dellakamp, 55

He is vice-president of a corporation, one of the country's most powerful. He is in charge of the Chicago area. Active in the city's civic and industrial power circles, as well as in the Presbyterian decision-making bodies, his is the classcial American success story.

He graduated from a West Side high school, and among his fellow alumni were Ambassador Arthur Goldberg, Benny Goodman, and Irv Kupcinet.* Editor of the school paper, he was one of the two boys in the stenography course attended by forty girls. This aptitude, in addition to his piano studies, led to the job of editing a trade paper for a drum company. He attended various night schools in the city, seeking out courses in marketing and advertising. During the Depression, despite a "brush-off test because they were looking for a college graduate," he won a job with the corporation.

He has been with the corporation thirty-five years. His most difficult decision was made after four years in the New York office. He had the choice, salary the same, of remaining in "the city of finalists" (a quote from Will Hays) or returning to his native city. "I decided to come back to Chicago and I have never regretted it."

I put the high-school ring on and I still have it. It's completely obliterated, but I think it stands for a lot of memories of why I like Chicago and why I'm so proud of

---

* Chicago's most widely read newspaper columnist.

this town. Everybody talks about the fact that if you can make it anywhere in the world, and if you've got anything, you can make it in Chicago.

Politically, we've improved so much, and this is a Republican talking. Under the last ten years, under Mayor Daley, the distinguishing thing of his leadership is that he has been able to bring the business community, the professional community, and the neighborhood pretty well together. It's brought a spirit of community.

Number two: a resurgence of civic pride. When I was in high school, we had entrepreneur types in industry, and they were a great factor. We've lost a lot of those. A management group has come up. I happen to be typical of this. Companies merged and some went out of existence. The Depression shocked so much of the leadership. They had a job of maintaining their own fortunes. So you got this stagnation, which we really didn't shake out of until after World War Two. It began around '48, '49, '50.

The day of the entrepreneur is still here but not to the extent that it was. I remember when I was growing up, William Wrigley, Jr., was a great factor in Chicago. You felt it was *his* company. Now it is *a* company with some very efficient and able Wrigleys. You look around—the people in charge of companies, all the big names, they're the professional managers, who have proved they can do a job. It's not quite as personal. It isn't the risk-taking sort of thing. It's a calculated man, who knows how to work with an organizaton, to get the most out of the people around him—but still is part of an organization, rather than a pioneer.

I know of two or three companies in town that still have the entrepreneur type. The fellow, his lawyer says, "You've grown so fast, you should become a public company, you should sell stock"—and he will pound the table and say, "This is *my* company." He's a vanishing American. There's a little bit of tragedy in it. But on the other hand, there are so many good things about the growth of the management class. I still believe in any organization there's room for the maverick. I don't believe that we're getting stereotyped, that we're all impersonal units in an impersonal world. We're approaching it differently, that's all. We set up research and development, goals and objectives. And that's all good. But I still thrill to the great leap forward from imagination, the risk-taking.

Here in Chicago, a wide group, an ad man like Fax Cone,* steel man like Joe Block,† people like myself, get into every sort of activity. It would be easier to stay home some nights. But you feel you owe it to this town, you're so proud of it that you want to do something for it.

I think the churches have got to be more in the mainstream. I don't mean only on the racial situation. I don't mean only in emotional outbursts. The solid day-to-day work. We can not ever forget that the best place for reconciliation is in the churches. I worry whenever I hear a churchman say: "This group doesn't belong. . . ." Sure, they're sinners, so am I, so's everybody.

I went through a racial change in the Presbyterian church I belong to. I'm not part of this community any more, I said, but I'm going to stay here until there's a leadership that can carry the church. I stayed four years. We had bought a house in the suburbs, but I was determined all I could to make it a real Christian church open to everybody. We were concerned with how to keep our church witness in the community. Did it stop serving because there were people of different color?

In industry, we all know the problem. I don't think most of us have done all that we could. I think we're growing and I think we're growing pretty fast right now. It took sort of an aggressive approach. People have to know they're welcome before they come in to apply for a job. Same thing in church. Except for a few that are willing to picket and storm the gates, the real solid progress is going to be made when you bring people in. I don't mean you have to sit by and wait for years. What I'm particularly happy about is the work of the Chicago Association of Commerce—the current merit employment committee.

I live in the city now. A week or so ago, Dick Gregory's troops marched by, about eighty of them. Nobody was worried about them. In fact, I think there was so much apathy, I think it bothered the leaders a little. I looked at that group and I had a reaction that I haven't seen any-

* Fairfax Cone, head of Foote, Cone & Belding, an advertising agency; chairman of the board of directors, University of Chicago.
† Joseph Block, head of Inland Steel Company.

body mention in the newspapers. I guess they call it the Dick Gregory hat. It looks like sort of a calypso hat, a wide-brimmed straw hat. And they wore blue coveralls. I thought: We have been hollering in my church work, in civil-rights work, in brotherhood work, don't stereotype the Negro. Don't stereotype him as a plantation hand. And, by gosh, look at these marchers. They're trying to fit the stereotype. I felt sad about this.

I'm unhappy about most demonstrations. I think people have a right to petition, right to parade if they want to. I'm terribly disturbed about demonstrations at a man's home. And this goes before the current picketing of Mayor Daley's house.* I don't think I have the right to disturb other people's peace. This is not my way of doing it.

Maybe if my experience had been different, maybe if I'd grown up in the labor movement, I'd think in terms of picketing first. I'll admit demonstrations have done one very fine thing for the Negro. They've called attention to his grievances and to his aspirations. It's the excess I worry about. And the stereotype either of the field hand or the revolutionary.

What are your thoughts concerning Martin Luther King?

I think he had a real cause in the South. I think he's now striving to find other causes. I think this happens to all of us. We grow. He's gotten a lot of world acclaim and I think most of it was deserved. He has a real problem now as to his next step. I couldn't suggest what it is. I don't think he really had a feeling about Chicago, while he was here† I'm sure he was deep down disappointed in his march. I think a lot of people gathered from curiosity. He was moving *for* something down South. He was moving *against* something here: a devil, that you put up in the form of Ben Willis. Down South, he was trying to get

---

* At the time of the conversation, CCCO, a federation of the city's civilrights groups, was picketing the Mayor's home in protest of the retention of School Superintendent Willis.

† A reference to a march on Chicago's city hall, led by Dr. King. Several months after this conversation, Dr. King set up residence on the city's West Side to lead a campaign for decent housing in the world's largest black ghetto.

rights for somebody. When he comes up here, he was trying to get a guy fired.

I'm not saying all is well, that this is the most beautiful place on earth. But I think people came to Chicago from the rural community, whether it be the plantation Negro or the hill white, or whether it be the Puerto Rican—they came here because there's more opportunity. We've got a lot of things to do, not *for* them, but *with* them.

Talk of violence bothers me—whether it be criminal violence, whether it be rape, whether it's been the teenagers in the suburbs. I'm terribly disturbed by a breakdown of the kind of respect for law that I think we had and that we're in danger of losing.

I think it's part of the breakdown of home standards. This is one of the problems that our civilization has got to lick. I don't think there's any easy answer. The Church has not been really doing its job. I suppose the Church has always had a sense of inadequacy, a sense of falling so short of the calling it has.

. . . I think I respect the job, though I get awfully mad at the man. I don't question authority so much as I question the use of it. I guess many organization men feel this way. When a decision is being made, I argue as hard and as long and as intelligently as I can to influence the course of that decision. I don't expect to win 'em all. When the decision goes against me, then I think I have to look at it from the standpoint: Can I live with it? I'm not going to question the authority that finally makes it. I get terribly disturbed when I hear a man in an organization going around and saying: *They* made a wrong decision. He should have tried as hard as he could to sell his viewpoint. If he didn't and just wants to criticize, he should get out and criticize it from the outside.

XI

CELEBRITY

•

*In the world of the celebrity,
the hierarchy of publicity has replaced the hierarchy
of descent and even of great wealth.*
C. WRIGHT MILLS, *The Power Elite*

• • • • • • • • •

Terence Ignatius Boyle, 45

*A gold plaque is on the wall of Boyle's well-plaqued office:
"For a little guy you really come on." There are photographs, all autographed: from presidents Truman, Eisenhower, Kennedy, and Johnson; from governors Stratton,
Stevenson, and Kerner; from Mayors Kelly and Daley; a
wistful likeness of the incumbent mayor, at the time he
was defeated for sheriff in 1956; a more ebullient group
shot of the mayor, Boyle, and others on a later, happier
occasion; from various judges, local, state, and federal;
from personalities of radio, television, and films; from
sports heroes; from celebrated figures of the city's demimonde; from successful businessmen; from Happy Chan-
dler; from others too numerous to mention.*

*The small bar is modestly provided with the better
brands of light wines, beer, and whiskies, though he rarely
drinks. They are tokens of esteem from dear friends and
casual acquaintances. On his expansive desk is a small
American flag, a green fez (a gift from the Shriners for
services rendered: "We need more programs today, the
way the world is because the devil is working so hard."),*

and two prayers, framed as diplomas. He reads one: "God grant me serenity to accept those things I can't change, the courage to change those I can, and the wisdom to know the difference." He says, "I try to look at that every day."

He came from a family of twelve children: "We were known as the Holy Family among the police department. I've always known policemen. The neighborhood where I came from, you always became a policeman, a priest, or the President. I always believed in my neighborhood and my country and my church and the people around me. They help you and you help them."

Born and raised on Chicago's Mid-North Side,* his was a boyhood of grinding poverty. "I was selling newspapers at seven, Clark Street from the river to Fullerton. I witnessed and saw the aftermath of the St. Valentine Day's Massacre. I sold a lot of papers that night. I did the night Dillinger was killed, thirty-one years ago, 1934.

"On my street was 'The Lady in Red,' Anna Sage, who turned in Dillinger. Midget Fernekes, the bank robber who initiated nitroglycerin, was also in our neighborhood. Down the alley from me was a fellow named Zangaris,† who as you know was the fellow who shot the Mayor of Chicago, Anton Cermak, a great mayor." Also from the neighborhood were Johnny Weissmuller, Frankie Laine, and "a young man named George Tozzi, who sang the background music for South Pacific.‡

"My father, when he died, he left something for everybody. When they said, 'What are you going to leave Terry?' he said, 'I'm gonna leave him everything from Fullerton to Diversey and from Lakeview to the lake.' Which turned out later to be the Park District. He had a great sense of humor.

"My mother, she said to me one day, 'As you go through life, never be heard saying anything about Italians, calling them dagoes, don't be calling Jewish people sheenies, and don't be calling the Greeks peddlers, and don't be calling the Germans heinies, because sometimes

---

* A radius of about three miles, extending north from the Loop.

† Giuseppe Zangara, who, in 1933, in Miami, fired wildly in the direction of President Roosevelt and killed Mayor Cermak, who is reputed to have said, "I'm glad it was me instead of you."

‡ Giorgio Tozzi, a leading bass-baritone with the Metropolitan Opera Company.

it'll be your own who hurt you the most and the quickest. It was not only the sins of the Jews that killed Christ, but all of us, and the sin that you may commit, and I hope and pray you won't, as you go through life.'

"My mother I'm sure is up in heaven watching over me. Every time I do something good, I think of her. Every time I do something bad, I worry about what she's thinkin'."

He has been elected and re-elected to public office on the local Democratic tickets. He conducts a daily radio program and in the spirit of public service offers reportage and opinions concerning city hall, civil rights, traffic, and race tracks; in the spirit of bonhomie, he frequently mentions the doings of friends and acquaintances, "whose name is legion."

My life has been a life of knowing everybody, regardless of who they are. I was forever getting ahead, and when you get ahead and accomplish something, you're bound to get in a little trouble.

In 1937, the President of the United States came here to open the bridge.* As the car made the turn, I jumped up on the side of it and had my picture taken. Skinny little kid with the President of the United States. About nine hands grabbed me and I flew right off again. That's how I got to know the Secret Service men. I had to do it. I had nobody who was gonna help me. I didn't know how to swim. There was no diving board on the Outer Drive. They made the turn, I happened to be at the right place at the right time. I thought the President would like to meet Terence Ignatius Boyle.

I wanted to be known, so my mother and father and my sisters and my brothers would all be proud of me. I was in the hotel room with President Truman, just before he whipped the little guy with the mustache. I was a precinct captain then. I said, "Will you do me a favor?" He said, "Everybody else wants one. You're the only one hasn't asked me. What is it?" I said, "Would you call my mother?" He laughed and said okay. I got her on the

---

* President Roosevelt appeared for the dedication of the bridge extending the Outer Drive. It was here he made his "Quarantine the Aggressor" speech.

phone and said, "Mom, the President of the United States wants to talk to you." She said in her brogue, "You're a danged liar." He talked with her for five minutes. Later on, at a big political meeting he said he had the honor of talking with the mother of a precinct captain.

I happened to be with Tim O'Connor the day he was replaced as police commissioner.* I was with Prendergast the day he replaced John Allman. And I was with Allman the day he replaced Alcock as police commissioner. So I was around the Loop pretty good. I'd be in the Loop with all fellows from all walks of life. They were from the area.

I would like to have been a lawyer, a criminal lawyer. I had to quit after a year and a half of high school. In school they picked other kids to go to the priesthood but not me. It was God's will. So I made friends with people.

I used to come Downtown and hang around the big shots and eventually became the office boy of Mayor Kelly. He liked me because he saw me around and saw me with bigshots. They gave me a job to keep me out of the way. They wanted to do something for me. The Mayor saw me everywhere. I was working as an usher for Andy Frain at the six-day bicycle races. I worked the walkathon, I worked the famous roller derby. I was the announcer for that later on. I worked the telethon on TV to raise money for a good cause. I brought Snite, the famous boy in the iron lung, Downtown. I brought the cameras out on the street, so he could make his contribution.

When I was around fourteen years old, I became a Postal Telegraph boy. It was across the street from City Hall, and I said someday I'm gonna have an office there.

Know how I became bat boy for the Cubs in 1929? I used to pick up the score cards that people dropped and I'd go to the L station the next day and I'd sell 'em. And I'd try to sneak in the park and Andy Frain got so tired of my sneaking in—he was one of my great friends—he said, "We might as well give 'im a job." There was a bat-boy job open on the visiting side. I was determined to bring home money, everyone had scrip in those days.

When I was with the Cubs, I got on the radio on Saturdays as the All-American Boy of Sports. I was with Gabby

---

* After the Summerdale police scandal, O. W. Wilson was chosen to replace O'Connor.

Hartnett when he hit that home run against the Pittsburgh Pirates in the dark in September, 1938.* The Pirates built extra stands for the World Series. Mayor Lawrence, who became a great governor, was giving away tickets already. It was awful dark. There was gonna be one more pitch when he belted it. The crowd and the players got so excited, they picked him up at second base. I ran out and said, "Put him down, he's gotta touch the bases."

At first for the Cubs was Demaree.

Al Demaree?

Not Al, you're going way back. Frank Demaree. Al was a great guy too. He was the one who put me in "Strange As It Seems." I was bat boy for every team in the major leagues by being visiting bat boy. Cubs Park. Sox Park.

You've always been associated with celebrated figures?

Hornsby was always hard to get along with. We did a radio show together. People said they saw me on TV when Hartnett hit that home run. There was no TV then. If I had a dollar for how many people told me—

They saw you SOMEWHERE, isn't that it?

I was a little guy. There was a screen behind home plate and the ball would go up there and I had to get in the game *someway.* So when the ball came off the screen, I'd go after it. Most bat boys didn't do that. I wanted to be somebody. I wanted to be in the game.

I was known when I was around the Cubs. I got known during the milk strike many years ago. The dairy I was working in was bombed. I picked it up, got a hold of it, and gave it to Jimmy Gallagher,† which wasn't very nice. But he threw it out and we saved the dairy. That's how I first got to know Walter Winchell.

I used to promote softball games between celebrities. I

---

* It was the celebrated blow that inspired the Cubs to overtake the Pirates and win the pennant that year.

† He became a sports writer on a local newspaper and later was appointed by P. K. Wrigley as general manager of the Cubs.

played a semipro game in Parky Cullerton's district. P. J. Cullerton, County Assessor, another one who's been behind me all the way, with the great Mayor of the city of Chicago, Richard J. Daley. I got a two-dollar bill from Hack Wilson * that day. They said I looked like him. I gave the bill to my mother and she put it in her prayer book. When she died that two-dollar bill was still there. It was a lot of money for me in those days.

It was very rough during the Depression, which lasted till the war. It takes a war to end the Depression and scare the reformer. A reformer is someone who's made a buck and got religion. I sincerely believe they're hypocrites.

When they start reforming, they start tapping phones, calling people communists and hoodlums, when they don't know what it means. I believe when they call a person something. I want to look it up, and I keep that dictionary right in front of me on the desk and I look it up and I study it and write it out and make sure I know what I'm talking about.

Too often you call a fellow a gangster, a hoodlum, a racketeer. A newspaper will say "alleged," but the person saying it won't. The loud mouths on radio and television.

If my sister or your sister or brother go to the stand to make a fifty-cent bet, they get arrested. Because they can't afford to take the day off to go to the race track, they can't afford to ride the railroad, they can't afford the fee to get in. Your bookmakers in the old days raised money for hospitals. The bookmaker today, you read the headlines. They say he's wrong, he's terrible. What did he do that was so wrong? I think they should pick up those people selling drugs and those rapists and correct that type of crime. Instead of tapping phones and trying to find out who's making a bet.

You read the headlines: Syndicate. Everything is Syndicate. There's a Crime Commission investigating stick-ups and bombings. Bombings go as far back as when I was a kid. Great guys I know have difficulties. Back in the old days, old fellows, who needed a buck, could vote a couple of times, whether Republican or Democratic. Today there's a law against it. They arrest the poor old guy.

In the old days, it was a different city. It's changed be-

---

* Pudgy home-run slugger of the Cubs in the "palmy days."

cause of the famous Summerdale scandal* which I was very sad about. A lot of those boys I went to school with. I don't think they did anything that was really that bad.

We need more prayers today. Civil rights, all these marches. If they would just teach youngsters the "Star-Spangled Banner" and if they would teach the Pledge of Allegiance to the flag, you know, that winds up with "under One God, indivisible, with liberty and justice for all." Live and let live. Then there's the famous prayer of St. Francis, who is the patron saint of everybody. (He reads the framed prayer on his desk.) "Lord, where there is hatred, let us sow love; where there is doubt, faith; where there is despair, hope; where there is darkness, light; and where there is sadness, joy.") With that and the "Star-Spangled Banner" and the Pledge of Allegiance— makes up civil rights. Without all the Washington affairs.

I hate to see violence. I think priests and nuns ought to stay where they belong. There's been a lot of noise in some parishes, you know. I cannot stand violence. If I was locked up for breaking a window playing baseball, why shouldn't a person be locked up for demonstrating whole-heartedly, tying up traffic and slugging policemen? Even if in their own hearts they think they're right. I believe in live and let live. We don't want riots. We want to improve the system. People should vote for more bond issues, for more monies for teachers, and more people should get back to church and listen to their ministers and rabbis and priests.

When I was seriously ill three years ago, Father O'Malley, Rabbi Binstock and Preston Bradley of the Pro-testant faith were all three at my bedside. I'm sure their prayers helped me a whole lot. When I was in the army, my appendix burst. I had last rites. God granted me the will to go on. I went into Special Services with a great guy like Joe Louis.

I came out of the army and started washing cars. I buried my uniform in Grant Park. It's under the monument for Henry Horner, the great governor of Illinois, that Ray O'Keefe built. The next day, I went to a radio station.

---

* Several members of the Summerdale District police station were convicted as accomplices of burglar Richard Morrison, after having been named by him.

I've met people like Colonel John Gottlieb, a wonderful guy, and Phil Regan, the singer, a friend of the Mayor's. I've traveled all over the country, announcing fights, wrestling matches, traveling with candidates for President. I interviewed Harriman on a dead mike and Estes Kefauver, who investigated crime everywhere but in his own state. We didn't have a live mike and I wanted to look important. They all wanted to be on the radio. There isn't a politician who doesn't want to be on.

In 1952, during the Republican Convention, I dressed as an Andy Frain usher and got on the platform. I put on a police officer's uniform once, too. The Chief walked by and said that was the smallest policeman he ever saw. I'm only five feet five.

In 1956, I assisted Richard J. Daley for sheriff. (He indicates wistful photograph: "To Terence, a sincere friend, Richard J. Daley.") We were defeated by a fine man, Elmer Michael Walsh. I played a role, running to get the veterans' vote.

Today, this is the greatest city in the world, thanks to Mayor Richard J. Daley. When he was first elected, the newspapers said this would be a city of ill-fame. Look at it today. New roads and highways. He gives people dollar for dollar for their taxes. He started from the bottom. Daley went his calm way, continued to be the family man he is today, father of seven children and lives in the old neighborhood, back of the Yards.

Here's a man becomes the Mayor of Chicago and what's the first thing he does: he wants to protect the women, the children, and the homes and that's most important to all of us. As I often say on my radio program, "Please be careful at the steering wheel of that automobile." Here's Daley driving carefully all over the city of Chicago. As he said, "No man walks alone." And he says, "Good politics is good government and good government is good politics."

In 1956 I wanted to be coroner. They said where'd you go to school. I said: De La Salle, De Clark, De Randolph, De Washington, and De Dearborn. And they said, "It looks good for you. Just go home and don't talk to no one." And my famous friend, who I can't name, said, "You be quiet. Oh, what we've got for you!" He's a wonderful man, he passed away.

I went home and said, "They want to make me coroner." And my wife said, "Fix the baby's diapers and look at the headlines, they don't want you for coroner." They picked somebody else.

So I took the next train and went back. And that's when my friends, the three party leaders, they put their arms around me: "Don't blow your top. What we got for you!" All three took me on the side and said, "I was for you but the other two were against you." All three said it, so I figured I might as well wait a while.

I waited a long time. I told 'em, "Now if you don't want me, let me know." In 1958, I was fortunate enough to be picked and to lead my own ticket. I'm the youngest man elected to this office.

Our department handles sludge, and I don't have to tell you what that is. We handle 280,000 gallons of sludge in a six-inch line. We're building sewers that can handle one truck sitting on top of the others. We're building further to protect the health and welfare of our city.

● ● ● ● ● ● ● ● ● ●

Ross Pelletier, 56

His office at the advertising agency, one of the largest in the world. It is after hours; the charwomen are appearing.

"I remember as a kid wanting to be a baggageman on a train. The D & I Railroad ran past our home, outside Duluth. Playing the field, we'd see these trains going by and here's a baggageman leaning against the open door and looking at the passing countryside. I thought, oh my gosh, what a great job to have. That was one of the early things. Later, when you get to figuring out how you make any money doing that, to provide yourself with a new pair of shoes and so on, you, like everyone else, start to think, well, maybe I can do a little better than that."

To me, an executive is a man that makes things happen. He's executive something, some plan. He also helped devise that plan of action, whether this is military, let's say, or business or social, or church group or almost any kind of gathering of two or more people. You have to have someone that tries to make it go.

So in my work, it's been hiring and training of other men. So the job for me is to spot that talent, somewhat like a major league scout looking in baseball, trying to find a fella that can throw from the outfield straight and hit the ball hard and so on. So my job is to find and train these men in creating television and radio commercials.

Advertising is a very fascinating business to me. We think it's a very important business, sometimes not fully understood. It's hard to understand the other fellow's business, because no matter what he's doing, you kind of wonder well, what is the importance of this? But advertising has been so important in mass consumption. . . . There's no sense producing if people are not going to consume what you produce in masses. You need mass consumption to make use of the goods that are turned out by the dozens in the store, you know.

A product must stand up in the consumer's hands. I could, by advertising, maybe induce you to try a product. But you will not make a repurchase if it is not satisfactory. I mean, if it's an off-brand, or if it's really too cheap a thing, you're not going to buy that coffee or soft drink or shirt or whatever it is. So you cannot put anything over —at least, not more than once. And who wants to stay in business putting something over once?

You have to tell a real story. One, is to sell him. But it's to let him know he has a choice. Our economy is an economy of choice. We, in this country, under this wonderful system we have, despite the fact that it has some faults, of course, have a tremendous choice. In worldly goods. And while life is more to it than just worldly goods, still, this man has appetites and needs. And here we have this great choice, be it a motorcar—you have a number of brands. They are all somewhat similar, but they all have their peculiar characteristics that make one of them maybe more desirable to you than another one would be.

Oh, another thing, business is quite competitive and people in executive life or even your good sharp clerks . . . you must be on your toes. At least, that's what I and millions of other people feel about it. That's the way we're built, I guess.

I think most people want to do a darn good job and be known for that and have your name mean quality. I want that. So, in a sense, they're seeking status. I'd like to be known as an outstanding, sound human being. I would like to shoot for that. I think most of our fellow citizens have similar views. They want to be the best plumber there is, or the best whatever it is. Manager of a store, a salesman, or minister, or Pope. President Johnson, I'm sure, is driven to being the outstanding President we've ever had, if he can. So to me, status is wrapped up in striving to do the best you can with the material you have.

Often I think, status is used as a term of . . . derision isn't quite the word. I think it stems from people who want to be known as this without putting in the sweat, let's say, to earn it. But people who have earned it, I don't think are thought of as status seekers.

So that means to me a certain amount of night work that I have to do. I think you would be a very smart person who could leave his problems at the office at night, and go home and not take his briefcase or his work home with him. I have not been able to do this. As a rule, I'd say, oh, eighty percent of the time that I take my briefcase home, and that is every single night, I will do some amount of work at home. Usually it involves the kind of reading and studying of business papers that I cannot handle in the office, because there's too many meetings, calls, conferences, and so on.

Again, this is violating a principle of my own . . . which I violate constantly. Thinking about retirement slightly more as the years go by, I don't yet have a plan . . . a particular hobby that would carry me through. I've seen and heard too much of people who go into retirement, finding themselves completely lost and just desolate. And finding themselves living without purpose. . . .

My other interest at night involves Army. I'm still in the Army Reserves. And that takes another night or so a week for much of the year. And in the summer months I go on active duty, during one of the summer months. Now that's the kind of a hobby you would not carry into retirement. . . .

This has been fascinating to me. When I was drafted, I was routed into the Army like millions of others. I had to start out as an acting private. I went down to Camp Roberts, California, an infantry training center. Many of my friends, it seemed all of them, had big deals. They became commissioned right out of civilian life. I went to the infantry. I decided, all right, if this has to be my lot, I'll try and be as fine an infantry soldier as I can.

So what I had to start out with was an acting private. And then I finally fought my way up to a corporal.

That was almost the hardest promotion I ever got, to be an infantry corporal, to teach machine gun and BAR and M-1 and so on, and drilling people, of course. And getting my work done. All my life I'm sure it's get-

240

ting my work done, whatever that work is. But anyway, I went to Fort Benning, Georgia, and was commissioned in the infantry after seventeen weeks there.

When I came out of the service as a first lieutenant, I thought I wouldn't stay in the Reserve, except that I didn't want to get drafted again if some other troubles came on the scene, and have to start back again as a private. I felt, by golly, I'm going to stay closer to this, because I saw already from my service overseas that the Russians were, oh, acting kinda tough. They really were. And I didn't know whether there'd be fighting or anything like that, but I thought I'd just better keep close to the scene. So I stayed there ever since, and that was 1946 when I got out of the service.

Here's what it's been since 1950: I've been in the Command General Staff College. I've been privileged, I claim, to be in it. It's a five-year course in the Reserve. You study all aspects of management and organization. The principle is the same, whether it be in business or, you know, military or political affairs. There are certain principles of organization . . .

In the military, you're studying how to serve on a staff, or be the commander of a unit. And you study personnel, all about it: from obtaining of personnel, training of personnel, the morale of personnel, and so on. It's all organizing men, training them to bring about the objective, winning battles. But that's what's so fascinating to me.

Let me reach over and get something and show it to you. Here's a book that's put out by the United States Army Commanding General Staff College. This is selected readings in management and in this book are articles by outstanding business and organizational minds, not necessarily military minds. Here as I flip through the contents, we find thirty-two articles in this book. And Ralph Cordiner, former president of General Electric, has an article in here. And there's one in here by a man from General Motors. And so on . . . Freedom, Authority, and Decentralization, there's another title for you. Managerial Skills for a New Age and so on. So, the Human Side of Enterprise. The Meaning of Control . . . where automatic data-processing fits into the Army future. . . .

You learn to be a commanding officer of a military unit. And to do it, it isn't just a matter of attention, right face, forward march. It isn't just marching men around. It's how do we organize the manpower of the country to preserve the country in case of an attack, let's say. That gets into mobilizing your manpower and your industry.

We've sent another division over to Vietnam, for example. All right, what kind of men, what kind of machines, what kind of weapons do they have? Where do they come from? How do you train these men? How do you exert leadership? How do you build loyalty and discipline? And how will a job get to be done? All those things are in this course. So having studied that for five years, I graduated in 1955 out of Fort Riley, and then was asked to serve on the faculty of our Chicago USAR School. And I've done that for the intervening ten years.

It's loyalty and discipline . . . serving the company then. But I don't think you set out blindly to serve or to just be a disciplined person. I think we all try to find expressions of ourself, an outlet. Also, I think most people want to do something for somebody, would like to do noble things, if possible. Now, most of all, of course we have to exist, I guess. That is, you have to earn a livelihood, let's say. So sometimes you do whatever has to be done.

So now the service years came next for me, the Army. Here I was with how many? . . . twelve million men in the total services. And so there I was, identifying with a tremendous group. So now out of the service and back to a firm like this. One of the largest agencies in the world. There are certain limitations, but it hasn't bothered me. I try to do the finest job of execution I can.

I mean, everybody can't have his own policy. There's never been a time, including our American Revolution, where every citizen thought that the policy was the best. But when the gavel falls and the policy is adopted, so to speak, we all want to—I think most of us certainly want to—to carry out this policy.

As a formal Catholic, I defer to what the bodies of the Catholic Church decide. I know in the matter of birth control, they are besieged by their own inner thoughts and by all the evidence that's mounting about the population explosion. And that we're going to control this, and control it in a way that will be an honorable way. But you have to support what your organization does.

In the same sense, you and I may not agree with what Congress and the President say, but we support it because they are our duly elected authorities. So I hope it isn't a war policy, believe me. . . . But as long as there is a draft going on, I think when a man is tapped, he should be given all the encouragement he can. And encourage a man rather than . . . Oh, wasn't it too bad a fella was caught, or something like that . . . you know.

Now, on the Bomb, I'm frightened by the implications of it, yes, and horrified by it, yes. But when I think you live with a threat or a horror for several years, or as many years as we have now, since 1945, and this is twenty years now, you begin to get adapted. They call it, like negative adaptation. Or you work in a foundry where they're pounding all the time, pretty soon you don't notice it. You don't hear it. The same with this A-Bomb threat. And I'm sure I speak for many, many people on this, don't from day to day worry and fret about it. We all hope that nothing will happen, but when you get so busy trying to work to support your family, or do some charitable works, or PTA or a youth movement, you don't have the time, thank heavens, to contemplate constantly the Bomb.

What I see coming is this wonderful conquest of outer space. Heaven only knows what we're going to find out there, there may be life out there and so on. But I think the opening up of outer space has helped ever so much in international relations, because if we find one speck of life out there, right away I think any agressor nation or the United States, will somehow feel a little more closely bound to each other against what may be a common threat or a common unknown out there. Even in race relations, I think this helps a lot: the fact that we're going together out into outer space.

The conversation was resumed at a bar, frequented by advertising men. After a couple of martinis . . .

Yes, so much today is made of the matter of guilt, about bearing the guilt, and so on. I think we ought to throw off this burden. You and I were born into the world as we are, different religions and the color we were born with. And had nothing whatever to do with bringing slaves over here or with crucifying Christ or with defaming Buddha or whatever. So we have our own lives to live here, and are trying to do the best we can with our fellow man. And so to heck with the burdens of the past and guilt that spans down to us. I reject that.

I don't think any Negro, a bright, young, forward-looking Negro, expects you or me to bear any kind of guilt whatever. You and I also don't look at him to be any stereotype. We think he's a bright, young, up-and-coming fella and he's gonna earn his own way, and he's gonna be given the right, just as you and I have these rights, to vote and to make our way in life.

Here's what I mean: there's a lot of excess baggage that we attach unto ourselves in life, called this matter of guilt. We should quit calling up this old baggage of the past . . . and all the old photos and all the old wedding gowns and stuff that you find in the attic, old picture frames and what not. Quit taking them from place to place. Why should we, white or black, haul them into our new, nice, burgeoning homes in the suburbs or in the re-built areas of the city? Leave that in the past and let's forge our ways into the future, on our own merits. And I expect that of the young white man and the young colored man. And by golly, they expect that of themselves.

Where is it better to be a young Negro than in these states today? It's an exciting future for them. They don't have to be solemn and belligerent. They are coming in now and learning. To me, to be a Negro today is tremendous. How could you want a greater challenge? How could you find squarer, fairer rules than we have in our society?

I have a few Negro acquaintances. I wish I had more. We've had quite a few Negro women that have come out, whom I really know mostly by their first names. But I think we've treated them always as equal. Not equal in the sense as when you employ somebody you have to tell them what it is you're employing them for. To do. So you spell out the kind of work involved . . . gardening or maybe washing or cleaning the house. My wife and I have had many, many relationships this way, but not in a haughty, you know, sophisticated way at all. At least, I don't think so. I could say I love these people and I hope we've treated them very fairly.

The kingdom of God is within you. Someone said this,

244

and I think it was Paul, who in turn was Saul, at one point and who was a prosecutor of the Jews, was he not? To subjugate the Christians or those who differed with him. I think that God is also within us, each and every one of us, and if we act badly with the gifts that he has given us, we become an anti-God or a devil or whatever you want to call it. But if we work for the good of our fellow man, we get rewards ourselves, and become a little bit of this omnipresent God . . .

. . . . . .

Charlie Landesfahr, 34

He is copy chief at a middle-sized advertising agency. With his wife and two small children, he lives in an upper-class North Shore suburb.

"My father discovered the other day that the Landes-fahrs came over in 1619, a year before the Pilgrims. I asked him whether they were indentured servants or something. He got kind of upset about it. I thought it was pretty funny."

He's a graduate of an Ivy League college; he was a Fulbright Fellow in Austria; and he toured Europe as a drummer in a jazz band. While working toward his Ph.D. in Germanic languages, he thought of going into teaching. He "discovered that faculty wives were possibly more shrewish than corporation wives." He came to the conclusion that the campus world was more restrictive than that of business: telling off a department head might hurt your chances for a job at some other college; the word is passed along. "In advertising, everything is so secret. If you insult the boss, he's not likely to tell the next guy about it, because he might be coming to you for a job three years hence. Three years is the average tenure at an agency." It enables men to blow up, without repercussions elsewhere.

On occasion, he writes articles, free-lance, for national magazines.

I find my job amusing. Soaps and cars, the differences are minute. If you're gonna write copy, *you* decide what the differences are gonna be. The dumb guys call it "image." The smart guys call it "a unit of communication." You become cynical, of course. One of our clients puts out a product in three different boxes. It's the same stuff, comes out of the same tube. It goes into different boxes with different labels. One advertising agency has one name to sell, another agency has another name to sell, and we have the third. Mrs. Housewife prefers one over all the others. If you approach it cynically, you find it amusing.

I know there's a guy, my counterpart somewhere, doing what I'm doing: trying to come up with a clever way of saying his is better than mine. A person is cynical if he is able to stand outside of the box he's in, right? So I stand outside and I say, "I'm doing what this guy's doing, and isn't he a funny man?" And I have to say, "Gee, I'm a funny man, too."

It takes a great deal of con to sound honest in this world. This is the crux of cynicism, I think. It's bigger than just the advertising world. The big lie is part of the outside world, too. Red versus white, yellow versus black, and what have you. This is the ball we're walking on. The big lie is promulgated by the advertising world, but it's a lot of little lies that add up to the big lie, okay?

It affects me both inside and outside. It affects me when I come home. There are some lucky ones who have a product that by its nature is unique. People are better off with it than without it. They're the easy ones. They don't make you feel cynical because you say, okay, I simply present this as *Consumer Reports* might do. My difficulty is that I get involved in something I don't believe in and I bring that cynicism home with me. You face ridiculous problems that nobody should bother to spend his time solving.

The great big white goods, the things that keep our economy going—refrigerators, stoves, all the things that used to be porcelain and white—they're now tinted. This is new. There's pop art that goes along with them. Very nice. Mandrake the Magician coming off the wall at you as you open your refrigerator to get your orange juice.

I'll use the word *creative* and bug you about that one, 'cause that's a gas, too. They're known as creative types in memos from heads of departments. "We just hired two more creative types." They don't say who they are or where they came from. The creative types have idols all right. Their idols are the modern communications heroes.

They can list maybe five or six agencies in the whole country and these are the guys who do the Volkswagen ads, Polaroid ads, American Airlines, and maybe a few others. Gee, they aren't insulting my intelligence, see? So us guys that don't like to have our intelligence insulted admire these guys. . . .

The work pays too well. As a young man, moving from one agency to another, you can make a whole lot of money fast. Glibness, good appearance, and social acceptability, these are the three things really. With these three things, a guy will get ahead, no matter what company he's in.

The advertising business, like so many others, is becoming computerized in areas such as consumer research, motivational research, kinds of things machines can do in part. Of course, sociologists and psychologists are cutting in on the cake, too. There's a jumping on the bandwagon. It's terribly dependent on fads. The Ajax commercial, with the guy on the white horse and the long stiletto, who makes people white, has begun a whole new trend. This will last another three, four years. A white tornado coming out of your washing machine.

The consumer is a great big gaping jaw we're all trying to fill up with whatever we can cram down there, and the great hope is that the jaw will keep getting wider and wider. And the more products there are, the more, you know . . . The population explosion is a grand thing for business, of course. My God, think of all the machines we can sell to more people. A third of the population is going to be under the age of twenty in another year or two, I imagine. They got all the money to spend, that's great. We can sell them records and we can sell them cars and dresses and brassieres at that age, and the whole bit. We can make the whole world like us very fast and make a lot of money on it. We can make it an American middle-class universe. Sell this product against that product. And what you do is try to find reasons why yours is better. If you can't find those, God help you. It takes time to realize they're identical. We're all conditioned to think this soap is different from that soap, until we go to the factory and see them coming off the same production line. There are times when I still believe they're different. It's a belief we have to hold on to.

Oh yeah, I'm established. And I'm digging tunnels like crazy to get out. Do I like my job? No. I deplore it. I hate it, I come home sick at night about it. I'm a pretty unhappy guy some nights. And a pretty mean father. I'm not able to divorce myself at five o'clock from what's happened to me all day long—or what I've been making happen to other people. As a consequence, evenings are not always pleasant.

I've discovered that I like writing. All right, a diaper pin's a useful thing, and ours is better than the next guy's because it's got a soft point and won't stick you. All right, we don't draw blood. What's wrong with it is you're not writing what you care about. You're writing what somebody else cares about. And you're a hack.

Call me a modern-day propagandist looking for a cause. When I was in college, there were no causes. We were known as the apathetic generation. All of a sudden there are a number of causes: civil rights, things like conservation, the population explosion, the H-Bomb.

The point is I've learned techniques, let's call them. Maybe I've even been brainwashed in a certain kind of way. Or I've learned how to use brainwash techniques, if you want to be cynical about it. Maybe it's just that I've learned a kind of persuasiveness and I'd like to put it to better use, okay?

It's a restlessness, something I've got to live with day in and day out. As you grow up, there are things more meaningful than others. Maybe it's because my dad took me to the North Woods when I was a kid, who knows? Trees, birds, wildlife—I don't want to call it a cause. But it's an important fact of man's existence, from which the urban community tends to cut him off. The more he gets cut off from certain roots . . . I'd like to do a series on conservation.

Maybe I'm ready to try to make it on my own. But at this point, it's irrelevant. I now have a family, two children, and I've got to weigh that balance against the other balances. I'm willing to take half the salary to do something I give a hoot in hell about. The trap, of course, is my past. I've been very successful writing for advertising agencies and I have a mortgage and a standard of living. . . .

Twice in my life I've reached for a knife, wanted to

stick it into a guy's gut. We hold ourselves in check, fortunately. You learn to count to ten and you do all kinds of things, you bite something. The doctor's told me my safety valve's my stomach. What I get, I get a very upset stomach. (Laughs.) That turns me off, that puts me flat on my back. You can't get in trouble there.

XIII

GOLDEN GLOVES

• • • • • • • • • •

Jesus Lopez, 42

He is a first helper at the open hearth, U. S. Steel Company. His work is highly skilled. He earns about $10,000 a year and is due for a thirteen-week vacation. On past excursions, he had visited relatives in Mexico, as well as his town of birth. "As I remember it, it was a big town; but when I went back a couple of years ago, it was just a tiny, little thing. It's nothing there, little shacks. It made me sick. Squalor, unbelievable, really unbelievable that people could live like that. You see rows of kids standing like that with their hands out."

His American boyhood was in Joliet and South Chicago, among "Polacks, Hunkies," and other Mexicans. "It was called the bush then. Oh, we had some grand old fights." He was a brilliant student at school, without too much effort, but he bypassed a chance at colllege to make some money fast.

He was once an outgoing person, with many friends and many curiosities: literature, politics. Today, he lives with his Anglo wife in a modest-income suburb, to the city's southwest. Their only child, a girl, died during one of their trips to Mexico. He is convinced it was malpractice.

He has had a few drinks:

I smash cars up left and right. I have a Corvair out there, you see it? It's all smashed up, not fixed. I got a Hudson sitting in a garage, one of these Green Hornets. It's green, too. And it's a Hornet. (Laughs.) And something's wrong with the transmission or something. I don't know what, and it has to be fixed. I got a '64 Le Mans in the garage that's gettin' fixed. That's one I'm gonna pick up Saturday.

It's mixed around here. Polacks next door. Over here's a German, I think. And next to that there, that's another Polack. And there's a Filipino.

I noticed a bar over here where other people were paying thirty cents a bottle and I was paying thirty-five cents a bottle of beer. I stopped goin'. I wouldn't bother to ask. I know. A lot of things that I would fight at the drop of a hat years ago, I just let go and think about it maybe. Like that business about the five cents. You may get sore inside, but you no longer make an issue of it, even though I feel sick inside most of the time. No, I've become a moral coward.

What do I mean by that? Let's say these principles and all that, I let them slide under to keep things at an even keel and all that. In other words, I've fallen into that pattern that everybody's cryin' about. That security. I'm forty-two years of age now. If I get fired from my job, what am I gonna do? How many first helpers do they want there in the back yard?

Like I happen to ride in Oklahoma City last summer and there was a motel, very fancy motel. They got those big neon signs and flashy lighted things around. And it was late, about 12:30 A.M. Drove in. I was with my mother. I was taking her down to Nogales. My sister's graduating from school down there. And there was nobody in there but one man. I asked for a room and I got it. I went and took my mother and got her settled and all that.

And there was some guy that looked like a salesman. Oh, when I walked in, I knew what he was talking about. About those people and all that business. When I walked in, he said the Negroes, you know. And the man who was behind the desk, he said, "We have to take them." I almost started to make an issue right then and there. Because I saw this guy looking at me and you sort of sense these things. I mean you get a feeling when you've lived with it. And I asked him, "How about let's say a Mexican citizen or something like that?"

He didn't know that the papers in my pocket says that I'm a citizen of the United States by Act of Congress. I put that in when I was sold this house. The real-estate agent . . . I paid a substantial down payment and all that business. Went to the loan outfit for the balance. The min-

251

ute we get back in the real-estate agent's office, after the thing was to be all settled, phone call. Real-estate agent answered the phone, he talks, then he asks me, "Are you a citizen?" (Laughs.) I told him "By Act of Congress. Who wants to know? Tell him by Act of Congress." And how many people can say that? By Act of Congress. In other words, I was made a citizen of the United States of America through service in World War Two. And I gotta put that in. When somebody asks me: Are you a citizen? I tell 'im by Act of Congress.

The guy next door, he mentioned to me that somebody came to visit him one time, and I was out mowing the lawn and he asked since when were niggers living around here? So he said, "He's not a nigger." (Laughs.) Sometimes in the summertime . . .

A couple time my car's been on blocks. One winter I had my car blocked, all four wheels, you know. I was standing on the corner, 95th and Central, waiting for a bus, and cars, kids: "Hi, Nigger," and all that. All I can do is forget it. A moral coward. Oh, well, I could carry a gun. Shoot somebody. I could carry a six-inch blade and kill somebody. Oh yeah, I used to fight at the drop of a hat. I used to be called the cock o' the walk. Yeah, I quit that long ago.

At the YMCA, I learned how to box. I became a very good boxer. I was small, light, I could move fast, I could hit fast. Featherweight. I was cock o' the walk for a while, and I found that a good feeling. You know, to be a big so-and-so in the Junior Golden Gloves and things like that. Yeah, it felt good.

Oh, did I have dreams! High school, sciences, mathematics, all A's. Did I have ideas! I wanted to be a violinist. I played violin and I was good. And then—I gave it up. Useless. (He takes a long swig at the can of beer.)

I'm a perfectionist, you know. That's a problem I found with my coworkers at the time. Let's say I don't lose my temper fast or easy. But when I want a job done, I want it done right and all things like that. Once in a while I see a guy lackadaisical or something, I'll go up to him and say, "Didn't your daddy ever tell you that if a job is worth doing, it's worth doing well?" My dad taught me that. I don't believe that, do I? (Laughs.)

But the work you do, you do. And that's another problem of this modern age. The majority that are coming up right now, they're gonna do the least they can and get away with. And I don't like that. I mean, I'm not built that way. This job of first helper, I try to do the best of my ability.

You can't go higher on the open hearth. From there you go to management. Being first helper is quite good for the ego, you know. You're the boss. 'Cause even bosses, I can tell 'em off. Quite a bit of independence. That's one reason why I like the work. Besides, we are men of steel, that could be. Actually, we're all soft, anyway, anyhow.

I run the furnace. Ostensibly I'm the boss of my second helper and the third helper. I say ostensibly because a lot of third helpers try to tell us how to run furnaces and things like that.

It's skilled, if skill is something you learn through practice. Half the moves we make are just an educated guess. We have seven doors and you have to be able to see in your mind what's happening in there and to interpret. We also take the temperature and test the carbon content. We're supposed to know exactly what moves to make. Intuition plays a great part. There's the son of a smelter foreman that's working there, he tells me it's an art. Well, it used to be an art before we had all these oxygen analyzers that will regulate your fuel. But they go on the blink a lot of times.

Actually the first helper is the man who's responsible. Two guys directly under me, and when I tap out the furnace, there's about seven or eight. If anything goes wrong, it's us . . . it's *we* (Laughs.)

. . . Oh, everybody's scared. Especially about this automation. You ought to hear it on the job. With these oxygen furnaces you know, they're gonna knock out all the open hearths. Well, it might. But I understand there will have to be some open hearths, because I don't believe oxygen furnaces can make all that steel, like some of the alloys we make, and things like that. But then I'm not a metallurgist. I'm just what is called an overpaid laborer. (Laughs.) That's exactly what they call us, overpaid laborers and like that. Actually we don't notice this fear among the furnace workers. It's the machine operators like the charging-car operators, the crane operators, and things like

253

that there. They seem more worried about it, I don't know why.

So . . . at work and all that, what do we talk about and have a few beers? Work. Problems we've had there and what somebody should have done and didn't do. Oh, once in a while you hear them about—what? What Johnson's doing in Santo Domingo? Well, nobody knows what the hell he's doing there. What's he doing in Vietnam? Nobody wants to know, either. That's a fact, they don't. Actually I've come to the conclusion that people are more indrawn toward themselves and all that business.

So I stick to myself and I'm sort of a loner. Once in a while I'll get with a couple of guys and we might have identical thoughts and ideas and something like that. But the majority of the time, I keep to myself. Everybody's concerned more about themselves and why that is I don't know. They're letting things like Major Daley and all that, let them take care of outside things. We'll take care of themselves, just "me."

Boy, these kids today are different. They're a hell of a lot smarter than when I was their age. Also a lot more belligerent.

I remember how shocked I was when I came back from the war. It was 1946. I was only twenty-three years old. I had a run-in with a guy at the bar. This character came back with a couple of friends and he was gonna take care of me. Couple of friends came that I knew. They were younger than I was. So we got in a corner and had a nice little fist fight. The guy that started it all, I wasn't involved with him. Another guy hit him and he couldn't knock him down. So I told him, "You stand out of the way. I'll show you how to knock him down." I did. I hit him and knocked him down. And then the two characters I was with, they started kicking him. And I said, "Hey!"

I remember when we had a street fight and we knocked a man down, we stood up there and let the man get up again, if he wanted to, and continue to fight. If he didn't want any more, he gave up and you were the winner. All of a sudden, it wasn't done any more. All of a sudden, why, the minute you get him down, stomp him, kick him, what the hell. Now mind you, I came back from a war where I was shot at and wounded and doing a little kicking myself. But still I had, what? You would call them

. . . ideals? Of a fair fight and things like that. Now what did I find? You knock him down, he was fair prey for kicking, kick him in the head, kick him in the ribs, kick him wherever, any place.

When you hollered "Hey!" did they stop?

They didn't answer me. They didn't give me an answer. Anyway, I quit getting involved in tavern brawls. I walk away. I remember the owner of a tavern told me about it once. The guys were saying I was chicken. "What the hell," I told him, "who's gonna profit? For what purpose? Look, I'm a grown man now, I'm not gonna get in a fight with anybody, and if I do, it's gonna be for keeps."

Have you found any hope, some other kind of people?

Hardly, hardly. When it comes to Negroes, I'm a little more than halfway neutral. (Laughs.) I can put myself in their shoes, because of things that happened to me. I did tell one, though: "You're not gonna get anywhere by wearing a chip on your shoulder." Any word that anybody says, you might say in a kidding way, they take it serious. I found too many people like that. But I don't care, that's the city of Chicago.

Is it true you don't care?

No, it's not really true. It's a world I have to live in, how can I not care? But the thing is *what can I do about it?* There we go. The Bomb. Nobody ever talks about it, nobody ever says boo about it. There's no such thing.

I was an idealist. I, oh boy! Now I feel we should all be happy as monkeys. No problems, just eat, sleep and— what's after that? It hurts me to think. For the last three years I just about given up thinking. I'm just going along day to day and day to day, like that.

What do you do in your leisure time?

I drink. (Laughs.) And read—*Playboy*. Look at the nude girls. I stopped being disturbed when I got over age for the draft. (Laughs.) Yeah.

(Astonished.) Why, don't you think so?

I have a sense of humor. In this day and age, how could you survive without a sense of humor? Ask my wife if I have a sense of humor. She complains I sit here like a bump on a log, hours and hours. I'm doing nothing but thinking. What am I thinking? I better not be thinking. I hate myself. I'm weak. I'm too weak. (Takes a long swig out of the beer can.)

XIV

SKILLED HANDS,
OLD AND NEW

● ● ● ● ● ● ● ● ●

Anton Faber, 75

A modern precision plant, employing about two hundred men. It is in a suburb, a mile or so to the northwest of the city, just off the highway. Behind is a small sports stadium, "Faber Field." We are in the sunlit office of the president.

I came to Chicago from Germany in 1912. I was born in a small town. My parents died when I was only four years old. At fourteen, I was learning my machinist's trade. I spent three years serving my apprenticeship. Another year in different plants, different shops. I made up my mind at the age of eighteen to go out into the world. What you call the wanderlust.

At eighteen, I already belonged to the labor organization. I was indoctrinated very young. I got the wanderlust again and wanted to see Switzerland. I wanted to see the mountains and snow. I landed in the middle of winter. I found out they were not waiting there to give me a job. But it didn't bother me. I got myself a job as a bus boy in a restaurant, sweeping the floor and doing anything that went along.

I found another job in the trade and I transferred into the Swiss Metal Workers Union. Being idealistic as a nineteen-year-old, I was elected shop steward in a company where employees ranged from fourteen to seventy. Very young kid, I was. I had experiences I don't want to express. Yes. I believe I had the first sit-down strike in history.

An older man worked in the cellar on a mixing machine, a mixer for asbestos. And the man took very sick. Well, I was then so-called shop steward, nineteen-year-old kid. I visited the old gent in the upper house. And his wife was scrubbing, working, making a few dollars, washing. So I became quite, you know, excited. I went to the superintendent and told him, now this man is improving and we want to give him a job as a floor sweeper and pay him whatever you can. But the fact that I was so young, and that I came there as a foreigner, didn't set so well. And I said, "Okay, I want to see the president." I waited for the president and he didn't see me for several days.

So I called a meeting of people and asked for a hearing from the committee and suggested by tomorrow morning at ten o'clock if we haven't got no hearing, we pull the switch and you all go to see the president. Okay. That happened and the president was all excited, when he opened the door and he faced the question. "What's wrong? Where's the committee?" "The committee was trying to see you but you didn't find it necessary, so the people are here as a whole. Acting as a committee." And he said, "Ach, you know that doesn't work." I knew that but I wanted him to say that. Now the result of it was we had a meeting, and it took us two hours, and while the hours was going on, the people were sitting on the steps and they waited for an answer.

I finally got an agreement out of them. Then they offered one month and then they offered two months' pay without work. They told me they're not responsible for the sick, that they're not an old people's home, never. And I kept on refusing. Finally the president of the company, who was also representative of the county, he gives us the promise that he would use his influence to give him a job in the county, and that settled my first labor battle.

The company later on was trying to influence me to take their side, and so I says, "You don't have to bribe me, when spring comes along you lose me in a hurry." From there, the next spring, I went to Vienna.

In 1911, I was involved in the biggest demonstration Vienna ever had. They were a wonderful city and nice people, but they were always hungry, never had enough meat. So they decided to import meat from South America, and a shipload was on the way. On the other hand,

Hungarian farmers, who had quite a bit of influence in the Austrian government, brought pressure to bear that the meat could not land in Austria, because they considered this competition a danger to their agriculture. And the result of it was the largest demonstration that I have ever seen. I think between five hundred and six hundred thousand people.

It was well organized; unfortunately, it got into a little bit of rough work; the city hall didn't have many windows left. In such demonstrations you usually find irresponsible people and people who hold out to responsibility. I was young and ready, but I still was responsible. The mass was trying to storm the government building next to the city hall. We had to build a human chain around the building. And we held that human chain for over an hour. Then somebody shot, a couple of shots, that aroused everybody, and the human chain was broken. The result of it was the police couldn't do much *or* the army came out and split the thing apart. I realized then that it was time for me to go home because I was a foreigner. (Laughs.) Unfortunately, it cost three lives, too.

And in a week or ten days, I was on the ocean. Okay, I landed in American. I had a brother here that helped me come to Chicago. That was, I guess, July, 1912.

I got a job, worked there three months, and the typical concept of manufacturers, capitalists, was to be rude to us workmen. I got the big sum of twenty-seven cents an hour, even though I had training from the age of fourteen to twenty-two. The people there were mostly German. In the trades, precision work, there was mostly the influx of Germans, the Scandinavians, and the Swiss. I asked for more. And the fella looked at me and he said, "You have a lotta crust. You just come over here and you can't even talk the language and you want more money." Of course I was rebellious. I looked at him and I said in German, "What does the language have to do with my work? If I could talk the language better here, nobody would understand me." And he fired me immediately. (Laughs.) But again, it did not faze me. I went out the next day and got myself another job and got ten cents more.

I also suffered. During the First World War, people became quite patriotic. One foolish boy in our union council made a motion that the business agent buys a flag and put it out. And some other fool boy again made a motion to lay it on the table. I was one of the first to vote and I was kinda handicapped. And I reported to the question: I refrained. The patriotism had penetrated so heavy, I was unseated.

But I never quit. I came back every meeting and I told them, in even the German Parliamentary, if a fellow wants to refrain from voting on a question, they wouldn't kick him out. (Laughs.) But it took me three months to get reinstated with a two-thirds vote.

There were many things in the American labor movement I did not enjoy. They didn't have enough sincerity in it. And I became a rebel. We had our training in Europe and we couldn't help ourself being what we learned. We had what we call a Labor Temple. In Europe they're highly respected and well run. And they do more to build up the workers and the respect. . . .

We had a library in the Machinists' Hall. But it didn't do us much good. The Americans weren't much interested in it. Ah, *ja*, the American laboring man, they didn't take too much time out. . . .

Wait a minute—I want to tell you how I switched from labor activity to the boss' organization. . . .

I got fired pretty regular, because anybody who in that day expressed an opinion on the right of the union or the right of anything, they didn't make much fuss. You had it. So a friend of mine was president of a small shop on Webster Avenue. He was also the same type man, came from Germany, learned his mechanics, and was still a union man, as a shop owner. He met me at the meeting and he said, "Anton, what are you doing?" And I said, "I got fired." So he asked me, they needed a man, I should come over and see his partner. And he said, "Anton, I want to tell you something. My partner is afraid of you." He says, "He's going to offer you ten cents less than scale, so you won't start." He says, "But will you start? I'm not afraid of you." "Okay, if you say that." I took that job. It was only about ten men.

I became so interested in the battle of that small shop, pretty near as much as the emancipation of the working class; and I helped the boys do the job, and it was a difficult job. I was unofficial foreman and unofficial shop steward. Yeah, I represented both sides. It was a small company. And more and more, I appreciated the battle of a small business.

So another year later, this partner died and my friend came to me and said, "Anton, how about you coming in?" And I asked him, "Are you crazy? You know that I don't fit." He says, "I don't know that. I can tell you that you're honest and you have strength to represent us and you find the right thing to do." Of course, I did help him build up his business. So that was the beginning. . . ."

I borrowed a little money here, and had a brother of mine coming in, and so on. In such striving for the eight-hour day, I worked eight hours a day and sometimes three, four, five on top of it. One never got paid for the three, five, four, because I was my own boss. (Laughs.) I finally left that company and in '29 started another. And the wrong time. (Laughs.)

Even though we had a capacity of a hundred people in the shop, at times during the Depression we had as few as six people. And still we did not go under. No, we didn't shut the doors. I had the determined will that as long as I was honest in paying what money I had, it didn't bother me.

I belonged to labor organizations for about twenty-five years. And now for thirty-seven, I've been with the bosses.

What disturbs me today is labor unions are more of an employment organization. So large, the individual man doesn't even get acquainted with what it meant, the battle of labor protection. It doesn't take enough thinking. He will eventually lead himself into more and more trouble, which will not do him any good, nor the manfufacturer nor the economy. You know, when you raise a child, the child gets so much more and more and more, what happens to him? This is, I'm afraid, the direction of the labor movement. It's associated too much by being used for the political end of it. They're protected, and they can go out on strike and then nobody gets enough protection. They don't have to suffer long, so why don't they have fun?

The greatest interest they have: how much overtime can I get in? Working here, most people get from eight to fourteen hours overtime which is the big thing: more money in the pay envelope.

Once in a while you find a good young man. I have a young man now, our shop steward, and he's a good religious man and he's raised three, four boys. He learned the trade here and he's grown up in it, so maybe that helped him. I was invited to a dinner, honoring a union president. So I bought a ticket for myself and the steward. They were down in the big hotel, and the big crowd. But I was disgusted to see the cheap politicans there and turn the union into a political meeting practically. I walked out.

The toolmaker, he had so much confidence in himself, this mechanical work, this engineering work, every time you face something you gotta lick it. It's not routine, if something develops. And he became quite important in his own strength.

Will automation have an effect on the tool-and-die maker, the skilled craftsman? Will this diminish his sense of personal strength?

Not much at the present time. We're part of building the automation. (He shows me the miniature of a machine.) This item here, see? In years gone by, gone through four or five different operations. Today it goes through one punch press. And all one operator. It doesn't call for less skill. It still requires the skill to produce the tools here.

Could the old-timer toolmaker work these machines?

It does not take much to work these machines. It's a matter of instructions. You can take a young man and run through there for a month and he's a damned-sight better than another man that's been there thirty years. It takes more will and sacrifice of a young man to go through in crafts and he's not paid more. He could be out making more driving a truck. They haven't been too eager.

I only look forward to retirement when I definitely fail at the machinery upstairs. (Taps at his temple.) When it gives out. What is retirement? Fishing I think is a waste of time. I'm not a good golfer, and card playing is also wasting time. When I came to America, I was looking for something. Just like I went from Germany to Switzerland, from Switzerland to Austria, then came here. The America, *Das Lander* . . . the land of dreams, of the impossible.

. . . . . .

John Robison, 57

A probation officer, attached to the juvenile court. He came to Chicago in 1932, after a boyhood in Fort Wayne, Indiana, where the leader of Negro society was the janitor. He had won various athletic scholarships, but wound up at the Negro university, Lincoln, in Pennsylvania, among whose alumni were Langston Hughes, Thurgood Marshall, and Kwame Nkrumah.

The only thing I could do to get money at the time was to play baseball during the summer with the barnstorming team. To a Negro baseball player, this was his whole life. Today, the modern baseball player, it's a job. He learns to do his job well, and after he does his job, he has another life to live. The Negro ballplayer in those days spent all his time trying to perfect himself as a baseball player. That was something that he loved. Forty or fifty dollars a game was nice, easy money, and so he lived that forty or fifty dollars a game. Everybody who knew a Negro baseball player didn't have to have a conversation with him to know he was a ballplayer. When he would go into a pool hall, well, there was just an air about him. I'm speaking of the late Twenties.

At that time, white baseball players were a different breed than they are today. The difference is that the white baseball player had it made out for him. There were organized major leagues. He knew he could advance himself and look to another life when he wasn't in baseball. But the Negro player never thought of living *out* of baseball. The old Negro baseball player, when he became too old to play, he either tried to organize a team of his own or else he just was a hang-on around baseball. That was his life, that's all there was to it.

I played in semipro and I played barnstorming and I also played in summer in the Negro major league, with the Indianapolis ABC's. Some of these players would have been top stars in the game today. Oh, I'm thinking of Buzz Mackey, the great catcher. Anyone who ever heard of Mackey thinks of him as a catcher. They played

Mackey at third base and anywhere they needed a ball-player. And each place that Mackey played, he was outstanding. See, in those days you had to be a *whole* baseball player.

We hear a great deal of talk today about the platoon system, a left-handed batter for a right-handed pitcher and vice versa. The manager decides what to do.

In those days he'd be half a ballplayer. I'm a right-handed batter. If I couldn't hit a right-handed pitcher, why I wouldn't make the team. I remember C. I. Taylor, who was manager of the Indianapolis ABC's. He was saying all the time that if they throw it across the plate, you should hit it. But if they don't throw it across the plate, you get a walk. So we felt that if it came across the plate, no matter from which direction, you should be able to hit it. (Laughs.)

A whole ballplayer can hit, throw, run, and field. Today —for instance, I was watching the game the other day, the White Sox—it was a late inning and they were trying to protect a one-run lead. So they put in a fast fielding man at second base, another in the outfield. Now these men were just specialists, that's all they could do. No, they could never have made the team back there.

They were a special breed then. I played aganst Josh Gibson, and I think he could hit a ball on a line harder than any baseball player I've ever seen. I've seen him hit a ball, it wasn't over twelve or fourteen feet off the ground, and when it hit that fence, it hadn't risen an inch almost. He slapped it off against the fence.

You may have heard of Buck Leonard, who was quite a first baseman. Again, thinking of the difference between the Negro ballplayer then and the white ballplayer. In order to draw crowds, well, I'd say white crowds, local fans expected something extraordinary and different out of the Negro player. Consequently, Negro players learned to clown. I'd say these were the forerunners of the Harlem Globe Trotters. Buck Leonard, great player as he was, why, he still clowned. Even in a serious league ball game, he would never catch a ball with two hands. He would always catch a ball with one hand. And you ask Buck, why doesn't he catch it with two hands? He'd say the ball was too small to catch it with two hands. (Laughs.)

They always expected something extra out of you and you were always trying to give them something extra. However, in many of these barnstorming trips when we played local teams, they wanted something extra, you'd better not give it to them either.

I guess it was in Paducah, Kentucky. They had a local white team there. Oh, I think they had won about forty games and they had lost only one of them. And so this was quite an attraction for this team that I was playing on. Well, when we came to town, it was talk all among the Negroes as well as the whites that this team was gonna skin us alive. Well, the Negroes hated to see us lose the ball game. They were pretty proud.

The publicity and local press had built this white team so high until the local Negroes thought they couldn't be beaten, and particularly by a Negro ball team. It was a pretty close game, and oh, I think it must have been tied in the eighth inning. Well, Long Tom Johnson hit a home run, hit the ball out of the lot. And when he hit that ball out of the lot, why a crowd of white people came running out of the stands as Tom was circling the bases. So Tom, knowing they weren't coming out there to shake his hand (laughs), why, he went over the back fence. (Laughs.) As I was saying, they expect something extra, but under the circumstances, they didn't like it.

You had to lose the game?

Oh, yes.

In order to leave the town uninjured?

Yes. Down in Lynchburg, Virginia, we were playing a local Negro team. This team was very good and they had a lot of white supporters. The ball diamond in Lynchburg was recessed in a valley, so that the people could sit on the hill and not come in. The white people viewed the game from that roost up there. There was quite a bit of money bet around the town, I understand, that these local boys were gonna beat us. Well, we played the game, so about the last half of the ninth inning, we were leading about five to one or something like that, so when we took the field for the last inning, well, our men on the bench began to gather up the bats and balls, and we were getting ready to go.

So just then, two large red-neck white men came over to the bench and said, "What are you boys doing?" We said, "We're getting our bats together because this is the last of the ninth." And they said, "Oh, no, this isn't the last of the ninth, this is only the seventh inning." Well, we began to get the idea. We played another inning and the score was still whatever it was and we were gonna leave. "No," they said, "This is only the eighth inning." So we get the idea that the only way we're gonna get out of that town was to let this local team catch us and beat us and that's what they did.

Oh, that happened many times. Particularly in playing white teams. It'd be a close game, and oh, you could hit a home run over the center-field fence and it was a foul ball. We'd have that happen many times (laughs) and then you learn you don't hit home runs when they expect you to lose.

How did your teammates react to you, a college boy with other interests?

This was a hard fraternity to break into. None of them wanted to see me make the team. Because that meant one of the regular fellows who was gonna play baseball all his life was gonna have to sit on the bench and instead of getting say, $30 a game, he was only gonna get $10. If you didn't play, you'd only get $10 a game. I wouldn't say they resented me. I was just an oddball. They tried all the tricks to see if I had guts, and any trick I'd fall for, they all laughed about it for weeks. Schoolboy did this, Schoolboy did that. But when they knew I was gonna stick, they took a great interest in helping me. The minute they began to give you a few tips, you knew you were in. When they were first testing me out, throwing dusters and things like that at me to see if I would show any fear, when I didn't, the joke was, "Ol' Schoolboy's gonna make it." They were kind of proud.

I don't know how you can fight the challenge of making a man feel proud within himself of a job well done. That he pleases *himself*. You can look at my size and see that I wasn't a home-run hitter. A couple of times I was lucky to get a home run. Of course, everybody clapped me on the back. Yet the hardest ball I ever hit, and I felt the zest of it, the ball was caught. But I knew I did everything perfect. The man who caught it was out of position at the time, his manager was waving him to shift. Now, nobody remembers me for hitting that particular ball, but that was the best one I ever hit in my life. Inside me, I felt good. I pleased *myself*.

Today, any kind of work, they do a job to please *someone else*, in order to hold the job. I mean, after the day's work is over, they pursue their own life. The *joy* of the job, they feel, this is just gone.

· · · · · ·

Andrew Bartok, 45

He is head of the New Products Division of one of the world's largest automated bakeries. In Budapest, through years of apprenticeship, experience as a journeyman, and stiff examinations by top craftsmen, he earned his certificate as a master baker. "At the time, in Hungary, there was a law that a person who does not have a master's certificate could not open a pastry shop. If someone invested money in a shop, he had to take in as his partner a master baker."

Always there was the master's personal hallmark in the ultimate craftmanship of his apprentice-pupil.

At one time, he had almost given up baking. "I looked around and I found that the bakers whom I knew looked much older than their actual age. They were tired people, they were disgusted. . . ." He studied mechanical engineering, "And then all of a sudden I realized that maybe there was a connection between this science and the art of the pastry chef."

There are many advantages to make a cake by machine. Number one: there is uniformity. No matter how skilled a craftsman is he will invariably make a cake slightly different each time. But if you make a cake by machine, you can make this cake, day in and day out, the same way. You can be sure that the cake looks and tastes the same.

There's another advantage. If you use a master craftsman to make a cake, maybe five, maybe ten cakes an hour. As a result, the labor cost per cake is extremely high. This is paid for by the customer. On the other hand, if you automate a bakery, the labor cost is very little. If you produce, instead of ten cakes an hour, a hundred or two hundred or maybe five hundred cakes a minute, the cost the customer pays reflects the ingredients of the cake rather than the labor.

Before automation, the baker sometimes could *feel* if the temperature was right. Few people can tell the exact temperature, but he compensates for his mistake as he goes along. Let's assume the milk is two degrees warmer than he should have. The dough will ferment maybe fifteen or twenty minutes faster. So he sets the refrigerator cold as he thinks it should be. The next day, the dough has not risen as much as it should have, he just opens the refrigerator door a little.

Let's assume he made a mistake and took the dough out a bit too young. He compensates for it by putting the pastry made from this dough in a fermentation box at a higher temperature to get the right size. What he's constantly doing he's correcting any mistakes. Even though he may have used six different techniques, the finished product is almost the same every time. Because he himself was his own computer.

When you mass-produce an item, you can't do this. You cannot change the temperature of the oven, you cannot change the fermentation box, you cannot change anything during this process, because you may ruin thousands and thousands of cakes. Everything has to be done just right. All this has to be recorded by a man trained in the sciences. He converts all these techniques into numbers, into procedures which can be simulated by the machine, and the machines will reproduce that every time the same way.

You have an art, which is nothing else than the product of a human being. Later on, he is routinely reproducing the same item. But I don't think the original product could be done by anything but a gifted human being. Through the marriage of art and science, it can be brought to the market at a lower cost. Ultimately, everybody benefits.

Computers, if asked the proper questions, can come up with the proper answers. I have not yet seen a computer which will ask the question. If that time will come, then maybe we are in trouble. Until then, we don't have to worry about anything.

We need skilled pastry chefs badly, because we have to make up these cakes originally by hand. We then have to devise machines to make these cakes. There is no substitute for the experienced craftsman, who then works with engineers and helps determine the characteristics of these machines, so that the finished cake will look and taste as if it was made by hand.

Before a large company would dare come out with a cake, it will produce the hundreds and thousands of different cakes, trying to come out with the very best one. They make thousands of different kinds, have them market-researched to find out whether the public likes this particular variety. It would be unwise to invest hundreds of thousands of dollars in a machine before this research is completed. So we need people to do this sort of thing, make cakes by hand. We call this experimental baking.

Unfortunately, there are less and less bakers being trained. We were looking for three experimental bakers for the last year and we couldn't fill the job. There are lots of applicants, but nobody can fill the job.

Let's assume a skilled craftsman would not want to work in a factory as an experimental baker. A large company produces a certain variety. But there is variety within variety that a small man can do. For a fine craftsman, there is always room in a small shop. But every week, dozens and dozens of bakers go bankrupt. One wonders why. Most of these places are run by half-skilled bakers, not really fine craftsmen.

The people who are unskilled or semiskilled, there is no need for them in an automated world. Such people cannot create the original cake with their hands. They are not needed for the menial tasks a machine can do. The computer mixes the ingredients, stores information, checks the temperature of the batter, the humidity in the oven and in the air. Just as the computer in the office does the billing and cost calculations and so on.

Unfortunately, what applies to pastry chefs is true of *chefs de cuisine*. More and more restaurants and hotels are buying prepared products, therefore eliminating the need for high-salaried chefs. So it is possible as we are automating bakers, we are automating kitchens where entire types of food are going to be mass produced.

There are several trade schools for baking. They learn things outside of actual baking, too. They learn a little about chemistry, biology, food technology, and bakery machines. When they graduate, they know a lot about little things, but they certainly are not master craftsmen.

If you look around in America, there are very few places which employ the old system of apprenticeship. Very few people want to become bakers, craftsmen. If they have the intelligence and dexterity, they try to become engineers.

XV

RETIRED

● ● ● ● ● ● ● ● ●

Ed Criado, 87

An apartment in the Mid-North area of the city. His wife and daughter live with him.

In 1893, at the age of fifteen, he left school and began his apprenticeship in a Boston machine shop. He was retired as a tool-and-die maker ten years ago, at the age of seventy-seven.

He holds a cigar between the stubs of two fingers of his right hand. "In 1917, a monstrous press came down on it. Eight or nine girls, working the punch presses, ran around screaming. It took four men to get my hand out. They wanted to cut off the whole business. I got compensation for the loss of the whole two fingers. But I said, 'Don't you take those off, I need 'em for my cigar.' I always smoke a cigar since I was seven years old. I'd steal from my father, who used to make the best Havanas. So they saved my fingers like that."

I'm doing things today at home here that I never done in my sixty years of married life. I wash and wipe dishes, I go over the place and I go downstairs to the laundry and put laundry in the machine and all. I never done that before. And go shopping for groceries. I never done that in my life. And it's all right, if you're retired and well situated.

Now when I retired, I had in the neighborhood of eight thousand dollars in the bank. Well, I thought, that's gonna keep me, I'm seventy-seven. I probably won't live another five, six years. Well, you know that's dwindled down to six hundred dollars in ten years. Between the sickness that I had, and her. It's absolutely out of order.

I got a couple of nephews, who argue about Medicare. They're against it and I fight with them. I say, you young fellas are talking now. When you get to be sixty-five, it goes, the money goes. At least, when you get sick, you got a place to go and the medicine done.

You take the medical cost today. My wife is in the hospital here only about two years ago. They never even found out what the devil was the matter. Only twelve years ago that I was operated on, all I paid for a private room, with bathroom, was $11 a day. My wife was in a room only two years ago and she paid $23 a day for a two-bed room.

Oh, those kids, I argue with them. I say, you young kids, you're still wet behind the ears, you don't know what you're talking about. And what would you have when you're sixty-five? You won't feel it now, but you'll feel it when you're sixty-five. But you can't tell them, they don't listen to you.

I can't visualize how young people are gonna live twenty years from now, with what we pay today. They claim automation is not gonna kill jobs. It's about 1955, automation hit the tool-and-die business. I never been in a shop since, to see it myself, but I know it's hit it.* It's all happened in the last ten years. I wouldn't last ten minutes.

To make a die today with the equipment they got, I wouldn't know how to start. The old skills are gone. Everything's done with these computers. Twenty years ago, it took about two dozen men to machine that motor block. Today, they have a machine that's as long as from that end of the room to here. One man does it today, he pushes buttons. I can remember when we had pretty near six thousand members in my local. I don't believe we got more than two or three thousand now. A lot of them retired, a lot of them had to quit because the machines put them out of work.

* Vic Horvath, of the National Association of Machinists: "In an automated period, the skilled man is the man that's needed. There is a shortage of tool-and-die makers right now. He is not made obsolete at the present time. There'll be a demand for the toolmaker for a goodly number of years, before he is affected by automation. It will not affect him in his lifetime."

And there's no new skill, no matter what they say. Unless they put them on something that requires individual work, like inspecting. Still, those new machines—they have those inspection machines that inspects a damned sight better than . . . I don't know. I can't describe it. But I'm living in another world today from the one I was brought up in.

You know, I was given the last rites of the Catholic Church three times. Three times, I was given up. The first, when I was nine years old. I had black diphtheria. I laid about four days and they'd given me up. And all they fed me was brandy. That's why I like brandy and whiskey so much in my later years. (Laughs.)

The next one was in 1944. I used to take my lunch in a restaurant on Madison Street. I loved rice pudding, that's one thing that I'd wind up a meal with. I went back to the shop, looked at some blueprints. I start to get dizzy. I lay in the hospital nine days. My doctor thought I was trying to commit suicide. He didn't know what the hell happened. They found out, by mistake somebody in the restaurant instead of putting in powdered sugar in this rice pudding, they put rat poison in it. I was poisoned, arsenic. Two policemen from the Sheffield Avenue station died. A couple of hundred sailors going to Great Lakes for boot training, they were all poisoned the same as I was. It was in the paper the next day, gave the name of all of them. And I understand that from that day to this, they never served rice pudding again.

Now, my third close shave, that's when they gave me up dead. That was in 1953. I told them I wanted to get a priest to come up here. The doctor showed me the photo and you could see on my left side a growth about the shape of an egg. "If that ever hits your liver, nothing will save you. You have to be operated on." I was seventy-five at the time. And I said, "What would an operation like that cost?" He says, "It's about $500." And I said "What would happen if I didn't have it done?" He says, "If you wait six months, you'll be a dead man. You won't be around to worry about it." My doctor still got those photostats in his files. He always brags how close this man was to—if it was an eighth of an inch more.

Know what happened to those priests who gave me the last rites?

Huh?

They're dead.

· · · · · ·

Herb Gross, 58

*A Loop brokerage house, early afternoon. It is crowded.
Groups of elderly men, some of seedy appearance, are observing the electronic quotes board. Their half-attention is
reminiscent of "had-it" horse players, small-sum bettors,
hanging around neighborhood books. The concern is
equally remote. It is a place to get in out of the rain.*

*We are seated in a small office, off the floor. He is wear-
ing an expensive silk suit and a pronounced Florida tan.*

I spend six months here and six months in Florida. Because of a heart condition, I can't stand the cold
weather, and I have to go South around November first.
And I have a wonderful day. My doctor's finally talked
me into playing golf. I thought it was a silly pastime, but I
learned to my great enjoyment, it's one of the most wonderful games in the world. You're out there, the fresh air,
the sunshine, the birds, all the other wonderful things that
Mother Nature has to offer. It's just wonderful.

And when I'm in Florida, I play every day. I pay little
attention to the market. When I'm in Chicago, my hobby
is the market. When I'm in Florida, my hobby is golf.

I've been retired now going into my sixth year. Oh,
there are times when you become mentally depressed,
when you see things go by and you're not in the swim, and
you see people making a success of their little business,
they become big businesses. This is fine. If I was physically able, I'd do the very same thing. So I've learned one
thing in life. Life is exactly as you make it. Because as
they said in the Bible somewhere, as you make your bed, so
shall you lay upon it.

I have made a new way of life for myself. I had to. Because the first two years I was retired, I nearly went out of
my mind. I was on the verge of a complete breakdown.
But I had to find another way and I was determined that I
was not going to be licked. And I found that way. Am I

having fun doing it? Having a lot of fun doing it. But then again there are days when you become mentally depressed, which is normal. This is the norm. But if you can throw it off, as I have been able to do up to now, have fun and reaping the benefits of my labor.

I wasn't the world's greatest salesman, but I was probably the hardest-working one. But when the other fella would stop, that's when I would continue. And I got my satisfaction in selling where the other fellow couldn't.

Without competition, what is life? Without a goal, without a challenge there is no life. But where you have competition and you're out to make a success of yourself, this is fun, this is sport, this is the greatest game in life. And there's no greater game in the world than selling, to me. This is wonderful. . . .

To me, this is important: When a man is working, you don't work from nine to five. He isn't there, if he starts working at nine. He starts at eight-thirty. He doesn't watch that clock at five. He's out there planning what he's going to do tomorrow, and this is what I always believed. My dad said if you're a street cleaner, be the best street cleaner. No matter what you do, try to be the best.

I had very little social life. For the reason that you can't serve two masters. You can't be out all day, work all day, and play all night. You burn that candle at both ends, as the old saying goes. They told me when I went into the advertising business that unless I drink or carouse, I would never make it. Now this was a challenge to me that was thrown down. I said, "I can't make it?" I said, "I don't have to drink. I've got a good product. A product that will help my fellow man. All I got to do is show him how to use it." Because a man don't buy your product because you buy him a dinner or you give him some little item. He buys because he's out to sell his merchandise.

There isn't a person living today who isn't selling in one way or another, 'cause life is all a matter of selling something. If you're selling something intangible, it's intangible, and I love the intangible, because with intangibles you can paint beautiful pictures. But one thing was a policy with me: I never promised more than I could deliver. 'Cause I found that if you promise the world with a fence around it and all you can deliver was the fence, you were a dead duck. But if you could just promise the fence and then deliver the world with it, man, you were on the right track.

I never made exaggerated statements and never lied. If I didn't know when a question was asked, I'd tell 'em I don't know and I would say like so: "I don't know but I'll find out for ya." There's no shame in saying I don't know. If more people would say I don't know when they're asked a sincere question, they'd be better and all would be better. Today I would classify myself as one who used to be a real pro.

I miss the challenge, the challenge of daily selling. I miss that challenge of going in and selling an idea. 'Cause I'm basically an idea man, selling an idea. This is what I miss, and I'm normal . . . I hope . . . whereby you get these depressed moods. I get them today, but I try very diligently to throw it off.

Your life, then, is recreation.

Fun. For example, when I leave here at quarter to three, I go to my club, I swim, a good steam bath, a good massage, I go home, have dinner. We play bridge at night, and incidentally, bridge is a very challenging game. And it's very interesting. I can play nothing and have a picnic. And then, come around the first of November, we head south. Every day it's the same way.

It's fulfilling to a degree, but, you know the law of compensation is always at work. When you gain something, you lose something. You must settle with life. If you don't, you'll be a very unhappy person. Now it took me two years of my retirement to learn this. But I had to, because my heart wouldn't take it. But we're having fun, enjoying every minute of it.

The basic thing about selling that was so enjoyable was this: I realized that in order to earn my commission, to have it coming, I had to do something for my fellow man. Not that I was a philanthropist or not that I was a great guy, but I realized in order to make a good living and to make it consistently, I had to think of my fellow man. I had to do things that were good for him, 'cause if it was good for him, it eventually became good for me.

The one thing I did do that perhaps the other fella didn't do, when I made one sale I said there was two, there was another one. When I made two, there was three. I was always looking for that extra buck. Many times, this is a feeling of many of our better salesmen: they go out and make a good deal, and then they play. Not Herbie. Because I had a credo when I was on the road for many years. Some SOB had to pay for my being away from my family. Thank God that I did, because you see I'm in a position today, and I have been for the past five years, and I can live off my investments.

You're here at the Stock Exchange every day. . . .

I'm here at the opening of the market. I'm here for the close. It's closed at two-thirty Chicago time. Then after the runoff, I go to the club. . . .

I found that finance was a very enchanting business. I wanted to learn about how businesses were financed from the embryo to the big companies we have today, and I found that everything was built around the dollar. And I watched little companies go broke, little companies and big companies.

For example, take Sears Roebuck or General Motors. I mean one of the top companies that started many, many years ago. If a man invested just a few dollars in those companies, today he'd be worth millions. I watched this country grow, and I felt, and I still feel, that in these United States, it's a privilege where a man has a right to invest in someone else's business and enjoy the benefits of good dividends and enjoy the appreciation.

It's a thrill to be able to watch the tape, seeing a stock start to move, you get in, you watch it move, you decide how much money you want to make, you work it like a businessman works his business. Well, on certain stocks I look for ten per cent, on some stock for fifteen per cent, and certain stocks twenty per cent. When I reach this objective, I'm out. In other words, I'm not trying to be piggish.

You've really found your thrill here.

The thrill and the companionship. The very wise people I'm associating with. I, too, in my humble way, make it my business to read my financial papers every day, and this has given me a very liberal education. Just think of it: there's over six hundred issues listed on the New York Stock Exchange. There's over nine billion shares outstanding. This is a fabulous thing. There's only the beginning of what will come. Things are gonna be bigger and better than ever, believe me, in this, the greatest country in the world.

Of course, you have our unthinking people who would demonstrate against our policy in Vietnam, 'cause if we don't stop 'em now, it won't be too long before they'll be over here. And you can be damn sure that that's right. If a person would just stop and look at a map of Asia, they would see how this finger points right into the Hawaiian Islands, Formosa, Australia . . . and eventually the United States. And we better stop these people cause, if we don't, we'll all be under another -ism.

My knowledge is garnered, *A:* from reading; *B:* from listening to the daily newscasts via TV and radio . . . open-end discussions, so to speak, among my friends, their opinions, their thoughts and my own. Most of my friends agree with me wholeheartedly. I have a few that are a bit more on the liberal side.

My social circle consists of men who are very successful businessmen, most of them with very fine educations, very good backgrounds. And fortunately, I have a daughter and son-in-law who border on the intelligentsia. We have some very lengthy conversations. You see, my daughter is a graduate of the University of Chicago. My son-in-law is a graduate of the University of Illinois and he has his two master's degrees. He's an electrical engineer. He's a brilliant man, and we exchange ideas. And their point of view is very interesting. They agree with me wholeheartedly. They understand. But, of course, many of their friends, who don't understand, disagree.

In the papers, you see pictures of Vietnam, you know, both sides. A kind of terror, you know what I mean? Somebody dying, a young American boy dying, a Vietnamese person, too. . . .

Look, you and I both know that no matter what happens in life, there's always winners, there's always losers. It's an unfortunate set of circumstances that our boys must

278

go on foreign soil and die. But this is life. It was ever thus. What can we do about it?

Could you offer a personal credo—as well as thoughts about yourself today?

There are times when I dislike myself immensely. There are times when I think I'm very, very good. In my youth, I was one of the most conceited asses that ever lived, but as I grew up I realized what an infinitesimal thing I really was. 'Cause up to that moment, I haven't contributed too much to this world. Unfortunately, I don't have an inventive mind. But as I walk through life I have one credo, though I'm not a religious man. My credo is this: I like to be treated well and the only way to be treated well is to treat the other fella well. 'Cause I also agree with another thing, a cliché if you will: I hear no evil, I try to speak no evil, I see no evil . . . and fourth, and most important, I will do no evil.

POSTSCRIPT
Several months before this conversation I had met him on a bus. It was morning. He was on his way to the brokerage house. I had remembered him from early Chicago radio days as a salesman, in the employ of a powerful station. He was terribly depressed. Life had no flavor for him any more. If only he could find a real interest. A suggestion was made, he shook his head: "You're talking about something where people cooperate. My life's been competition. It's in my blood. I can't do this other. . . ."

• • • • • •

Charles Wilhelm, 61,
insurance underwriter

I'm due for retirement in three and a half years and I'm looking forward to it. I have a feeling that when I reach sixty-five, if I just have sufficient wherewithal to get along, I won't have any trouble at all finding things to do and enjoying myself. I know there are other types of men that simply can't give up. I have the feeling that after I've run the race, if I've got enough to get by. . . .

Everybody kids me at the office. They say, "Well, when the time comes, you'll be looking for another job"—and things like that. But I don't think I will, because I love so many things. Sports. I bowl, of course, in the Insurance League. And baseball. We're a card-playing family. We love bridge. We were all raised on that, thanks to my father. There again, other people would criticize us and say, well, playing cards is a sin, it's a waste of time. To us, it wasn't. I mean, it's just a way you look at things, I suppose. And I love to read, and I'm sure I won't be bored.

I hope I'll be here a few years to enjoy it. Fortunately we have a fairly decent pension system at the company where I work, and God willing, if I happen to be around for a few years, I know darn well I'm going to enjoy myself.

You're not afraid of retirement?

No, and I think there are a lot of people that really are. I feel so sad when I hear of these cases, or see them in the obituary column where a fella had just reached retirement age, maybe he's had a year or something like that. And he dies and I feel so sorry because the fella has worked so— let's face it, everybody has to work hard these days in order to get by. They work so hard to arrive at that age where they can enjoy themselves for a few years, and they suddenly pass out. Now whether the fact that they can't make the adjustment has some bearing on their running down, I don't know. Maybe the ones that find it difficult to make the adjustment just don't last too long.

I see it in the office so often. We have a case in our office, a chap reached sixty-five years old and he was due for retirement but he had no other interests besides work, and he petitioned to be left on at least another year. And they're going to, I suppose make it a year-to-year thing. I happen to have a friend that works under this fella in the same department, and he's perhaps thirty-eight or forty, five or six children. I don't think it's fair for that younger man, to hold him down.

This older man, I know him real well. And he has no . . . he doesn't like sports, he doesn't like cards, he doesn't like a drink or two, which we haven't mentioned so far, but you can put me in that category. I like a drink or two, I sure do. But there's a man, he's a single guy that never married. His sole interest is the insurance business. Now I don't suppose I should say it, but I feel sort of sorry for a fella like that, because I suppose he would be lost, as you say, if they forced him to retire.

· · · · · ·

Valerie Bosard, 73

A retired nurse. She keeps house for herself and her sister. She has been retired seven years.

I've enjoyed retirement. It didn't turn out the way I thought it would. I became involved with church, neighborhood, friends.

There aren't any easy nursing jobs. I never had time to read or walk down the street or anything. Never went out during the week, always busy reading professional stuff. It's nice to have your own time and do what you want to do. I keep house and cook and belong to a little group that's studying French. I wish I had more time.

I belong to a neighborhood group. I think that's the solution to the impersonality of the city. Our minister wanted a neighborhood library. We have no branch of the public library here. You have to take a bus and walk two miles to any of the nearest. The library turned us down. She said, "You don't have a reading neighborhood." Not too many people have library cards. And we found it was all too true. We have to educate people to read books.

I didn't approve of the idea at first. But finally we got started. The library turned down our plea for a mobile unit, too. We thought it wasn't fair. There weren't enough card holders because of the distance to a public library. We actually didn't realize that people didn't care.

Anyway, we had a day when the Boy Scouts picked up books. We were swamped with them. Of course, we don't have the newest. We're collecting S & H green stamps for a new encyclopedia. There were about twenty of us volunteers. It doesn't fulfill the function of a public library, but it's better than nothing.

Grandchildren are just wonderful, they stormed the place. It's the adults we have to encourage. I think they've

281

never read very much. The man next door is a truck driver. This is a neighborhood of truck drivers. He's obviously an intelligent person. I think he could have been almost anything. His wife has a better formal education. She comes and gets books and says he's a non-reader. One day she said, "This is an interesting book. Read it." And she said at two A.M. he was still reading.

I know the names of most of the children on the street, and the adult's. The teenagers are off by themselves. We were afraid when we opened the library, we might have trouble. We had young hoodlums, but the ones who come in are very well behaved.

My close friends are not in the neighborhood. Once in a while, we get together and talk about what we're doing and settle all the affairs of the world. We fight like anything about local politics. We don't agree at all. But we agree that our foreign policy is terrible. I think there's a lot of this feeling. We talked it over with our landlord and our neighbors. They feel this way. Something is terribly wrong.

War toys bother me. The children around the neighborhood have them all the time. I scared a little boy almost half to death the other day. He stuck a gun at me and said, "You're dead," I gave him such a lecture, he ran down the street as fast as he could. I said, "You're bad if you shoot anybody." (Laughs.) Maybe we ought to have a neighborhood meeting on it.

We don't intend to always live here in Chicago. We're leaving. I think Chicago is a fascinating place. I'll miss it a great deal, the excitement of living here. Probably go back to Iowa. We want a garden. I want a more quiet life and get away from Chicago problems. We want to live in a pleasanter place, where living isn't quite so high.

• • • • • •

Clyde Fulton, mid-eighties

He lives with his wife in a three-room flat on the first floor of the Dearborn Housing Project. A pension from Swift & Company and social security benefits are his source of income. He had been a cowboy in Nebraska and a dining-car chef for Illinois Central before his work at the packing-house, where for many years, as a boner, he was consid-

ered by the whole department as a "real artist with the knife."

He was retired fifteen years ago. "The foreman says, 'We caught up with you at last. You're fired for stealing.' What the heck, I've always had a very good name with the company. So you know how bad I felt. So after they had their fun, they said, 'You damn fool, don't you know what you been stealing? You been stealing a young man's time.'" (Chuckles.)

If them doggone doctors would let me alone, I'd be working now. Them confounded doctors—I turn around and say, I'm gonna get me a night job or somethin' like that, her and the children give me a chilled look. (He gestures thumb toward his wife, who looks heavenward as she shakes her head.) And the son tol' me, he said, "You're getting by all right, dad, you're not broke. What the heck do you wanna go to work for?" Oh, lotta people would be so happy to get off and not have to do nothin'. You know what I'd like to do? I'd like to go back to using a knife. Boning.

(Talks with enthusiasm here.) Now you take this, there's three groups. They have a knife man, a butcher, and a boner. Boner gets the best pay of any of 'em. It's the idea is this: it's not just cutting the bone out, but don't scar your meat up and leave a whole lot of meat on it. You've got to take it off clean, not being cut up. You take them big fellas out there in the office, they go out huntin', come back with a deer, bear, somethin' like that, they wouldn't let a person touch it but me.

Aren't some of these jobs being done by machines now? Automation?

Oh, Lord, why bring that up? That's highway robbery. When I was young, they were talking about machines boning, no, they never did that. You go out there and see now. I would be willing to bet that at least twenty-five percent of the work out there now is did by machines. One man, he's up on that truck, and he will knock out twenty-five men trucking.

You think the machine bones as well as you did?

283

The last time I seen it, I could answer that very plain: no, they did not. For the simple reason is this: you take with the machine, it would pull. And the consequence is you would tear the meat. (His tone is the proudful one of a master artist.) You see, when I got through with it, the meat was virtually trimmed, the meat wasn't cut, it was just marked with the bone and followed that thing.

Is there one moment in your life you remember most vividly?

To a great surprise?

Yeah.

Down at the World's Fair, when they put me in an exhibit down there, with all those fancy cuts and meats. You know actually I was scared, it was such a surprise. I thought I was hearing things. I was a darkie, putting me up there.

The other time was in Tampa, Florida. It was a few days before Easter, and I was trying to make up my mind what kind of suit I wanted to get for Easter. I was merely standing there lookin' at the window. And this man grabbed me, and he said, "Say, nigger, don't you see that white woman standing there?" And I said, "Oh yeah?" "Then you take the sidewalk." Yes, I let him have it. I walked on. Well, I'm on my way anyhow, waiting for the train for Chicago. I walked down to the station. (Laughs.) And a crowd around there. "Well, then, what's all the excitement? What's happening?" "Oh, a crazy-ass nigger knocked a white man down." (Laughs.) I just walked around and went back to the station. Caught the train and came back to Chicago when I get that kinda stuff, in some kinda way I'm gonna knock it. I'd figure out a way. (Laughs.)

Some noticeable changes since I been in Chicago, almost fifty years. The first job that a Negro had on the transportation system, they'd taken the job away from some Italians, and I'll tell ya how it happened. They were laying that track from 51st and South Park to Cottage Grove, and there wasn't a man in the bunch that would say good morning to you. None of the colored boys was workin'. And some of 'em said, "What the hell are we gonna do?"

So one of the fellas said, "Follow me." So they fell all in line right there at 51st Street, and that gang of men walked up to them fellas that were working and take the shovels away from them. And told 'em to get the hell out of here. They'd taken them jobs, they'd been working on the surface line ever since. . . .

The biggest part of my time is spent over there at the clinic, from this one to the other. And the doctor's office. Then I love to walk. I catch hell about it, too. "Oh, you got no business doing all that walking." I do have asthma and a bad heart. But I love to walk. You take the majority of them, I could name you four or five in this here building, they go down the street, they'd get in the car and drive down. I light out here and I walk, two, two and a half, three miles. And I forget that I'm walking, I must enjoy it. I think if I'd given up, I don't think I'd be around here.

And I still love to be around children, and every one of them here in this project, almost: "There's Mr. Fulton." (Laughs.) One reason I work so damn hard with these little kids is to try to work some pride in 'em. Meaning of that, keeping the home and the vicinity around the home, keep it decent. It's not something to throw a lot of mud at and let it go. Because you go to a home and that home is neat and clean, right away you give that person living there a pride in themselves. Now of late, I haven't been able to, I've been laid up. . . .

You wanna know the other surprise? Here I am surprised again. You coming to me for information or something like that. (Laughs.)

Why shouldn't I? Why are you surprised?

Why am I surprised? Well, for the simple reason is this: I didn't think I was qualified. I'm not a speaker . . . I'm afraid I say something I ain't got no business.

XVI

"SEARCH FOR DELIGHT"

• • • • • • • • •

Barry Byrne, age indeterminate

A disciple of Frank Lloyd Wright, his is an honored career as a church architect. His home in Evanston, where he lives with his artist-wife, is "a house of delight," created early in the century by George Maher of Chicago's Prairie School.

Self-educated, he went to work at thirteen. His father was a railroad blacksmith, who read Shakespeare out loud, wrote poetry ("Nasty little prig that I was at ten, I didn't think it was good"), and fought along with Gene Debs in the Great Railroad Strike of '93. He was killed by a locomotive.

"Certainly I'm my father's son. His miscast lot, his thwarted ambition, is probably what drove me on. All I knew is I saw what I would be and that I would be desperately, desperately unhappy if I could not be that." *At the age of ten, he came across a book of plans and buildings; to be an architect was to be his life.*

"At fourteen, I remember standing in front of the Carson Pirie Scott Building,* as a woman, evidently of the upper class, passed by. She said to the man, "Aaahh, too gingerbready for words." I turned to my younger sister and said out loud, "This is one of the most beautiful buildings in the world." It was a "feeling" the boy had; "I thought this belonged."

An insatiable hunger for culture drove him to the library

---

* The Chicago department store built by Louis Sullivan in 1903-1904—"the jewel in his crown."

—*"Reading, reading, reading, I'd have read the telephone directory if it were the only book available"—concert halls, and the art institute. It was there he saw Wright's first exhibition of works. "After that, there was no architect for me but Frank Lloyd Wright." A series of letters and an amusing contretemps led to his employ in the home-studio of "the great man." He was seventeen. "I'm the little boy with the adolescent pimples in his autobiography."*

After seven years with Wright, he took off for Seattle to start his own practice. There were periods of travel and work in various parts of the world. He has come home to continue.

When I left Wright, I was twenty-four. I can't overrate what it meant to me in my life. To me, the place had always a sort of magic. It was too cold in the winter. You had to depend on the fireplace and the heat in the fireplace smoked. The floor had no basement under it and therefore was cold. All this was nothing. There was delight.

It was an easy going atmosphere. They had five children who raced through the studio back and forth. The father would pursue them and threaten them with dire happenings. One day somebody said, "What would you do if you caught one of them?" "Well," he said, "I really don't know. I'm very careful not to." Perhaps it was this feeling of—of improvisation that evoked a sense of delight.

Yet the Chicago I knew was vast and squalid. It was an inexpressively dreary city, without any delight. But again, you're caught into a sort of beat, you always move. Chicago was a place where things were done, a working place, probably too much so. It was a place where people initially came to make money. But it must also have that element in it that makes *living* in it an experience. To me the delight was to go to Lincoln Park and sit on the breakwater. Of course, it was an escape from surroundings that were not so good.

Slum clearance hasn't improved it. They have substituted a more sanitary type of squalor. It is not a shantytown any more, but possibly something worse. It is based on the mistaken premise that you can create a home environment if you give people all the "sanitary" necessities; that you therefore create an atmosphere in which they feel they can live. This is not true. While no one regrets the vanishing of the old slums, we also remember we once had neighborhoods. They have vanished, too. Without them, there can be no such thing as a city to which one feels held.

Chicago now? It's still in the throes of being born. Like every other city. Mumford is right. We haven't learned how to create cities; a city should be a place to live. I always feel a chest-swelling when I drive along the lake. I always respond to it. And yet I know four blocks over, there is desperation: the sanitary slums. Park Avenue in New York has become a slum with door-men.

I visited Logan Square* recently. It looked like a neighborhood. Then I realized it was in transition to something else. In modern life, everything works against the neighborhood idea. We are now a race of nomads. On our block here, there's a pleasant gentleman next door. Suddenly he's gone. Real-estate signs. Three other people, they're gone. They're gone.

The city is in a state of flux. The great problem is getting cars in and out of the city. The evil genius of the neighborhood is the car. We are passing into a society without roots. We must conquer the city or be conquered by it. Just as we must finally conquer the automobile and the other technological developments. Or become enslaved by them.

Architecturally, these housing developments are nothing, except that they look like institutions: an asylum, an orphanage, or a prison. Once we lived in a community. These sanitary prisons are not communities. There is an element of horror in these buildings. I deplore it, but they really belong in our age, they do. The monstrously ugly high-rises that are going up, they do belong.

The UN Building, what is it? A huge filing cabinet. That's what every office building is, a huge filing cabinet. The thing of living has gone from it. Its function in a society becoming dehumanized is to express that society. Its closeness to reality is in itself the indictment.

Ironically, then, form is following function?

Yes, if our function is a living death. No, if our function is life. And if advertising is our prime function—ad-

---

* An area on the city's Northwest Side.

vertising, our great curse—then form is certainly following that. This may be the chief cause of our age never having lived. Unless some big transformation occurs. In the highrises today, we don't have a piece of architecture, we have a piece of advertising.

There must be something akin to passion in a thing if it is to move you. What passion can you have for Prudential Life? Louis Sullivan transmuted his commercial buildings into something else. Advertising was not as dominant in our lives as it is today. . . .

In building Carson Pirie Scott, was he not serving a mercantile master?

No, no. He was expressing his own feelings in architectural terms, in mass and detail. It was effervescent. It is this that is missing. We are victims of our time. Even our greatest living architect, Mies van der Rohe. Sullivan made a *building* quite without reference to the display element, which is the essence of advertising.

His Auditorium* was a delight, with its infinite variety. In Wright and Sullivan, something of that was always there. You felt that thing you called inevitability. It lifted you to another plane and satisfied. Today, architectural form is just a bad manner. One fashion to be supplanted by another. The thing you wear today, you throw away tomorrow. It doesn't matter. But architecture is so damnably permanent. It lasts. It has the unhappy, unfortunate fate of lasting. Thus, it must have life-sources. Fashion does not.

As for passion or lack of it, consider church architecture today. How can there be religion without passion? You either believe or you don't believe. There is no middle ground. If I have a job designing a church, it is to make it indubitably a church. Today, as we look at the buildings around Chicago in the modern idiom, they could be anything. You put a cross on it to make certain they know it's a church. There is so much anonymity of purpose today that a church without a cross could be an office building or a factory. Its true purpose is not expressed.

---

* The Auditorium, concert and opera house of another day, built by Adler & Sullivan, is being rehabilitated.

Wright did not build the Unity Temple like one of his houses. The manner, the style, the man is all there. It was his way of *expressing what* the building was to be. *Organic* was his favorite word. When you look at a tree, it is a magnificent example of an organic whole. All parts belong together, not by labels or intellectual means, they just belong, as fingers belong to one's hands.

My vision—that's a glorious word for boyish thinking —came out of what Wright did. Not that he ever said it or taught it: he took the facts of existence as we know it in this country and we lived it; he saw its components, put them together freshly, and made them a new thing.

With Sullivan and Wright, it was highly personal. These depersonalized cults . . . Society exists—or should exist— for the person. Not the person for society. There is a coldness to our time. The warmth of personality is in every damn thing Wright ever did. I visit Katherine Lewis* out there, all I could do is just sit there and let it soak into me. This is it. You couldn't say it was this thing or that thing, the view of the Des Plaines River—you were just experiencing delight.

My first memory of Chicago was a neighborhood of the lower middle class. There was squalor, but it wasn't so to me because I could visualize a different life. While I'm not a Horatio Alger hero, what operated in me, operated in most of young America. We saw this and something better and desperately tried to climb out of it. Out of it but not *away* from it.

It was a place where people lived for quite a while. We knew everybody on the street. There was a tie of self-respect. They were aware of what hardship, a strike, might bring to a family, as it did to mine. But there was always a desire to help people—who were really so damn proud they didn't want help.

There was a snobbery in the process of rising. You want the greener field. Only when you reach it, you know it isn't so. To be more comfortable, that seems the end. When you get it, you know that isn't what you wanted at all. You meant excellence in something, something more spiritual. You get among the people that have the money, but

* Widow of Lloyd Lewis, Chicago historian, drama critic, and journalist, living in a Wright house.

that isn't what you meant. So you're willing to kick it away to go after the thing that is somewhat clearer to you now: a thing that more fully represents what you were struggling for.

I've always been guilty of a certain artistic snobbism: like pushing out of sight all the members of the Prairie School when I got to know Wright. Because they didn't fly as high as he. Only during these last few years, in remembering my boyhood, I can see how unjust I was to all these people. They didn't approach Wright in talent, but they were doing what they could do and were honest in their efforts. Some did it with charm, others not. So you finally respect not the lesser thing, but the man who does only what he can do. And, in some cases, you felt a letdown in certain men, whom you regarded as highly talented, but didn't measure up to what they had. And you know that life and the necessities of life had done the job with them. They've taken the lower level to live. See, the problem of making a living. (Laughs.)

Life pushed my father into being a blacksmith. He would like to have been a writer. Yet he met Eugene Debs. His god. It's a curious thing, today, with labor organized. And management, too. I think that's the one thing that marks us Americans apart. We are magnificent organizers. And that's what this age is a monument to. It has served a purpose. Finally it must be a question of whether this will be the thing that throttles us. We create the things that usually end up in getting us by the throat. This is not too happy a world. They talk of escapism. What's wrong with escapism? In true escapism, you're out of the material push, necessities. You're a man for a moment and you achieve peace.

Why did you return to Chicago?

This is the place I knew. I didn't want to experience new cities. This is the place where I feel at home. You go to the place where you feel at rest in. In a physical way, it may be a better city. Yet a question of values arises. Is another tradition coming into being—not like the one you regretted and thought should be changed—but equally as bad? Those virtues, so necessary for living, too.

We're caught in a treadmill we created. There really

isn't too much any human being can do to change it. If we, as St. Francis of Assisi, were of that simplicity of spirit, it might change. But that is not the way the world is, see?

And yet, in the individual must lie the way out, because he is society. It can't be ordered. It must be achieved. The achievement is so simple. It probably will not be done. Everybody looks for miracles, wonders. We live in an age of wonders. You long for something not wonderful, for something that is simple, yet is *yours*. You get tired of wonders. In the simplehearted person, finally, is the solution. A society so pervaded will make it. Not the doctrine of the announced idea. The man must listen to man himself talking.

I feel I've had a good life. I've had extraordinary enemies and extraordinary friends. And I'm still searching for delight. (Laughs.)

XVII

TEACHER

• • • • • • • • • •

Janice Majewski, 25

She was born in the house where she lives with her parents. Her brother and sister are married. It is in Bridgeport, the Mayor's neighborhood. Most of her married contemporaries—third generation Poles, Lithuanians, Italians, and fourth and fifth generation Irish—have moved to the suburbs. She suggests status-seeking as the primary reason rather than fear of change. She herself welcomes the changes in the city: more respect for the police, highways and high-rises. "I am a progress-minded person."

Though her parents fear and resent the imminent encroachment of strange peoples of strange colors, she, as a "student of history," accepts, indeed welcomes, change. "I see the American process at work again." She is engaged in Slavic studies at the University of Chicago and is amazed at people's ignorance of the richness of Polish literature, history, and culture.

She has but one fear: "Failure in life. My goals are many. This is my problem. I am very ambitious and very aggressive. It's not so good because this is pretty much a man's world. I always tell my students: I could desire with all my heart to be President of the United States, and have as much brains as the next man. By the very fact that I am a woman, I will never be President. I believe in tempering one's ambitions with one's sense of reality.

"High-school teaching is not the aim of my life, no. It is merely a transitory period."

I teach at John Marshall High School. It's about ninety-nine percent Negro. There is very little desire to expand themselves. The desire to learn is not reinforced in the home. So you have many problems with these students, because they feel they're serving time in high school, waiting until they're sixteen and can get out.

I'm quite satisfied with my relationship with my students. There is definitely no question, I am sure, in many of their minds, as to who establishes the order in the classroom. Whether this is a saving grace or not, I don't know. I don't like to use the word . . . well, let me use the word, authoritarian figure. Of course, this is a figure they understand. At home, their mother is often very strict, and many of these students, big boys oftentimes, stand in awe of their mother. She is *the* power figure at home, and outside the home there is always another power figure—the police, the gang, the biggest boy in the neighborhood. So power is something they will understand very well. One works with what they understand.

And I establish this order, very few rules in the classroom. As long as they obey these rules, fine. If they break these rules, there will be consequences. They understand this. Of course, you will have people who will break the rules, but they also accept the punishment, because they know they have done wrong. Establishing a power structure, that is what they understand.

I don't think the problems which arise in a school such as where I am would arise in a suburban school, such as rebellion—not rebellion, but a questioning of the power structure, and a real attempt to see how far they can get. I doubt this would occur in a suburban school.

When I say I'm dictatorial or authoritarian, it doesn't mean I don't give any leeway. No, really, I'm rather pleased with my relationship. It's a joking relationship with the students, it's not above saying: "Gee, why don't you take off, Miss M?" or "Don't you ever get sick?" or "How come you came today?" So we're on this joking relationship. But when it comes to their not doing their homework, and why should they do their homework, they don't like this. One does it because I have told them to do it and that's it.

I think they're rather happy. These students, like any adolescent child likes order, likes a sense of security, likes the feeling that someone is interested in them.

One thing that a teacher who has taught in a suburban

school mentioned. He was always surprised, when he walked in they would—five or six students would just come up and stand around his desk, and you know, just stand there. Some might say a few words to him and others would just look. They would for a few minutes just stand around him while he got his books out or his papers or chatted and so forth. They would just stand there, wanting to, say, be near the fountain of power, let's put it. Wanting to have the warmth of someone they knew, and someone who's in a respected position, talk to them. In a suburban school, you walk in and everyone is in his seat, they might say good morning and that was that. No one ventured to come up in the class to the desk unless they had a serious problem. No one wanted to come up to the desk.

Which type of student do you prefer?

I can't honestly answer because I have not had this one kind. I respond rather well to a human response. If someone needs you, you respond to them. Now I would like my students to be more intellectually inclined. I myself am this way, and I get very annoyed and very frustrated at times because they have no intellectual curiosity. They will barely learn what you put in front of them. This is, of course, not at all pleasing, and probably in this respect, I would have a greater sense of accomplishment in an area where students are halfway interested.

Within every class, there's one person who's worth it. This is what keeps most of us going in the final analysis, I suppose. Maybe there's more sometimes. But usually there's at least one, who now and then will do something, or show in some way, that your efforts are not totally in vain.

I am coming swiftly to the conclusion, in many of these areas, the type of education is not the correct kind. Rather more of a vocational would give these students . . . these students are frustrated themselves . . . it's beyond them to learn. The litany of American presidents is beyond them to learn. What the New Deal was or what effect Roosevelt had on the American society, they're not interested. It won't help them in any way.

Yet teach them, giving them a trade like printing or carpentry or the electrician, this is bread and butter. This they understand. They understand in dollars and cents. This is what will give them status. Certainly not the fact that they can name the presidents from Abraham Lincoln on.

You teach history?

Yes, American and European.

Do you ever tell them about the Negro and history?

Oh yes, they're very interested. I bring it in whenever I can. Almost none of our books have anything on this, but I think the Board of Education is contemplating within the next year to use history books that have inserted a chapter on Negro history. Yes, I bring this in, and we have discussions often in class. These students at this school. . . . I think it would be different on the South Side, because the South Side is more militant. The West Side is very lethargic, and many students in some of these classes you'll ask them who Martin Luther King is, and they will know he's a Negro, but exactly what he is or who he is or what he has done is very vague in their minds.

But, you see, it's not so much especially a history of accomplishment, is it? It is simply . . . they were slaves and in 1863 were set free, and since then they haven't accomplished much until 1960. Now and then, here and there, there has been a scattering of notable Negroes, yet these are few and far between. I try to constantly get them to—I will give them certain names, like Ralph Bunche, who was he? Well, no one's ever heard of him. He is, you know, Assistant Ambassador to the UN, a very highly placed diplomat in the present American diplomat corps. They have very little curiosity, you know. In the middle-class Negro areas, I venture to say this would, of course, be different.

Are home problems ever brought forth in class?

Oh yes, oh yes. Because the child doesn't have his homework in. Why? He works from three-thirty till one o'clock. He's the sole support for his family. Or, Why are you late to school? "My father is sick and he's living on the South Side and I had to stay up all night with him." A child is truant for two weeks. Why? He ran away from home because his mother is a prostitute. And he couldn't stand it any longer, coming home and finding her with a different man. And so forth and so on. These things, this is very much the way of life.

How about your colleagues at the school? Do they share your feelings?

Yes, I think Marshall has quite a decent faculty. Many of them are very devoted people, fairly young and quite understanding. Of course, there are, naturally, individuals who are not so enthused, don't really care. Perhaps mine is not overbounding enthusiasm, but I feel a sense of responsibility whether I enjoy the job overly or not. I will do it as best as I can.

No, I don't enjoy it too much. It leaves much to be desired. Now I will say it has been a very profound experience, and one I don't regret. It has taught me an awful lot about life in general. There is so much you can learn from books. But after that you have to get out and grapple with it yourself. I always tell my students, I do not recognize aristocracy of birth. I only recognize aristocracy of character.

• • • • • •

Judy Huff, 24

Like Miss Majewski, she teaches at Marshall High. Last year, she taught general science. This year, math.

She was born and raised in a small Florida town. "I was a very stubborn child who always liked to take the other side of the question. As far back as sixth grade, we had debates: integration versus segregation. Some not terribly bright teachers, who thought we'd evenly divide up, said anybody could take whatever side of the question they'd like. Very often, it was twenty-nine for segregation and me for integration. Mostly because I was so stubborn. I argued so hard, I became in favor of it. Which did not please my family terribly well."

297

She came to Chicago four years ago and with it, "my first chance to even meet and speak to a Negro person as another human being." She is married to a young Methodist minister. They live at the Ecumenical Institute, a seminary located in the heart of the black ghetto on the West Side.

I'd rather teach here than any place I can think of. I love it. I'd keep on teaching even if the pay stopped, you know. I just enjoy it. Oh, I'm strict when I have to be. That's usually on first contact with the students, so they'll know I'm serious.

There are some students who would never get their work done unless you're strict with them. It's kind of puzzling, because in the same class they get rebellious if you're too strict, and don't do anything. So you sort of coax them along, you sort of love them, and oh, I sometimes feel like I have to go hold their hand: yes, go ahead, you can do the work, I know you're ready to do it. It's a very individual thing. I like to get to know all my students plans for the future and impressions of the school and the city and so on. It's hard, there's very poor attendance, but I make strong efforts to do this.

This lack of interest in school strikes me as being in some ways good as well as bad. It's almost delightful to see the lack of mean competition and wanting to get ahead and so on that you get in a suburban school. I think there's a lot less cheating in Marshall High than in a suburban school. The students haven't placed such an unrealistically high value on grades or getting to college to get ahead. They don't go out of their way to cheat for a higher grade.

There are plenty of students here that are very bright, excellent. They'll go to college. They're honor students, they don't need to cheat. Besides, there's no one around to cheat from. The people with average ability or less don't feel this push from their parents to get ahead, to get better grades, to go to college, like your average student does in the suburbs. It's the average student that does so much of the cheating in the suburbs or small-town high schools. I know. It happened in my own school. They go to college to make the grade. And nobody knows where they're going. It's the parents that want them to.

Here, ADC mothers would like their children to go to college, too. But they don't have enough money to support them. Unless the student is bright enough to win a scholarship. There's just not the push anywhere. Those that aren't capable don't overwork themselves trying to do what they're incapable of doing. Of course, there are some that don't think they're capable that I think are. I do my best to prod them along a little.

The main thing is to give them a feeling that if they really put their whole self in working for it, they're going to be able to do it. I shocked every student the first day I walked into math class. I told them all: "If you want to pass math, you can. Anybody in this class who wants to pass bad enough, really put work in it, I'll pass you. If you aren't doing quite well enough, but I can see you're putting your whole effort into it, that's fine. And I hope everyone who fails will come up when the semester's over and say, 'Mrs. Huff, I really didn't want to pass math.' " (Laughs.)

It's a young faculty, both white and Negro, and, I think, with a very exciting attitude toward teaching. Of course, there are exceptions. Complaints not very plainly put, but side comments that they don't expect much from these students; you know, Negro students are like that, naturally lazy, they don't care. This has come from very few teachers here. But from enough to make me wish they weren't here, that they'd find themselves an all-white suburban school.

Then you prefer teaching at an inner-city Negro school than at a white suburban school?

Very definitely. Many teachers here agree with me. It's more of a challenge. And then, this horrible, unrealistic competition isn't there. I've heard teachers say they don't like the spotlessly clean, beautiful suburban schools with everything just so, that they were happy to be back in the inner city. The students running around . . . I'm not quite sure how to explain it.

It's less the high social type. Of course, it would be exciting to work with suburban students doing work comparable to college work, projects or whatever. But somehow the students here are more down to earth, more real-

299

istic about life. They know there are problems, the slums they live in. The suburbanites are oblivious to this. They know intellectually they're there, but they have no *feeling* about it.

I've never felt any fear here at all. I don't know why. It never occurred to me. This year, two great big boys, much larger than I, were yelling at each other and starting to swing. I just calmly walked over and stood between and told them to cut out the nonsense. And that was that.

Any idea how your students feel about you here?

The last couple of days at school, I let them all sign my yearbook. And the comments were just ridiculously flattering. It's *impossible* for all the students to think I'm their favorite teacher. (Laughs.) I'm sure they write in ten different teachers' yearbooks: You're my favorite teacher. I expect to be somebody's favorite teacher, but not everybody's.

I like to take a lot of extra time with students. Some don't like me and are very clear about it, because I expect them to work. As long as they're willing to work, I'm willing to go all out. Come in two hours early or stay hours late, if necessary. In fact, I might push them into staying: "You don't understand this? You darn well better be there after school, so I can explain this to you."

. . . I took a week off from school to go to Selma. My thinking was I could come back and tell something they were really interested in. It makes it much more exciting to them to know someone who was there personally, who could tell them what the teenagers were down there and doing.

Did they ask you a lot of questions?

All kinds. I know I got carried away explaining it, because one boy was very impressed when I used a few slang words, about how I met "these really swinging people." Since then, he refers to me as "that cool-talking teacher."

One of my students, Douglas, was telling me how he earned his money. Gambling, pool, stealing. He's reformed now. I asked him what he was going to do with all the money when he got it and he was puzzled. He didn't know. He'd give it away to people, his grandmother, his mother, and then he'd go out and get some more. You had to have money to be something. But once you get it, you don't know what to do with it. He was a strange and wonderful student. Among other things, he explained how one lives by cheating at dice and warned me to watch out: that I'd be smart to play on a rough surface, like a sidewalk. (Laughs.) I sometimes learn a lot more from them than they do from me. (Laughs.)

I taught Douglas to do long division. It was part of a tutoring program, where a student having trouble comes in one or two days a week. He's a freshman in high school and seventeen years old. When I was teaching science, he was in my class and did absolutely nothing. He'd come in with his black leather jacket, which is against the rules, and his hat, and he'd go to the back seat and sleep or pretend to be sleeping. But he came so seldom that as long as he wasn't bothering anybody, I wasn't going to bother him.

The next semester he came back and ended up in my math class. The first day he walked in with his black leather jacket and his hat on, he didn't look very changed. He went to the back seat and slumped down. Halfway through the period, he sat up and looked at me. He raised his hand and says, "Say, aren't you my science teacher?" (Laughs.) He really wasn't very sure. I said, "Well, you ought to know. Am I your science teacher?" (Laughs.) And he said, "You sure look like her."

For the next two weeks he became a completely changed person. He'd slip into the room and strut around and make some bright wisecracks in a completely incomprehensible slang. One day he said, "Say there, you just crawl out of the old shopping bag?" (Laughs.) I said, "I don't know." I had to figure what in the world do you do with people who say things like this. So I made it a habit of asking him what they all meant. That one meant: Are you accusing me of being something wrong? I told him these sayings were so interesting, I'd go home and try them out on my husband.

All of a sudden, he became, you know, a *student*. He worked at his work and so on. He came up with no idea how to do anything you expect of a high-school student in math. He did passing work, which was quite an accomplishment. After seventeen years of not paying attention in class, it's kind of difficult to get back in the habit. He could do problems that very few other students in the class were capable of doing. He's constantly explaining to me ways of doing things. He doesn't know his multiplication tables, but he can figure any combination in such a weird, roundabout method that makes little sense to me. It takes him a while to do it and he draws all sorts of pictures and diagrams, but all of a sudden he pretty well knows what he is. He's one of my most promising students.

He was what we call under contract. Being over-age and having been kicked out of school once, he was allowed back in on only one condition. For the first year, he was not to fail any course at all, not to cause any trouble, and not to cut classes. If he got into any trouble he'd be permanently kicked out and not allowed back into Chicago schools.

Since I'd been working with him, I was naturally concerned, and wondered how he was doing in his other classes. I kept asking him: "How are you doing? Are you gonna pass?" And he'd say, "Oh sure, I'm doing fine." I knew that wasn't quite true. Marking time came up, and I kept saying, "Douglas, how you doing? Are you gonna make it? Are you gonna pass everything?" Finally, about two days before, he said, "I'm doing all right in everything, but I'm not too sure about the shop class."

I talked to the shop teacher that afternoon. He was not aware that Douglas was under contract. He had planned to fail him and that would be the end of his high-school career. So he agreed to give him a D-minus, on condition that Douglas would do extra work to make up for what he hadn't done. So he made it through on straight D-minuses that time.

The next time through, I decided I couldn't go back to the same teacher and ask for mercy again. It was the understanding that Douglas would get to work. All I could do was ask him: "Are you really working?" And he'd say yes. And I would hope that was the truth. The last day came. Douglas was still swearing he was gonna pass everything.

The grades for all the students are laid out on tables in the library. The students aren't there that day. I was so worried about him. I'd take turns putting my grades in and running back to see what grades had been put in his book. Little by little, his grades got in. All passing, mostly D's, a couple higher. They were all in, except this one shop grade. I was getting more and more fidgety. And then fiinally it was there. It was a C. Not only had he done acceptable work, but he had really come up quite a way.

I was just so delighted, I went skipping down the hall sort of childishly, almost singing. (Laughs.) You know, "He did it! He did it!" Like I had done something great instead of him. It was almost as if I had passed the course myself. (Laughs.) It was a great victory.

• • • • • •

Marlene Dexter, 26

She is currently a playground instructor in the employ of the Chicago Board of Education. She has a degree in physical education, and at one time was working toward her master's degree in education.

She has lived all her life in Chicago. Her father was a barber and her mother was "almost a nurse." After working hours, she attends a local charm school. Appearance is very important to her. "I like fashionable things and I like nice clothes. Because of my father—the professional aspect—you have to be neat and clean. I was brought up like that. Walk properly, feet forward. You don't walk like a duck. Don't slump over. How to hold your hands, how to take out a coat, how to carry a purse, how to get in and out of a car properly, how to sit with a cup of coffee in your hand, how to sit on the floor and get up gracefully —this education is something they can never take away from you. I tell all my friends these hints. I'm not selfish about it at all."

When in college, it had been suggested she become a model, "but it's too rough and tough and your looks don't last that long and it's dog eat dog." She loves her job.

I subbed for six months at Marshall High School as a gym teacher. But then I quit, the neighborhood was too much. Ninety percent colored. I was so outnumbered. I felt uncomfortable because I was a white girl. It all stems

303

from my background. My father was raised in Louisville. I minded my own business because my father always used to say: If they say hello to you you say hello back, but you never turn your back on 'em. Because you can't trust them. In other words, they might stab you in the back, you never know. All through this bein' brought up with a little bit of this Southern prejudice, it kinda worked on my subconscious mind.

This is when I was twenty-four, when I just got out of college. And anyway, all the fellas I was going out with, they warned me to be careful and park my car. Because they see a blonde walking out and a new car and everything—I was just a little leery. Fellows I've gone out with, they wouldn't appreciate my working with colored children.

There was other things beside it. When I was in the school, the teachers that were there were old enough to be my mother. Here I was just out of college and I got the dirty work. The jobs they didn't like—taking the pool, working the house classes and some of the gym classes that they didn't like. I just felt, "I'm on an equal basis with you. I went to college, too. Just because I'm young, you shouldn't give me the dirty work." That's the way I felt about it.

I had no trouble with the students. You blew the whistle when you told them what exercises and what to play. There was no trouble there. Maybe I didn't give it enough time, only six months. No trouble as far as that goes, but the idea of it . . .

If I had the opportunity of going back into schools, I would take the Far Northwest Side school. I'm not too prejudiced, but I like working with those type of white children. Your mediocre-class students. Because I feel that these parents are more concerned about their children. If their children are failing, they want to know why. And if they're not in school, you can call up home and find out what's the matter with them.

If a Negro parent came from an upper-middle-class neighborhood, they would take the time, too. But in the school system, they need teachers in the lower-income bracket, where the parents are from ADC. They're divorced and you don't know who the father is and they don't care about their children. They're in a tavern or they're out working. To me, they just don't take the time.

They don't care about their children?

Oh, they do. I guess in a way any parent . . . but maybe they feel so down and that the world is on their shoulders. They just do the best they can, and if their kid gets in trouble, they'll rationalize or make some kind of an excuse.

Right now where I work in the playground, I can name you ten little girls whose mothers and fathers are divorced or they're in the tavern drinking. And they're white people from Chicago. I don't think they're satisfied with what they have. They're displeased with their husbands or displeased with life. They have to go sit in a tavern and have a man go sit next to them and buy them drinks and build up their ego. These whites are also doing it but it's not that well known.

I would say a lot of your white teachers refuse to work in the colored area. Most of my friends are teachers, and they don't like to work with colored children. As far as your athletics, you'll find your Negroes are tops, especially your track, your high jump, and your broad jump. But when it comes to discipline problems, those little kids carry knives around with 'em.

I work with girls. I like the ones that have ability but maybe they're a little lazy and you have to push 'em and drive 'em, because I like to push 'em and drive 'em and make 'em work. I like to work with a child that has the ability but they don't think they have the ability. I like to encourage them: they can learn how to smack a volley ball or hit a baseball or learn how to swim. I like to give them a sense of security. Right now, I would prefer working with white children. Because I'd feel more secure myself.

· · · · · ·

Nell Robison, 47

John Robison's wife. After her father's death, she and her mother came to Chicago—1924. They were related to the two most prominent white families in the Mississippi town. "An old man used to come to the house and say, 'I'm your grandfather's daddy.' He was white." It was no secret to the town.

Most of her white friends are involved with civil rights and peace. Her middle-class Negro friends are not concerned. They are ashamed and resentful of the project people. "There's a certain kind of poverty they don't understand. They don't understand the poverty of spirit that comes from this, no hope. The middle-class Negro takes on the white man's mind. He thinks these people really are undeserving. They admire Martin Luther King because it's respectable to do so. They don't admire SNCC. 'You must be careful not to associate with the wrong people.' They don't like the uninhibited feeling. They think you should suppress your feelings.

"I think I was born a little rebellious, perhaps. As a child in Mississippi, we were very poor, but there were other people who were poorer. My relatives looked down upon the other people. My mother at the time thought very much as they did. I'm very happy to say, she's grown." (Laughs.)

At Wendell Phillips High, I just remember being a scared little girl. One of my big memories is not being able to understand the Northern speech. It was quick. I became very sensitive about my own, especially since I was from Mississippi. People made fun of you if you were from Mississippi.

There was one teacher, Mrs. Cutler. She could read poetry, oh, very beautifully. She told us about Negro poets. Langston Hughes was popular at the time and so was Countee Cullen. She made poetry live for you. I had always been very poor in English. I think it was probably due not only to my background but to my fear. I felt that anybody in America could do anything better than I. When we had to write a book report, I thought I couldn't, I just couldn't. I had never written anything before. I remember one night being rather sleepy. I just sat down and wrote fast, but I wrote down what I really felt and handed it in the next morning. I was so afraid and I was ashamed because I had put down what I had actually felt. The paper came back and there was an E on it. (Laughs.)

In working with mentally handicapped children, I found that many of them were afraid. They were timid just as I was. That's why it was such a challenge to me. I felt if you could put them at their ease, if you gave them confidence, you could get a great deal more from them. I've been working with them now for ten years.

When they come in, they're usually very unhappy. They know this isn't just another room. Some of them call it the dummy room. But later, when they're given work they can do, they enjoy it. You can't keep a child in as a means of punishment, because he likes it. I've tried it with children and the next day they say, "Oh, I'm not going out to recess. I'm going to stay here with you." (Laughs.) They like the attention they get.

If they think you care about them, they don't mind any punishment. The children you've had to correct the most are the ones who love you the most. They come back to see you year after year. There was a little boy in kindergarten who was quite troublesome. When he went to first grade, I was so happy. But every day at recess, he came right down to the kindergarten,* and every day at noontime he was down there, and at 3:15 he was escorting me up to the office to sign out. Later he was transferred to a Catholic school. They're out at 11:30. So at 11:30, there he was, knocking on the window of the kindergarten. (Laughs.)

The children with the greatest problems—who seemingly would be afraid that I had something unpleasant to tell their parents—are very happy when they say, "Miz Robison, my mother's coming to school! She's coming to school to see about *me!*" They get to talking about the bad things they've done and they'll say, "Oh, you know I did this and my mother nearly skinned me alive!" They seem proud of the fact that the mother cared. They can't bear indifference.

They may not progress very rapidly academically, but they have a good sense of values that is frequently lacked by "normal" children. They have a good sense of loyalty toward each other. Sometimes one child looks at another with such understanding when there's something he's

---

* Mrs. Robison taught kindergarten before taking over the class for mentally handicapped children.

trying to get and can't get. There's a sympathetic understanding. They don't make fun of one who stumbles. When a child achieves something that's very difficult, they're very happy about it. They're proud of it, the child who's made the game.

There's one little boy who sits in front of me. He never smells very well. I think he sleeps in bed with the baby and in the clothes he wears during the day. But this boy can read my mind. Before I can speak of what I want, he's handing it to me. He seems to anticipate everything.

I like music. So I give the children a lot of it. One boy, who was not interested in school and not very clean, liked the music. He'd put his hand on his chin and listen to the tape-recorder. One day I had a tape on from the Jubilee Singers. And after, Maria Callas. I thought, oh my goodness, this boy, he isn't going to like her. He'll probably make fun of her operatic voice, he's not used to hearing it. But when she came on, he looked up and said, "Oh now, she can really sing, can't she?" (Laughs.)

I remember playing some of Copland's music, *Billy the Kid,* and they said, "Oh, listen to the cowboys, listen to the cowboys." And they began making motions of riding around on ponies. (Laughs.)

Some parents are ashamed of their children being in this room. They will not accept it. They usually think the child is lazy. Some are ambitious for the children. They don't want them to do the kind of work they're doing. They tell them, "I want you to be a schoolteacher," or, "I want you to have a white-collar job when you grow up." It's very difficult to make the parents understand.

Causes? Many. Sometimes it's due to brain damage that occurs when the child is being born. Prenatal care, if the mother doesn't get the proper treatment . . . of course, the low-income family frequently doesn't get the proper care. It's an all-Negro school.

We talk a lot about races because they're big children and they are very aware of things. When a white person does something for Negroes, I make a point of talking about it. They came to school talking about the three boys who were murdered in Mississippi. They come and tell you about it and describe it. So I wrote Mrs. Chaney and Mrs. Schwerner and Mrs. Goodman a letter. They answered. I read it in class to my children and told them about the boys: what kind of boys they were and anecdotes from their lives. We use their names frequently, especially when we have phonics. I'll say, "Give me a word that has an *a* short in it." And they say, "Oh, like in Andy." Or a "long *a* like in Chaney." We make a point of using these names whenever possible. My children became very interested in them. They'd say, "Miz Robison, do you know what this boy has done? That's not the sort of thing Andy Goodman would do, is it?"

You get to appreciate other qualities than just the mere ability to read very well or do arithmetic. You yourself develop just being with them. How warm and how small they are. How human. It gives you some faith.

I don't think there will be any Utopia. I think there will be progress. However, I realize there can be retrogression. In Germany, the Jews were highly respected. They had education, economic independence, they had all the cultural attainments the Negroes now are seeking. Yet there was a depression and along comes Hitler. I don't think the future's really too bright. . . .

Religious people have such faith. It's such a solace to them in times of tribulation. I'm sure those dark days will come and then what do I have? Do I have any faith in something to cling to? Do I have something to believe in? I have faith in a few individuals that I know. I have a faith in people who are working for ideals. When I make a contribution to these things, I wonder if it's worthwhile. But I think of the person who is following a dream and I can't let him down, even though he's in a very, very small minority. I suppose they're the fortunate ones, the ones who have a dream.

XVIII

MAKING IT

• • • • • • • • • •

Gene Willis, Revisited

Now he is one of the owners of another tavern on the Near North Side; his clientele, the same sort of "swingers" who patronized the place where he had worked as a bartender.

You make your own break the best way you can. If I had to shovel streets for some guy for ten years and finally I can move up and own the sidewalk, I mean that's the break you take. I have many more things I want to do. I hope to get in real estate and buy some more things. But this takes time and I'm just a young guy anyways. Buy a couple of apartment buildings and let 'em pay . . . just like anything else. As soon as I can. It costs me a lot to live. I'm not a millionaire but I'd rather go first class and go out once a week than go out and spend forty cents a night and sit around and worry about having a good time. Find a good-lookin' chick, a few bucks in your pocket, and you can go many ways. I'm a high roller.

A high roller is after I've had a couple of drinks. If I walk into a bar and I see three guys and they're with ten people, I buy everybody a drink. I always leave a deuce or three bucks tip because I been in the business. Always paid my way. That's a high roller. I can't see a guy that worries about a nickel or a dime, because then he's in trouble.

I have a nice apartment that runs into a lotta dough. Very high-rise, seventeenth floor, overlooking the whole thing. My average day? After I kick my girl out . . . I get up at ten o'clock, breakfast, shower, the whole bit. Then we get a golf game going and we play in the afternoon. Then I cry for an hour while I have a drink, while I count all the money I lost. Grab a date about five o'clock for a drink or so. Dinner. Then I go to work. About nine now. I'm through at four. Whatever's happening, of course, you never know what's happening around Near North. You always try to grab something, so you never know what you're doing.

My philosophy is that I have only one life to live, and it's enough the way I'm doing. I don't have room for anything else.

A ginger man, he recounts his early life and some pica-resque experiences. Father, a burlesque comic, alcoholic. Mother, several bad-luck marriages. All-state basketball player out East. "We used to get CARE packages from Europe, sort of that kind of family, that's how poor we were." Coast to coast, after the army. Bellhop, fired for "pushing booze, pushing broads." Bartender at posh joints and those less so; pocketing about $125 a week on the side; shilled at a Las Vegas casino; swung all the way on a Diner's card left by some drunk at a bar; running up $600 hotel bill, friend stuck with it, but getting away with "tow-els, peppermills, dishes, glasses, the whole bit." Arrived in Chicago a year ago.

Do you ever feel guilty about this stuff?

About what stuff?

You know, when you . . .

No, shit, no. I believe the world is based on gettin' a little bit of the pie, everything's hunky-dory. But as soon as you're not gettin' it, the first thing you say is, "Why aren't I in that?" And of course it's not right. But show me a person that's not makin' a few bucks on the side, god-dam it. I believe that everybody, if they make a little bit more, get a little greedier, and they want a little bit more. There are a certain amount of straight arrows, they don't know any better. But they got a lotta dough or they don't care. But give like a guy that come up and he's up there by cutting a few fences, he's not gonna stop cuttin' fences.

It's too late for him to stop cuttin' fences. When you cut a fence, you have to involve somebody else usually. So everybody's always helping somebody, one way or the other. Most guys I know would do anything for a buck. (Laughs.)

Like Vietnam. People think the reason whoever are get-tin' their ass shot off, we love the other guy. I don't know anybody who wants to get his ass shot off because he loves somebody else. It's not that way. The pressure is on us from the guy with the big buck. We have a lot of money invested. You have to go that way. With more power, you make more money. The Russians want the same thing. How does it change? Take the guy that sells peanuts. He's tryin' to make more peanuts, that's all. Or take the guy with more dough that's selling gold bars, it's the same.

Chicago is the only area of a big city that I've ever been, like in the Near North where I know everybody. They're all good people. A lotta bullshit goes on there, but you have to pass on it. I have a brother I brought back with me. He's bartending. He's a nice kid, but he's got so much shit that it's unbelievable. He's just a dreamer. He never had anything, you know. He bought a T-Bird, so he can impress the girls. He tells 'em he owns planes, yachts, and all this sort of stuff. Fantasy. A terrible dreamer. I don't mind it, but when I'm talkin' to a broad, I don't want him to lie.

Suppose one of your bartenders did what you did?

Impossible. You don't swing in this area, because you don't work in this area again if you do. The difference is in L.A., you can go anywhere and get a job with no refer-ence. There are thousands of bars in L.A. and it's so spread out. Here a guy who swings wouldn't go anywhere. You can't get away with anything here.

But I don't bother anybody and I don't like anybody to bother me. If I were walkin' down the street and they were robbin' a bank, the guy would walk out and say, "Hi, Gene, how are you?" And if I knew him or didn't know him, I'd say, "Hi, how are you?" And as long as he didn't step on my foot while I was walkin' by the bank, let him do what he wants to do. It's none of my goddam business. I could care less. (Indignantly.) Nothin' bothers me more than people that are tryin' all the time to say, "Oh, did you see what he did over there?" It's none of your business, he's not bothering you. If nobody hurt me, let them do what they want to do. I'm glad they're gettin' away with it. If they can get away with it, all the more power to 'em, that's their business. If I were a police officer, then of course that's my problem. I'm pleasant, get along, courteous.

I'll tell you what I want in life. I'd like to have a nice home in Evanston, on the lake. I'd like to have a ranch in Mexico, where I could retire a couple of months. I'd like to have a girl with a lot of qualities: intelligence, good-looking, which is tough to find, a little common sense, which could be very important. With high ideals, which you don't find around here. Morals. Broads around here, Christ, they screw you one night and they wanna screw someone else the next night, and they could care less. And they lie to you. I got all the broads I can handle now.

I'd like to find somebody that could be a companion. Some girl that you have to bend and sway. The way I am now, I could care less with the girls I meet. I'd like a girl you can discuss things, you can do things together, the important things. Respect and faith. Respect is the most important. You can't do anything in this life without respect for the other person. Once you lose respect for anybody, you can't go anywhere. If I find the right girl, I'll marry her tomorrow.

What kind of people would you like your kids to be?

Just like me. I want 'em to work like I have. I want 'em to be open-minded like I am. I want them to be respectful and respect myself because I demand respect. If you don't respect me, I don't want you because I don't need you. I want the kids to have a good education which I never got. And I want a very close-knit family, because the close-knit family is the whole thing.

I like people. If you know somebody, you can give him an even break, and if you don't know him, you screw him. When I wake up in the morning, there's only one person thinking about me and that's me. If I were God, I couldn't say anything else that's different, because where else could you go? Everybody's human. You have to change the

313

human being to change the world. The world is beautiful in itself, terrain-wise and etcetera. Everybody has greed, lust, and wants power, so you can't do it differently. As long as there's man, then that's it.

• • • • • • •

Norma Blair, mid-fifties

We're in a three-room flat, to the rear of the grocery store owned by Norma and her husband, Horton. They came to Chicago from western Tennessee in 1943. They have been on this corner sixteen years. It is on the Northwest Side; an ethnically mixed neighborhood, it's latest arrivals are Appalachians and Puerto Ricans. Negroes work in the area, but don't live there.

They own two buildings on the block, a two-flat on this side of the street and, kitty-corner, a four-flat. No vacancies. "We got a guy, he keeps comin' back, bought his own furniture. 'When's them people gonna move. I'm gonna sell my furniture an' move in. That's the on'y place feels like home to me.' There's two or three guys beggin' for a place." They own a rooming house "back home" in Tennessee as well as a large private dwelling, surrounded by a lake.

Her mother was a "widder woman with eight kids." Though she was a sharecropper, they always had "plenty to eat and plenty to wear" because her mother was a good "seamster." Flour sacks and grass sacks were dyed and looked like linen clothes. "She worked in the field and stayed up till one o'clock sewin' for us. I don't know how she done it, but she did it."

Horton works days for International Harvester, building heavy construction machinery. She runs the grocery store. He belongs to the Masons. She's about to join the Eastern Star. They are childless.

I guess I worked all my life since I been big enough. So that's all I think of doin'. I worked on a farm till I got old enough to work in a shirt factory. I wouldn't know what to do without it. Sometimes I get the idea I'd like to sell this place. Even if I'd get ready to retire, I think I'd keep it open two, three days a week. I worked in a little town. I'm workin' in a big town. I'm no more comfortable here, as far as that goes.

I watch television if I get a chance. I don't get much of a chance, runnin' this store. You open six or seven o'clock, you run till eight that night. I'm sorry I don't go to church much. I don't have time. I could close up an' go, I guess. But people around here won't let me. If I'm not out there, I think they'd have the police lookin' for me. Sundays, too. If I didn't stay open on Sundays, I'd just have to close my doors. I make more money on Sunday than I will three days in the week. So if you got a job, you gotta do it, that's all.

I don't go out too much but people tells me it's awful bad out. 'Course when I go, I go in the car and just come right in an' out of the car an' come back in. I don't think I'd want to get too far from home, out walkin'. That's the way that people are *sayin'* it's gettin'. They say they snatch their purses, knock 'em in the head, an' beat 'em up and things like that. It's never happened to me. We've never been held up or robbed or anything.

I spent an awful lot of time here by myself. I don't think about bein' afraid. I just come back here an' lock all my doors an' go to bed. He stayed in the hospital fifty-six days, I was here every night by myself. I never thought anything about it.

Biggest majority of people works around here. We've got a few who don't. I just run my store, take care of my place. There's a lot of women around here that works. It seems that their children is under better control than those that don't work.

It seems every year the kids get worse about swipin' things. Just aggravatin' ya, slammin' doors an' hollerin'. They used to didn't do that way so bad. I guess there's just more children around or something or other.

I don't think their parents are bad. I know these women, they're good women. But they just set in the house all day long, they don't pay no 'tention how many times the children goes out, how many times they comes in or even come in. They're nice people, you know. But somehow or 'nother, it seems they don't care what times the childrens comes or goes.

If I had children, I'd see they wasn't out with a rough gang and then I'd bring 'em in, feed 'em, make 'em sit

315

down an' read books, or look at television or go to bed. Course I don't say these women drink or maybe their husbands go in the tavern or maybe they got double jobs. Maybe they work day an' night. Some of these women, they just don't know how to get along when their husbands are not there. They just set there an' brood. Maybe they figure they're out with another woman. They just don't pay any attention to the children.

I don't know what they do. They don't get out an' go to the store. The kids'll come home for lunch. They gotta go to the house, get their money, come over here and buy soup, bread, stuff for their lunch, and I cain't see that. The little ol' kids, they gotta come an' get that, then they gotta go back and they gotta fix it an' then they've gotta rush back to school.

All the mothers thinks other kids are mean and their children's okay. If they happen to ask me, I can tell 'em. They cain't tell me one's better'n this or that or the other. Because I put up with 'em all day long. I got 'em more'n their mothers. I correct 'em more'n some of their mothers. They mind me pretty good. Some of them mothers tell me "If my kids do anything, you just let 'em have it." I say, "You know I will, with my tongue." "Well, spank 'em." I says, "No, I ain't gonna do that." They wanta get them outa *their* hair.

Swipin', that makes me mad. If they were hungry, if it was food, but it's not food. It's somethin' other. We had two boys walked in here, and by golly, if they didn't take a hundred foot of that clothesline, and you just know they're not gonna eat that. They throw it down in the street. It's just: I bet I can get away with somethin' you can't. I don't think they really care about it.

Only thing I know is maybe their mothers and daddies are in a big squabble at home and maybe not gettin' along, so they're not payin' any attention to their children.

We had our business in Tennessee before he went off in the service. We was thinkin' of gettin' a ten-cent store. We looked into it, but there was a man ahead of us had his bid in. We coulda went to Mobile, Alabama, we coulda went to southern Illinois. We went to see this broker about another store an' he told us of this one. So we bought it.

I had colored people come here in the store but they don't never bother me. As long as they stay in their place an' don't try to mistreat me, I haven't got nothin' to say against 'em. I have a lot of colored customers. There's a factory down here works nothin' but colored. They work two and three shifts there. One man's money's as good as the other one.

We all born in the world, we got our place, I suppose. Fact of the business, I was practically raised by a colored woman. My mother was sick. There was on'y one colored family lived in our neighborhood. She practically taken care of us kids. Fed us, washed for us an' everything. And spanked us. I never did feel bad toward them.

We had our own business back home. We had a house-to-house route, sellin' milk. The colored boy would lift all the milk for me. When Horton went into the service, I'd just drive and collect all the money and he'd do the work for me. I used to make Nigger Town. And the niggers'd say: "You all be quiet, here come Miz Blair." They'd be raisin' heck in that dance hall, I'd walk in an' they'd be quiet. I'd ask what they wanted and I'd collect my money. They never bothered me. They'd always call him Fat Blair. One nigger woman tol' me, "Honey, they'd never bother you as long as you Fat Blair's wife."

But I wouldn't run off down there an' get into a lotta this an' put myself in a place to somethin' happen to me like that woman did from Michigan. If she'd been home with her five children where she belonged, prob'ly she'd be livin'. A woman's got five children, she didn't have no business down there. I've got this grocery store, if I wanted to lock this store up and go down there an' mess around, my husband, if he'd do what he should, he'd knock me in the head afore I went. I'm not gonna close *my* store an' go down there an' mess around in with 'em. I'm neither way, for 'em nor against 'em, I'm gonna take care a my part and let them take care a their part.

I'm not gonna move out an' run if they come here. I don't think it'd be right for me to rent 'em. 'Cause if I rent 'em, people that comes into this store, they'd kill me. But if somebody else rents, it's their property, not mine. But I'm not runnin' from nobody. Maybe they'd wanna run *me*, 'cause I'm a hillbilly. They tease me about hillbillies. It makes some people mad, but not me. Oh yeah, some of em, you'd just as well slap 'em in the face as call 'em hillbilly. To me, it don't make a bitter of difference. You are just what you are, that's all.

If they're respectable people, I don't care if they're niggers or Germans or Polacks or what. I don't have no beef against 'em at all. I don't want to have anything to do with Southern trash, if they're no good, red-neck, or Northern trash or nigger trash. I don't have no time for them. But if they're good people, I like 'em. I got two houses, and I think it's my business what I do with 'em. As it stands right now, there ain't but one way I'd rent 'em. The whole neighborhood gets colored an' then I'd have to rent 'em. I'd be kind of the last. I've got a girl friend did live in this neighborhood. She lives at North now. They got an apartment building in a colored neighborhood an' she says they pay good. She's got no trouble at all collecting.

I don't give nobody no credit. We used to give out credit. *No more.* I used to set on their doorstep and hound them an' hound them. An' I said, "That stuff goes." So no credit. I'd almost turn my brother down. I'd say you come back here and I'd feed you but I won't give you credit.

There's one thing you can't hardly do is collect a grocery bill. You can collect a whiskey bill or a beer bill better'n you can a grocery bill. Because they wanna pay off so they can get some more whiskey.

• • • • • •

Horton Blair, mid-fifties

It's all the same to me. It don't make no difference where I'm at.

Do you enjoy your work?

Yeah.

Day passes by quickly?

Pretty fast.

Anything gripe you?

No. (Long pause.) It don't do no good to talk about it.

Remember your boyhood?

Farmin's all.

Watch TV?

Nothin interests me.

Read the paper?

Scant a headline is all.

Anything bother you about the headline?

No.

Bomb?

No.

Negroes?

No.

Is there any one thing that makes you sit up and take notice?

No, I don't know if there is.

What would you like to do when you retire?

Don't have any idea.

No idea?

No idea—wait till the day comes.

You play it day by day?

Day by day.

(Norma Blair interjects, "He's the really educated one. He went to high school.")

What about high school?

History was my favorite subject. Civics and science and history and mathematics. I had the idea of being a teacher. Could never work out. Other things always seemed to do better for me. Teachin' didn't pay anything in those days. I could make two, three dollars to one compared to what I could do teachin'. So I took to sellin' work.

And that changed your mind . . . ?

Money.

• • • • • • •

Bob Skinner, 39

General manager of a drug-and-cosmetic firm, owned by S. B. Fuller, "the last of the rugged individuals. He started in 1935 with $25 and a suitcase and now he's the head of a corporate structure of fourteen companies, including a chain of thirteen newspapers"—one of which is the Pittsburgh Courier. *Although he is a Negro, most of the company's employees and customers are white.*

He lives with his wife and daughter in an integrated housing project. He came to Chicago in 1942, by way of St. Louis, from an Alabama farm, "nothing but pine trees and red clay." His father was a mule-skinner at a sawmill. His mother, in Chicago, worked as a power-machine operator.

In Chicago, he encountered de facto segregation in the school, offering Negro children a worse education than schools in St. Louis of the Thirties and in the South, due to the indifference and transience of the teachers. Nonetheless, he was a superior student.

"I always thought we were better than white people. I thought the whites were afraid of us, and were trying to place certain handicaps on us so we couldn't catch up. I always remember as a child, whenever there was hard work to be done, we did it. When there was a heavy load, we did

320

*the lifting. I said, 'The good Lord sent white people here
weak and he sent us strong.' I remember Joe Louis as the
world's greatest fighter and Jesse Owens was the world's
fastest runner.' And I just knew that any Negro boy given
the same opportunity could beat the white boy. This was a
reverse inferiority complex, I guess."*

*His first revelatory moment—before his meeting with S.
B. Fuller—came when he was sixteen. He was earning
thirty cents an hour for the same work that paid white
high-school boys fifty cents. When he produced more than
the white boys, he was paid their scale.*

Why must I measure up more than someone else? It
always bothers me to give some poor-white the
idea that his very presence has value to me. I don't need
him. I'm a productive citizen and I'll be an asset to any
community. I can survive either way, with complete segregation or complete integration.

I think just as dangerous as the bigot are the do-good-
ers. The people who tell me I'm a poor helpless handicapped Negro and I can't survive in a competitive society
unless I have social help. All I need is the same rules. I'll
measure up. They'll say we'll change the system because
you won't survive. They'll tell this Negro boy: "I know
you stole that watch, but you poor handicapped, helpless
little fellow, you couldn't help yourself." He stole the
watch because he wanted the watch and he didn't want to
work for it. It's just that simple, and he should be pun-
ished just as any white boy would.

I think every man has the ability to accomplish much or
accomplish nothing. I can accomplish, or I can very easily
drift on and become a derelict. I think Getty is no more
involved with his millions than a bum on Skid Row is involved with getting the wine bottle. It's just a matter of
which way he directs himself.

We take two workers. Each gets $75 a week. One takes
care of his bills and he goes an' boozes it up. He drinks
$25 a week in booze, gambling, and all this. The other
person takes his $25 a week and he banks it. Every month
he has a hundred dollars. In a year he has $1200. He
takes his $1200 and buys him a used sewing machine and
he starts to make sheets. He stays up all night sewing

sheets. He sinks all this in—he invests. One day he looks around and he has a million-dollar business, hiring a thousand people.

S. B. Fuller says we are as obligated to make jobs for little Negro boys as the white man is to hire him. More so. The problem with America today is not a scarcity of jobs but a scarcity of job-makers. The Negro ten percent of the population need not be dependent on the whites for jobs. We've got to become manufacturers and leaders. We've got to control our own community.

He says we must let the people see that we can run businesses, we must hire white people and show how we can be good bosses, we must clean our communities and then there will be this acceptance. We must be prepared to survive independently of the whites. When we reach this point, we'll be able to contribute something.

It'll be more difficult for a Negro boy to start a business today than forty, fifty years ago. The economy isn't as free as it was. We don't have a free-market economy in the fullest sense of the word any more. Too many federal restrictions—taxes, particularly.

When the incentive was there and the possible return was there, the little poor boy could stay up all night trying to do one thing better. And when he got this one thing, he'd go into business, and he'd put somebody out of business, naturally. He would go up and he would build factories, he'd support schools and hospitals, and he'd take care of his family. Now we're fast reaching the point where poor boys can't do this any more.

The whites have their place in the economy now, they're in a controlling position. You have your General Motors and your U.S. Steel. They're established. They can always invest their money in tax-free securities and survive. But you take the little Negro boy now with $100. If he buys $100 worth of sheets and he sells the sheets and he gets $200, he won't be able to invest his money at the rate people could forty, fifty years ago. So we'll never catch up.

We weren't moving at the time our economy was open. So now we're ready to make our move and we can't. I believe the Negro boy can build businesses, he can run businesses. And if we must—we have twenty million Negroes

322

—we can have an economy within an economy—if we must.

I don't think there's any white-consumer reluctance to buy merchandise from Negroes. However, with the government crowding in now, you're going to get more integration on the worker level than you will on the management level. You won't be able to get many Negroes in the NAM.

The one ruling class in America is Mr. and Mrs. Consumer. All this protection for the consumer is nonsense, a lot of hogwash. If you don't please him, if you abuse the consumer, he'll break you. He'll put you out of business. The trend in our society has always been toward the elimination of the least efficient producer.

I don't worry about automation. All you got to do is take the pressure off the economy. Leave enough incentive there and the poor boy will think of something better to move up. Remember Studebaker was making wagons, and the automobile came, so now he was making automobiles. Remember some of the old refrigerators don't wear out, they're still working . . . however, refrigerator manufacturers, they paint them pink, blue, they put handles on both sides, anything to make you buy it. These people will keep the economy going. The people in Washington are not going to make the people decide. It's the producers: our poor boys trying to make something better. Build the better mousetrap. Appeal to the only ruling class in America, the consumer. If he's fooled once, he'll put you out of business next time.

I agree that there must be some legislation, however Ayn Rand says it's all bad. I realize that large ones may abuse the small ones, so there must be some legislation. Senator Taft said, "Liberty is the right of self-discipline. However, when people refuse to discipline themselves, they lose the right of self-discipline." This is the flaw in the John Birch Society. It's misunderstood. Its great fault is giving solace to bigots. It says people never lose this right: If the Negro is not allowed to vote, the government has no right to interfere. *This* is where I disagree with them. My philosophy is Taft's. If the conservatives were at all sincere, they'd be in the forefront of the Negro's fight for equality, for it is purely a conservative fight.

Because of abuses, lack of self-discipline, this legislation is coming in on us. Can I survive in my business with bureaucracy crowding on me? The little Negro boy now that's coming . . . he has a better academic background now, the economy is expanding more, he's ready to move up. However, the way the government now operates. . .

In the name of giving the Negro his freedom, we are getting legislation, and legislation means less freedom. However, equality is the thing we're after. We'll be more equal before all the laws we have made. Inevitably, it means total enslavement of the people—we'll all be considerably less free, but more equal. When you get a crusade going in the name of good—I forget the exact quote: "We can protect ourselves from men doing evil in the name of evil, but heaven protect us from men doing evil in the name of good."

S. B. Fuller and I have one difference. He says the white man doesn't try to keep the Negro down. I say he can't keep us down, but he tries. The philosophy I would like to see Negroes have is the one held by the Unsinkable Molly Brown: Nobody could keep her down because nobody wanted her down as she wanted herself up. I believe this: Nobody wants me down as much as I want up.

At the same time, I have conflicts. I am in a state of transition right down the line. . . .

I recently saw a map of places covered by different [American] Indian tribes. I always believed this was barren vacant land and the Pilgrims moved into an area that was uninhabited. This was not true at all. We took the land from the Indians and said this was ours, it belongs to us. And this thinking process, it's what gets me in so much trouble. How can you have a free-market economy unless you have some form of rugged nationalism? I have a tremendous amount of conflict, yes, yes.

I would like my daughter to do anything that pleases her, to be a sound, productive citizen, to have a good sense of values, and not be torn by this conflict I have inside. I worry about the sort of life she's going to live and the abuses I had. I don't want her to experience—I can remember my mother walking down the street and the names drunken white men called her. I would never want her to go through this. I don't believe God sent me down here handicapped. I wasn't born with a bridle in my mouth and a saddle on my back and a white boy with whips and spurs. I think with equal opportunity, I can do all he can. I don't need him just because he's white.

• • •◦• •◦• • •

Edward Gilroy, Jr., 37

"From the time I was about six years old, I wanted to be a radio network announcer. I used to sit in the tile bathroom and say 'This is NBC, the National Broadcasting Company.' During the early part of my childhood we were probably what you call lower middle class and eventually reached the heights of middle-class Irish people on the South Side of Chicago. This is my father's thirty-ninth year with Western Electric.

"I don't know if you'd call it status. I know it's wanting to walk outside the line, as an instructor does in the Army or a drill instructor in the Marine Corps. Where everyone marches along in the column and there's someone walking just as far, but they're walking outside the column. I've always wanted to do that.

"I finally found out after I did get into radio that every announcer, if he's good, is a salesman. And I found out there's money talking to the individual customer, being able to go in, not as a salesman but as a helper. To go in and explain, 'Here is how I'm going to help you make more money.' When I was selling air filters, we didn't sell air filters per se, we sold the man clean buildings.

"Everyone sells air filters, and my air filters are no better than the competitors' air filters when you come right down to it. But we could say, 'Now this air filter we recommend for your particular building and this is how much it costs. If you want something better, I can sell it to you, but it's going to cost you money. If you want something less expensive, I can sell that to you, too. We can sell you air filters that will take out all the dirt. I also have a line that I guarantee will take out no dirt. Depending on how much you want to pay.' We felt this gave the customer confidence in you, that he didn't feel he had to call anyone else. You were right there and you were Mr. Filter.

"We come up with actual mundane phrases, but they were catchy. 'Don't shoot the breeze, we clean it.' 'It's an ill wind that doesn't blow through our filter.' It's surprising how many people believe it."

Actually, in America today people are sales-resistant. You come to the door and say, "I want to show you . . ." and they say, "No, I don't need it," because all America is saying Buy Me, Buy Me. Billboards, television, Buy Me, I'm going to do this for you. And people don't believe it because they've been disappointed so many times. I know my children, they watch television. They're eight and six now. They don't believe the toys they see on TV will actually do what they infer.

Children eight and six become cynical about this?

Certainly, certainly. They send in the back of a cereal box and it's described in glowing terms to children who are just learning how to read. And they believe it. And they get their quarter together with the box top and they send it in and they get a little plastic toy that will last for half a day and breaks. Eventually, they'll send in for the next one and the next one and the next one. . . [but] they also begin to realize that nobody gives them something for nothing.

How good does a salesman have to be overcome this resistance?

That depends on what you're selling. If you're selling Bibles, you can narrow it down. It's going to cost about ten cents a day. You can compare it to a cigar smoker. "Well, you smoke at least one cigar a day, and that's ten cents. Now you mean to say you don't have ten cents you can put toward this particular purchase?" When you convince them it doesn't cost too much, that's when you should have the pen in their hand and have it ready to write their name on the contract. They have the pen in the customer's hands, that's when the salesman, if he has to bite his tongue, should sit there and not say a word. When he's put the monkey on the customer's back. The customer has the pen and he's ready to go. Then the salesman has to be quiet, because if he says another word it relieves the prospect. I've seen people sit and actually faces become red, sweat, and finally they write their name on the contract.

I've been to the front door and had it slammed on me, and people didn't want anything at all, and it's the people who scream and howl that they don't want it, that you know they probably do have a need for it. And then you go to the back door, and as soon as they open it and you don't give them a chance to say a word, you say, "Oh, I'm so glad *you* answered, who's that mean guy that lives in front?" And this throws them off guard and sometimes you make a sale.

The greatest thing for a door-to-door salesman is to learn just a few simple techniques. If they ring the bell, when somebody comes to the door, especially a homemaker or a housewife, when she comes to the door, if you take one simple step backward as you say hello, this relieves all her fears about who is this fellow at the door. Because of you taking that one step backward, she realizes that you're not there to do her any harm.

You should always call them a homemaker rather than a housewife. Because the expression *housewife* is used by so many people. If you listen to the radio and television quiz programs: What do you do for a living? Oh, I'm just a housewife; and that's how these people feel. So you have to glamorize their position, because, well, any of the Sunday supplements will tell you how much a wife is worth to a husband: $25,000 a year, because she's the nurse, the cook, the chauffeur, the maid, the mistress, all these things combined into one. You have to make her feel that this is a very responsible position—which it is.

With one hand, he flips open a matchbook, removes a match, casually flicks it against his thumb, lights his cigarette and my dead cigar.

A neat trick. Very impressive.

It's part of creating an impression. Where you're calling on the purchasing agent, and ten years ago you took him to lunch, today he's got too many invitations and more than likely if he's a big enough man, he won't go to lunch with you because he doesn't want to become obligated. But lighting his cigar with one hand, he's gonna remember you. Maybe he'll forget your product, but he'll remember you. And the next time he sees you, maybe he'll go home and try and burn his hand himself, and maybe he'll remember the next time he sees you and he'll ask how you did that. When you call on him the next time he'll see you, because he wants to find out how you did it.

I'll tell you it's a funny thing about this particular trick. For a long time, I saw a man Downtown in Chicago on an elevator, it was in the 333 Building, over on Michigan Avenue, and we both got on at the twentieth floor. And he had one arm and on the twentieth floor he rolled a cigarette with one arm out of a Bull Durham bag. He had rolled it by about the tenth floor and by the fifth floor he had it lit because he lit with one hand, like that. (Repeats trick.) And I figured that would be a good thing to learn, and eventually I learned to do it, not only with the right hand but with the left hand, too. And take the match out of the book. I find it's rather impressive.

. . . Today, with the way America is producing, no one really has a better product. For every good product on the market, there are nine other competing products that are every bit just as good and all in the same price range. So the problem is, the man's going to buy one of them, and if you come in and create the need . . .

Lots of things I quote I stole from somebody else. I worked for Dale Carnegie, and his famous line was "I've never had an original idea in my life." The greatest truism in sales to me is this: To sell John Smith what John Smith buys, you must see John Smith through John Smith's eyes. That's whether you're selling to the president of a corporation, to a janitor, or if you're selling to a homemaker.

What did you think of Death of a Salesman?

I think in today's day and age people have a rough time really feeling. Today I don't think the boy could have that much confidence in his father because we live too close to the radio, television, and other things that . . . I know. My little girl is eight now. When she was six she had a lemonade stand, this was the big thing. We lived in a dead street surrounded on three sides by forest preserves. And there's no foot traffic on our street at all. So I got home from work that night and I said, "Well, Leila, how did you do?" And she said, "Well, I made a dollar twenty-three profit." And I said, "How could you make a dollar twenty-three profit selling lemonade out in front?" And she said, "Well, Daddy, I stood there for a while and nobody came by. So I started shouting, 'Lemonade for Sale' and still nobody came by. So then I put my orange crate and my lemonade and my glasses on a wagon and went up and down the street shouting 'Lemonade, lemonade.' And you know, Daddy, nobody came and bought some. So then I went door-to-door and I knocked on the doors and said, 'Don't you want to buy lemonade?' and almost everybody bought some.' " This is what you have to do today. You have to go out and find the business because it's a buyer's market.

I really don't think she had thoughts of what Daddy would do. Oh, at that time she knew what profit and loss was. I had taught her that when I was selling filters. I would make up a number, say a nickel a filter. "How much money would you make on a filter, Daddy?" I would say a nickel. Well, by the time she got to be six, she could transpose anything into a number of filters. If something cost a dollar, my son, Dennis, would say, "I want that, Daddy." And Leila would say, "Well, Daddy has to sell, let's see, twenty filters, in order to buy that for us." Which I think is good. Others don't.

There's another thing in sales. If you find out somebody is from a particular background, you have to find out first if he'll appreciate what you're going to tell him. If you know somebody is of Jewish extraction and you know some Jewish words, well, you have to know first how he's going to take it. It's something you ascertain just by talking to him. And there are some people that you would use these words with and it would enhance you, and others, it would cut you to death. Same way with an Italian. Well, you have to be able to almost guess, well, how's he gonna take this? Is he going to . . . is he proud of being an Italian, first of all. And if he is, you know you can go ahead and use an Italian phrase. Is he proud of being Irish? Is he proud of being a Bohemian? Depends on what it is. This goes right back again to when you sell John Smith what

John Smith buys, you must see through John Smith's eyes. And if you can get to the point where you are looking out at yourself through his eyes, then the sale is a cinch.

As a salesman, I sometimes don't feel free to have any of my own opinions. Now, I'll call on one fella, now say he's a purchasing agent. That's one of the first things you have to find out: Is this man able to give me an order? Don't ever talk to the guy who has got to go to somebody else. And he'll say, "Oh my gosh, did you hear about those colored people? Here's what they're doing now. They're ruining this and they're ruining that." And, as a salesman, you say, "Yeah, isn't that awful? How about that?" And you get an order. And fifteen minutes later you're in the office of somebody else and they'll say, "I don't know what is the matter with the rest of my white brothers. Those people in the South. We know that all of our teaching says that these people are created equal to us and if given the opportunity they can provide and contribute to our society." And this is a fella who is on the other end, and he's waving the flag for equal rights for Negroes. And you have to sit there and say, "By golly, that's right. I hadn't thought of it that way." And you get an order there. And you get home at night and you think, gee, do I really have an opinion myself? Will I allow myself to have an opinion, or is the sale more important to me? You can't be overenthusiastic about any cause, but you certainly can't be opposed to what your potential customer thinks.

Rather than express an opinion, you have to be able to argue either side and be well-read enough to be able to come out and say, yes, what about this or that, or that recent thing in Selma? Many were against it, many were for it. And you have to be able to talk intelligently about it. Perhaps you don't have to be as enthused as they are, but let them know in diverse ways that you agree with them. Because you do run across people whose mind is running in the same channel as yours, and then they're not really sure of you, whether you're really expressing your opinion or not. You've not only got to roll with the punch, but to anticipate it. It goes back to seeing the man through his own eyes.

Eventually you come to the point where you have to psychoanalyze yourself and find out, "Why am I thinking this particular way?" Is it because I think I'm going to make another sale tomorrow? Is it because this person is going to like me better? But I've been able to have opinions of my own. I've been far to the left and far to the right and I feel that if this is going to affect me, my life, and my family, well then, perhaps I'll keep my opinion to myself.

. . . I worry mostly about my children. I worry about the kind of life I am making for them. What kind of life are we as a generation making?

I've never been able to sit down myself and say: You know, what do I want? I've been just too busy eking out a daily existence. I think all of us have goals. Those that have a fixed goal, I find rarely reach them. I have a father-in-law who worked for the telephone company for thirty-two years. He went to work when he was eighteen. His whole thought in life was to retire to Florida via trailer and live there from the time he was sixty on. And he died when he was fifty. So I'm kind of afraid of long-range goals.

I think people are not as honest with themselves as they used to be. Whether they're better or not, I don't know. We're all in this rat race, trying to keep the income up with the outgo. I've been in it for years, and you wonder. Fears? Yes, there's a great fear. Am I going to be able to continue this? And the more you make, the more money you spend. You see, basically there are two types of people in the world: those who lend money and those who pay it back. Those who give interest and those who pay interest. And it's a big step to jump from one side to the other. Once you reach the point where you're not paying interest, then you're collecting it. This is a very worthwhile thing. There are some people kid a great deal about the Bohemians. I have a number of Bohemian neighbors and these people make their regular trips to the Savings and Loan, they drive a 1955 Chevy and they've really something in the monetary sense of the word for the children. They're working, as their parents did for them, for their children. I have great respect for them. I for one quite often go deeply into a hole on things that I really can't afford.

With me, the more I have to earn, the more I earn. Perhaps that keeps me on streets an extra hour a day. And perhaps if I know I've got to make so much money this week, that means I can't lay in bed until eight o'clock in the morning. So perhaps when the pressure is on you, you go out and work a little harder than when the pressure isn't on you.

You're only thirty-seven. Fear of age, has that ever . . . ?

The only time it worries me is when I pick up the Help Wanted ads and now . . . I always read the Classified, I read the Personals, I read the Auctions, I read Help Wanted, all these ads. And I see more and more Men Wanted, 22 to 30, 22 to 35, and I look and say I wouldn't take that job anyway. But how about the fact that they wouldn't even interview me? That makes me stop and think. I think I've got enough in me personally that I'd be able to convince this person that I would do a better job than the twenty-two-year-old he's looking for.

This is the great thing I have to offer, myself.

· · · · · ·

Frank D. Haley, 44

He is a study in brown: a four-in-hand tie, a fedora, lapel handkerchief. He is smoking a panatela, a well-advertised brand. The archetypal "dapper gent." He could pass for a small businessman in any American community.

At one time I used to be called Young Frank, and now I'm thinkin' of considerin' myself Old Frank. But I'm happy-go-lucky, carefree; I'm just happy. I feel terrific. I don't ever worry about growin' old. I think it's something that comes naturally and, like I say, worry isn't gonna help. I just live one day at a time, as though it were your last day and you don't need to worry. You've seen this picture on the Squirt bottle of some funny little men that says, "Why worry?" I found out that worry just makes bills.

I work at the post office at present. I'm hopin' to work tomorrow. They sent me home the other day. But he told me to be back Friday, and I'll be there.

I always wanted to be my own boss. I wanted to have my own business, and I hope some day that that dream comes true. And I think I'm in the right spot. I do believe, you know, the breaks . . . and if you're there and they need you, then you get in. And I think it's a break that I came to Chicago when I did, because I met some darn nice people in Chicago.

I came to Chicago in '61. A man told me that anybody that wanted to work could find work in Chicago, and I think he was right. 'Cause I found work. It hasn't been suitable work all the time, but I found plenty of work. I've been working at, what do you call them? I call them slave markets, where they pay you the minimum wage which, thank God, they have to.* Supposing you were the man they sent me to, and your regular rate was $2.50 for your regular employee. In case he didn't show up that day, you called the number and they sent you myself. You pay that regular $2.50 an hour to the company that's sent me, and I did the work, and I got $1.25 an hour. . . .

Then I quit and went into business for myself, and I really did hurt. But I was independent and I was carefree and happy and contented. Window washing, painting, carpentering, anything that anybody wanted me to do. So I still know that I can go out and dig up customers that I've lost, 'cause I did have a big business going. Then I went into the hospital for a hemorrhoid operation, and I came out and then I went back to the post office. I started at the post office for Christmas, and I was aspiring for sixty days in the post office so I could become in the union. If they send me home again, they'll at least send me home with ten dollars.

I like Chicago . . . if it doesn't happen, stick around five minutes, it might. I mean that's what they advertise and it seems to be true, I've been from coast to coast practically. Hitchhiking. I did. I took one American Airlines plane ride and I think that's the greatest way to travel, by airplane. But it's expensive. I get a kick out of the way they advertise now: Fly Now, Pay Later. And some day I hope maybe I will.

I've picked apples, I've topped onions, oh boy, what I haven't done is hardly worth mentioning. Scrubbed floors,

---

* Employment contractors who supply companies with casual labor and temporary help.

did dishes, short-order cooking, various and sundry other things.

I'm from Butler, Pennsylvania. It's a city of about thirty to thirty-three thousand people. It's called the Glad Hand City. It's a town where everybody knew everybody, everybody spoke to everybody. I think Armco Steel is what's holding the city together. And then there's a family that has a gas company, and they also, they're millionaires. I admire these men because they must have had something or they wouldn't be where they are. I think they weren't just born that way.

I have a brother that's a retired football coach and he worked every minute for his. He was a self-made man. Of course, he had some help, too, he married a rich girl. But he kept on working.

My father was in the oil business. He was a tool dresser and he never made more than a dollar an hour. He worked in Michigan and New York and Ohio and other states; he was home long enough to have twelve children, though. He was a good Irishman.

I mean we're Catholic and ten of them are married, and I think about seven of them married non-Catholics and five of the seven became Catholics. You be the judge.

I hope some day to meet the right woman. Truly. I'm crazy about women. I'm now in the Third Order of St. Francis of Assisi down at St. Peter's Catholic Church, and I'm invited to a party on my birthday, and I hope I get a nice-lookin' girl to go with me to the party. Oh, heavens, I could stand up to marriage. But, like I said, happy-go-lucky, carefree. And I do want to take on the responsibilities of a father or a home because I'm gonna get old, too. And the only thing I can look forward to now is a pension from the service. But I want to definitely build my own nest egg.

I tell people watch out, they can be replaced by push-buttons. I think automation is definitely here, like the automat elevators, it's fantastic. But why worry?

That's what that Bomb can do also. It could replace us all. I happened to ride back to Pennsylvania for a Christmas visit in Harrisburg, P. A., with my sisters. And I met this young soldier on the bus and we got talking. And he had been to Vietnam, and he told me they were issuing the soldiers steel boots, steel shoes, and I said, "What for?"

334

And he said, for those bamboo poles, rods that the guerrillas, the communists, are sticking out of the ground with poison on them. That must be terrible, walking around in steel boots. They must be pretty heavy, I imagine.

So there again, I'm thankful to God that I'm, as I've said before, I'm over the hill now, I think, for the services, and I feel sorry for my nieces and nephews. I've got several nephews in the service now, but I think they're pretty smart, they got in the Navy. But I'm just happy all my experiences are behind me, I hope.

Thank God, I'm still living and I'm still happy and I'm still carefree and I'm still in debt. Yeah, room rent, but they aren't pushing me now, but they know they'll get it a week from tomorrow. And I thank God we have relief because I just got off it, I'm happy to say off, and I reported myself off, because of employment.

I mean, I'm working now, but there was a period when I wasn't working, and maybe you might say I was living above my means, which I don't hope I'm not. I'm paying fifteen dollars a week room. And the only reason I took that room is it had a bathtub and I needed to sit in it when I first got out of the hospital. It also has a telephone in the room which came in handy for my business.

I think maybe I'm makin' history in the Wilson Avenue area.* I don't know if they're kidding me about it, but they say I'm the Mayor of Wilson Avenue. But I don't believe them.

Why do they call you the mayor of Wilson Avenue?

Well, I can't read their minds. Because I wave at a lot of guys. I know them by their first name, Les and Ray and Nick. I don't know nobody in the hotel but the maid. That's the only person I know there. I'm in that type of hotel that I think it's best that I just stay and mind my own business. I get in my room and go to sleep. I get up and get out early in the morning, and I stay out till sometimes late at night, and I don't get a chance to fraternize or stick around there too much.

And I'd just as soon not. I mean, because in this partic-

---

* Wilson Avenue: one of the main arteries of the North Side transient-Appalachian area.

ular neighborhood you don't know for sure who you're running up against. Well, the brass knuckles and the pistols and the stilettos and the switchblades. So I'm happy that they don't bother me and I don't bother them. And then there's the yo-yo's—somebody that I don't care to go any further with the relationship. Not that I think I'm any better, but there's so many people that they're content, and they're satisfied with what they are, and they always seem to want what you have: they want a sandwich or they want a cigarette or they want a quarter. So I can do without those kind of people. I'll try to help them. One yo-yo, I bought him a hamburger and bought him a pack of cigarettes, and I'm so happy that he's in one section of the city and I'm here. . . .

I keep to myself. I keep busy. I used to go every night to the movies and sometimes I'd miss work to go to movies. But recently, now, of course, it's Lent, and I have to give up something. So I gave up movies. I have a radio and I read the papers. I read 'em . . . sleep . . . sometimes I write letters. I have quite a correspondence built up.

When I was in the hospital recently, I had taken voice lessons and she said I had a wonderful octave or whatever, I don't know. She's a paraplegic, she goes around in a wheel chair and she donates all her time just teaching patients. I guess she realizes there are people worse off than she is.

That's why if I'm not working, I'm at a meeting. AA. That's my life now. I know if I take a drink, well, that's the end. I feel I've had my last chance as far as drinking. In 1958 I took my last drink of anything. I've lost the fear and remorse and the nasty thoughts that go with drinking. Heavens, yes. I wake up in the morning, I know where I was the night before.

But now I'm happy all that's behind me. I'm free. . . . I still have hopes of owning one of my own cars by the end of this year yet. And I still think if I stay where I am now, I'll have it. And today's a great day. I got my new choppers today, and as I've been hearing on the radio, it's income-tax day. Maybe I'll earn enough to pay next year.

But this is especially a good day for me because of my new teeth. The last time I was home, I went home without my lower choppers. And my sisters were so humiliated and angry they told me never to come back unless I have a full set of teeth. So I hope to be back to visit them in July or so. They thought I was negligent in having them broke, and I broke them playing with some orphan kids up the street here, but I still wanted to see my sisters and nieces and nephews, and I saw them without teeth.

I think that's the first thing a person looks at is people's teeth or their shoes shined or the crease in their pants. I think it adds to their appearance. I try to keep clean, shaved, hair cut. It was drilled into me, I guess. My mother used to tell me, she'd say. "Show me the company of people and I'll tell you what you are." And she'd say, "If you laid down with the dogs, you'd get up with the fleas." And they've also taught that cleanliness is next to godliness, and soap is so cheap, it's too bad that more people don't spend more money for soap instead of this dog-gone wine.

I think if you set a goal and work toward that goal, and when you've reached that goal, that is success. I think a man that is successful is a man like Clement Stone* who borrowed money from that insurance company, turned around and bought the insurance company with their own money. Right now he's a pretty fabulously wealthy philanthropist and a wonderful man. He helps. In the Bible, I think it says whatever you shall sow, ye shall reap. And he certainly is all merciful with anybody and everybody it seems. His heart is almost as big as his wallet.

But there's another great man, that Cardinal Meyer was. Well, I got to see Cardinal Meyer, and that was the first Cardinal I ever saw. Yeah, down here on State Street. And I got up especially one hour early that day just to go see him, thinking I was gonna go to work. And as it turned out I could a gone to the funeral, because they sent me home from work that morning. But that was an impressive sight for me. I mean, I'd never seen a Cardinal laid out like that. I've seen any number of priests, but as I recall I don't think I've ever visited a nun that had died.

Tomorrow's Good Friday.

Well, that's the day that Christ died. And it's the ending

---

* A local insurance executive.

of the beginning. A sad day, but then Holy Saturday and then Easter Sunday, all is risen, Christ, Easter . . . it's too bad He had to die for rats like us. . . .

. . . .

Phil Eagle, 55

His shoes were caked with mud. His suit was rumpled. A pencil protruded from his lapel pocket. A thick wad of bills appeared, fives, tens, and twenties. He casually flung one on the table. The restaurant tab was $1.80. The tip was a dollar.

"I used to have great faith in America till Franklin D. Roosevelt. I am symbolic of the greatness of the struggle in America. There is so much opportunity if a person can get away from this craziness of politicians supporting him. America was a wonderful place when I was born, and I don't think it's gonna be so wonderful when I die. We've become lice and bedbugs and parasites."

Born in an area of transient men on the outskirts of Chicago's Loop, he ran two newsstands at the age of eleven. He published racehorse information sheets at sixteen. He worked as relief clerk in men's hotels Saturdays and Sundays, while managing a variety of other jobs during the week. "In the depth of the Depression, when other people got on relief and all that craziness," *he worked for a traveling salesman, offering his employer many ideas at turning a profit. He had rejected get-rich-quick offers from the Syndicate to manage taverns, because of his distaste for beer, liquor, and cigarettes.* "I haven't had a drink in twenty years, and I haven't smoked a cigarette or drank a cup of coffee in twenty-two years."

As a young boy, he sold dirty postcards to workingmen, and it has been on his conscience ever since. Often he's had bad dreams and nightmares. "How can a puritan be a puritan if he sold dirty postcards? I'll carry that to my grave. My church is in my mind and my conscience. I'm honest enough to know I've tried to buy my way into heaven."

His greatest luxury is to "lay in bed and read different facts and in different ways I use it for material advantage. I've spent thousands of wonderful hours, learning facts."

338

His wife and he have "a combined IQ of 300." He is in the process of divorcing her.

Twenty-two years ago, I met a beautiful girl accidentally in a Clark Street saloon. And we fell in love under impossible odds and built a beautiful life under impossible odds. I was making $28 a week. She was married at that time to an immature boy, who left her to go on a fishing trip with another woman. She was a part time 26-girl at this saloon, on a vacation from Montgomery Ward. She was a collection correspondent, which she worked up to in a very short time from a typist.

We met with no thoughts of sex, and on the second night, we wound up running away to Crown Point.* It was the beginning of a life that had eighteen of the most wonderful, wonderful years that any two people could have. During that time, we started various small businesses and struggled together. I worked in a factory nights, my wife worked in office days. We took turns running a little business and taking care of our baby daughter. And in the end, we wound up to spend a happy wonderful decade, from 1952 to 1962, golden, golden years in Prairie City, Illinois, roughly a hundred miles from Chicago.

We created a business that give us an income of thirty thousand dollars a year on a three-day week. And along the way, my wife—when she was a kid worked on a farm in Michigan for a dollar a day, ten hours hard work, weeding onions—she became probably the greatest commercial auction buyer of shoes and clothing and drapes and dry goods and curtains and things like that in the history of the Chicago market.

She came to Chicago with five dollars, borrowed from a neighbor with no help from her mother; her father was dead. She rode the elevated lines in Chicago all night, to be decent and not a prostitute, which she could have become very easily.

To be an auction buyer, you have to be cruel and cold-blooded and merciless and almost with no conscience, and boy, oh boy, she fits all of those. Very unusual. You have to be smart, you have to be fast, you have to be shrewd, you have to be a gambler. Along the way, I gave her con-

* A nearby town in Indiana, long noted for "instant" marriages.

fidence. In every business I've ever had, I had momentum. I was always able to have action.

We went into this gradually. My wife went to an auction house with a paycheck from Montgomery Ward and stood there for two, three hours, just looking and looking and looking and probably driving the auctioneer crazy, wondering what is that beautiful blonde doing there. And he put up something like eighteen shirts and asked for fifty cents and she came to life. And, by God, he sold it to her. And then an hour or so went by, eighty pair men's socks for four cents a pair—boing!—she came to life. She was terrific. She didn't gamble, she invested. And the merchandise she bought that day, I hauled back two, three days later with a streetcar and put it in a little corner of our store.

We had back-number magazines, two for a nickel. We used to trade magazines, one for two. A couple months later, we moved around the corner to a big store, with nothin' in it, but we filled it up eventually. We used to sell comic books two for a nickel and bubble gum free. We sold sherbets, ice cream, two scoops for a nickel, and novelties and school supplies and balloons. Everything we've ever sold has been a bargain and guaranteed as clean as Marshall Field's. Cleaner. We've always done a legitimate business. My wife eventually grew with the momentum and the financing that I manipulated, scheming. My wife eventually became such a buyer, she earned in her career a thousand dollars or more a day, at least fifty times.

We struggled together and we learned together. Along the way, she absorbed many things from me that she could never have started this thing herself. The financing, the borrowing, the having two different bank accounts and writing checks from one bank to another. I created a system of picking up merchandise from an auction on Friday afternoon. No matter when we bought the merchandise, we wouldn't pick it up till Friday afternoon at two o'clock. And what the hell is the auctioneer gonna do with the check on Friday after two o'clock. He's gonna deposit the check, in most cases, on Monday. By that time we have the merchandise. And Saturday, Sunday, Monday, and Tuesday, by the time it reached our bank, ninety-nine cases out of a hundred the check was good. We sold the merchandise to finance the clearing of the check.

We grew from all kinds of tricks and financing. We grew to a $21,000 credit in the Prairie City Bank on my signature only. We grew to a $20,000 credit at Sears and a $10,000 credit for the Eagle Store in Wisconsin. We grew to a Dun & Bradstreet rating in the last seven, eight years of C 3½, which means $50,000 to $75,000 credit. Fantastic for a business which started with ten dollars.

We wound up in Prairie City in a three-day-week store. It eventually became a $30,000 income. With a twenty acre park we live at. I encouraged my wife to have her own car, her own bank account, her own bowling team. Along the way, I even gave her as a birthday present a regulation outdoor tennis court. I encouraged her to have a housekeeper, which we pay our housekeeper more than any doctor in the county pays his nurses. We have thousands and thousands dollars' worth of merchandise, sometimes in the basement. We wanted a higher class woman or no one in the house.

My wife had turned into a marvelous woman, a wonderful mother. We share a daughter in common who is very uncommon. When we washed her diapers in roadside parks, she became one of the most outstanding students in the history of the country. When she graduated last spring, she was among other things the saludictorian of her class. That's number two. She was elected by the teachers of the entire county as a Daughter of the American Revolution Good Citizen. Our daughter was the drum majorette, which is unusual for the class saludictorian. Our daughter was in the prom court, almost the queen for beauty. She was in the homecoming court, almost the homecoming queen. Our daughter got nineteen medals, mostly gold medals, state music competition, playing the trombone. She was given the highest award Illinois can give a high-school student. She was given a four-year scholarship at Bradley University, where she is now. And on top of everything else—with extreme pride—when she went to college, she went with enough money that she earned, owning and operating her own business, Betty Ann's Teen Shop in Prairie City. She had a wonderful business career from the age thirteen to seventeen and she accumulated thousands of dollars. And she is now heading toward being a housewife or a teacher of music.

I'd like my two boys to be like Yukon Eric. I'd like

them to be outdoor men. I'd like them to have a wonderful chest and a fine body and lead a clean life and the hell with the money. Three children, I've been an unusual father, I've come home from a $400 profit day and washed the diapers.

At this point, he mentions his wife's temporary condition that made connubial duties impossible. "So I went into the Chicago underworld and came up with a good-looking prostitute who didn't smoke and didn't drink. And that's the only woman I have any use for is a woman who don't smoke and don't drink. I tried to reform her. When I saw it was impossible, I gave up and returned home. Instead of cutting off my tongue, I confessed. My wife took this very hard. I'm positive this was the turning point in my life. My wife that night drove wild and almost tried to kill herself. Eventually, she tried to forgive me and start life anew." During their "second honeymoon," they fell in love with a location in Wisconsin that had even greater potentialities than their Prairie City enterprise. He didn't realize that his wife had the intention of "dumping me, where I'd wind here and she'd wind up with everything else."

I was stricken with a serious disease. In the middle of the night, I woke up paralyzed on the neck. I was released as a hopeless cripple four years ago. I wasn't able to work and my heart was broke. At the depth of my sickness, my wife suggested, out of a clear blue sky, no argument, with deep thought, she suggested I go to Chicago and sell newspapers. She wanted to keep a hundred percent, all our assets, and our twenty-acre home.

When she suggested that I be eliminated, it gave me incentive. The medical profession credits my hundred percent recovery to my will power. I latched on to an idea. The idea is contained in the book, *F-O-L-K, Folk Medicine*. The book is almost a hundred percent concerned with apple cider and vinegar and honey and water and eating fish. And using Lugol, *L-U-G-O-L*. A solution which can be bought for pennies, enough to last for a year. In any drug store. Which everybody should have a drop or two drops a week. Following this book and changing my diet and eliminating sugar from my life and pop and orange juice, I recovered my health.

342

That's one of the things that helped break up my home. My wife is against preaching or trying to help anybody or trying to do good. She isn't gonna go to anybody's house and ask them for anything, and she don't want them to come to her house and bother her.

I own fifty percent of the stock and she owns fifty percent of the stock. Along the way, we accumulated $220,000 of assets in eighteen years. From a ten-dollar start. When I was crippled up, she came over from the house and took over physical control of the business. Unbeknown to me, she announced to the workers in the store that she was the sole owner of Prairie City Stores, Incorporated.

I'm one of the most widely respected men in the county. I was the only citizen in the county to fight the sheriff who was running a whore house. I advertised in the papers begging the people to vote for an honest, decent, sober, respectable man for sheriff. It took the combined political parties to return him to office. The whore house has been eliminated. I've cooperated with the Illinois State Troopers, and I'm instrumental for at least seventeen or eighteen people being put in jail for burglaries.

I've done thousands of good deeds in the county. Any hillbilly family with children that had a fire, I'd send a check for a hundred bucks, or a letter certifying they can come to our store and pick out a hundred dollars' worth of clothing for the kids. I never turned down any honorable request. In none of these have I ever expected sex. In thirteen years in that county, I've never touched any woman, except my wife. Except for that prostitute in Chicago.

My wife is almost friendless in this battle, except that she has the almighty buck behind her, in bank accounts and in safety deposit vaults. From weeding onions for a dollar a day, ten hours, she found herself with a $30,000 a year income and a wonderful home—five vehicles: two cars, two big trucks, and a Volkswagen station wagon, bank accounts and the Prairie Stores, Incorporated Bowling Team.

As far as money, when I was making $28 a week and we went out to eat in a restaurant and I couldn't afford to leave a half a dollar tip, but she would make me leave a dollar tip. Now when I can afford it, she's against me being the biggest tipper in the county.

Counting $3500 or $4000 or $5000 every Monday morning, piled up on the table, in cash on the table, apparently affected her mentally.

The only thing between her and all this wealth is my heartbeat. Three different times she threatened to kill me over this battle for money. She was carrying a gun in the glove compartment of her car. The state troopers warned her if they caught her on the highway and if this gun was found, they would put her in jail. That scared her. When she wouldn't let me in the store that I'd given my life to building, on a peaceful mission of inspection, it resulted in a fist fight. With my Madison Street experience, I clouted my wife a few good ones after she made a pass at me. It's reached a stage where a man who never struck a woman before, I want to choke her one night, involving a $7000 transaction. I tried to run her down once when I was on the truck and saw her on the road.

I'm suing her. A man from the gutter who's taken all he can from a woman that he loves and that he created and built up and developed into a tremendous woman and then to be thrown out like a piece of toilet paper. It's a horrible, horrible feeling.

It's been a fabulous, fabulous career. And a full life. And now I face a bitter age. As a small boy I always had ambition to serve the public with values and bargains. Today, the average lady customer in Prairie City owns twice as many shoes as the Marshall Field customer. They buy ten for the price of one. I've enjoyed serving.

My wife and I shared rich and rewarding memories. In the eighteen years, I feel we have accomplished in mercenary things a miracle from our humble beginnings. I'm crazy about her.

In order to overcome the mental shock of being alone and thrown out, I really think I'll go from this thing to the heights in business.

XIX

FALLAWAYS

• • • • • • • • • •

Dave Williamson, 43

Why did he and his wife, Julie, give up the "good life" of a North Shore suburb—a before-dinner martini on the patio, genial neighbors, a good job? They had lived in Northbrook, an upper-middle-class suburb, "where everybody's a VP of something."

His father was a bond salesman, "almost a Southern-gentleman type person." He hardly knew him. "When I came back from overseas, we had one beer together and he told me one dirty joke, and that was that."

"I was brought up in South Evanston where, oh boy, if a Negro or a Jewish person was anywhere in sight, all doors would slam, real-estate offices would lock their doors, and janitors would pull down the shades. My parents were from the South. My parents called them niggers."

He was an artist-designer with one of the city's most respected architectural firms. His salary was in five figures. His wife had a well-paying secretarial job. They are childless. They were active in suburban Presbyterian church circles.

They now live and work at the Ecumenical Institute in the heart of the city's black West Side ghetto. He does artwork for its publications and teaching, as well as "emptying waste baskets, cooking, running the printing machine, and janitorial work." His wife does a variety of jobs there. "We thought we could offer our bodies and our hands and our energy."

I seriously doubt that we could ever move back to North-brook. It's not that we don't love everyone who's there. It's not that we don't appreciate what we had there. It's just that there's a job to be done down here and there are not enough hands to do it.

Sure, we had it made. But underneath all the affluence —and the beautiful women at the advertising agencies and all that—I had a feeling there was something missing in my life. I wasn't really satisfied. I rationalized the need for making a good income. I felt there's nothing wrong with this. Certain everybody around me was doing the same thing. Yet there was something missing.

We were becoming more deeply involved in church work. I was putting in an eighty-hour week, forty at the job and forty at the church. I disassociated a Christian life from a man's vocation. I saw a Christain life in which a man would think of the church as a building and not really relate faith with being involved with people.

About a year ago, we canceled a bridge engagement and a party and spent a weekend at the Ecumenical Institute. It changed our lives. It opened up to us the thing that we both wanted. Only we couldn't put our hands on it, a way in which you could give your total self. You didn't have to go Downtown and work your forty hours a week and come back and try to figure some way to make your life more meaningful. We found a renter for our house and came here.

When we first told our friends about the move, it was met with: "My word, you guys are nuts." (Laughs.) I guess everyone's image of a teacher or a church worker is one in which you live out here and you commute out there. This is a horrible thing. You've got to *live* with people to understand what their problems are.

Some of them were quite shocked. A lot of our friends thought, "Maybe, but I doubt it." Once we made the move, we ourselves realized we were no longer in doubt. Our friends knew we could no longer be with them socially as much as before. We work an eighteen-hour day and, of course, our weekends are the most busy. And this is the time we used to party and so forth.

The thing that struck us most is the different way in which we see our friends. It's almost strange. Things that were so important before appear to be superficial now. Utterly meaningless. Economic gain, status gain. Most of the wives are pushing the husbands all the time—either doing it directly or telling you how he's been promoted, an increase in income and the travel, the chatter about night clubs and parties. The same old thing.

"We've noticed when we've visited, it becomes boring, almost. When we try to get the discussion toward what we think is meaningful, there's resistance. When we bring up the subject of the Negro or Vietnam, they shun away. They escape with words, abstractions. They use every subtle means to shift the subject. Or transfer the responsibility. Or consider it unimportant. They don't even want to become involved in a *conversation*.

We're living in two different worlds. Occasions have arisen when we visit close friends of ours, a couple. We can't help but talk about the inner city. They'd immediately get us off the subject. There's a horrible guilt in the minds of almost everyone here. A guilt about running away from life. Seeking some kind of retreat. Getting away from having to make decisions. They move there not so much to *go* some place as to *get away* from some place. Just like we once did.

When you're running away, as a retreat, into a suburb, you *can't* say you're concerned. You might give a token response, in economic help or a few hours a week. But you can't convince me you're concerned. Most of the problems are discussed in the abstract. They intellectualize a great deal. Whether it's the atom bomb or integration or housing, it's always out *there*. Away from *them*. It becomes obvious as they use things such as percentages and, oh, it must be done slowly. Specifics would challenge them to be personally responsible. If you say you're aware of something directly, then you carry a responsibility.

You see, we moved into Northbrook just months after the Deerfield incident.* We're just south of Deerfield. There was much talk and concern, naturally. There are only eleven Negroes living in Northbrook, and all of them live in the homes where they work. The majority of people

---

* Deerfield became the center of controversy when a builder bought land for an integrated housing complex. After a series of town meetings, a referendum was held. The area was declared public domain. It is now a park, with swimming pool.

claim there is no problem. The reason is they've never confronted themselves with what they would do if something like Deerfield happened. Most of our friends are church-affiliated. But when it connects with life, it become uncomfortable.

I don't think they really believe that the situations we talk about exist. They don't want to believe it. There's some fear that we might influence them, of coming down to visit, of showing them what life is really like in the inner city. They hesitate to step foot into a situation that might gobble them up. In the abstract, they can talk about anything without becoming committed. Unless a person investigates something himself, he knows nothing about it. You can't do it intellectually. You can't go on pure study. A person has to get his feet wet. Once you get your feet wet, then you decide whether you want to throw yourself into it or avoid it. If you escape responsibility, you're a victim. You're not free.

To be free, you must find out who you really are. It took me all these years. Wanderings . . . I was in the gutters of Madison Avenue for a time.

Gutters of Madison Avenue?

I meant Madison *Street.*

You said Madison Avenue.

(Laughs.) Yes, I know. It was 1944, after the war. I signed for meals at Salvation Army hotels. I was flat broke. Without direction, a person falls into all sorts of traps. At twenty-two, I was under the impression I was something I wasn't. I allowed my past family history to represent me rather than thinking in terms of me representing myself.

He recounts his years on the bum. In the city's Skid Row, bootlegging, time in jail, digging ditches, scrubbing elevator shafts, running away to the deserts of New Mexico, working as little as possible, walking from one Indian mud hut to another, "a bum in bare feet, a rope holding my pants up. I was really running away from life." Eventually, through the encouragement of his high-school sweet-

heart—his wife—he enrolled at the Harwood Foundation in Taos, studying art, sculpture, stained-glass work. He graduated with straight A's. "And what did I find in the suburb? People in a rat race, busy running away from life."

In my life on the streets as a bum, I was running into everybody and finding likenesses of myself. In people of different color skin, some good friends, some bad friends in people I would have admired because of their blond hair and blue eyes and the others who were not like I was told they were. They were all likenesses of myself. I recognized their fears, my fears, self-preservation, the manner in which they survived. Without being conscious that something was happening to me, it was happening.

My car was broken into a couple of weeks ago. My television set was stolen. The person took something that didn't belong to him because he had nothing. I could put myself in his shoes. My friends'd be shocked, naturally. They'd say, "Well, this is the inner city. It's stealing, lying, irresponsibility." I see the desire to change oneself, one's living conditions, as necessary for all human beings. If a fellow fills out a false application for a job, he's stealing as much as a man who goes into a grocery store and puts a piece of meat under his arm. The most obvious fact is that he's hungry and can't pay for the meat. It's not a natural thing to steal, although there is something in all of us to deceive at one time or another. The worst of all is to deceive yourself.

As I see people in the neighborhood, I see a real, deep desire to *become* themselves, to be recognized as someone with a name, as someone with potential. Sometimes it's in the way they walk, sometimes it's in the way they speak. Or sometimes it's in stealing. They're all seeking to be recognized as being able to do something different than what they're doing, something better. To be accepted, to be desired.

When you can see all men, no matter what part of the world they live, no matter what condition, as having these common desires, then it's easy to face the fact: Gosh, they're just like me.

. . . Yes, the city's a threat. It's a horrible threat to all mankind. And yet it's the most beautiful thing there is.

There's more creativity going on in the city than anywhere else in the world. Unless a person allows himself the privilege of living deeply in the city, he's missing a great deal of life.

POSTSCRIPT

"Our friends are anxious to know when we're coming back: 'I suppose you'll be back pretty soon, won't you?' There's that guilt, again. One of my neighbors said, when we moved away, 'Dave, it wouldn't bother me one bit if you were to rent your house to a Negro.' She would welcome the idea, but is afraid to do it herself. There's that fear again—of what others would think: not 'What do I think?' "

· · · · · ·

Hal Malden, 35

He was in jail, sentenced to one year and fined $700. The charge: defamation of character. The victim: a celebrated Negro performer. Malden, at the time of the misdemeanor, was a member of the American Nazi Party.

He came to Chicago in 1954 from a small Arkansas town. His family was lower middle class. His father, a car dealer, had lost all his money and now held a minor county job. "I had never really known a Negro personally. I had never known a Jew, although there were two Jewish farmers nearby. I once dated the daughter, but I didn't know she was Jewish.

"When I got into this Fascist bit, I had to cover up a lot of unanswered questions. I had to cover up a lot of things that didn't make sense."

After serving five days, he was out three years on bond, was retried and sentenced to serve out the remainder of his term. At the time of this encounter in jail, he had three months to go. We had met originally at a house party, knowing little of each other. We were drawn together by our mutual admiration of Big Bill Broonzy, a Negro blues singer.

He had been attending various colleges, off and on, for the past ten years, majoring in Spanish. "I always enjoyed

350

being with Mexican people." He had a couple of unfortu-
nate marriages.

*"I wanted to be an individualist: a person who feels he
does what he should or wants to do. I'm in jail as a result
of doing what I thought was right—at the time. Kind of
like the fellow who drove his car into the store-front window on Saturday night. When he went to court Monday,
he told the judge that when he did it, it seemed like the
right thing to do. That's kind of the way I was."*

I worked three years in Chicago for an insurance company and hated every minute of it. It bored me to
death. I came to work one Friday, it was payday. I hated
it so much that I took my check and went and cashed it
and walked right out and got on a highway and hitchhiked
to Mexico City. Just to get away. I just felt I was gonna
crack up, if I came to that office one more time. The work
was of no consequence. As a matter of fact, business, period, just bores me to death. I came back trying to make
the nine-to-five bit again. But I couldn't. That was about
four years ago. I felt lost. I was groping around, I didn't
know what I wanted to do.

I joined the army in 1957. I had some sort of an idea
that maybe it was a panacea. I thought that a professional
soldier was an ideal man. He's in an honorable profession,
he's looked up to. I guess I got my idea of the army from
movies. (Soft chuckle.) I found it to be vastly different. In
twenty-four hours, I saw that it wasn't what I thought it
was gonna be. I found it was just about like anything else
I'd run across. People just doing their job, making a livin'.
I found it to be just as petty as anything else. Much more
conformity. Everyone was afraid to do anything on his
own. I got out on St. Valentine's Day in '58.

*He recounts the various jobs he had: a grocery store, an-
other insurance company, college for a semester. "I still
didn't know what I wanted. . . ."*

I joined the American Nazi Party in 1961. To me, at
that time, the world was a very confused, disorderly place
that was on the brink of falling apart. I saw that as the
only thing that could bring about order. I really don't
know what I honestly thought. I told myself something

would happen. . . . I wasn't what I wanted to be. I didn't have what I wanted to have. I couldn't accept it as my own fault, so obviously it was someone else's fault. I felt frustration. I thought this would bring some kind of order: everything as it should be, where it should be.

Did you wear the uniform?

No, I never did. I didn't feel that I had the right to wear it. I've always been very sensitive about having something that I don't feel I have the right to have. I would be very uncomfortable if I thought somebody attributed some ability to me that I didn't have. I'm always careful to point out to people that I didn't graduate from college, that I don't speak Spanish fluently. If I see that someone is assuming that I can, I tell them that I can't. I don't want to be thought of as being a phoney.

I always felt that I was somehow awkward or clumsy or something, that I was inept. I really don't know why. I don't think I am now, any more than anyone else is. And if I am, so what? At the time, I was very, very sensitive about it.

But I did wear an olive suit and a white shirt and a black tie. I just happened to have one. Maybe I was trying to wear a uniform without really wearing it. It's like a badge. I laugh at some of the funny things that I used to take so seriously. It's actually funny. A monkey in silk is still a monkey. Clothes don't make the man.

I didn't make speeches because I didn't feel I had what it takes to get out there. About all I did was any time someone came to town, I would always put them up with me.

He recounts a sequence of events that led to the incident, the cause of his conviction. Things were getting tight: an ex-convict member in California was found with a machine gun and sent up for several years. Colleagues were frequently getting thirty days for disorderly conduct. Ironically, he was about to pull out. "I told Rockwell I had lost interest."

A Loop movie house was showing a film featuring a celebrated Negro performer, "who could easily be a target of any racist group. He's about everything they hate,

*everything rolled up into one. And he's got money and
seems to be having a hell of a time with his life."
(Chuckles.) "A perfect target." The theater was picketed;
the signs were defamatory. Malden was away from it,
across the street, "to see if I could get an objective view."
He was recognized and arrested.*

You meet quite a few worried people in this thing.
There's always somebody around willing to drive a car for
a little thrill or something. One thing that everyone
seemed to have in common was a terrible frustration.
There were no really happy people in this whole thing.
Someone always had some kind of a bug. Of course, at the
time I could overlook any fault. You'd be surprised in the
city of Chicago, there are literally hundreds of people like
this. I know people who are on social security, who send
five dollars every month every time they get their check,
to someone like Rockwell.

They have this enemy called "they." You ask one of
them who "they" is. They'll say "Well, the Jews." You say,
"Who?" "Well, you know." If you say, "No, I don't know,
tell me," they become very frustrated; they get agitated
and they say, "Hell, you wouldn't believe it if I told you."
"They"—the Negro, the communist . . . "They" is someone who is keeping them from their rightful place in society.

When I came to jail here, everyone knew who I was,
July, 1961. They had just seen me on TV. Some kids in
here thought I was going to organize an American Nazi
Party in jail and they wanted to join. It's funny, quite a
few Puerto Rican and Mexican kids were interested and
some Italians. For one thing, it would distinguish them
right away from the nonwhites. I told them to stay away
from me.

I was whacked a few times by some Negroes. I honestly
thought I was going to be killed. I thought when night came,
I was going to get my throat cut. I stayed up all night just
expecting any minute for it to happen. I was sent to maximum security. A funny thing happened. A Negro man
came over. We talked a few minutes and he left. And nobody bothered me. A few days later, I found out it was
Big Tom. Somebody told me, "He runs the place here. If
you're all right with him, you're all right with everybody."

All the guy did was just come over and ask me if I still felt the way I did. I told him very honestly I didn't. My whole system of values and everything else was shaken up. I didn't know what the hell I did believe in, but I didn't feel that way about anybody any more.

After five days in jail, he was out on bond, pending appeal. He was free for three years.

It was like coming into the world again. I believed with all my heart there had to be something more to the world than what I had found so far. I was trying to see what it was all about. I found people were willing to accept me. I got a job tending bar in Old Town. A jazz place. I always loved traditional jazz and folk music. I had the greatest summer of my life.

I met Little Brother Montgomery.* I got to hear him every night and play poker with him. Of course, they were of all races and religious backgrounds. I didn't know until the end of the summer that these people knew about me. Most of them knew who I was, but they hadn't said anything. It was an awakening.

I don't know if this had anything to do with it or not. I met a Negro girl and really fell in love with her. She taught me a lot that I had never really thought of. She showed me a world, another society that I didn't know anything about. And I showed her. She had never met a Southern white. I think we taught each other about different kinds of people.

I've always been searching for some way to live so that I was comfortable. I still haven't quite done that. One thing I have learned now is that I can learn something from almost anyone. I can set down to some derelict here, who will probably be coming back to jail the rest of his life. But I could probably learn something from that fellow.

That's the reason that as soon as I get out of jail and I get a few bucks together, I want to go around the world —if it takes forever. I want to know what's goin' on. Learn about other cultures and other ways of life. I started saving money. I still have the idea of hitchhiking

* A Negro blues pianist and singer.

354

around the world, to see if I can make it—working a little here, there. Go out for maybe two years to wander around and see what it's all about. Looking for something, I don't know what.

He returned to college, majoring in sociology and anthropology. One teacher, in particular, influenced him profoundly.

I heard of a job as interviewer in the slum areas, teenaged boys and their mothers. I had no idea if I could do the job. I had never talked to anyone before. I was told to call a Mrs. Newman. I thought, well, here goes the job. (Chuckles.) She had to be Jewish. It turned out Mrs. Newman was Negro and a very intelligent woman. We got along very well. She hired me. I went to work on the Near West Side and on State Street.

I loved every minute of it, going to people's homes and talking to them. Many of these people were Negroes. I don't know if it was my Southern accent or what, but I found I could establish a certain rapport with them. I was interviewing quite a few Mexican kids, too, and I liked that. And I interviewed some Southern white kids and I liked that.

After about a year and a half, the fellow I was working with thought I would do well in social work itself. A job came along, working with high-school dropouts. Everything was going great for me.

I forgot all about my case, my troubles. I had severed all my connections with the American Nazi Party long ago. It was almost like it never happened. Like it happened to someone else. I was beginning to feel comfortable with myself. One day while waiting for my laundry to dry, I picked up a paper and saw my name in it: "Pair sought by police." I almost fell out right there.

He gave himself up. The appeal failed. His $1500 savings toward the round-the-world trip went to the lawyers. He was back in jail. "Quite a few people feel I could do something useful on the outside."

I don't know who knows about me here and who doesn't. It's been three years since the arrest. In that dorm over there, if anyone wants to spell a word that's difficult, he comes and asks me. I've written quite a few letters for people. In a certain way, they look up to me. I'm getting to like myself more all the time. I'm accepting myself, my shortcomings, my failures. . . . I don't want everybody to love me. All I want is a chance to do whatever I can do.

My family back home doesn't understand it. All they know is I'm up here in the North in some kind of trouble with the law and it has to do with some civil-rights stuff. (Laughs.) I'm gonna wait till I can get home and I can sit down and explain it to them when it's all over. To me, it'll be like when somebody comes home from the war and tells them about the way it was over there. I'm gonna go down and tell 'em how it was up here.

They'll be very surprised about my feelings. It'll be very interesting for me to go down and see what's actually gonna happen when schools start integrating in Arkansas. I would like to be down there and see it. I'd like to be down there to ease the blow if I can. (Laughs softly.)

I look at this city differently now. There are things here that I never noticed before. I never had time, for instance, to go down to the lake before. I never had time to go for a long walk. I was always looking for action. I'd go out of my way to see a fight—if it was nothin' but a drunk bein' thrown off a bus, I would stand and watch. I spent time in Skid Row, just looking, kinda like lookin' at a movie. Life, I was observing it before. I want in it now. I want to be in on it.

I feel there's enough beauty in the world, there's enough ecstasy, there's enough of these good things to make up for the rest. To me, one of the most beautiful things in the world is an Oriental rug or a flower. They're the epitome of whatever they are, the peak. I don't mean something should be perfect. I wouldn't want anything to be perfect. I like that one little flaw. It's said they never make a perfect Oriental rug and they leave a little flaw in 'em. Beauty is something that gives you pleasure. Blues like Big Bill's . . . It's the opposite of the order I was lookin' for. It's the human touch. I don't feel the world could ever be perfect, because if it were, it wouldn't be human. It would be nothing at all.

POSTSCRIPT

Since his release, Hal Malden has been doing social work in the inner city. He is highly respected by his colleagues. As one put it, "He has a rare sense of compassion."

XX

GRASS ROOTERS

• • • • • • • • • •

Jim Campaigne, 25

He has lived in Chicago three years. He comes from a middle-income family; his father, an ex-marine, had been a traveling salesman who became a journalist. His brother, an ex-marine, now at Naval Academy, had attended an old Eastern college "and got fed up, a pack of atheists and everything like that over there."

Jim himself had gone to the same school. "I'm a little down on it. It's been taken over by radicals, really. They don't educate. They're promoters. That's what Max Rafferty* calls them. A diluted Marxism prevails." He *"went in swinging and started a conservative organization on the campus and really had things cooking there."* (Laughs.) "I got myself hauled up before the board of directors, because I was telling the alumni the teachers were indoctrinating instead of educating." *He feels many colleges are like that today.* "The real intellectual must have a dispassionate mind."

The five intellectuals he admires: "Really fine-tuned minds, I'd say: Milton Friedman, down here at the University of Chicago. I'll throw Bill Buckley in, even though he hasn't written a magnum opus. He's a superb human being." *In addition, Elisio Vivas, a Venezuelan professor of philosophy at Northwestern, a German historian, Eric Voegelin, and C. S. Lewis.* "Ayn Rand is good on the attack. She's a very good critic of the inconsistencies of the liberal mentality. But she's got a blueprint mind and I shy away from that sort of thing."

---

* California's superintendent of schools.

He is one of the city's leading spokesmen for Young Americans for Freedom (YAF). "It grew out of a group that masterminded Draft-Goldwater-for-Vice-President, in 1960. All youngsters, a significant number from Chicago. We went off to Connecticut in September, and Bill Buckley loaned us his mother's house for a couple of days and he went off to sail somewhere. We sat around and hammered out the bare bones of the organization."

He is editor of a series of neighborhood newspapers in the Calumet area, on the Far South Side of the city: "Steel plants, strips of homes, and more steel plants." The people work in the mills and in affiliated industries, "heavy Eastern European and a large Mexican community."

I talked with a Mexican woman last week, she's put five or six of her kids through college, by saving and work, and keeping them upright and this sort of thing. They're very conscious of trash and seem to spot a so-called intruder. (Laughs.) They're respectable people and don't like the people on welfare.

I think most of us recognize the mark of the beast on people. It's not a color problem really. There are beasts everywhere. Boors or uncivilized people. Civility is something that touches a man and rubs off his rough edges, his antagonisms, his feelings of aggression, and either channels it along constructive lines or mutes it.

I don't want to sound too hardhearted about welfare people. You can't categorize all of them as a bunch of shiftless skunks. (Laughs.) That would be wrong. But as Al Capp said in *Playboy*, the system has degenerated into something maudlin and mindless and is creating the worst kind of human beings in the world. And not because they're black, because a lot of them aren't. You've got hillbillies on ADC, as well as Negroes. Fellows that call themselves young studs and have a wife, let's say, in three different locations. And they drive a Cadillac (laughs) for the money they pick up, getting a subsidized house for $36 a month and renting out half for $15 a month.

Most of our people are gregarious, very rough, they've got a sense of humor—Serbs, Croats, and Slavs, your breadbasket-of-Europe people, very friendly. But at the same time, they're very home-oriented. Well kept up. They're the most charitable people in the world. The

Lions Club has raised churches and put kids through college. They do more good things than you can count on all your hands and toes.

They're both warm and cold at the same time. Suspicious yet openhearted. Even I'm an outsider. Educated, went to college, and this sort of thing. They suspect intellectuals, and it's a healthy suspicion.

You don't commit yourself, just like you didn't commit yourself to the bunco man of the old days. Everybody is regarded as a stranger until he proves himself. I think this is very healthy for a community. A stable community has a lot of assets. People know each other. When old Joe down the street's wife dies, thirty women who knew his wife will come in and cook for him and take care of the kids. It gets back to the voluntary thing that Tocqueville talked about. It's now being grafted onto the conservative movement in this country.

Do you discuss civil rights in your papers?

They're thin-skinned about it here. We knock civil-rights agitators, or whatever you want to call them, when we see them.

Would you describe Martin Luther King in that manner?

I would say King is a demagogue first, last, and always. There are all kinds. There are Ku Kluxers and Hitlerites and Jew-baiters, all kinds of demagogues, left and right, middle-wing. They get caught up in it and become messianic.

Is this pretty much the feeling of the people in the community?

They don't know that much. All they know is they don't like him, that he's disruptive and trying to change things.

What's your feeling about the Birch Society?

I think Robert Welch is kooky, but there are an awful lot of good people in the Society. Most of them, if they find out you're a good guy and sincere, will admit they don't really go along with Welch. I think most people regard the Society as the only adult anticommunist group in the country, and they'll put up with an awful lot if they can use it as a point of communication with other conservatives. The Birch Society is just a thing of the moment, a political necessity of the moment. The conservative attitude is something that lasts longer. There are Birchers among the teenagers in YAF. It caused a problem at our last convention. It was scary, almost. Of course, I was that way when I was younger, a lapel-grabber.

Would you describe YAF as a grass-roots movement?

Oh yes. These are doers, the people that care about issues. In the high-school level, the kids are general anticommunist, that's the first impulse, the first little bud of the conservatism instinct. In college it gets more sophisticated. You get into the problems of religion or oppressive Marxism. In communities, it's politics. Those are the three ways YAF operates and vibrates.

We're against 75 percent of the same things SDS (Students for a Democratic Society) are against. They call it corporate liberalism, I call it incipient fascism. This is the fruit of the fifty-year labor of the same kind of people that started the Fabian Socialist movement. We're *against* the same things as SDS but not *for* the same things. We're for free enterprise, for example. I have always thought the Birchers were crazy when they thought the Commies would take over this country. Nothing of the sort. It's international socialism. We're on the road now, with creeping controls. It'll be a native variety of Naziism.

SDS is naive with respect to its positive program. Some sort of participatory democracy, they talk about. It doesn't take into account expertise. Everybody should vote, they say, even though some people may not know what to vote about. That's democracy, and damn the consequences. I've always thought that was sort of a foolish thing. I'm not for suppressing it. If anybody wants to say anything about it, that's fine. It's naive talking about the poor taking part in the antipoverty program, especially when it's my money or yours.

People that know what they're talking about ought to be able to have a say in the way things are done. I'm not for one of those crazy schemes like H. L. Hunt's, where the more money you have, the more votes you ought to have. (Laughs.) That's pre-posterous. But if you're gifted with brains and talent, you should kick some of it back into the system. Right now, people with talent are being bled white by a confiscatory income tax that confiscates proportionate to their success.

Are you thinking of an elite?

In a sense that noblesse oblige should be expected of people. Not institutionalized. You see noblesse oblige everywhere. Good heavens, look what the Elks and the Kiwanis and Lions are doing, and the small-town type people in big cities. It's as old as de Tocqueville. A voluntary approach as opposed to one that is imposed from the top down.

I'm putting out a newspaper in a steel community. The lack of familiarity with public issues by the average Joe is astonishing. Even among your North Shore housewives. They don't even know their congressman's name.

The average Joe cares when it gets to the sticking point. This is the way human beings are made up, to look after their own interests, their bowling league, their housewifery. No, I don't think the human being is perfectible, if that's what you're driving at: that man is a lump of clay with all the same potential under the skin. I don't buy that at all. Sure, people can always behave better, but how are you gonna bring it about? From the top down or the bottom up?

Bottom up? Isn't that the SDS approach—participatory democracy?

Yes and no. Yes and no. The conservative wants to protect the family unit and the community unit. Perhaps one day there will be international government, but the most important thing is that the first unit is a family. I happen to be quite religious. I'm not a pusher, but I think the religious approach is the sane approach. I took a lot of religious courses in college from a young Lutheran, who impressed me very greatly. The whole idea of the clergy involved in the civil-rights movement is a denigration of reli-

362

gion. It's a perversion or a heresy that traces back to your agnostic Manichean heresies. It's a heresy.

You wouldn't go along with Pope John's Pacem in Terris?

Yes and no. You have to read the right translation and that sort of thing. It doesn't come out quite as liberal as some of the popular media have made it out to be.

Does YAF work in communities the way SDS does?

No. We're too busy trying to hack back the tentacles of government to worry—I don't mean worry about it. Efforts have to be concentrated on both an immediate threat and a long-range threat. YAF people work in neighborhoods, individually. A lot of conservatives are tied to their church. They may be working with the Kiwanis or Jaycees or Elks on a charity project: getting a wheel chair for some kid that's paralyzed. The same sort of thing that SDS is doing, except they're doing it as an organization.

What are these immediate and long-range threats?

The corporate liberal trend. The phrases: general will —general welfare—the state fusing the will of the nation. But I don't believe in the devil theory, either. Right-wingers are accused of being paranoid. It's a handy phrase these days. A smear. The left has as many fears about secret conspiracies as the right has. I believe there are conspiracies, but I don't lock everything into one great conspiracy.

They do draw what we call spider webs. They take a long list of people and a long list of associations and hook them all together. The daughter of a John Birch leader was on the YAF Board. Because she used to be on the Board and I'm on the Board, I'm by implication a Bircher. This is neat.

(Long pause.) What are your thoughts about the late Senator McCarthy?

You can be humorous about it or you can be serious.

Noel Parmenter, a wit that writes for *Esquire* once in a while, thought McCarthy did a lot of good. He scared the communists out of about ten years' growth. McCarthy was a net good in some ways and a lot of harm in other ways. Eisenhower, not McCarthy, destroyed the Republican Party in my opinion. He had these great lights in the Party, some a little more uncouth than others, McCarthy perhaps being one of them. Ike cut the floor out from under them. Taft, for instance, by turning the Party a fifty-degree course toward the middle of the road. In Russell Kirk's phrase, Ike was a golfer. (Laughs.) Not anything else.

He quotes Milton Friedman of the University of Chicago in pin-pointing the cause of the Depression to the Federal Reserve Board's irresponsible policies. He pleads the case of elderly people living on their savings, opposes Medicare in not allowing the elderly to make their own choices; he views with alarm our drifting foreign policy, calls for "tightening the screws": a blockade of Hanoi, sinking allied ships that try to sail through, suggesting Chiang Kai-Shek's armies be sent to Vietnam as well as to the Chinese mainland ("the northeast coast is seething with revolt"), the bombing of China's nuclear facilities. "It seems to me sensible to lock the barn door before the cow is stolen."

There is a frustration that is horrifying. In my community as well as anywhere else. You can't pin it down to one thing. Some people worry about the big problems, some only worry about the little problems. You listen to the chatter of people in supermarkets, on trains, everywhere. You find people living pretty close to their own immediate concerns.

I like Chicago, albeit a city with an awful lot of problems. It has a lot more than other big cities in terms of people. I found New York oppressive, it's people becoming dehumanized and ugly. I'm talking about the upper classes more than the others. Chic, but unattractive, hard, mean, with no feeling of community or good will about them at all.

I hate to give Dick Daley any credit, but a strong man like him, not a captive but a boss, has done well. Even more responsible has been this fantastic, enlightened business community that had really worked out and hassled the bare bones of a program and made it the city it is. I'm more at home here than in any other big city I've seen.

As for re-creating the world, I'd leave it the way it is. It puts an awful lot up to man. A guy has to develop *himself* to be a whole person. Nothing's done for him. No, I wouldn't eliminate war. Then you have to eliminate some of the good qualities of man and the bad qualities also. You have to exercise to toughen your body up and you have to take knocks when you're a kid to get to be an adult. Man's got to have hardship and he's got to have drives and there's always gonna be people who fall away, people who Christ even said are no damn good.

If there were no war, we'd have an awful lot of people around. Some scientists have worked out theories of stress and proximity of populations. When the nuclear pile reaches the critical stage, bang! Things might thus weed themselves out. Who's to say?

I'm not gonna lose any sleep over the Bomb. It bothers me the same way the possibility of getting killed in an auto bothers me. As far as other people goes, the more people you love, the less people you're gonna love intensely. I tend to not be a great brotherhood-of-man guy, except if I'm going to love humanity, I'll love them one at a time. These are my feelings vis-à-vis the human race.

One of the maxims my father gave me was that things have to get a whole lot worse before they'll get any better. I think we're in for hell-fire and brimstone within the next fifteen years. Economic disorder, international disorder of the worst sort, and then perhaps things will settle down. Pushing the button will kill a lot of people, but it won't mean the end of civilization.

It sounds scary to have bombs falling all over the place, but sure there'll be a victor and he'll come out clean. Just like the ants repairing a crushed anthill. (Laughs.) I tend to be a take-it-or-leave-it type person.

Jeane Dixon tells us we're going to have a new Christ. (Laughs.)

Think He'll be crucified again?

It could be the KKK or the Vopo team in East Germany or somebody like Stalin or Mao.

Would we crucify Him, you and I?

Well, *I* wouldn't. (Laughs.) I happen to be very easygoing. I try and pull people rather than push them. I'll associate with anybody, talk to anybody. As far as my soul goes, I think I'm on the right track.

A person like myself tends to be lonely. There aren't too many people you can talk to because I think a lot, I read a lot. I spend a lot of money on education and self-education. I've got an enormous library, and I actually read some of the books.

Do you have any friends?

Not a great number of *close* friends, no. I was president of the varsity club in high school and that sort of thing. But since then I have that itch. It's the thing inside you that pulls you on—to know. I want to know.

· · · · · ·

Anne Grierson, 26

A flat on the third floor of a run-down building in the Uptown area of the city. All the tenants are Appalachian, except this one. The flat is shared by several members of JOIN (Jobs or Income Now), a subsidiary of Students for a Democratic Society.

The furniture is hand-me-down, much like that of the other tenants. There are all sorts of books, especially well-thumbed paperbacks, strewn about: C. Wright Mills, Danilo Dolci, Ernst Cassirer, Gunnar Myrdal. Young people wander in and out; the phone rings often.

Anne talks, while nursing her baby, Sarah, whose lusty yowls and occasional purrings provide a varied obbligato to the conversation. She and her husband, Glenn, have been in the city five years and in the neighborhood seven months. She's from the East. At the University of New Rochelle, she had joined the Young Christian Students, a liberal Catholic group: "They worked on problems they saw around the campus. Say, investigating whether the cafeteria help was underpaid. Or picketing some local place that discriminated. We tried to find out what students could do about it."

For me, this is a religious thing. As Glenn puts it: This is the only group that we've ever been in that can talk about love in a very concrete, real sense. It surprises us a little bit because we've been in and out of a lot of religious groups that don't seem to have the same hold on us. What we're trying to build is a society in which men love one another. A society which has not exploited man, although we're not really sure just what it could be.

I think we're a tiny percentage, if you look at all the college students who are apathetic, interested in cars and girls and getting a good job. That's still the majority. But we're a very quickly growing minority, I'd say.

Here in Chicago, we work with the white poor. CORE and SNCC are organizing the Negroes. We improvise very much. We're not here to be their leaders, and shy away from talk like that. What we hope to do is have a community in which everyone is a steward, helping make decisions on things that affect their lives; that everyone in the group understands what he's doing and not that he's being in some way duped.

Each of us takes a block. My block is the one we live on. What I simply do is go door to door and say I'm from JOIN. And see if we can solve some of the problems we have in common: poor housing, bad schools, and dirty streets, because the city lets the area go, and no playgrounds for children. The only playground in this whole area is on the street the Sisters* live on. It's an island in the middle of traffic. There's about a kid killed every year on this thing.

We have a newsletter, the staff mimeographs it but the community people write it. If anyone has a gripe or a particular perspective, we ask him to write. And if they don't feel comfortable writing, they'll dictate it to us, their words, their thoughts. Seeing their name in print . . .

* The Glenmary Sisters.

We talk to all our neighbors. We have the problem of people working all day and don't have a telephone and also these people come home exhausted. They work six days a week, long hours and hard jobs. It seems like the people who are most enthusiastic are also working such long hours that they're just too tired to go knocking on doors at night.

There's also failure involved, of our not reaching the people yet. We've recently discovered we're not getting anywhere with this door-to-door technique. What we're doing is talking. Somehow this is not working because we're not friends with these people, we're not part of their lives; as one guy put it, maybe getting drunk with these guys on Saturday night.

Now, I just take Sarah on my arm and just go up and have coffee with the lady down the block and talk about her son, who she's afraid is going to be a delinquent. And I just have coffee with another lady and we talk what it's like back home. Not just gripes they may have, something wholly unrelated, personal. At meetings, we have country music.

We were surprised that nobody questions our being here. We thought they'd feel hesitant about a bunch of ex-students, who dropped in on them and were here to change things and all. The people are very friendly and open and accept us. The problem is often apathy: people who often welcome you with a smile and say, "Fine, I'll be there," and they never show up. Then you realize you've never reached them and you have to go back and try again.

We're trying to create a countersociety, unlike the society that exists, but something we would like to see happen. To make people as free as possible to be creative. Even on our own staff. My husband is working as a photographer now, because he has a special skill. He doesn't feel comfortable door-to-door and talking with people. We're making personal discoveries.

There's no facility for child care for working mothers. Most of the women here work full time because their husbands are unskilled factory workers who make a dollar and a half an hour. We've tried to get the local War on Poverty office to open a daycare center—very unsuccessfully. Several women on one block are getting together and plan to open one of their own, each of them to take turns; they're the poor women of the neighborhood. A chance for them to use whatever skills *they* have to create better lives for themselves.

Our relationship to the Urban Progress Center is strained. (Laughs.) They didn't publicize its opening here at Uptown. So we picketed it in protest of its undemocratic nature. It was brought in from the outside, it made no attempt to ask the poor people what they wanted. It's just another welfare agency. If they find a lady with five kids who doesn't get enough income, they tell her where she can go get relief. It's not telling this woman that her society should be reconstructed so she doesn't have to live on welfare. And when a man's out of work and thinks he's too dumb or stupid to get a job, they should give him a sense that it's not him . . . a sense of some self-respect.

My husband and I have no other plans. We find this work more meaningful than any other we can imagine. I grew up thinking people went to school and had very exact notions of what they were going to do with their lives, all laid out from the start. I've found out it's not true. It's not true for us and not true for anybody else I know. Even friends of ours who are in professions, that to all outward appearances look like they know where they're going in life, are full of conflicts and doubts, and wonder whether they should pull out and do something else. And a lot of them don't have the courage to chuck it and find something that's more meaningful. And so I guess in a sense we're improvising. We'll stay here as long as . . .

My father thinks we're wasting our time. If we had a good education, we should go ahead and get a good job. Why are we wasting our talents for nothing? That we should have a good income and enjoy good things in life. Glenn's parents feel the same way. My mother understands very well and encourages us and is really very good about it.

My mother, since I've grown up, has become a more devout Catholic than she ever was. I mean, her concern for other people. Love is the primary force in her life. She's stuck in a little one-horse town, in which the parish is a scandal. The priest there doesn't know anything that's going on. She's the one who brings these ideas in. She writes letters to the editor of her diocesan paper. She reads intelligently and very widely. She had two years of commercial high school and had to quit to work because she came from a very poor family.

My brother next to me is a Goldwater conservative. He's in South America in the Peace Corps, but he's only there to get out of the draft. He wants out of life a good job and to make money. He doesn't see himself wasting his time in the army, it's just for stupid people. My second brother is much like myself.

We expect to have a lot of children. And whatever I'm going to do, the home comes first, if possible. I never have ample time to be a good housewife and mother and it puts a big pressure on me. It creates lots of tensions in me.

We just get room and board here. We have no income except what people give us. We ask unions, but we've been largely unsuccessful in getting money from them. I guess we're largely dependent on the good will of older people, who are willing to dig down and help us live.

We have very little leisure time. We often go out on Saturday nights to a movie and on Sundays we go to church and visit some friends. We get, together, six dollars a week spending money.

We're upset with the local parish church because the sermons have no meaning and the liturgy is in poor taste and it's a huge struggle with us. . . . When we hear a sermon that talks about our being on time for Mass instead of talking of peace in Vietnam or civil rights or simply loving our neighbor . . .

I never attempt to defend the Church or explain it away. When friends ask why we go—because we always complain about it—we go because we believe in God and want to worship. What can we say? We're always questioning and re-examining ourselves. We're not always sure.

I don't believe that men are basically selfish. I have to be an optimist . . . if the world's going to last . . .

POSTSCRIPT

On the day these notes were written, there appeared an item in the Chicago Daily News, February 5, 1966: "The headquarters of JOIN was destroyed by fire Friday night. 'But we're not going to let this stop us,' said Todd Gitlin, a

JOIN staff member. 'We didn't come this far to be scared by fire.' He said a new headquarters would be ready for Wednesday's regular meeting. JOIN currently is conducting a survey of housing-code violations in the Uptown area."

XXI

THE INHERITORS

•

I love life,
I only wish some of it
would come my way.
—LUCKY MILLER, 19

● ● ● ● ● ● ● ● ● ●

Chick Marmor, 19

He "boards" with his parents; he comes, he goes, there is no communication. His father is a clothing salesman for Robert Hall; his mother works as an accountant. A quiet younger brother works from nine to five and goes to bed early. His parents retire early. When his friends visit, they talk or listen to records, always softly.

He attends Central Y College, Downtown, and hopes to become a social worker.

On his muscular left arm is a tattoo: a skull, a sword, a rattlesnake, a bandolier, and, rippling above, the legend: "Born to lose." He explains, "I put that on my arm to prove to myself that I'm not born to lose. I was fifteen when I put it on. To continually remind me that I won't lose. And it's a good reminder, too."

Nowadays, a kid is pressured to a point where they don't know . . . he's either a kid, a teen, or an adult. I just didn't want to be classified, so I moved out. For five years I lived with my boy friend in a coach house, off Wilson Avenue. I got the feeling of being an adult. I was fourteen.

My boy friend's mother had a nursing home. So for four years I worked, nursing patients. I learned how to care for them, dispense medicine.

When I first moved out, it was a fear of being cast in an outer world. A lot of kids feel that, if they leave home, something will happen. They might fail and their parents won't take them back. They just have this fear, a lot of parents have built up in the minds of the child: Until you reach nineteen, twenty, twenty-one, we'll keep you under our wing, we'll watch you, we'll give you money and so on. I didn't want this, that's all. I wanted to live by myself. My parents felt bad at first. But after that, it was nothing, as if they went on a vacation and left me at home. I don't believe in depending on anyone, because the minute they leave, you're lost. Some day my parents are gonna pass on. . . . I felt now's the time to build myself up an attitude of survival in the world, that's all.

I knew I had to go to school, and living by myself, I learned you wake up in the morning, you get dressed, you go to school. There's no messing around. You want breakfast, you get breakfast. I was independent when I was old enough to realize . . . Both my folks worked, you find things to do, you go out with the kids and so on.

I never had the feeling that I was being ruled down by anybody. I just wanted to be able to say I could stand up alongside of somebody possibly a few years older than I am. And be in the same category. That I lived what they lived through. Yeah, I had trouble with the Authorities, one thing or another when you were a kid.

I wasn't really close to my parents. Of the two, I was closer to my father, because I felt that my mother had no reasoning with me. She felt I was too independent, that I could get into trouble. But I had no feeling of getting into trouble. In other words, I got into trouble, I really didn't care. If I got in trouble, fine. If I got out, I got out. If I didn't get out, I didn't get out. She felt I really didn't care. So I would avoid her and go to my father. But my father worked days and nights, so he wasn't really there, either. So I built myself to a point where I could survive on my own.

When I turned about sixteen, I sought someone I could see. I lived in a boy's home for a while, and I met a social worker. At least, he'd give me forty-five minutes to sit there and listen, you know, concerned or not. It turned out he became very concerned. In my mind, he took my image as a father and a mother.

This was before the coach house. I agreed, to satisfy my folks, I'd try a boys' home. I went and visited the place. It looked nice. So I lived there for seven months. I didn't fit at all. Number one, a lot of them were raised in this boys' home. They had no feeling of love, of looking out in the world. They were completely dependent.

The boys' home was their parents. They wouldn't move without someone saying: All right, you can do it. A herd. I didn't want to be with the herd, that's all. My mother, my father, they conformed into a herd. They would work all day and toil, and if the boss would say something to my father, he'd just kneel down and take it, and I couldn't see that. I can't see one adult stooping low to another adult because he has more authority.

My mother always wanted a house. So when we got the house, she went nutty over the idea of gardens all over the place and this kind of stuff. Because you know everybody else on the block has this, she wanted this. She moved from one environment to another and she fell from one herd to another.

I couldn't see it. I feel if you're lucky enough to be brought into the world, then you should see what part of the world you want. It's all in front of you. All you have to do is take it.

What did you mean, there was no love in the boys' home?

There were boys there, nineteen, twenty years old, that had never kissed a girl. Or if they kissed one, it was a quick kiss and they ran away. I was out on the streets and I had seen kids thirteen, fourteen ready to go to bed with girls, and so on. Yeah, I had a very early sex life. That was due to seeking love, I would call it. I had no parental love so I turned to someone I felt I could love. And I'd find a girl and I felt that I loved her, and then sex developed, and after that it was drop her and look for another and another.

My motorcycle is my big interest. I've had a motorcycle since I was seventeen. It's been something I could constantly work on. When I lived on Wilson Avenue, I didn't want to get in trouble, so I felt I had to have something. So I got a motorcycle, completely wrecked it and I built it. I had no knowledge of it. So it took me five times longer than it would take anyone else. And I fell in love with 'em. I wanted it and I wanted it bad. After that I sold it for a car. I swapped it for more money and finally I ended with another motorcycle. I fixed it up, I hopped it up and I customized and I sold it. And I got another one. I want to ride in tournaments with my motorcycle and race for trophies.

I have boots and the black jacket, yeah. When you see a kid in a black jacket, it's not bad, really. They're not killers. It's for protection. I've spilled off my motorcycle four or five times and if I didn't have a jacket, I'd rip my shoulder completely off. The boots are for the motorcycle. My motorcycle is now hopped up to the point where you kick it over, if you wear street shoes, you could break your leg. You put on a heavy boot, you have better kicking power.

When I ride, I dress three, four ways. If I'm hill-climbing, I wear levis and my black T-shirt. If I'm going out on a Sunday, I put on nice pants, I wear very short Italian-cut boots, a nice shirt, a tie, sometimes, sunglasses.

There are motorcycle gangs that shoot for trouble. I've rode with a lot of them, but I didn't want to be part of it. I'm gonna join a club this summer, I hope. They belong to the American Motorcycle Association. Decent clubs belong to this. I haven't gone up for nomination yet. They judge you on how many traffic tickets you get, how you ride, if you're a maniac or not, they judge you by your attitude toward adults, toward people on the street. If you wear the club name, they want to see how you're gonna wear it. They don't want any trouble. They're a respectable club instead of being a gang.

When I was young, I wanted to be another Marlon Brando, you know. Because in the movie,* it was funny. He was an independent as I wanted to be. On weekends, he'd leave the herd and he'd go ride, which is the same feelings I had. But I felt good and bad about it both. Nobody likes to ride alone.

* The Wild One.

What's your feeling on a motorcycle?

Freedom. I guess you'd call it being out in the world. You have no protection around you except yourself. There's more freedom than a car. Complete control over something much stronger than you are. It's a thrill. You have to learn how to harness it, just like you have to learn how to conform to certain rules of society. A motorcycle is the same way.

You don't see much "chicken" played with motorcycles. You have to have a sick mind to begin to do it. I saw two motorcycles headed for each other and they both chickened out at the end. Which is smart to a point. When you see death staring you in the face, you don't actually ask for it. It's going to come eventually, why push it forward?

Vietnam is a big discussion among the kids now. First of all, a lot of girls are losing their boy friends in Vietnam. There's varied views. A lot of kids would like to go over there and just wipe it out. Others are satisfied with the way it's being run. I have no feelings. I run in a different circle.

Day by day, we find something new to discuss. What did you do over the weekend? Whether there's a party coming up. Will someone help you do this? Does someone need help on that? Like my motorcycle, I want it pinstripped. So I asked one of my boy friends to come and help me. I helped another boy friend build up a transmission. Just like adults, I imagine, help one another. If someone needs help with his lawn, if they need help with their car, you ask your neighbor. We do the same thing.

Our motorcycle clubs are all mixed. I haven't heard of any clubs to my knowledge that are all white or black. There's one Puerto Rican club which was last year, which was from around five square blocks. I don't even know if it's still that way. The club I used to belong to, our leader was Negro, all the high officers were Negro. My friends are all mixed. We have a completely mixed school, Central Y, Downtown, where I go.

My parents have no discrimination. The South Side they were raised was at the time white, Jewish, a very high-class neighborhood. In those days, a Negro was just a Negro, that's all. I mean, you avoided them. And they can't see me going down there now to what they feel: I'll be walking down the street and someone will see a blur of white and kill it or something. Which is not true, but they can't see this idea.

Politically kids are just letting it ride for a while. A lot of kids have said it: It's the adults that run it, they started it, so we'll see what they do about it, that's all. You figure we're drafted before they are. They're gonna get the young before the old. When they get drafted, they get drafted, there's no argument about it.

I don't think about the Bomb. I think about Vietnam, what I would do if I was drafted. I'd go into the Marines. To me they're the strongest of them all, which is what I enjoy. They carry the most force and they're the first on the beach, which is what I'd want to do. I'd want to take boxing and judo and so on. If you're gonna spend four years somewhere, you might as well enjoy four years.

What do you think of your parents now?

My parents are people, that's the way I classify them. They're people, they're adults. There's no strong feeling. I never had, I'm not gonna fall into it now.

Do you feel they missed something in life?

Yeah, they missed me. They missed me by a long shot. What else they've missed is their own fault. Not mine, I can't help them now. They're past it.

. . . . . .

Bill Lahr, 18

He was a star athlete at high school; he became editor of the school paper. A middle-class suburb, immediately northwest of the city.

Too many of my fellow students are interested in appearance. Tomorrow night is our senior prom. I think the prom is a fine idea, don't get me wrong, I'm not opposed to it. But for the last seven weeks, you hear nothing but, "Where are you going prom night?" "What's going on prom night?" If you're not going to a beautiful restaurant, if you're not going down to do something really posh, why then you just aren't in at Niles East. I just can't go along with that.

The important thing for them is to be "neat." Do something everybody else does, you're "neat." If you do what they do you're considered "neat." And who is "they" I don't know. I suppose "they" is the class in general. They never consider themselves as individuals. They're a "neat" group, they do things together. If you wear a madras shirt, that's "neat," because everybody wears madras shirts.

I was guilty of this for a long time. The important thing in my life was what other people thought of me. Was I well liked? All of a sudden, this year, I realized the important thing was whether I was well liked by myself. It's a big change.

My mother, who is interested in the social life herself, is always glad when I take an individual stand. I'm afraid she's glad whether it's good or bad. (Laughs.) She just likes an individual stand. For instance, she's bragging this week that her son *isn't* going to the prom. "He doesn't even care for that kind of stuff." So it's funny. (Laughs.)

• • • • • •

Amber Ladeira, 20

A woman living in the neighborhood recalls her first encounter with Amber:

"I didn't run into Amber. She ran into me. I was just standing talking to neighbors, and Amber came running like a deer. Her hair was flying in all directions, and she was panting, she was so tired from this chasing. I said, 'Where are you going?' and she said, 'I'm chasing my brother, I'm looking for my little brother.' And then we started to talk.

"She seemed rather harassed at the time because she said she was responsible for taking care of her brothers, and she was in high school herself. This was about three years ago, she seemed quite young but she must have been seventeen.

"I thought she was marvelous. She seemed very open, very friendly. Kind of freedom about her that I thought was just wonderful, and not very many people have. At *ease with talking to people and just giving out and telling about herself. There just seemed to be a tremendous freedom.*

"And I was a stranger, she'd never seen me before. We talked and I found her very lively and very pretty, too. In fact, quite beautiful. Even under her flying hair . . . I think it was her interest in everything that was going on. And I thought it was very refreshing for a young girl to feel that way."

I hated Chicago when I came here three years ago. I despised it, I despised the schools here, everything. Academically, this high school wasn't rated very high. But monetarily, the parents of the children who attended the school were rated very highly. You know, fraternities and sororities that people wanted to get into, and they cried when they weren't admitted, and cried when they were admitted. I just couldn't see any sense to it.

You see, that's one thing, when you've had kind of a tough life—not as tough as many, many people, I haven't been to Siberia, for example—when you're constantly uprooted all the time, like in my case, then the key to survival is adaptation. If you can't fit into the situation that's at hand, then you're lost. You either have, well . . . like the duckbilled platypus, if he hadn't been able to form all those strange things on his physiognomy, he wouldn't still be here. Why does the kangaroo have a long neck, you know? (Laughs.) Giraffe; I'm sorry.

One way or another, I make it. For example, the job I have now. I'm working for a carpet company and I call people up from lists in the phone book and I say, "Good morning, this is Mrs. Smith?" And she says, "Yes? And I say, "Well, how do you do." Oh, we have a standard pitch, it runs something like this. I say, "Good morning, Mrs. So-and-so," and she says, "Yes?" and I say, "This is Mrs. Miller." What *do* I say? I hate it so much I can't even remember.

Yes, even though we're single, we have to be housewives, you know, to identify with the housewife. The whole thing is a market-research bit, and all that. You have to be a con artist and I just hate that. Our spiel is something like this: "Good morning, we have a marvelous inventory sale going on now of all the top-quality name

379

brands of carpeting, discounted up to forty percent. We'd like to give you a free estimate, no obligation . . ." and so on and so on. Essentially it boils down to this, you get the salesman into the home, they show carpeting, they say this is McGee's or Bigelow or Alexander Smith, but it isn't at all. Everything seems to be fake somehow or fraudulent or false advertising or exaggeration or anything you want to call it, but it's not right.

How'd you get the job?

I saw it in a neighborhood newspaper. So I tried it, and then I began to realize that we didn't have the name-brand carpeting and we just said anything to the people to get them to buy, and that's an expensive item, you know. I've had people tell me, yes, we've bought from your company and it wears out in a year.

This one gentleman I called said, "Well, what are these brands that you have?" Well, I said, Lee, McGee, Bigelow, Karistan, and, naive me, I thought we really did carry them. And he said, "You don't carry Karistan," and I was wondering why he was so positive and I said, "Well, how do you know that?" And he said, "Well, my dear, I'm the representative for Sears . . ." blah, blah, blah. He said, "I wonder if I should take legal action on this," and then he started laughing, and in a patronized way the way some executives do when they think they have something on you, and they did have something on me, but not directly, because I was more or less an innocent pawn.*

I had a job at an employment agency. Now you would be surprised. . . . The girls come in, like I did in this one place. I was looking for a receptionist job. And they sent me here, there, and everywhere. And they told people I could type fifty words a minute, and I cannot type a word over thirty. And the people didn't hire me, naturally, because I wasn't qualified and I wasn't going to lie and tell them I was. And then they couldn't find me a job, so they were in need of a counselor in their agency, so they offered me this. They said, "Well, girl, you have something to offer, so we'll hire you, and you'll probably do pretty good."

* She quit the job shortly after this conversation.

So it starts off. They have certain companies that they call up: We have qualified girls, blah, blah, blah. The girl comes in and they don't know how to do a thing, and the counselor tells them you've got to look like this, and you've got to act like that, and you've got to convince them that you can do it. All kinds of conning again. Now we'll call up and you get what's called the job order. Now do you know what the employer wants?

First he tells me, "I don't want a Cleopatra type, talkative, I don't want a fat girl, I want an All-American, clean-cut, pretty girl." He starts telling me all the qualifications he has on the personal side, you know, some of them want live-at-home girls or girls on their own or girls boarding, they even have requirements like this. What does this have to do with her qualifications for the job? Nothing, but that's in the job order. I could show you tens, hundreds of them like this.

Then they say a little code, DBE, that means dark brown eyes, no colored people, don't send us colored applicants. Or they had another one, no green eyes, that would mean Catholics. I've forgotten all the codes, but they had to do with the eyes, blue eyes, green eyes, and DBE—I remember that the most, because that infuriated me the most. Yes, and many companies would say: "No DBE's, no, that's not right, send us some, but use your own judgment." In other words, the most attractive, the most white-looking ones.

For instance, you have a job order, say job number 10, they'll give you the rundown: the appearance of the girl, and then at the end of this, they'll say, "Oh, we want her to type sixty words a minute." That usually comes at the end. It's the *type* of girl actually that they want. They want a type. It's funny on the phone, they'll start running off at the mouth about how she looks, where she lives, and what type she is. It's funny.

I worked for them four weeks, and it's straight commission and I didn't get a penny, because I left before I could hire a girl; and I thought the whole thing was so fraudulent and so prejudicial and everything, I just had to leave.

Just before I became an employment counselor, I went there and they sent me on different little office jobs, receptionist supposedly, and you know, file clerk and everything. But, you know, dressed just so in the business thing.

Not too colorful, not too gaudy, just right, the hair up just so and everything, didn't talk too much, sounded bright but not too bright, I'm a secret actress, but unfortunately, they seemed to sense something. I wasn't their type. That's the whole thing. I wasn't their type and they knew it. Even though I was dressed just like the rest of them were, I wasn't their type and I wouldn't fit into their scheme of things, so I wasn't hired.

In every company, there's an average, you know: dresses well, a little business, collegiate stuff, flirts a little bit but not too much, knows when not to put her foot in her mouth, is discreet and tactful and will be an asset to her boss, and this kind of thing. And very, very seldom do they want an independent girl. They're uncomfortable, too. It's really a very natural situation.

I have an opinion our free enterprise is gonna survive for a long time in some fashion, shape, and form, because it seems to go on with the unfortunate things that we have in the world, little, big, grabby, and we all want something to our own little selves. I've never seen a society that's ever lasted that was really marvelous and based on things in human nature that would be nice.

I worked in a factory. It was a very enlightening experience. This was a couple of months ago, just after I came back from Brazil. I visited my grandparents. I needed a job and I noticed that in the neighborhood, they had a cap-and-gown factory. I always wondered how this worked. But what's more interesting than anything else was the people who work in a cap-and-gown factory.

People assemble things together and they talk very frankly, very earthy terms are used, and many of the people work at this humble job at a dollar thirty-five an hour are hillbillies and they call each other hillbillies in a very fun-loving way. I called them that, too. I got to learn a little about factory life and about different people like the hillbillies, for example, and they had different ways of living and different ways of thinking and loving, and it was nice.

A week before I went to Brazil, I was looking for a job, just for a week. And I saw an ad in the paper, a family wanted a woman to take care of a little boy in the house. I went down there, Chatham, a nice Negro section. I worked for a week as a housemaid, of my choice, to see whether I was really prejudiced or not. See what I could learn.

I was the domestic and she was the one, the Negro woman, that ordered me around. And I didn't mind it. I disagreed with things she did, because I didn't like the way she was doing them, but not because she was a Negro lady, and I learned at last that everything I crow about is really true.

Suppose this woman and her family moved next door to you and a hostile, threatening crowd gathered?

What would I do? What would I do? I would maybe address them through some kind of megaphone and say: "What are you trying to do? Are you throwing stones at someone that has a different color skin than you, what's the difference? If they keep their house clean like you do, what's the difference? The real-estate values aren't gonna go down, that's ridiculous."

And say all this through a megaphone?

Probably. What's to be afraid of? I walk down the streets late at night and I do things that people just wouldn't do in a big city, because I don't believe a word of everything I read or hear. I walked once from Sin Corner, which is 63rd and Cottage, to 83rd, twenty blocks, no one bothered me. A few whistles and catcalls, that's just about it. If you comport yourself right . . .

Yeah, everyone I know thinks I'm strange. I don't think I'm strange at all. I like to be left alone a lot. I like to write and stay up till five o'clock in the morning and sometimes I talk to myself and have a good idea and I'm reading something and I'll explain something out loud and go jot something down. . . .

And maybe the reason I did all those jobs is deliberately because I wanted to learn from everything. I have a very good friend who was very high up in the Poverty Program, he's quitting suddenly, he's going to be a free-lance photographer, then he's bumming his way to Europe, then he's coming back to have another completely different kind of job. And it's marvelous to be able to do this.

I was invited by a girl friend to live on the South Side.

Well, I didn't like the way she lived, because, well, you know, she had different values than I did, and all sorts of men were wandering in and out of the house and I didn't care for it too much; I didn't object to her doing it, I just didn't want to be there myself. Anyway, I met a guy, a very sad case, he lost his wife and little daughter within a year of each other. So he had a large South Side Hyde Park apartment, and it was just him and his fifteen-year-old son and he said, "Would you come and live with us and be a homemaker here?" And I thought, why not? Well, don't I do just that. And everyone was screaming: Oh, you'll get a reputation, and oh, my God, what's going to happen to you. . . . I went anyway. And I had a room to myself and a bath, and I cleaned the whole place up, and I did cooking and entertaining. I learned to cook very well from this.

They all thought I was rather strange. You know, I look kinda different. I'm small and I have long blond hair and I usually leave it down, and I'd cook great big dinners, you know, simple stuff. I'd bake chicken and put all kinds of garnishes on it and.

How'd you learn to cook?

I had to. You know, things just come natural, if you've got to . . .

Just take any problem at all, and use the brick wall as an analogy. If you've got a brick wall and it's around you, you either have to sit in front of it and think for a minute, you've got to do the best you possibly can. If there's a door, you'll go through it. If there's an opening above and you can fly over it, you will. If you can break it down, you break. But if you can't, you can't. Then you must wait for someone to break it through to you. Then the only thing you can do is just sit there and wait until you see your way to having another solution. You cannot butt your head against a brick wall. And the trick is not to sit and wait forever. 'Cause that's apathy, and you've got to be careful, that's all.

Molly Rodriguez, 15

Mexican; one of eight children. She is seated on the sofa with her Anglo sister-in-law, seventeen-year-old Lorna, her brother Ernie's wife.

What do I do now? Nothing but laze around the house. That's all. My thoughts? Oh, my thoughts are a lot of things. Especially about school, and how it will be in the future. There won't hardly be any work because all the machines are taking over and you have to have a high-school education for this and ya have to have a college education for another thing. And that's just it, you ain't got it—well, you're just gonna sit there and just rot away.

Any hope? Oh, maybe that I get married and I find a boy that is not that smart, but at least he went to high school and he'll know what's happening and all that.

There's some colored people that are all right and there's some that are just no good. To me, they're like dirt. I just don't go for them. I'm actually *scared*. 'Cause you walk in their neighborhoods and what do they do? They throw rocks at you and all that. But then when they come walking in ours, they just want you to sit there and do nothing about it. If it's that way, why do they do it to us? We can't go all over the world, because they're all over. I mean, we can't fly over them either.

What kind of world would I like to see? A world with all white people, no colored or nothing. That's all. I mean, I just put Mexicans and Italians and a couple of Irish people, that's all. I wouldn't put no colored people in there.

• • • • • •

Frankie Rodriguez, 17

Molly's brother. He has been arrested several times; a drop-out. In a parked car somewhere in the neighborhood, about one A.M.

Why should I worry about the world? I figure it this way: Who's gonna take care of you? Nobody! And you figure these people that don't wanna take care of you and you ain't got no education, what're you gonna do?

I wasn't learning nothing in this school, nothing at all. Just sit back, watch the teacher say something, and what not. He never asked me to say anything. He never told me to do nothing. Just as soon as the bell rings, go to another class. That was it. I even asked one teacher, "What's this?" You know. And he wouldn't even answer me. It was a drag.

What're you gonna do? You gonna be walkin' the street? So I figure like this: If I can't make money the right way, I'm sure gonna make it the wrong way. I'll be livin' in jail. (Half-laughs.) That's my home, that's my next home. Because look it, if I pull a job, I have it real nice, you know. If I get away with it. If I don't get away with it, I'm in jail.

What can I do in the street? I don't wanna be walkin' the street. Because you walk the street, and you see these young guys, like they wanna go bum-huntin'. Ha. They might just grab you one of these days and beat you up. So I figure like this: Why walk the street and look for your dimes and nickels and pennies on the sidewalk, when you can be robbin'. And if you rob and get away with it, you're lucky. But you can't be robbin' all your life, an' then don't get caught. So ya figure like this: You're gonna spend a couple of times in jail. But you ain't got no education, so that's it. It don't bother me. 'Cause I don't really care about the world, and the world don't care about me.

• • • • • •

Dan Fowler, 20

A student at Northwestern University. Background: upper middle class. Says Dan: "I respect my father very much. He was able to go from relatively nothing to the vice-presidency of an auto corporation. Knowing him, he will set out in another enterprise that will about equal the amount of work and challenge. He's a tremendously dynamic per-

son and when he gets to work, I don't know how to describe it, it's unreal."

There's no place on the campus for me. It's always remarkable how no one says goodbye; they always say, "Have fun." Northwestern students are too cool to get involved in anything. You can't show up at mass meetings, that's very uncoolish for them. Although if there are enough people there to be seen, a lot of people stepping out and making the scene, checking out and everything, to use all the jargon . . .

It's indicative of the North Shore Country Club type society that's going to grow up in a rich suburban neighborhood, who get their vice-presidency in a corporation and they're going to live in a $50,000 house. They're decked out in the madras, regard themselves as being in the "in" group. It's just a kind of complacent indifference to everything. It's not only a nonengagement, it's a nonthinking type of existence.

Do they laugh at the kids who picket?

No, I think they may even feel a little guilty about it all, because they know it's right, you know. But I don't think they do much thinking about it.

And there are the kids who are deeply engaged in study and stuff. I don't know what to think about them, because I don't know very many. There's a possibility that they're not accepted with some peer group on the campus and they feel they're some outcasts or whatever. They plunge themselves into their studies.

A lot of them don't worry too much about the prospects of nuclear war. I feel they take it for granted so much. I feel, just what does it take to scare this clown?

You're scared, I take it?

Well, let's say I'm not thinking of getting married at the moment. (Laughs.) And I'd like to. I think about whether I want to bring kids in the world and all that. If the Bomb does fall, I'd like to be around. Maybe we can kill off all the generals and get a more selective breeding. (Laughs.)

I attended a teach-in recently, and what bothered me

387

was the outright emotionalism. It didn't change my thinking. I mean, there's blood flowing in that land, these poor people are being bombed. We've napalmed, burned up the kids. Another VC installation bombed today. I mean, who are they trying to kid. But at the teach-in, it was like a game of intellectual volley ball. None was listening to the other's arguments, really. Ha, I won this point, this intellectual point, rah, rah. The only reason I'd give a rah was when the poor Vietnam people stopped being bombed and killed.

I respect the man who does little action but tries to stay outside society and gain insight into what's going on. I think this will somehow all blow over while I'm developing. My values are forming slowly and when I'm ready . . . Of course, it's easy for a twenty-year-old from a comfortable WASP community . . . (Laughs.) Most people don't realize decisions are being made, whether they're choosing or not. Because if you don't decide about an issue, inevitably something will happen. I'm just soaking in; I imagine most young men are.

What do you think of the kids who went down to Mississippi?

My first reaction was, I wonder if it's going to do any good. I can semi-understand the Southern position, while I sympathize with the Negro. I tutor down at Lawndale. I felt I wanted to do something for myself. I knew that if I could teach these little kids something I knew, I would get satisfaction out of it. Of course you don't really get much done. I mean you're just deluding yourself if you think you're uplifting Lawndale with your great one and a half hours a week. You're lucky if you can get the clown to sit down in a chair long enough to open a book. They're from six to about thirteen. And it kind of baffles them to know somebody's concerned. This is the only thing I've really enjoyed . . . the kids give me such an uplift. I mean they always come through for you. . . .

What's your father think about this?

He's not too excited about the civil-rights movement. He's got his own problems now. When you're a high-pressure executive living in a high-pressure world, you don't think that much. I knew he wouldn't be interested, and I didn't care what he thought. He's developed this tremendous drive. He has what I call salesman ethics. You know, sell, baby. His moral system is incompatible with mine. But I wouldn't say that mine would necessarily be mine, if it weren't for the easy time I had of it. He values things, I take them for granted. Now, if I was at Lawndale, I don't know how I would be. . . .

. . . . . .

Jimmy White, 18

He came to Chicago from Birmingham, Alabama, at the age of seven. He lives with his grandmother in a housing project on the Near West Side. She runs an elevator at one of the hospitals in the Medical Center nearby.

He dropped out of school about a year ago. At fifteen, he had been a street fighter and acknowledged leader of a neighborhood group, the Counts. "Just fightin' anybody and everybody. It wasn't because I had a dislike for them. It wasn't that I'd go jump on some white guy, it was anybody, people of my own race. You want to be known. You want to feel you're important. If you can't get attention one way, you get it another."

A neighborhood street-worker took an interest in Jimmy. "Now, there's a little boy's club I took up with. Kids about seven, eight. I'll take 'em out to the beach, you know, to places they haven't been. We go to the park, play ball. Little kids are pretty much easy to please. I would like to do this job here, I really would."

I get up in the morning, most of the time I take a cigarette. After takin' a cigarette, I'm pretty sick then. (Laughs.) I probably won't even want breakfast. I walk around a little while. Talk to the lady in the cleaners. She ask me if I'm married. She know all the time that I'm not, but she just hold conversation. We might talk about anything and everything. I go back to the seventh floor of the building, talk to some neighbors. I come here to see who's in the neighborhood.

I ride bikes or something. You know, it's pretty childish. (Laughs.) But there's nothing else for a guy that's eighteen. You don't feel like bein' around a whole lot of guys that's younger than you all the time. You feel like goin' places and doin' things. Things I have never did before. Like down in Old Town, the chauffeur drive you down with the horse and buggy. It's comical. It's somethin' you see in the movies.

Most people pattern their whole lives on the movies, you know. They see a pitcher. Tarzan, Superman, anything. They see it on television and they try it. I'm pretty much like everyone else. I want to do 'em. Go to exotic places, places I haven't seen, may not ever get a chance to see.

Everybody dreams. You dream that you're rich, you have all you want. My dreams are usually a penthouse. I'm up on the last floor, I have all the money I want, I have all the pretty girls I want. And then again, you change the dream sometimes. You walk down the street, you may see somethin' that may cause you to dream about it. Of course, everybody dreams, just about, at night. But I mean daydreamin'.

Sometimes I dream about bein' married to a girl and she's real nice. I come home after work and she'll know just how I feel, you know. She'll bring my slippers out or somethin'. She'll have me a beer or somethin', you know, in the movies they can really get you all shook up, make you think how perfect marriage is. But then again, you know it's not that perfect, but you can still dream about it. Like myself: I'll come in, and here's my slippers. She's standin' there waitin' to kiss me or somethin' like that. And food's prepared—or she may even be preparin' it when I come in. And she'll say, "Jimmy, dinner'll be ready almost any time. Why don't you sit back and drink the beer and watch television for a while." Or even read the paper or take out a book you like. And maybe you'll have kids. In marriage, kids suddenly come up, you know. You don't be expecting it, but suddenly they spring up.

But then again, from dreaming I want other things. Downtown in an office, where I won't have to worry too much in the day, pull my hair out. (Laughs.) I want to do a whole lot of different kind of jobs. I want to be an executive, sometime a lawyer, sometime a doctor, you know. I usually wind up doing something else that I never thought I would really do.

Like my problem was, there was a restaurant and they always played music and I like to dance. Certain music make you be in different moods. Some music make you have laughter, make you happy, and other music make you sad. And other music make you feel like you're a Casanova, you want to love, you know. Music has a strange effect on people. . . .

Miriam Makeba, she's unique in my way of thinkin'. Uh huh. Here's a lady who's come all the way from Africa. These people are struggling for their rights and freedom and things just in the same way in the United States, with white and colored alike. I feel the whites are struggling, too, you know. They're wondering. It's really a struggle, for you to think: "What should I do? Should I go along with these guys? Are they really up to my standards?" I feel this way about her. She done come all the way across the ocean and she has proven herself good.

There's one record, "Wimoweh." I think that's great. It means that's a Zulu lion hunt. When I listen to it, I can imagine this hunt. You could almost feel that one of the natives might be scared, you know. He might have fear in his heart. Every record have a peak: where you go up so high and you hit that peak, and then it comes back and it relieves you. This is what she do.

You could have a whole lot of fun at this restaurant. So for a long time I'd cut classes, I'd go there. But each day I'd start out for school you know, in the morning. You'd say. "I'm going to school." But you wind up, here you are at the restaurant. All the kids thinking the same way you are. Here we're gonna have some fun. You start out, like with me. I get on that bus and I be four blocks from home. All of a sudden in your mind, you visualize the music. You start tapping your feet, your feet get itchy, you want to get there, where the rest of the kids are.

You say, "Oh, I can miss my first class period. What's that? They won't even notice I'm gone." But you really do be intendin' to go to the second class. When you get over to the restaurant, you start dancing. Pretty soon the whole day is gone. And here you are, you're saying, "Well, tomorrow for sure I'm going." And this'll continue and it'll continue and pretty soon here you are, you're out of school.

And then there's the other problem that comes in. The restaurant used to be jampacked with kids my own age. Here's the kids, they're smaller and smaller each year. You say, "Well, here I am. I'm old. I'm older than these kids." And you gotta look for somethin' else to occupy your time. You're not in school any more, so what are you gonna do?

You worry about what's gonna happen when you grow older?

I guess everybody worries about it. I worry about it more than most people. I want more things. I don't mean material values, like home, yes, security, yes—but you know, will I be a bum? Will I end up drinkin' wine like a lot of my friends? I see them everyday, they're doing the same thing. Just go over by the tavern and stand there, somebody's gonna buy a drink sooner or later. They cut out from school, you know.

The teacher, she says, "Here's a book, read so much out of it. I want you to go home this evening and write a report." You figure like this: "I don't feel like writin' no report. I don't even feel like readin'." You find yourself nodding in class. You go to sleep. Daydreaming. You wind up thinkin' you're a million miles away. Then when you catch yourself, the class is all over and here you are, you haven't did anything. You try that last-minute rush to get somethin' on your paper. You wind up with D's, or whatever the lower mark is.

I remember there was one teacher, she used to take an awful lot of interest in me. I passed her class. I *really* did. I passed her class. I'm not tryin' to down teachers, you know. But they don't all do the job they really could. One they really trained for. I guess they sort of figure, "I can't beat this guy, you know, so I'm not gonna waste my time. I'm gettin' paid. If he don't want to learn, it's up to him. It's not hurting me."

In order to be a teacher, you have to think about each person as an individual. You can't use them as a group. You can't say, "Well, I'm gonna give all these guys the same thing." I don't think this is doin' 'em any good. You have to think of them all as one special person. You have to care about each one of the students.

When you're learning to be a teacher, you learn you're not supposed to get involved with your students. I think in order to be a good teacher, you *must* be involved with 'em. You have to *feel* somethin' in your heart in order to be a real teacher: saying, "Well, I want this guy to grow up to be worthwhile." So you can turn around and say in a later day, "Each guy, I really poured myself into 'em. If he don't make it, it's no fault of mine. I tried, I really tried. And he knows this, because while he was here I really cared about him as personally as a person. As if he was someone close to me, even in my own family maybe." This is the way I feel about it.

Did you ever think you might be a good teacher?

I guess you do dream about it. Like most students, they say, "I could handle this class better than that teacher could any day." I've seen a lot of teachers that I think I could do a better job than they could. Then again, maybe I couldn't, maybe this is all in my mind. But yet and still I have the idea that I could do a better job.

Everybody's strugglin'. Complainin' too. My grandmother, every time she start complainin' about somethin', she must like it. She don't ever have a good thing to say about anything she like. She might say something good about the bad things. She likes her job, you know. It's because you don't want money from nobody. You got the feelin' that people are always doin' somethin' for ya. They say, "Ah, gee whiz, they ain't no good, they lazy." They down these people on welfare. It's just like a guy that loses a race. He's downed because he loses the race. But they never tell him there's another race, you know. It's the same way with people on relief. You get treated in a different way. You can't do as much as you want to do if you was working. If you was working you could have a free mind.

With my grandmother, she would almost enjoy having to come home and say, "I worked hard all day. Gee whiz, I'm gonna quit that job." Knowing all the time she never leave. Yet and still, she says, "They work me hard. I'm damned tired from it." She blow off steam, you know. (Laughs.) And then she go and think to herself, "This is

what I'm gonna do with my money when I get paid."
Then every weekend, "Oh, am I glad this week is over."
And then she say when the week starts, "All right, here
come another hard week." But you know, you enjoy it,
because it's yours. This is yours because you worked for it.
It's nothing where nobody can say I gave you this. You
say, "I earned this. I came up and did it myself. This
money is mine."

Pride, that's it. I guess you gotta have your pride, no
matter what. If you don't have pride, you pretty lost. This
is where your faith come in. This is sort of like your
strength. You gotta believe in something. Everybody gotta
believe in somethin'. If you don't have nothin' to believe
in, you just walkin' around here and you just might as well
be dead. If it's no more than theyself—if they just believe
in theyself, they really have somethin' to believe in.

We get along okay, me an' my grandmother. Until one
of us gets rubbed the wrong way. If I'm displeased in my
daily course of life, I might come home and take it out on
her. You know, the slightest thing she say, and then boom!
there's a big explosion in our household. I don't be intendin' for it to just about last all night. I figure I'm gonna be
throwin' off a little steam and it'll be all over. But grandmother don't like it like that. (Laughs.) Sometimes she
puts me to sleep, she argue at me so loud.

Yeah, we do a lot of talkin' at times. She tells me some
pretty corny jokes, though. Her jokes are not what I call
authentic. (Laughs.) One time she told me when she was
a little girl, she saw a man standing in the middle of the
road with no head, and he had a casket on his shoulders.
(Laughs.) She knows I'm gonna laugh, because anything
like that is humorous to me. And she get a kick out of it,
'cause sometimes in bed I hear her laughing to herself. . . .

I find myself dreamin' I wish I was there when President Kennedy was shot. I could walk up to the guy that
did the shooting and take the gun away from him and
hold him until the police come. I feel that he was sick. I
don't think you should kill him, you know. 'Cause I don't
approve of capital punishment. I think that God didn't put
no one here to set themselves up to say, "You deserve to
be killed. You should die." This is like sayin', "I'm God."
You're *not* God. Who are you to say he should die?

You're only a person yourself. This guy Ruby that killed Oswald, I feel he was all wrong. And it's all wrong for him to die, too. Yet and still, all of 'em made a mistake. The only person that didn't make a mistake was President Kennedy. He didn't have a chance to.

Suppose you were God?

I'd have it so, when somebody goes to kill anybody, whatever they're usin' wouldn't work. And they couldn't kill nobody. They all go out and work together and grow food and stuff. They'd have fun together after workin' hard. No one person could set hisself up as lord and keeper. I know you can't please everybody. (Laughs.) 'Cause right now I try to please a lot of people and I never succeed. Someone always gets hurt in it.

And with this, I'd create a love for each other. Such a love where it couldn't be unbroken, you know. And they wouldn't want to hurt each other. This is my world. But this is yet again dreaming. If I could do it, I would.

Most of all, I know I could never stop people from hating people and I could never stop people from killing other people. And people dying. I know pretty soon the people I love most will die. When my grandmother die, I want to die the same time she die. When I was little, I remember I used to say all this all the time: "When my grandmother die, I want to die the same time she die. Then I wouldn't be here lonely." But you can't do this, you can't. If she die, you gotta go on livin'. And know that she did do a good job with you, that she really made something out of you.

'Cause I really don't want all that much out of the world. I don't figure the world owe me nothin' at all. If anything, I owe the world somethin'. You know, there's a lot of things for me to do, a lot of places for me to see, a lot of people for me to meet. Different people, people I like and people I won't like. I guess I be lookin' forward to it.

POSTSCRIPT
Jimmy is now in the army, somewhere in Vietnam.

• • • • • •

Lily Lowell, 16

A black heart is tattooed on her pale arm: "Somebody told me, 'You ain't got no heart.' So I put one on my arm." (Laughs.) She digs protest songs like "Universal Soldier": "It gets through to you." She associates with "way-out people" older than herself: "They're what you'd call a searcher, I guess. They stand apart and they have their own views and they say what they have to say. I've sort of been gathering up my own thoughts: Everybody's goin' a straight line, everybody's followin' everybody else. We leave this world, we go into another world. Like Seventh Heaven. You just shoot up with them." She has been drinking since she was twelve. "I don't drink to make myself drunk but to free myself. Sniffing glue makes you high, but it deadens your brain. Grass* is a lot better than glue."

She quit high school after three months: "I was involved in some kind of trouble." She acts as a "governess" for four small children, whose middle-class parents travel a great deal. "The biggest thing is comforting them when they're hurt. Or reassuring them when they wake in the middle of the night that their mother will be there. I like getting through to the little kids, giving them security that they're not alone and things like that.

"Like today, Edward hit Irita because she wanted the toy and he wouldn't give it to her. I slapped his hand and told him God didn't give 'im his hand to go smacking people when they weren't doin' nothin' to him. (Laughs.) And then I told Irita that she should learn to share her toys and she should not want to keep all the toys in the yard for herself. Blending."

When she is not "away" in other quarters of the city or in state institutions, she lives with her thirty-nine-year-old mother, stepfather, and ten brothers and sisters. Among her peers, in a lower-middle-class white neighborhood on the West Side of the city, she is a leader. Often, she draws, writes poetry and long letters to friends. "I found the easiest way to acquaint myself with words was to read the

* Marijuana.

dictionary. I haven't gone through it yet. I have a very big
dictionary."

When I was away, I wrote a poem to my mother. It's
titled, "I Ask You, My Mother."

> Why must you and I grow old?
> Why must we die and grow cold?
> Why must you cry? Why must we say goodbye?
> Why can't we stay young and free?
> Oh, mother, why can't it be?
>
> Why must we suffer the pangs of hell?
> Mother, why can't I be well?
> I ask you as your child—
> Tame me, don't let me be wild.
>
> Mother, don't let me say things
> that will make us part
> and you go away.
> Mother, help me see the things
> that are best for me.
> For some day you will be gone
> But I will live on
> To suffer for each mistake.
> Mother, I give you my heart,
> Please don't break.

I mailed it to her. She sent it back to me. (Laughs.)
She didn't say anything. She just sent it back to me.
(Laughs.) I sent her two poems. I just put it back in the
folder with the rest of 'em. I wrote it to her, 'cause she
always asks me to tell her things. And I can't talk to her,
so I wrote to her. She sent it back, so I didn't write her
any more. I wrote her two and that was all.

Did you ever talk to her about it?

She better not try to talk, I'll pop her on the lip.
(Laughs.) She better stay away from me. I don't want to
hear her. I don't think there's any way to clear the air any
more. I wrote my poems to my mother when I was sober,
because I was locked up when I wrote them.

My day? My mother's up before I'm up. I go and I get dressed. I don't say nothing to her, I'm too tired to talk. I go to work. I come home at a quarter after five and I'm outside by six-thirty. So I don't see much of the family. I just don't like 'em. My mother . . . (Laughs.)

She calls me Joe, see, that's my father. All through my life, everybody told me all you'd need is a mustache to be your father. She told me, "I don't want to hear you, you sound just like your father, and I had to listen to him and I had enough of him. Why don't you go away, you duplicate, you carbon copy?" And all that good stuff. I don't want to hear her either. I didn't tell her to marry him.

I think my father's great. He lives in Peoria with his third wife. His second wife was my mother's sister. I see him once in a while. He doesn't come to our house when he's sober. I wouldn't show these poems to him because he knocks everything.

I think adults are as confused about things as their children are. But they don't want to let on they're confused. They want to make it sort of like: I'm older than you are, so I know more than you know. They don't think you know anything, that's what I don't like about 'em. They take too much for granted.

When a gang fight or a holdup, involving young people, is reported by the newspapers and you see the word punks, *what is your reaction?*

Feeling I get is this was written by some big guy who smokes a cigar, and he's got a big tuxedo on and his foot up on his desk and he sits there and he says, "I don't got no kids, but I still know what they're like. I can tell ya they're all no good." That's how I get a picture of people who write things like that.

Kids, thirteen, fourteen, and so forth are pushed into an adult world. But they still want to goof around. Sort of like a vise, you know: one side you want to be an adult, and the next day you don't want to be. You just get so tangled up that you really don't know what you're doing. You just sort of lose contact, because it's a struggle. They are children, but they don't want to be children. They want to be adults. Then, they don't want to be adults, they don't want to be children. They don't know what they are.

There's so many things expected of them. The kids they hang around with don't expect nothin'. You try to search your soul, man, and the answers just don't come. You just don't know what you are.

Most of the kids around here, who do they have to identify with? Every child is supposed to identify with something or someone. Or they try to identify with so many people that they get confused. And you have to give respect to get respect. Most of these kids, they'll tell their mother or their father: "I don't want to hear it," just as soon as look at 'em. I don't think there's any respect for parents in this neighborhood.

(Laughs.) No, not really. So they rebel against parents, police—authority.

What are they looking for?

Security. Reassurance that life may get better. That they can make something of themselves. Confidence, they need someone to push it up just a little bit. And they just don't get it.

A fifteen-year-old boy, Sugar, sitting nearby, interjects: "I'd rather be dead. I wouldn't mind dying. This world's no good."

This is a famous saying around here: everybody wants to be dead. But they don't believe it and I hope you don't believe it either. Because none of these kids want to die any more than I do. I got some finks around here said, "I'd like to be dead," but when you get right down to wanting to die, you think about a lot of things, like you'll never see those people again, you'll never see your little sisters, and you'll never see nothing again, then you don't want to die any more. Because if you kill yourself, you can go to hell.

If I was God, I'd make the language of God easier to be understood. I would try to alleviate the pressures of living in a way that people would understand [that] when they made a mistake, it wasn't the end of the world. They would get another chance. And they wouldn't have to be a Catholic to get to Heaven. As long as you believed there was a Hereafter, you would get to Heaven. And I think people who disagree with the word of God and yet maintain their own convictions and stuff like that, they should get to Heaven, too.

What's Heaven to you? What's going on up there?

(Softly.) It's like pink and it's blue and when you die, you get to be a baby again. You go to Heaven and there's just little children runnin' around up there. (Laughs.) No adults, and there's no presidents, there's nothing like that. There's sort of like a peace. They're not all the same color and they don't all look alike. But yet they don't have any wars or anything like that. It's just sort of a freedom. Never knowing about war and murder and things like that. They'd just live in a sheltered world in Heaven.

The idea that you'd like to start all over again?

(Laughs.) I think you're prying.

(Laughs.) I am. I'm sorry.

When I was a baby, my mother used to take care of me when I was sick. She used to baby me, spoil me. That was the only time she was by me, when I was havin' attacks or something. I used to fake a lot of them, too, so she would come by me. That's when I was a baby.

Do you believe in Hell as well as Heaven?

Yeah.

What's Hell look like?

It's just hands, reaching up, trying to get out. With sort of fire around them. The more that people on earth pray for them, the higher their hands come out and finally it touches God and He brings them up to Heaven.

We've talked about Hell on earth, is there a chance for Heaven on earth?

Yeah, there's a way. You just shoot up. Meet the right people and just shoot up with them. You're in Heaven with them. Right, shoot up. You gotta get mellow. To live in this lousy world, play it cool.

There's no other way?

Not that I can think of.

She reads a long letter she had just written to a fifteen-year-old girl friend, who has been "away" for two years —in a state hospital. She recounts her own "youth" as a runaway and "swinger." "Believe me, I was a good girl once, and at times still am. I was trying to put the cork in the bottle, so to speak. But every time I do, someone from the past pops up and it starts all over again . . . So I sit here, smoke in one hand, bottle in the other, regrets, and pain in my heart. . . . Don't go on like you do, or you will end up like me, a big fat zero in the eyes of God. . . . All your chances aren't up yet, don't waste your life in a Godforsaken place like that. You've got to do it and no one can do it for you. Don't let the devil's disciple play with your pride, intelligence, and human reasoning. I know it's a slow process and there will be backslides, but keep one foot in front of you on sure ground and you'll come out of the black forest into the streaming sunlight and green pastures."

Do you think you're a big fat zero in the eyes of God?

Yes, I do. Go to confession, all kinds of stuff like that (laughs), then go out the same night and get drunk. That's being a hypocrite.

All the kids in the neighborhood respect you, look up to you. They don't think you're a big fat zero in the eyes of God.

Because they don't know me. They know the *outside* of me, they don't know *me*.

Oh, brother, the world's a mess. A complete mess. There's people fighting in Vietnam and most people around don't even know why we're fightin'. There's all kinds of things happening. The everyday Joe doesn't even know why we're doing things. I mean, I don't know. (Laughs.)

It's gonna take a lot of stuff to iron out the world. And I think before you iron anything out, it's gonna be to late. Something's gonna happen and the whole world's gonna go whoosh!

What about those songs you like: "Universal Soldier," "Eve of Destruction" . . . ?

This is the teenagers' revolt, the young people's revolt. The young at heart, they're revolting, too. But it's not gonna prove anything. There's something somewhere, but who's gonna find it? This is God's plan that there might be a solution somewhere. But you people have to find it, even if you go around blowing each others' brains out. So, I don't know. Sometimes I think His plan is pretty ridiculous.

There's good things in life. You just can't go on telling yourself there's nothing good about life, because there are some beautiful things in life. Art can be so . . . so expressive, so beautiful. Poetry can just elate the mind with beautiful thoughts . . .

This poem is titled, "For Myself, Myself Alone" I was fourteen when I wrote this.

> *I'm not a child of my mother nor of God,*
> *But a child of my own.*
> *I live not of the soil or sod.*
> *A child of independence, no one holds my hand,*
> *A child not of this earth nor belonging to this land.*
>
> *I am not a child of the father nor his will,*
> *Neither a child of song or the night's cold dark chill.*
> *I am not a child of joy or of tears*
> *Nor of happiness nor the years;*
> *Now I leave you with one thought, my friend.*
> *This is by all means the end.*
>
> *If I am for myself alone*
> *What am I?*

EPILOGUE

● ● ● ● ● ● ● ● ● ●

Jessie Binford, 90

Tall Corn Motor Motel, Marshalltown, Iowa: population, 23,000. She returned to her home town in 1963, "when Hull House went down." She had come to Chicago at the invitation of Jane Addams in 1906 and was a Hull House resident until the day of its demolition.

"The day isn't long enough for all I want to do. I can't begin to tell you my new interests: the people who work in this hotel, the college students from little towns around here, who come to see me and talk. And I have a tremendous correspondence with old friends from Chicago and from people I've come to know, when I was with the Juvenile Protective Association, perhaps twenty years ago. People don't forget.

"I'm usually alone and read a good deal in the evening. I rarely go to bed before midnight. Twilight are the hours I like best. I've been doing lots of thinking. . . ."

From her two-room suite, we see the brick building in which she was born.

Here it stands, as fundamentally strong as the day it was built in 1874. And beautiful. The story we loved to hear my father tell was when his father came out from Ohio to see the new house. They sat out on the steps talking. And finally my father said to his father, "It's getting late, I think we'd better get to bed." And his father stood up and said, "I have yet slept in a house with a mortgage over my head and I don't intend to do it tonight." And he wouldn't do it. He was a Quaker. And my father often told us it was the proudest moment of his life when he said, "You don't have to go tonight, the house is

403

paid for." That kind of morality, I hardly know how to express it. . . .

You think of the joy it must have been in those days, to build a house for his family, to help build a town. And what a wonderful beginning for a child's life. You can't get much joy out of the city any more. They've scattered the people, they're wrecking things. You'd have thought there'd be enough people in Chicago who wouldn't let them cut down those trees, just to change the route, to make it a little faster by car, to save a few minutes.* Our whole sense of values has changed. It's reflected here, too, in a small Iowa town.

Nobody walks here any more. He jumps into his car, of course. I walk more than anyone else in this town. I'd much rather get out in the evening at sunset and walk here then get into a car, with probably all the windows closed, because nobody wants her hair to be blown, and just drive around the city's streets. My sister gets into the car and drives to the grocery store instead of walking.

It applies to everything. Nobody seems to care about the things we feel are wrong. Take a town like this. Most people are pretty comfortable here now. They're putting lots of money into schools, especially gymnasiums. A huge, awfully expensive high school here, and the teachers complain about the lack of educational facilities. But people don't want to take any responsibility, you know. Don't bother us, we're comfortable.

Yet, the commonest thing I hear in a town like this is a fear of the unknown. They've got just that one word, Communism. Fear, fear. They don't even know what it means. They know something's wrong, why do we fight over there in Vietnam? They're just scared to death. I think they'd even accept the Bomb. I just stopped talking to lots of people, because I just didn't get anywhere. They say why worry about it? There's nothing we can do about it. That's the problem. I ask too many questions.

We began pretty well here in America, didn't we? When you think of all the promise in this country . . . I don't see how you could have found much greater promise. Or a greater beginning. So nothing stays the same. I don't

---

* The city authorities cut down 800 trees in Jackson Park to facilitate auto travel in the area.

know, do you? We should have the intelligence and courage to see the many changes that come into the world and will always come. But what are the intrinsic values we should not give up? That's the great challenge that faces us all.

Elmer is one of the so-called houseboys in the hotel. He's very quiet, no one pays much attention to him. But I've always liked him and we talked now and then. The other day, he said, "You have lots of books, haven't you?" And I said, "I have only a few. I wish I had all my books here." He went over and stood there, looking at the titles, and he took one book out and he said, "What's this book about?" It happend to be *What Can a Man Do?** and Elmer read the title and said, "What does that mean: What Can a Man Do?" I tried very simply to explain and he put the book back. He didn't ask to take it. He could have if he wanted to. But I wasn't sure, because he's somewhat retarded. But of all the titles, that was the one that attracted him. It seemed to mean something to him: What can a man do?

Everything is so organized today. The corruption itself has become organized. Everything, it's part of our whole fabric. Drugs . . . the first day I came to Hull House in 1906, a mother came in and asked for Dr. Alice Hamilton, who was living there at the time. She was worried about her boy staying out of school, sleeping. Dr. Hamilton found he was taking cocaine. So we campaigned against the sale of drugs, which was carried on in the school yard. But those were individuals. It wasn't organized then.

I arrived in Chicago on an awfully hot July day. Every other place was a saloon, the streets were dirty. The air was heavy. I had left the beautiful Iowa countryside, and I wondered if I hadn't made a mistake. And no one paid much attention to me. The next morning I said to Miss Addams, "I want you to tell me what I am to do." And then she said what seemed to me the most wonderful introduction for a young person: "I wouldn't do anything if I were you for a while. Just look around and get acquainted and perhaps you'll think of something to do that

---

* Milton Mayer, *What Can a Man Do?* (Chicago, University of Chicago Press, 1964).

none of the rest of us have ever thought of before." I don't know, it gave me a kind of freedom. Of not having to conform to an organization right away.

Miss Addams didn't start with any blueprints. She didn't start out with getting money for a foundation. Everything grew from the bottom up. We lived where we worked. And the place belonged to everybody. You learned life from life itself.

It was her understanding of why each person had become what he was. She didn't condemn because she understood what life does to people, to those of us who have everything and to those of us who have nothing. And now we're getting further and further away from this eternal foundation on which individual life must rest. And community life.

Miss Addams realized a whole world outside her gatepost. As a child of four, she heard her father talk of Lincoln, on the day he died. He wept when Mazzini died. And she realized then that we didn't have to live close together or know each other to be really brothers in things that matter most. Her dream of world peace became her life's goal. She paid a great price for this. Even her name was taken off the roll of the little church she belonged to, right next door to Hull House. They just struck it off. . . .

I feel most sorry today for our young people that are growing up just at this time, and the current despair they feel about lots of things. They're rebellious against they know not what. But I've come to feel, especially out here, that our great hope is in them, the youth who I think are concerned and even the ones who are confused. But they're getting a feeling of something that may affect the whole world. I don't know, I just feel it.

They know that in the huge colleges today, they're not getting what they want, what they long for. They have a feeling of sort of unreality about it.

I know a young boy who's just wandering around, a boy with Beatle haircut, a brilliant student. He's been through college. He'd rather hitchhike than take a plane, which he could easily do. He feels more comfortable. He hasn't any plans. He's like many young people today, he's restless. He's resentful about so many things which he feels are wrong—and they *are* wrong. I think there are thousands like him. But not all of them. Some just give it up, for something they don't really want. He's resentful, he can't tell you just what—but it's something pretty big.

When you look to the older people for what the young should find in them, it isn't there. Nothing's there. Do we have to wait for these young people to grow up and awaken those who are older? Or those who are in control and make all the decisions? To help us clarify the eternal truths which America seems to have forgotten? They'll meet opposition, no matter what they do.

Oh, the terrific waste! We've forgotten the spirit of youth, in things we permit to happen to them. I mean, if we're ever going to fulfill the possibility of life for all men, not only in Chicago, but in America and in the world, the spirit of youth must not be neglected. It must not be injured. It must not be killed.

POSTSCRIPT
Jessie Binford died July 9, 1966. She was buried in Marshalltown, Iowa.